VOLUME 3

by
Nami Akimoto

HAMBURG // LONDON // LOS ANGELES // TOKYO

Ultra Cute Vol. 3
Created by Nami Akimoto

Translation - Emi Onishi
English Adaptation - Hope Donovan
Retouch and Lettering - Mike Estacio
Production Artist - Jihye "Sophia" Hong
Cover Design - Monalisa De Asis

Editor - Troy Lewter
Digital Imaging Manager - Chris Buford
Production Manager - Liz Brizzi
Managing Editor - Lindsey Johnston
Editor-in-Chief - Rob Tokar
VP of Production - Ron Klamert
Publisher - Mike Kiley
President and C.O.O. - John Parker
C.E.O. and Chief Creative Officer - Stuart Levy

A  Manga

TOKYOPOP Inc.
5900 Wilshire Blvd. Suite 2000
Los Angeles, CA 90036

E-mail: info@TOKYOPOP.com
Come visit us online at www.TOKYOPOP.com

ISBN: 1-59532-958-7

First TOKYOPOP printing: July 2006
10 9 8 7 6 5 4 3 2 1
Printed in the USA

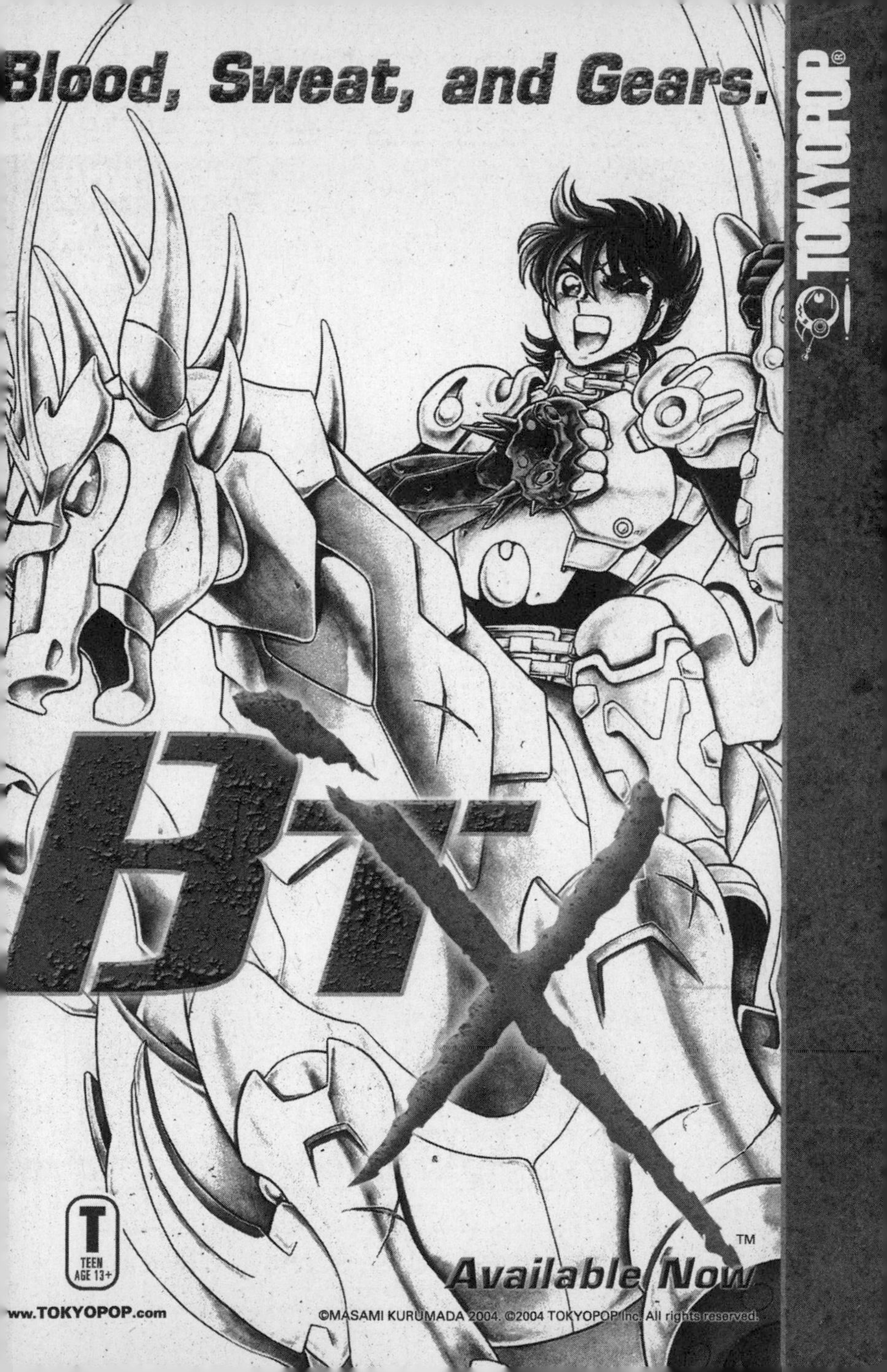
Blood, Sweat, and Gears.
TOKYOPOP
B'TX
TM
T TEEN AGE 13+
Available Now
www.TOKYOPOP.com
©MASAMI KURUMADA 2004. ©2004 TOKYOPOP Inc. All rights reserved.

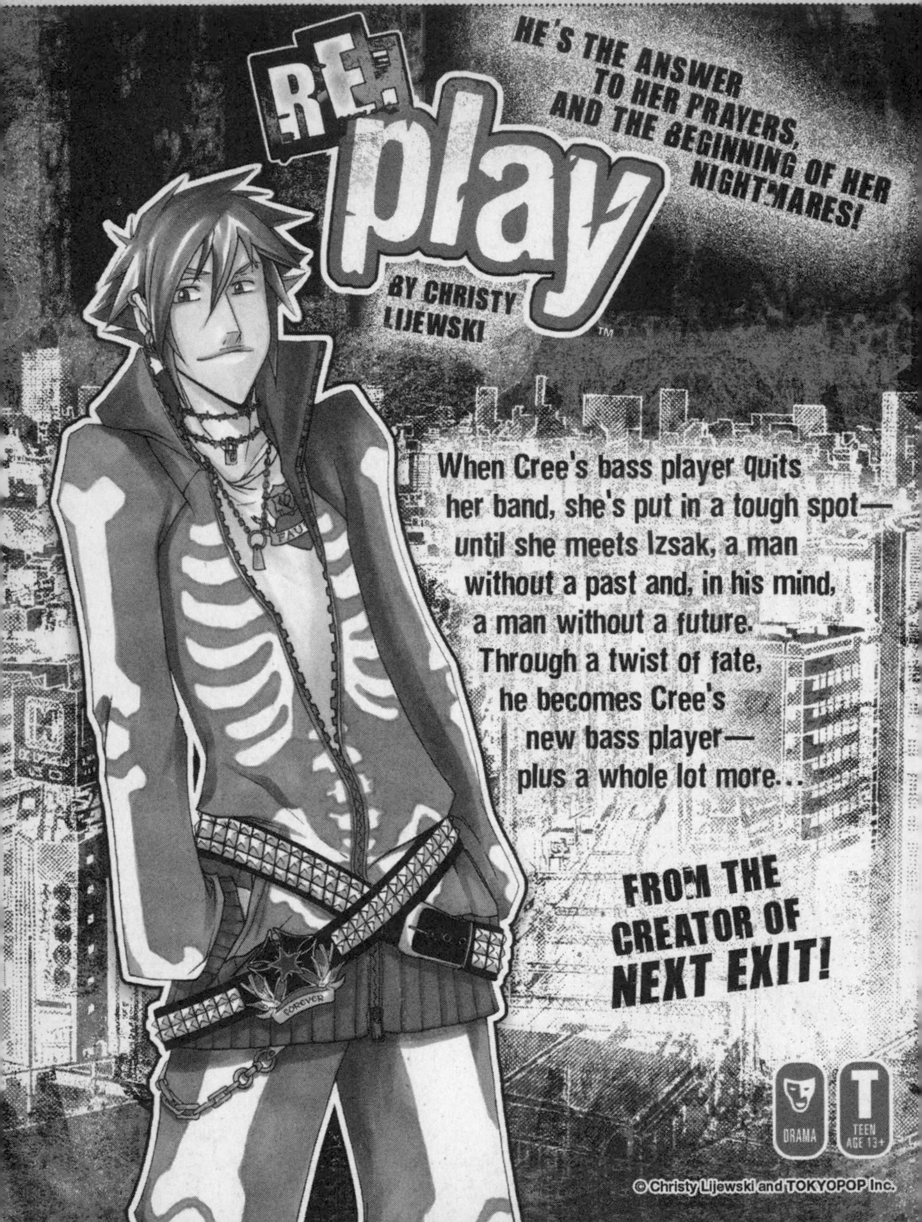
RE: play
BY CHRISTY LIJEWSKI
TM
HE'S THE ANSWER TO HER PRAYERS, AND THE BEGINNING OF HER NIGHTMARES!
When Cree's bass player quits her band, she's put in a tough spot—until she meets Izsak, a man without a past and, in his mind, a man without a future. Through a twist of fate, he becomes Cree's new bass player—plus a whole lot more...
FROM THE CREATOR OF NEXT EXIT!
DRAMA
T
TEEN AGE 13+
© Christy Lijewski and TOKYOPOP Inc.

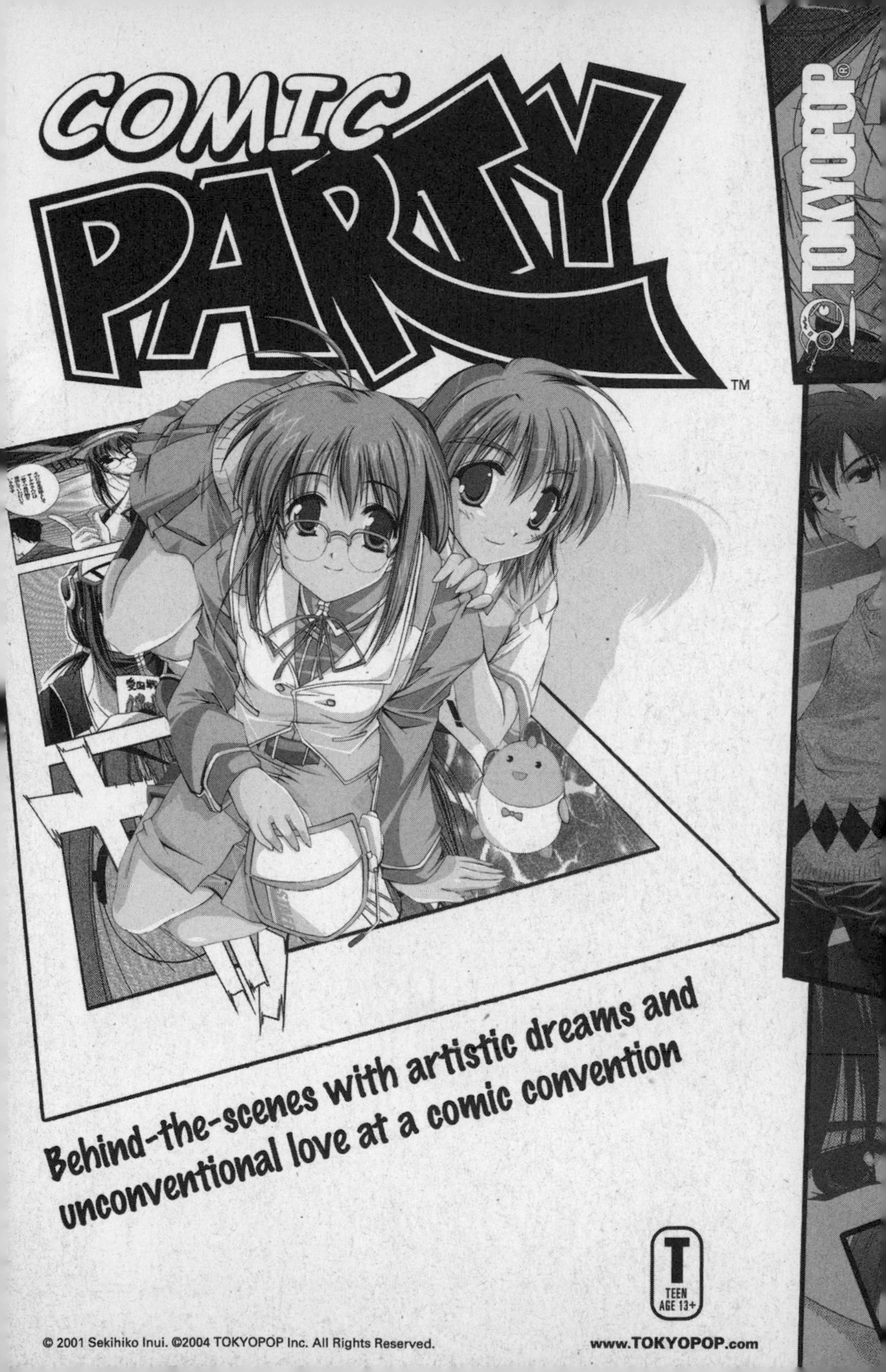
COMIC PARTY™
TOKYOPOP®
Behind-the-scenes with artistic dreams and unconventional love at a comic convention
T
TEEN AGE 13+
© 2001 Sekihiko Inui. ©2004 TOKYOPOP Inc. All Rights Reserved.
www.TOKYOPOP.com

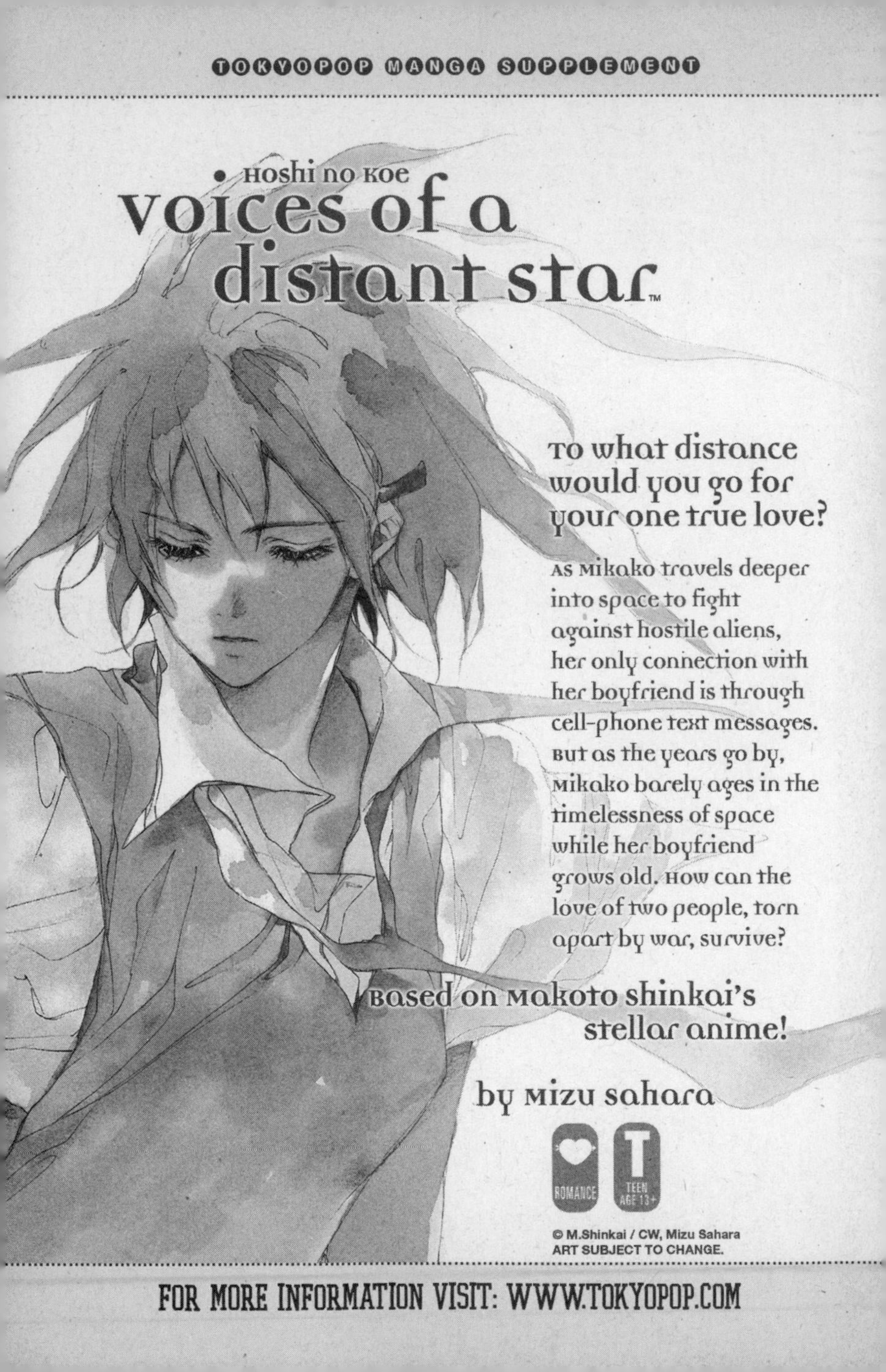

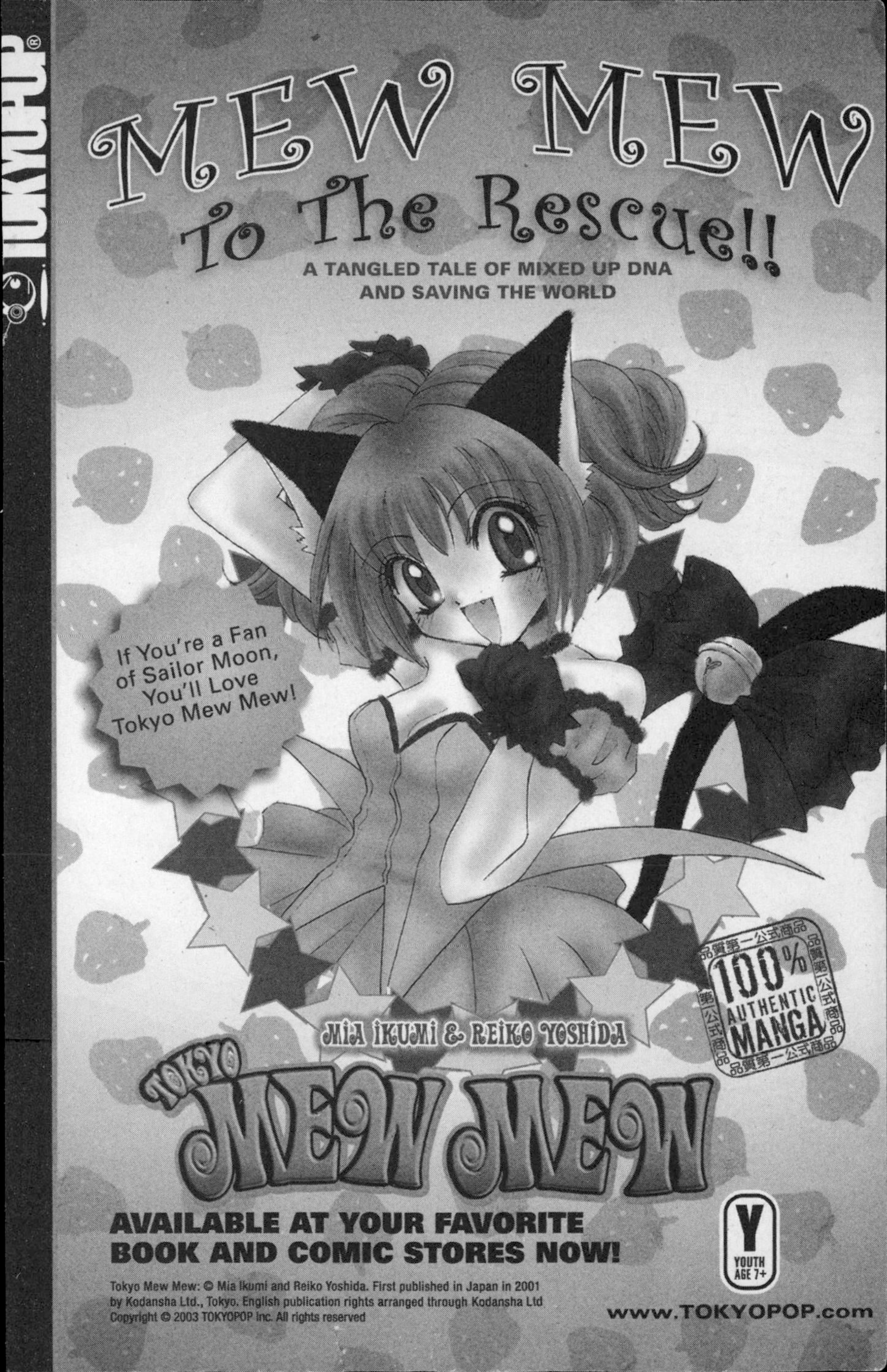
TOKYOPOP
MEW MEW To The Rescue!!
A TANGLED TALE OF MIXED UP DNA AND SAVING THE WORLD
If You're a Fan of Sailor Moon, You'll Love Tokyo Mew Mew!
100% AUTHENTIC MANGA
MIA IKUMI & REIKO YOSHIDA
TOKYO MEW MEW
AVAILABLE AT YOUR FAVORITE BOOK AND COMIC STORES NOW!
Y YOUTH AGE 7+
Tokyo Mew Mew: © Mia Ikumi and Reiko Yoshida. First published in Japan in 2001 by Kodansha Ltd., Tokyo. English publication rights arranged through Kodansha Ltd Copyright © 2003 TOKYOPOP Inc. All rights reserved
www.TOKYOPOP.com

THE QUEST TO SAVE THE WORLD
CONTINUES IN THE BEST-SELLING
MANGA FROM TOKYOPOP!

AVAILABLE WHEREVER BOOKS ARE SOLD.
www.TOKYOPOP.com

IN THE NEXT VOLUME OF

ULtra CUTE

AMI'S PLAN TO MAKE THE "LEGEND" COME TRUE AND
CONFESS HER FEELING TOWARD TAMON IS IN DANGER OF BEING
SABOTAGED BY THE VINDICTIVE MIKA...WILL AMI'S DREAM
OF ROMANCE TURN INTO A NIGHTMARE? AMI ISN'T THE ONLY
ONE WITH RELATIONSHIP WOES, AS NOA MAKES A SHOCKING
DECISION ABOUT HER AND TOMOHIRO'S FUTURE...

IT'S ALL IN *ULTRA CUTE* VOLUME 4!

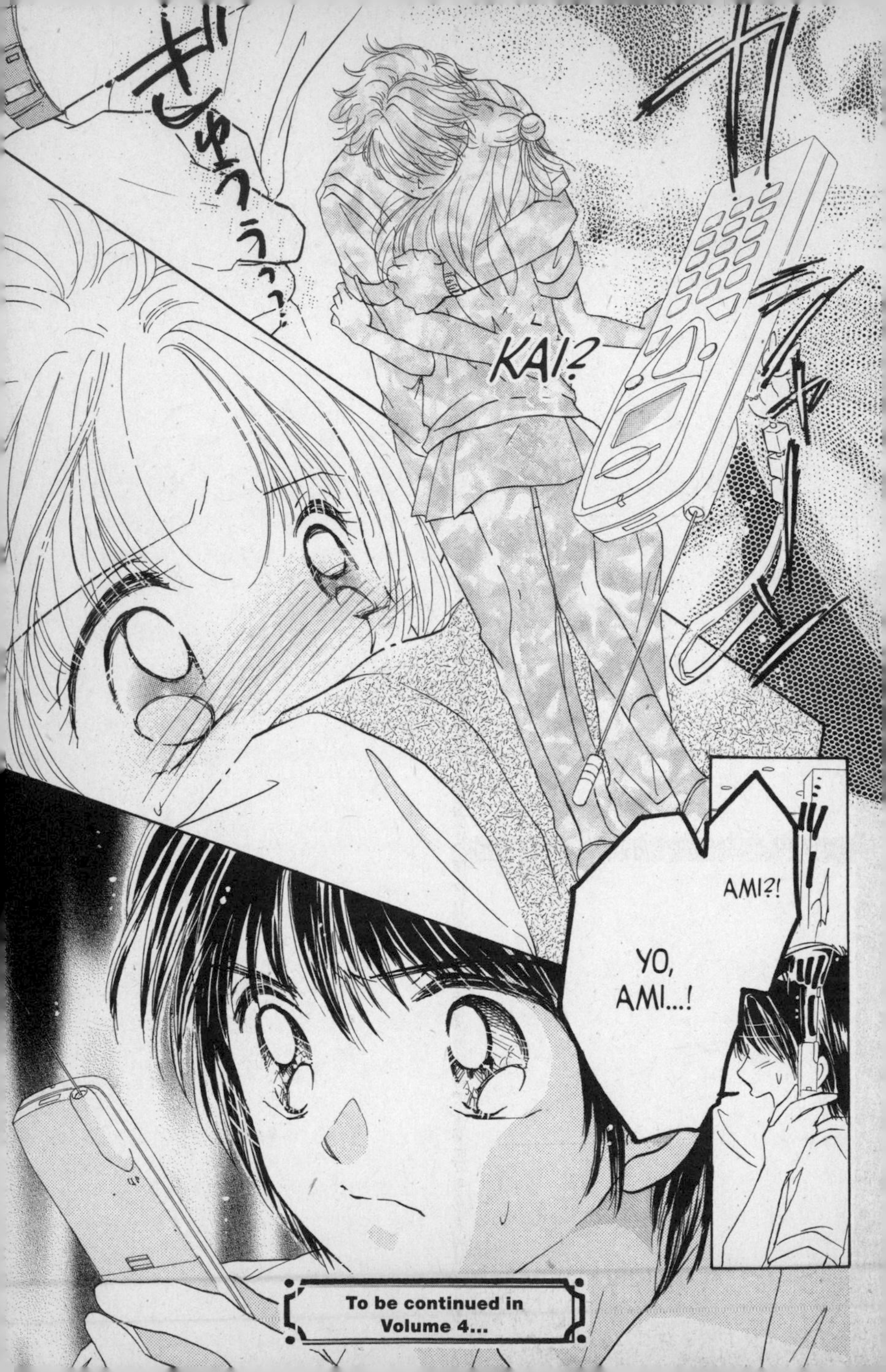
KAI?
AMI?!
YO, AMI...!
To be continued in Volume 4...

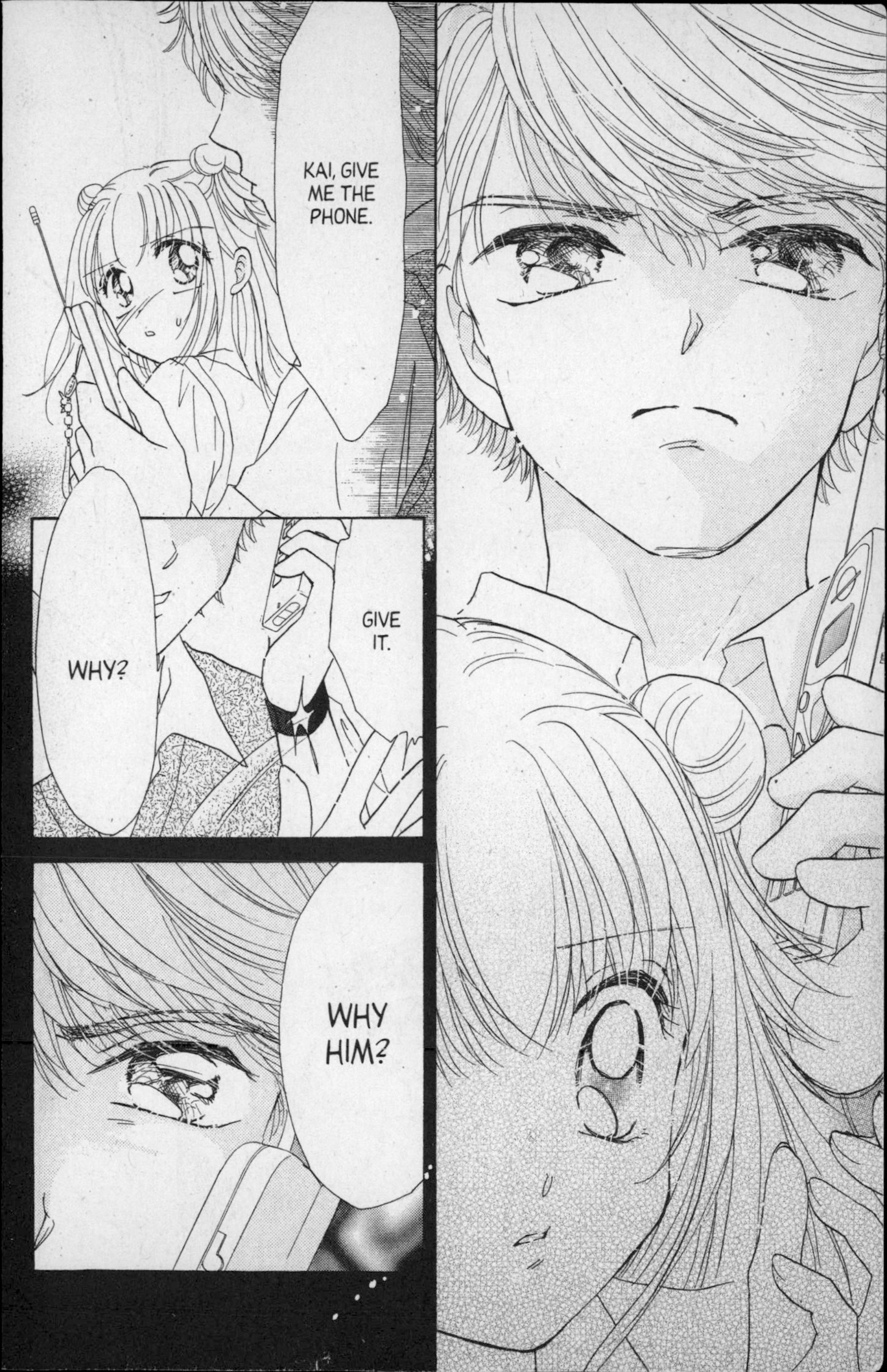
KAI, GIVE ME THE PHONE.
GIVE IT.
WHY?
WHY HIM?

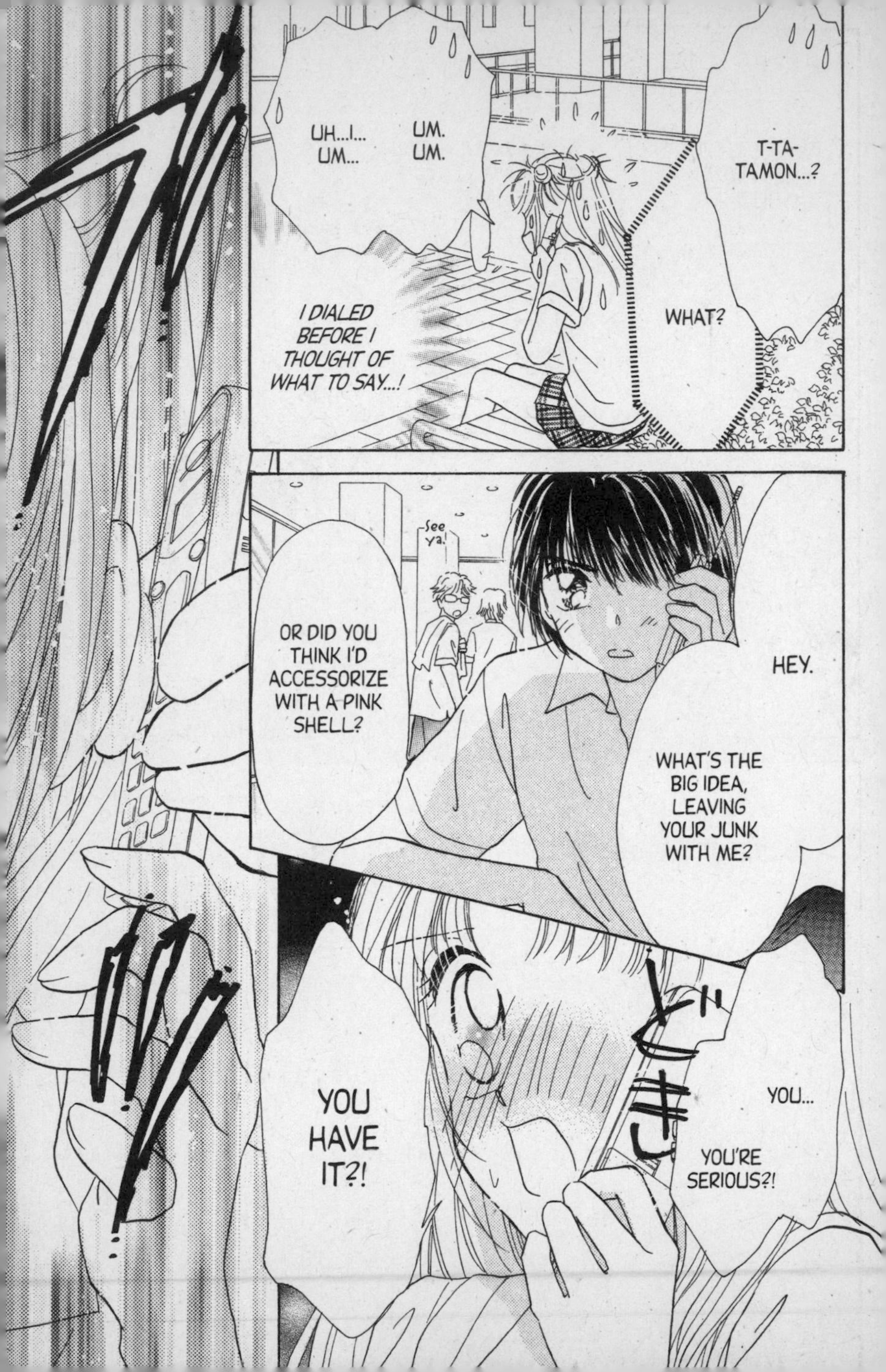
T-TA-TAMON...?
UH...I... UM...
UM. UM.
WHAT?
I DIALED BEFORE I THOUGHT OF WHAT TO SAY...!
HEY.
WHAT'S THE BIG IDEA, LEAVING YOUR JUNK WITH ME?
See ya!
OR DID YOU THINK I'D ACCESSORIZE WITH A PINK SHELL?
YOU...
YOU'RE SERIOUS?!
どき
YOU HAVE IT?!

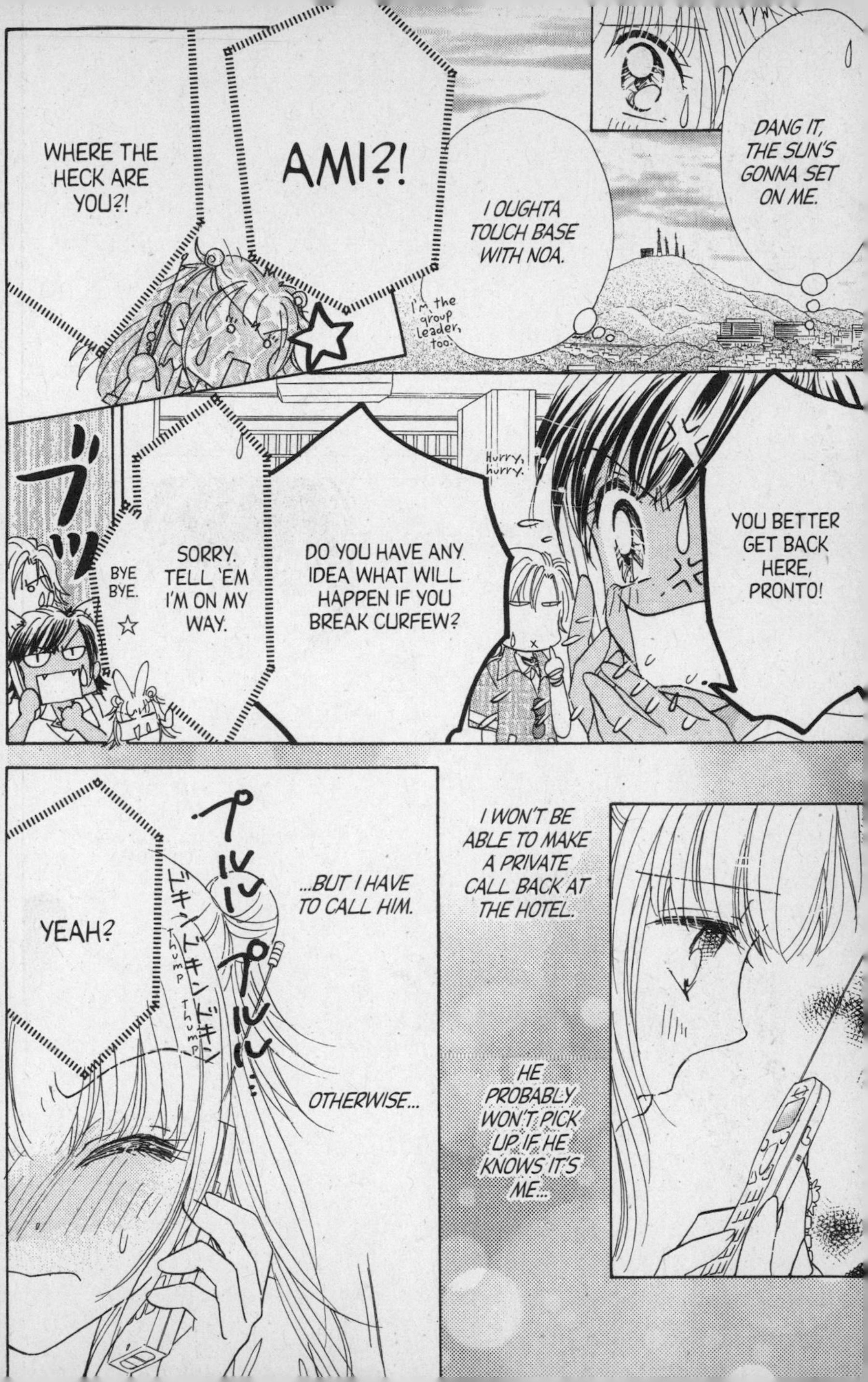
DANG IT, THE SUN'S GONNA SET ON ME.
I OUGHTA TOUCH BASE WITH NOA.
I'm the group leader, too.
AMI?!
WHERE THE HECK ARE YOU?!
YOU BETTER GET BACK HERE, PRONTO!
Hurry, hurry.
DO YOU HAVE ANY IDEA WHAT WILL HAPPEN IF YOU BREAK CURFEW?
SORRY. TELL 'EM I'M ON MY WAY.
BYE BYE. ☆
ブツッ
I WON'T BE ABLE TO MAKE A PRIVATE CALL BACK AT THE HOTEL.
HE PROBABLY WON'T PICK UP IF HE KNOWS IT'S ME...
...BUT I HAVE TO CALL HIM.
OTHERWISE...
プルルプルル…
ドキンドキン
THUMP THUMP
YEAH?

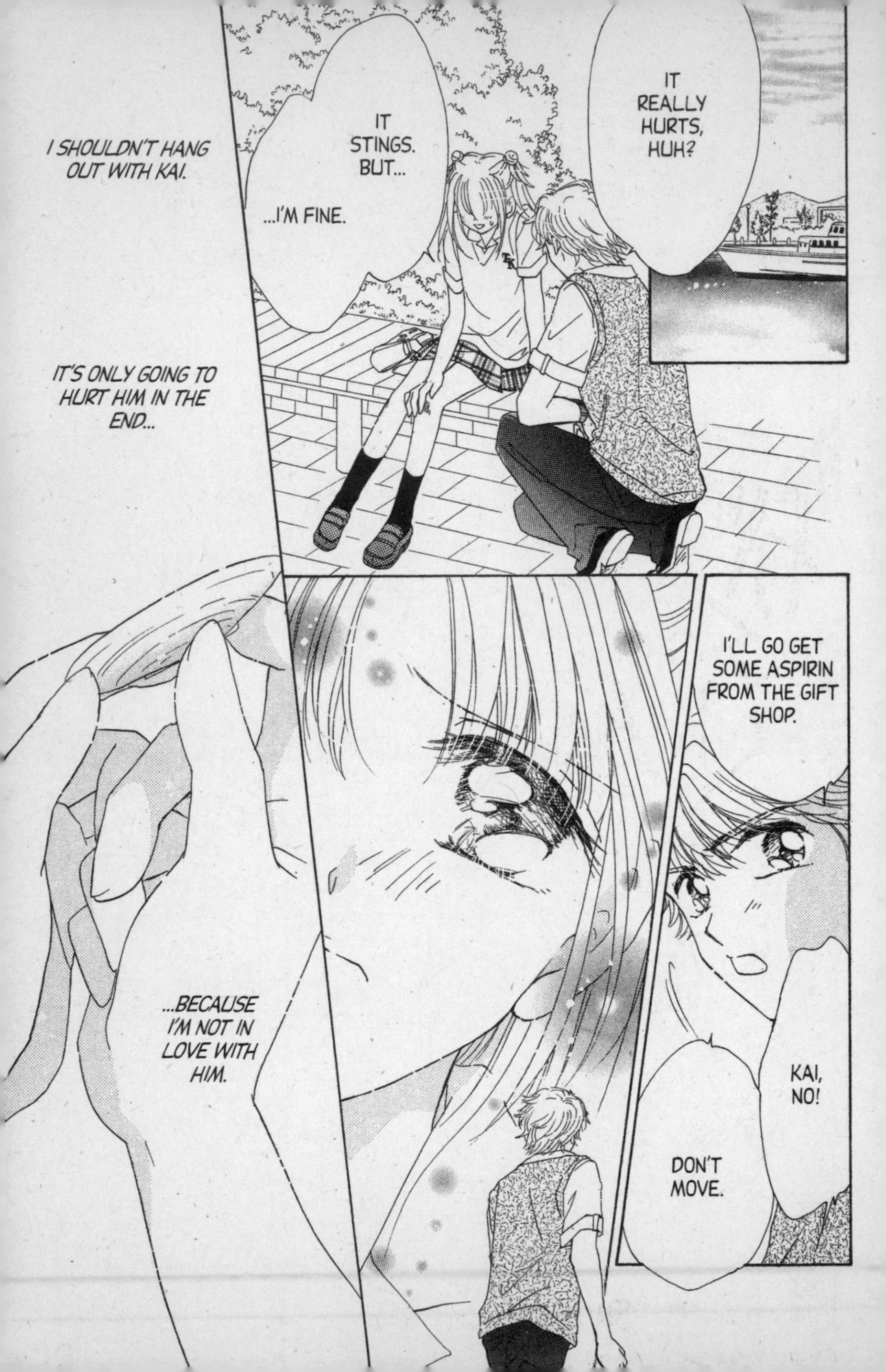
IT REALLY HURTS, HUH?
IT STINGS. BUT...
...I'M FINE.
I SHOULDN'T HANG OUT WITH KAI.
IT'S ONLY GOING TO HURT HIM IN THE END...
I'LL GO GET SOME ASPIRIN FROM THE GIFT SHOP.
KAI, NO!
DON'T MOVE.
...BECAUSE I'M NOT IN LOVE WITH HIM.

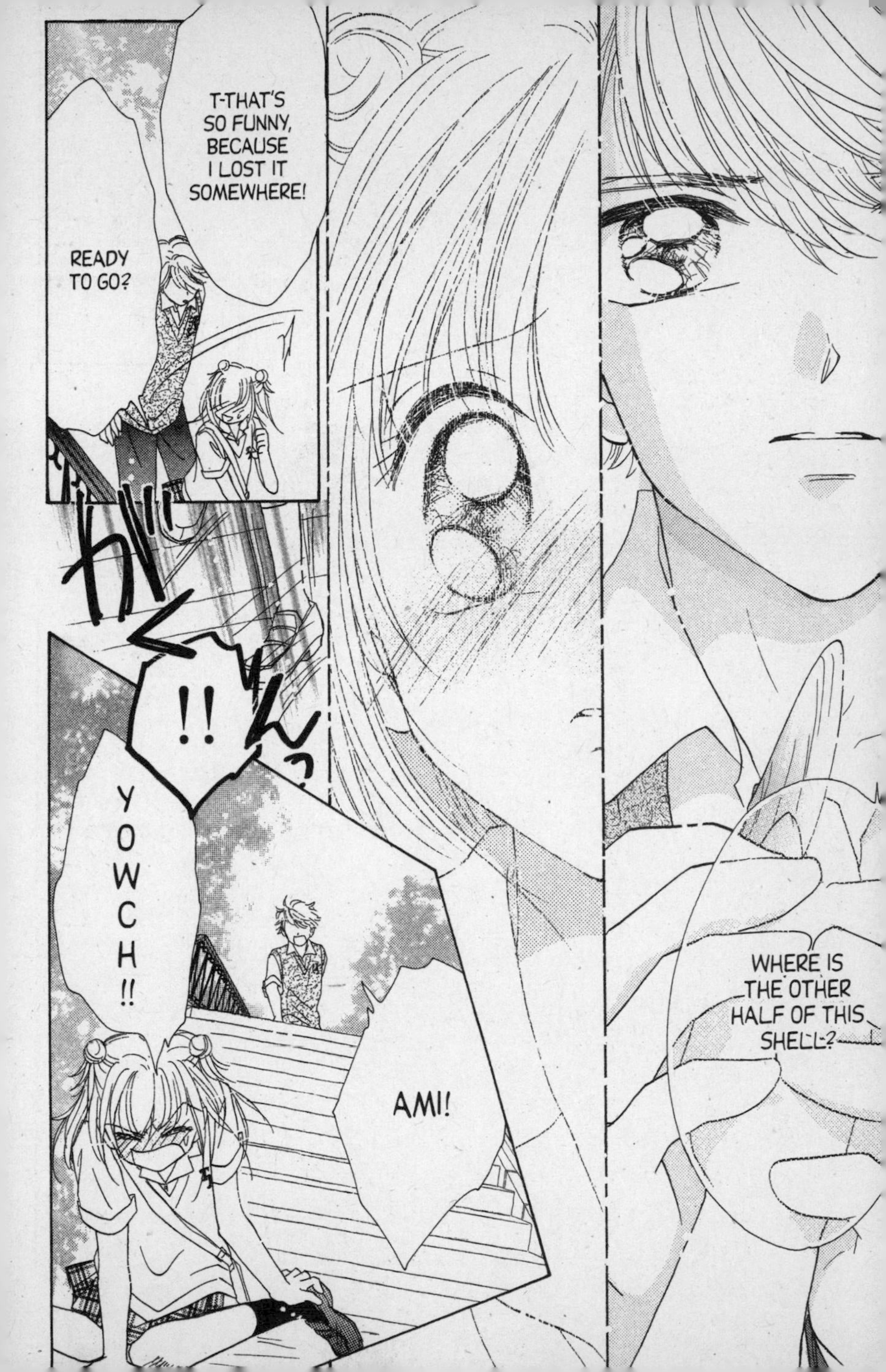
WHERE IS THE OTHER HALF OF THIS SHELL?
T-THAT'S SO FUNNY, BECAUSE I LOST IT SOMEWHERE!
READY TO GO?
!!
YOWCH!!
AMI!

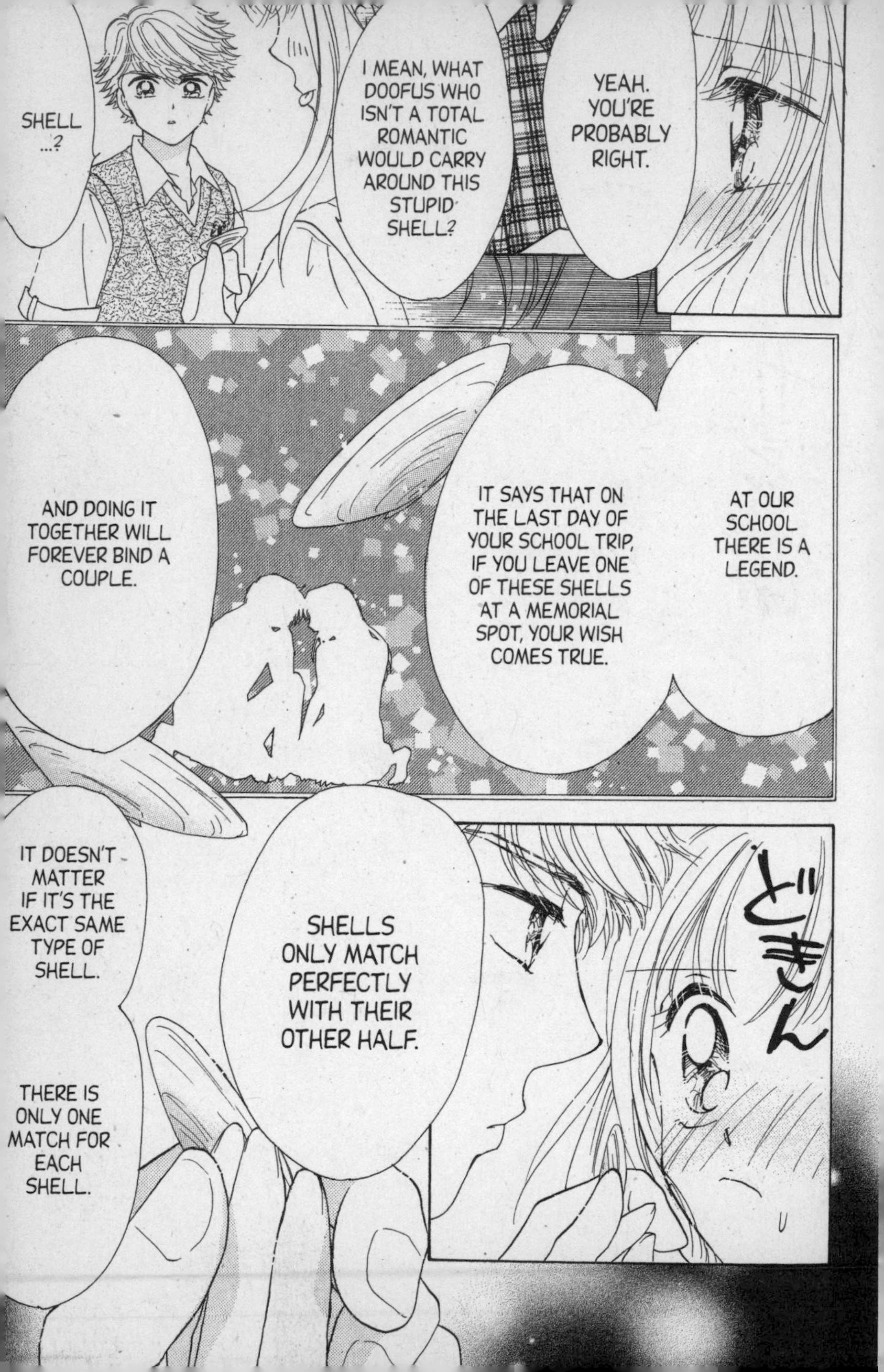
YEAH. YOU'RE PROBABLY RIGHT.
I MEAN, WHAT DOOFUS WHO ISN'T A TOTAL ROMANTIC WOULD CARRY AROUND THIS STUPID SHELL?
SHELL ...?
AT OUR SCHOOL THERE IS A LEGEND.
IT SAYS THAT ON THE LAST DAY OF YOUR SCHOOL TRIP, IF YOU LEAVE ONE OF THESE SHELLS AT A MEMORIAL SPOT, YOUR WISH COMES TRUE.
AND DOING IT TOGETHER WILL FOREVER BIND A COUPLE.
どきん
SHELLS ONLY MATCH PERFECTLY WITH THEIR OTHER HALF.
IT DOESN'T MATTER IF IT'S THE EXACT SAME TYPE OF SHELL.
THERE IS ONLY ONE MATCH FOR EACH SHELL.

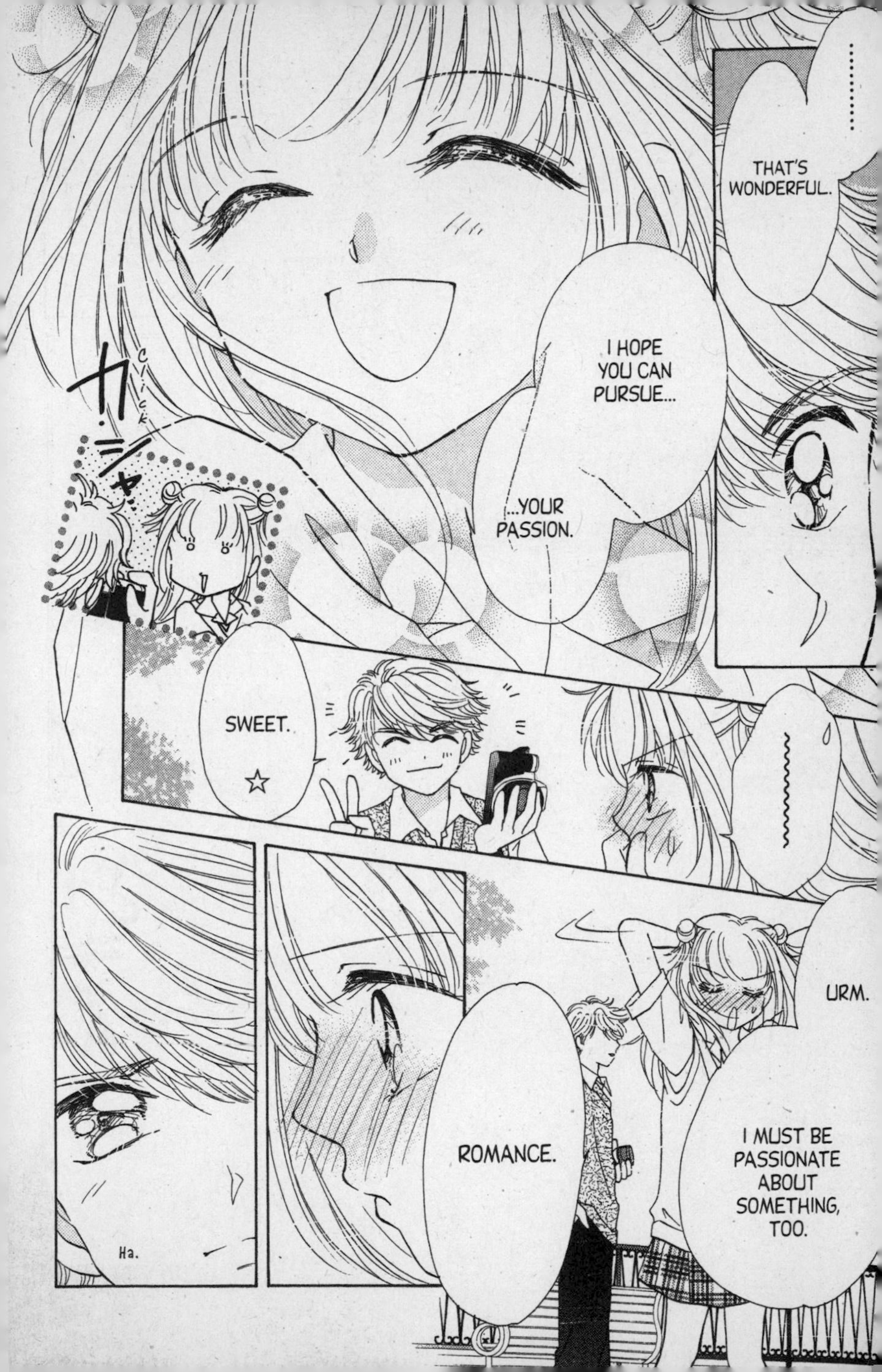
......
THAT'S WONDERFUL.
I HOPE YOU CAN PURSUE...
...YOUR PASSION.
CLICK
SWEET. ☆
URM.
I MUST BE PASSIONATE ABOUT SOMETHING, TOO.
ROMANCE.
Ha.

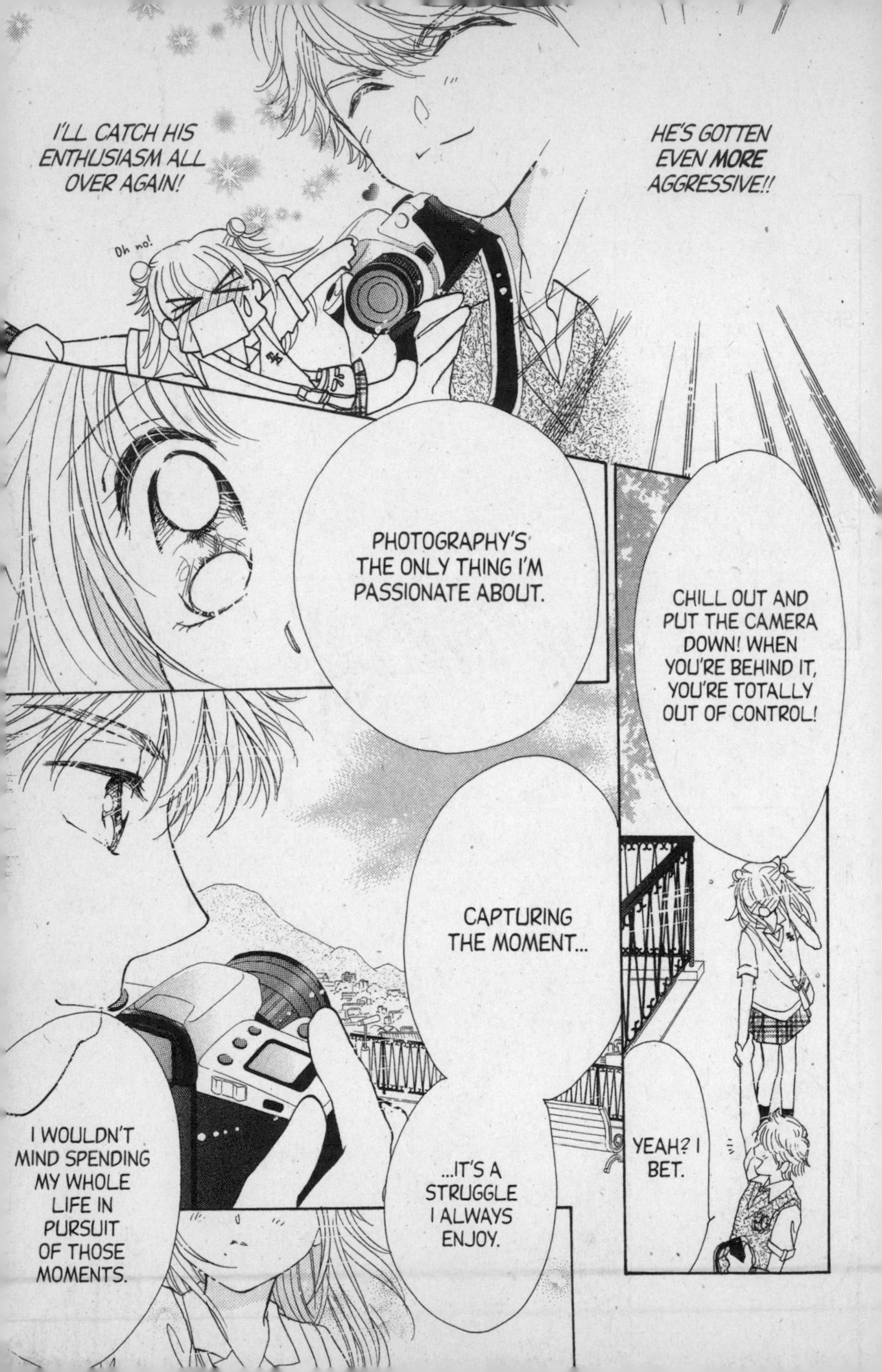
HE'S GOTTEN EVEN MORE AGGRESSIVE!!
I'LL CATCH HIS ENTHUSIASM ALL OVER AGAIN!
Oh no!
CHILL OUT AND PUT THE CAMERA DOWN! WHEN YOU'RE BEHIND IT, YOU'RE TOTALLY OUT OF CONTROL!
YEAH? I BET.
PHOTOGRAPHY'S THE ONLY THING I'M PASSIONATE ABOUT.
CAPTURING THE MOMENT...
...IT'S A STRUGGLE I ALWAYS ENJOY.
I WOULDN'T MIND SPENDING MY WHOLE LIFE IN PURSUIT OF THOSE MOMENTS.

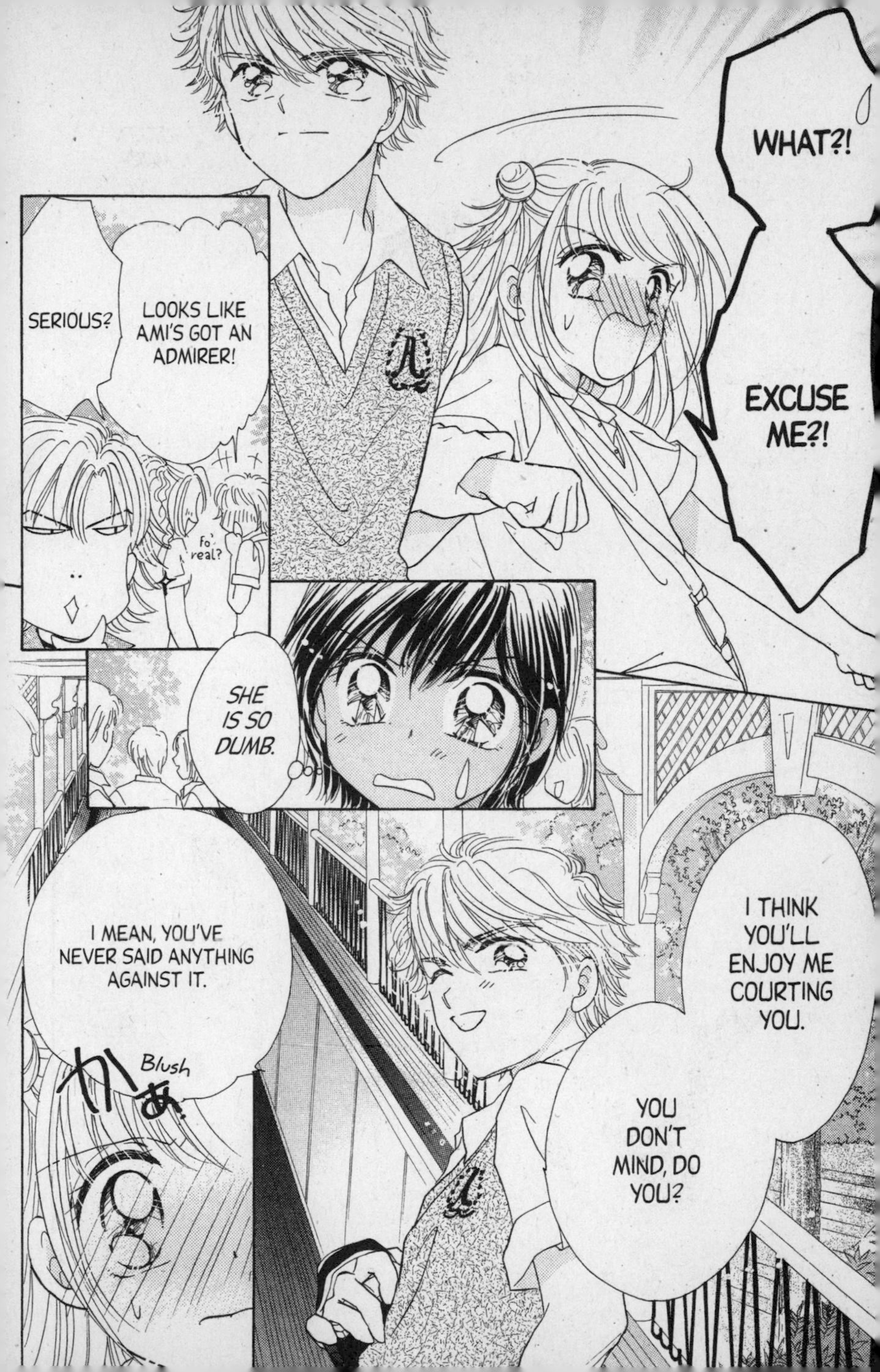

WHAT?!
EXCUSE ME?!
LOOKS LIKE AMI'S GOT AN ADMIRER!
SERIOUS?
Fo' real?
SHE IS SO DUMB.
I THINK YOU'LL ENJOY ME COURTING YOU.
YOU DON'T MIND, DO YOU?
I MEAN, YOU'VE NEVER SAID ANYTHING AGAINST IT.
かあ
Blush

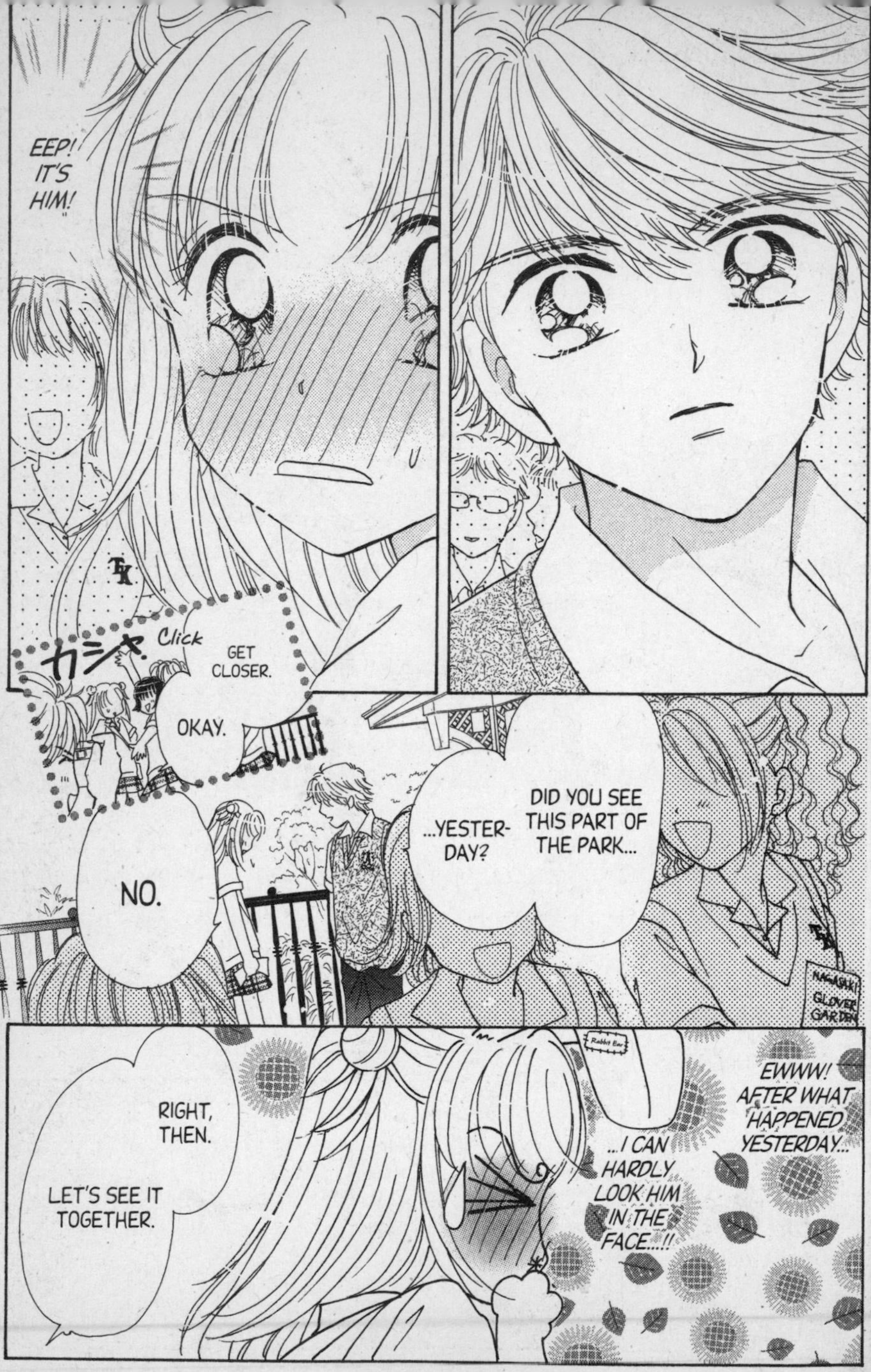
EEP! IT'S HIM!
カシャ Click
GET CLOSER.
OKAY.
DID YOU SEE THIS PART OF THE PARK...
...YESTER-DAY?
NAGASAKI GLOVER GARDEN
NO.
EWWW! AFTER WHAT HAPPENED YESTERDAY...
...I CAN HARDLY LOOK HIM IN THE FACE...!!
Rabbit Ear
RIGHT, THEN.
LET'S SEE IT TOGETHER.

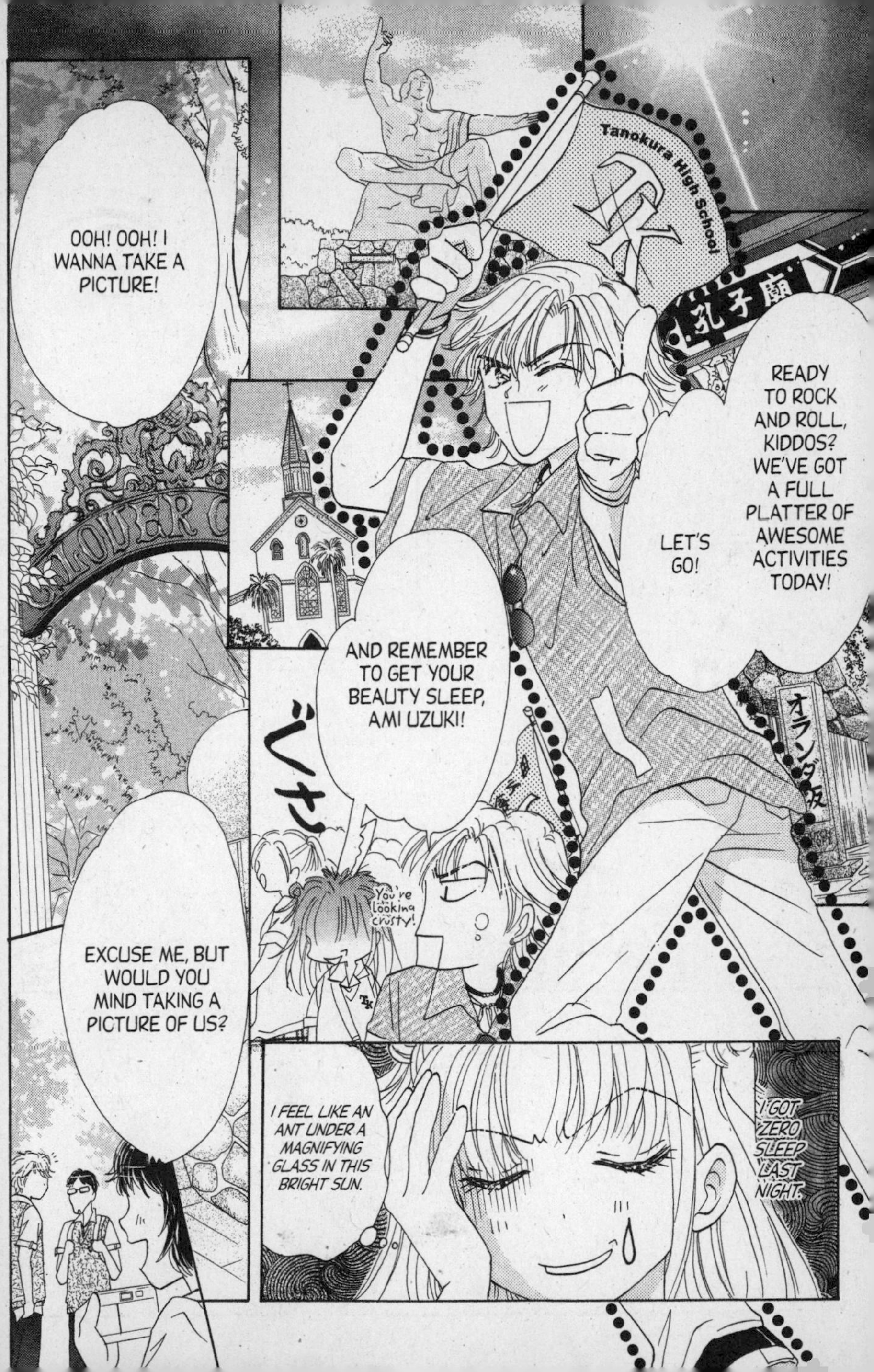
Tanokura High School
孔子廟
READY TO ROCK AND ROLL, KIDDOS? WE'VE GOT A FULL PLATTER OF AWESOME ACTIVITIES TODAY!
LET'S GO!
オランダ坂
AND REMEMBER TO GET YOUR BEAUTY SLEEP, AMI UZUKI!
ぐさ
You're looking crusty!
I GOT ZERO SLEEP LAST NIGHT.
I FEEL LIKE AN ANT UNDER A MAGNIFYING GLASS IN THIS BRIGHT SUN.
OOH! OOH! I WANNA TAKE A PICTURE!
EXCUSE ME, BUT WOULD YOU MIND TAKING A PICTURE OF US?

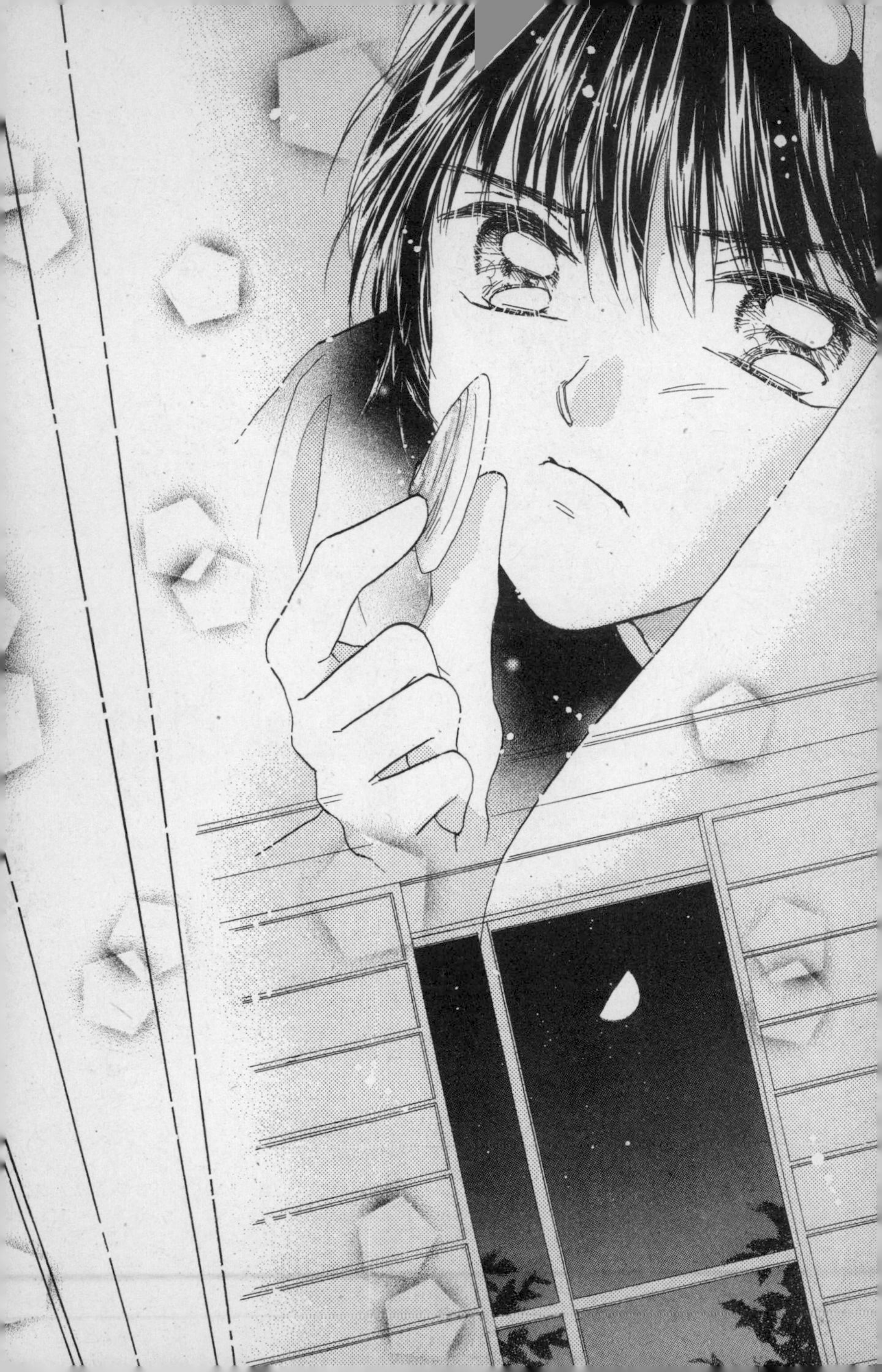

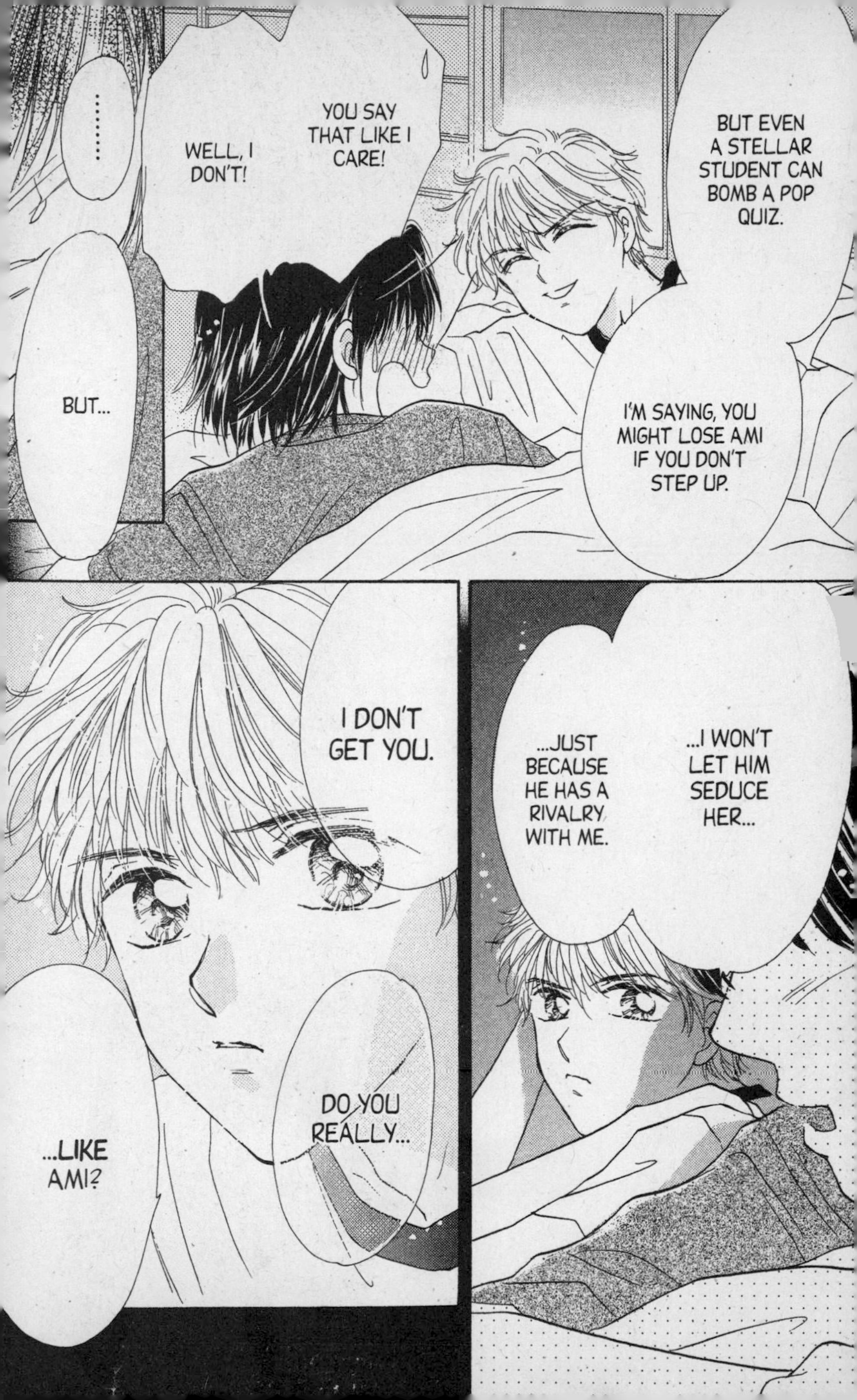
BUT EVEN A STELLAR STUDENT CAN BOMB A POP QUIZ.
I'M SAYING, YOU MIGHT LOSE AMI IF YOU DON'T STEP UP.
YOU SAY THAT LIKE I CARE!
WELL, I DON'T!
......
BUT...
...I WON'T LET HIM SEDUCE HER...
...JUST BECAUSE HE HAS A RIVALRY WITH ME.
I DON'T GET YOU.
DO YOU REALLY...
...LIKE AMI?

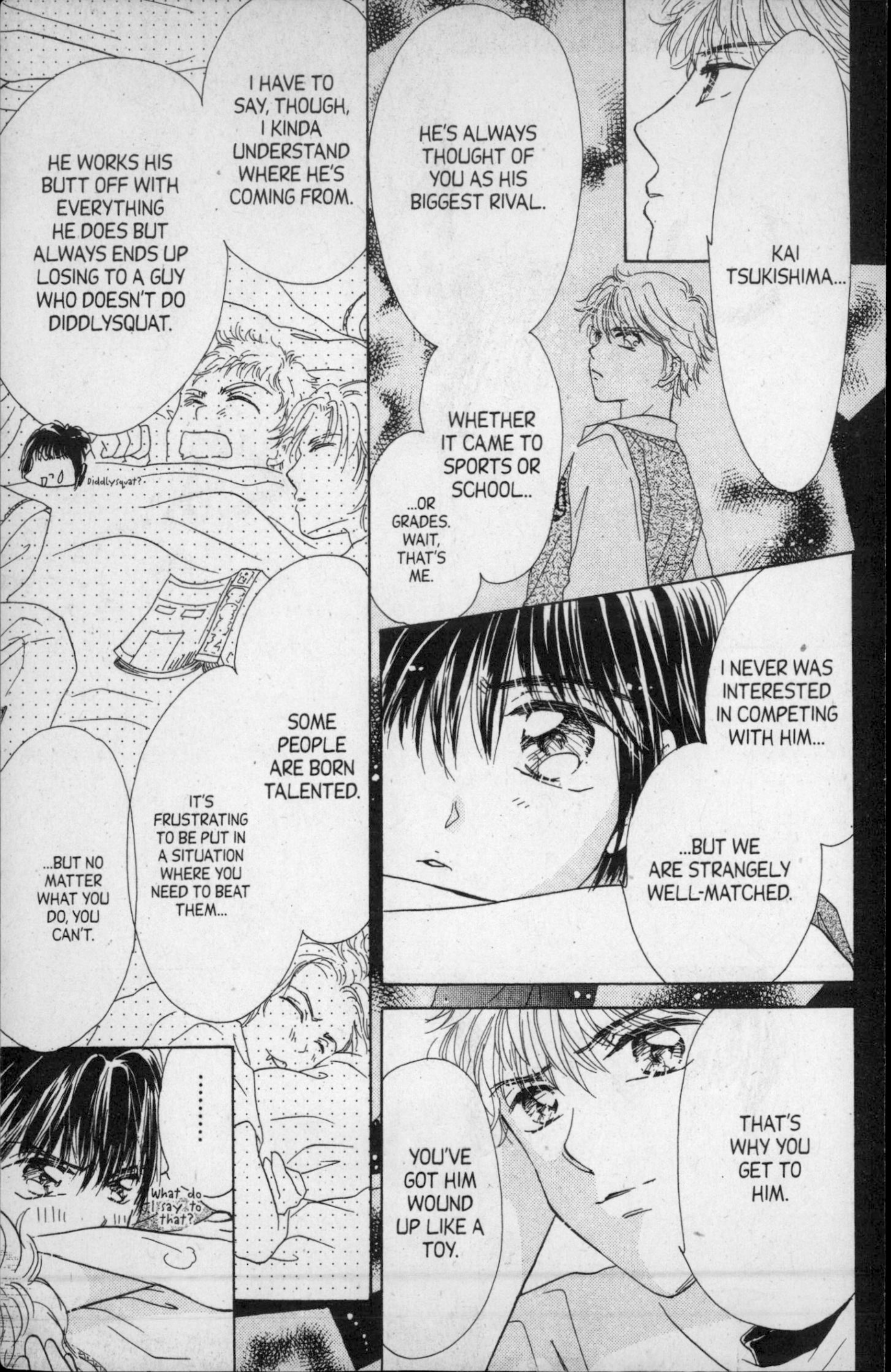
KAI TSUKISHIMA...
HE'S ALWAYS THOUGHT OF YOU AS HIS BIGGEST RIVAL.
WHETHER IT CAME TO SPORTS OR SCHOOL..
...OR GRADES. WAIT, THAT'S ME.
I NEVER WAS INTERESTED IN COMPETING WITH HIM...
...BUT WE ARE STRANGELY WELL-MATCHED.
THAT'S WHY YOU GET TO HIM.
YOU'VE GOT HIM WOUND UP LIKE A TOY.
I HAVE TO SAY, THOUGH, I KINDA UNDERSTAND WHERE HE'S COMING FROM.
HE WORKS HIS BUTT OFF WITH EVERYTHING HE DOES BUT ALWAYS ENDS UP LOSING TO A GUY WHO DOESN'T DO DIDDLYSQUAT.
Diddlysquat?
SOME PEOPLE ARE BORN TALENTED.
IT'S FRUSTRATING TO BE PUT IN A SITUATION WHERE YOU NEED TO BEAT THEM...
...BUT NO MATTER WHAT YOU DO, YOU CAN'T.
......
What do say to that?

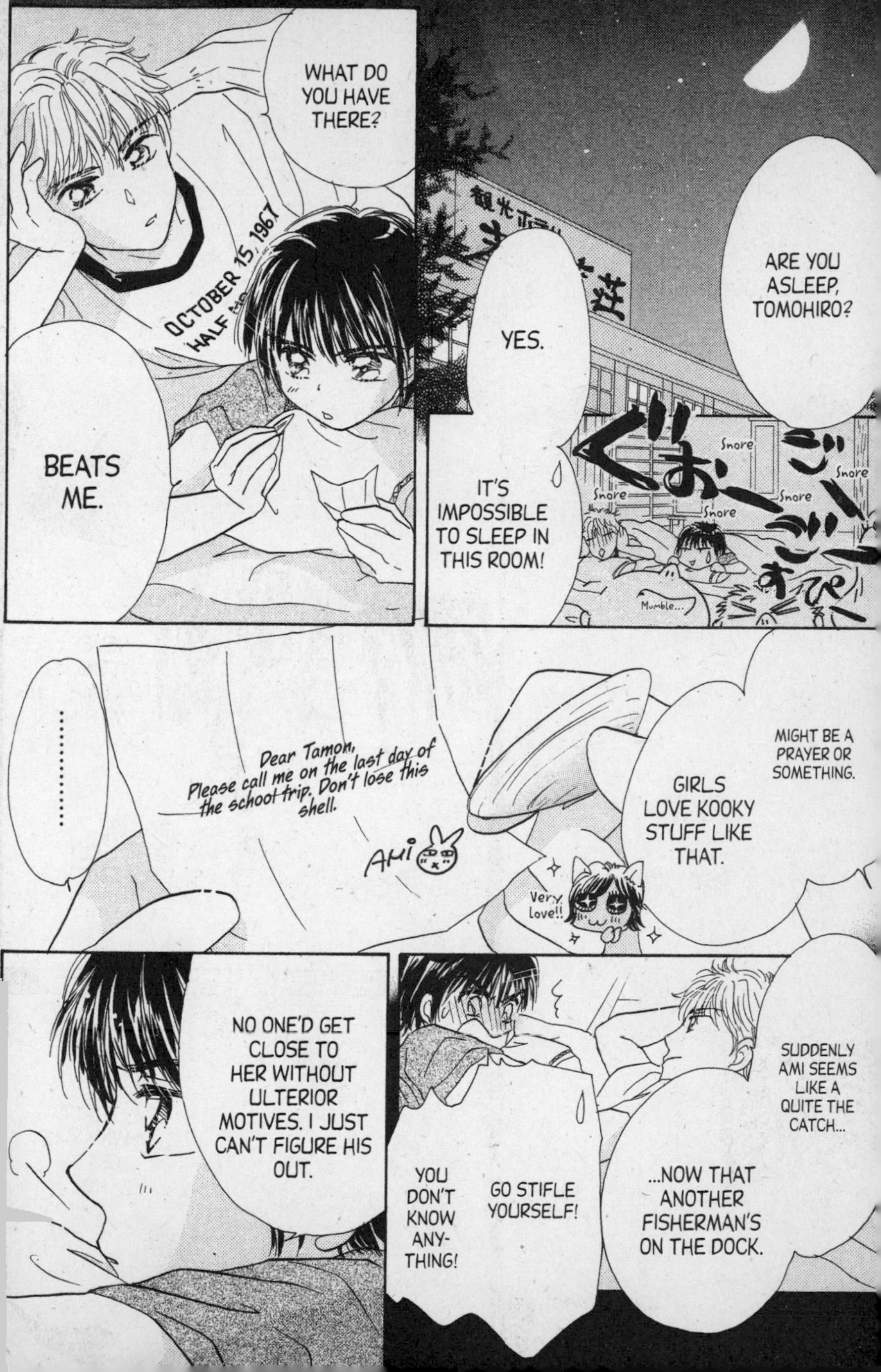
ARE YOU ASLEEP, TOMOHIRO?
YES.
IT'S IMPOSSIBLE TO SLEEP IN THIS ROOM!
Snore
Snore
Snore
Snore
Snore
Mumble...
WHAT DO YOU HAVE THERE?
OCTOBER 15, 1967
BEATS ME.
MIGHT BE A PRAYER OR SOMETHING.
GIRLS LOVE KOOKY STUFF LIKE THAT.
Very love!!
Dear Tamon, Please call me on the last day of the school trip. Don't lose this shell.
AMI
......
SUDDENLY AMI SEEMS LIKE A QUITE THE CATCH...
...NOW THAT ANOTHER FISHERMAN'S ON THE DOCK.
GO STIFLE YOURSELF!
YOU DON'T KNOW ANY-THING!
NO ONE'D GET CLOSE TO HER WITHOUT ULTERIOR MOTIVES. I JUST CAN'T FIGURE HIS OUT.

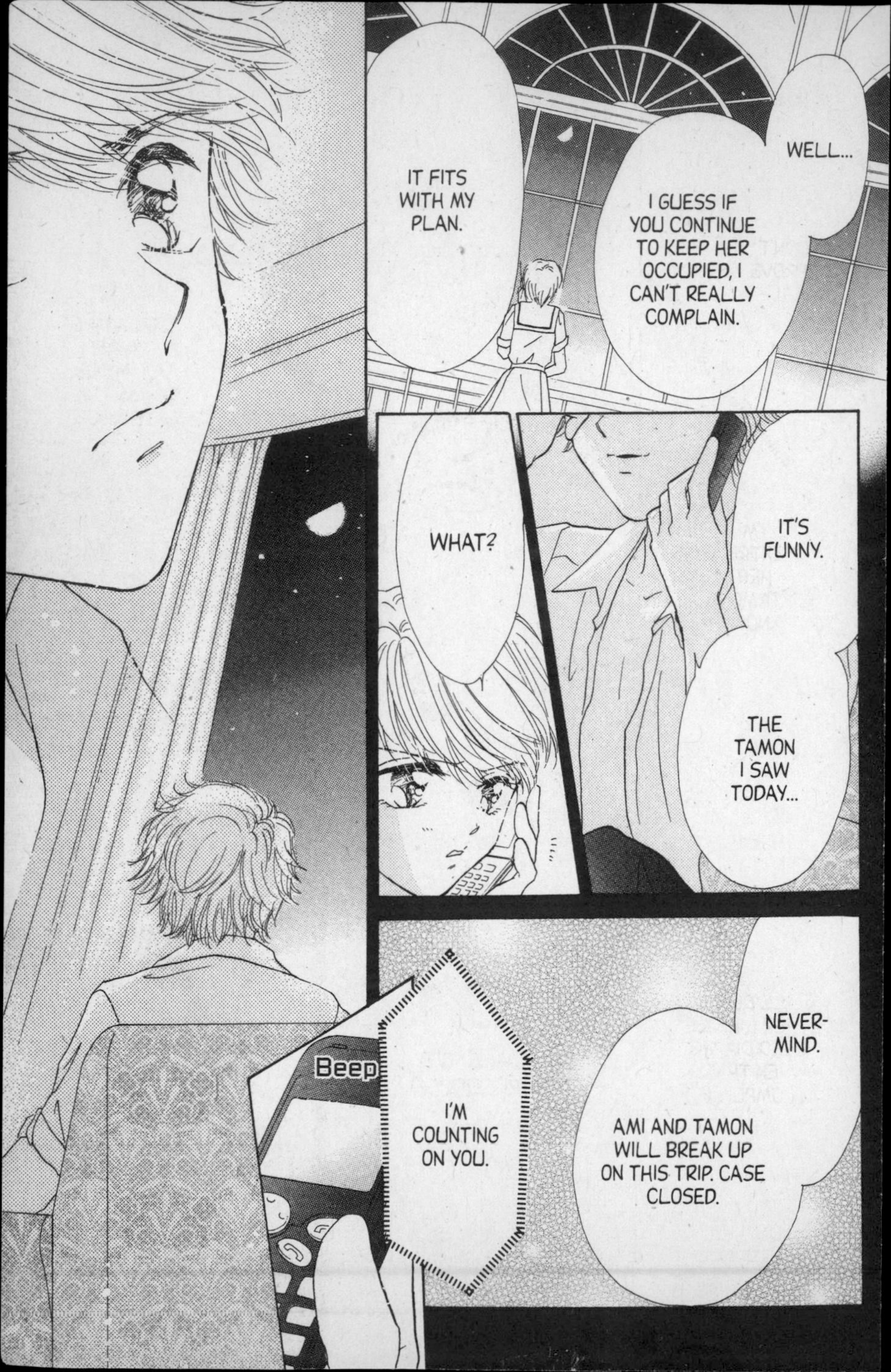
WELL...
I GUESS IF YOU CONTINUE TO KEEP HER OCCUPIED, I CAN'T REALLY COMPLAIN.
IT FITS WITH MY PLAN.
IT'S FUNNY.
THE TAMON I SAW TODAY...
WHAT?
NEVER-MIND.
AMI AND TAMON WILL BREAK UP ON THIS TRIP. CASE CLOSED.
Beep
I'M COUNTING ON YOU.

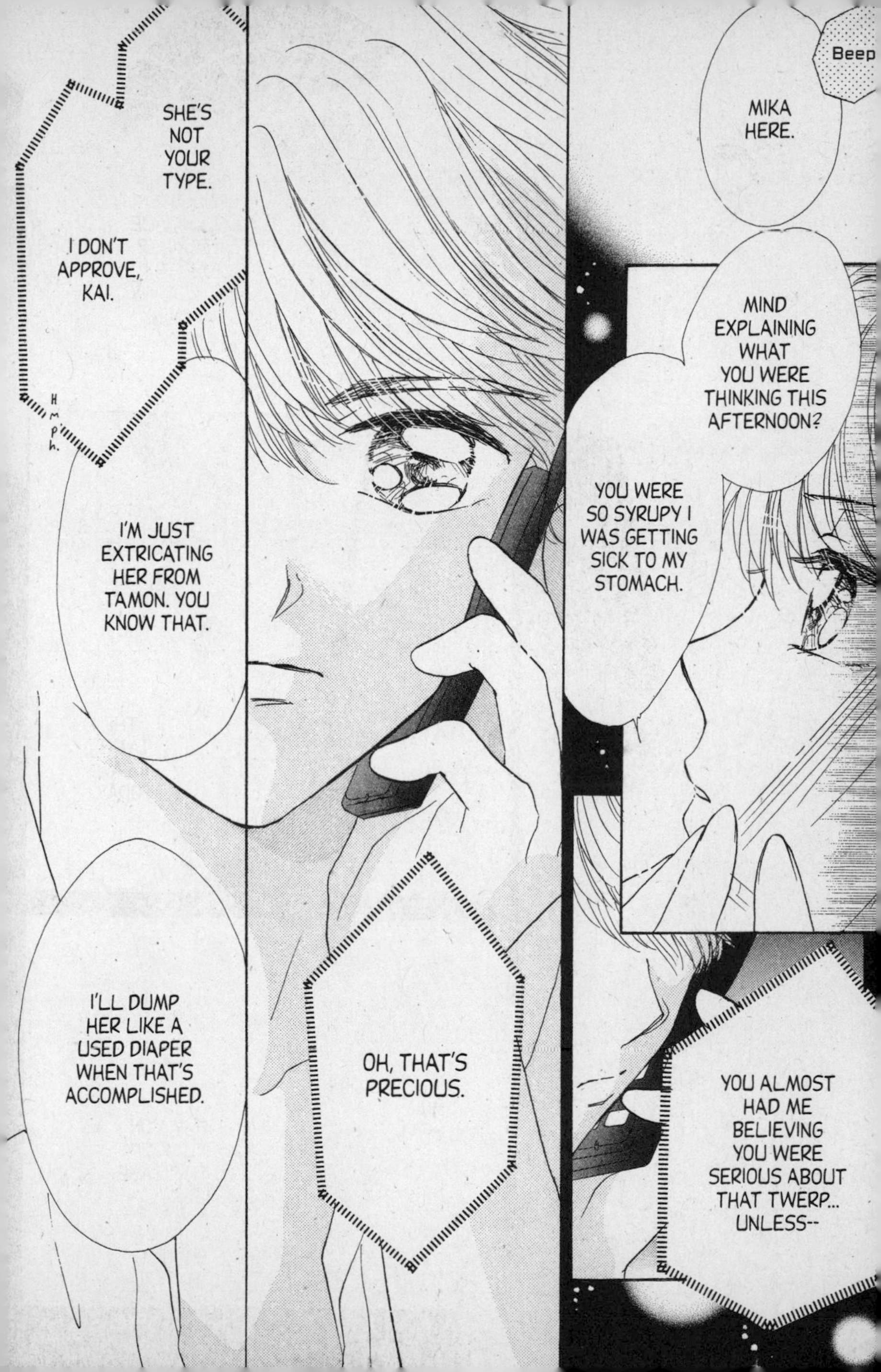
Beep
MIKA HERE.
MIND EXPLAINING WHAT YOU WERE THINKING THIS AFTERNOON?
YOU WERE SO SYRUPY I WAS GETTING SICK TO MY STOMACH.
YOU ALMOST HAD ME BELIEVING YOU WERE SERIOUS ABOUT THAT TWERP... UNLESS--
OH, THAT'S PRECIOUS.
SHE'S NOT YOUR TYPE.
I DON'T APPROVE, KAI.
Hmph.
I'M JUST EXTRICATING HER FROM TAMON. YOU KNOW THAT.
I'LL DUMP HER LIKE A USED DIAPER WHEN THAT'S ACCOMPLISHED.

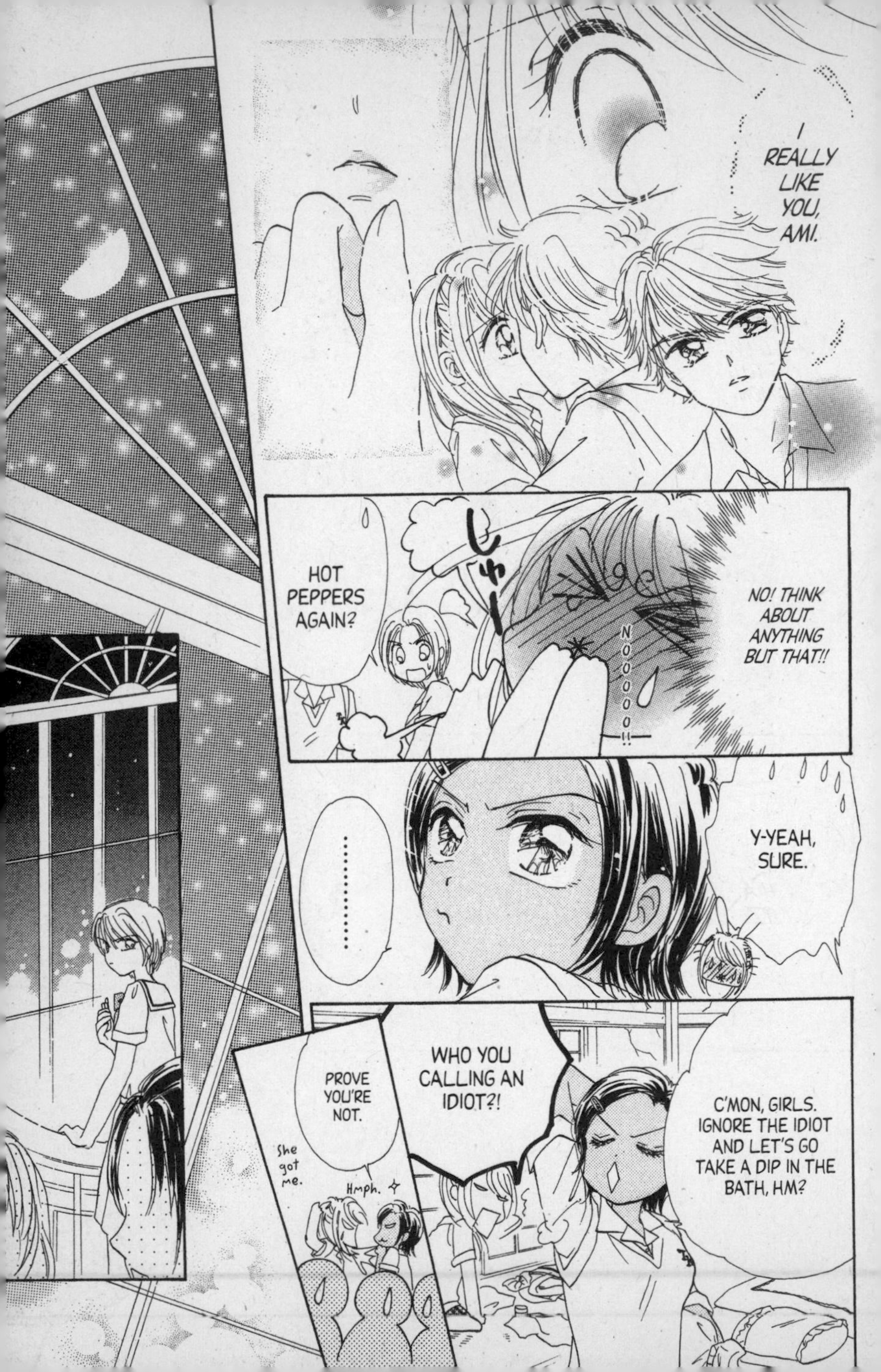
I REALLY LIKE YOU, AMI.
NO! THINK ABOUT ANYTHING BUT THAT!!
NOOOOOO!!
HOT PEPPERS AGAIN?
Y-YEAH, SURE.
......
C'MON, GIRLS. IGNORE THE IDIOT AND LET'S GO TAKE A DIP IN THE BATH, HM?
WHO YOU CALLING AN IDIOT?!
PROVE YOU'RE NOT.
Hmph.
She got me.

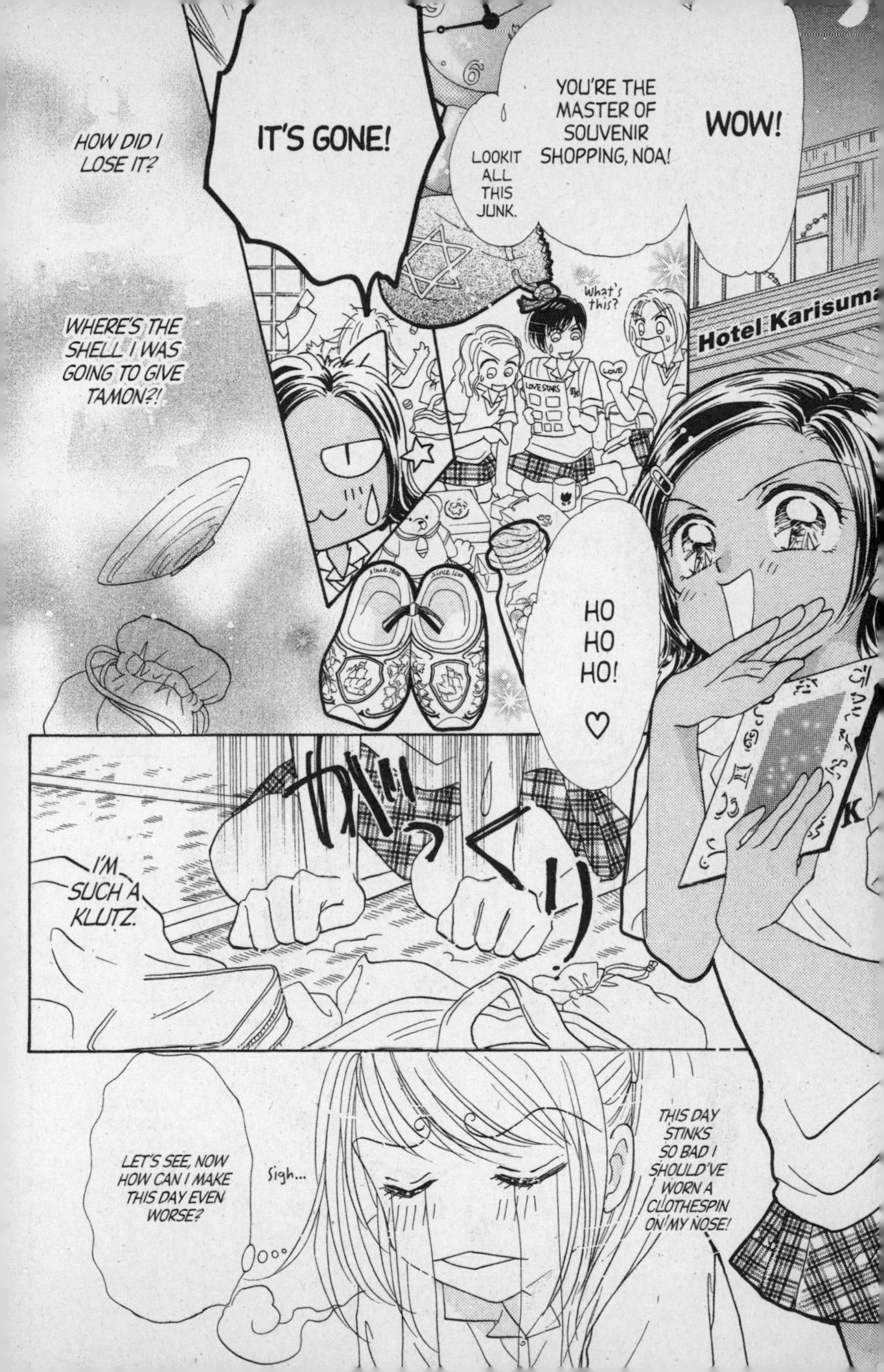
WOW!
YOU'RE THE MASTER OF SOUVENIR SHOPPING, NOA!
LOOKIT ALL THIS JUNK.
What's this?
Hotel Karisuma
HO HO HO! ♡
IT'S GONE!
HOW DID I LOSE IT?
WHERE'S THE SHELL I WAS GOING TO GIVE TAMON?!
I'M SUCH A KLUTZ.
THIS DAY STINKS SO BAD I SHOULD'VE WORN A CLOTHESPIN ON MY NOSE!
Sigh...
LET'S SEE, NOW HOW CAN I MAKE THIS DAY EVEN WORSE?

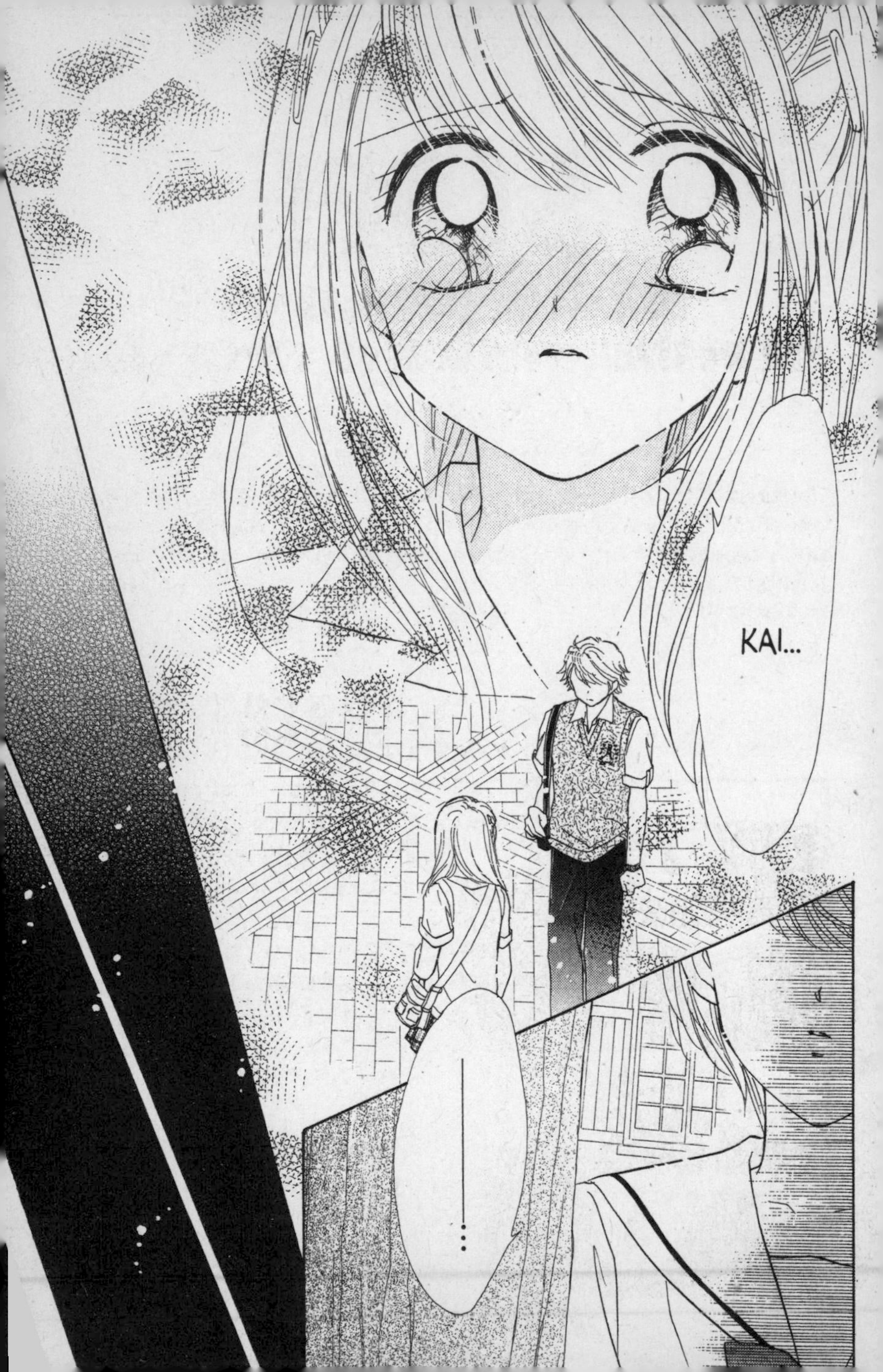
KAI...
......

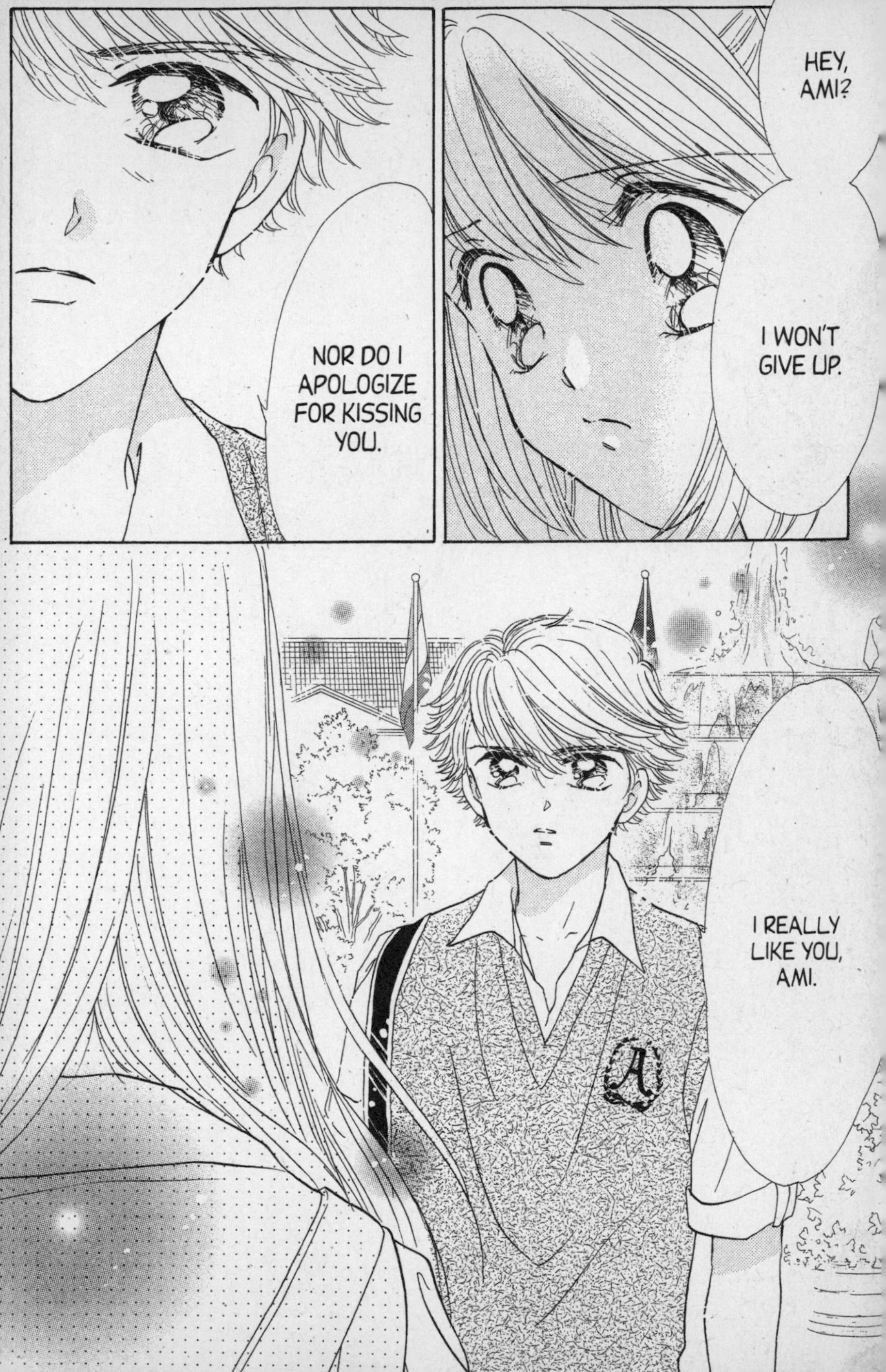
HEY, AMI?
I WON'T GIVE UP.
NOR DO I APOLOGIZE FOR KISSING YOU.
I REALLY LIKE YOU, AMI.

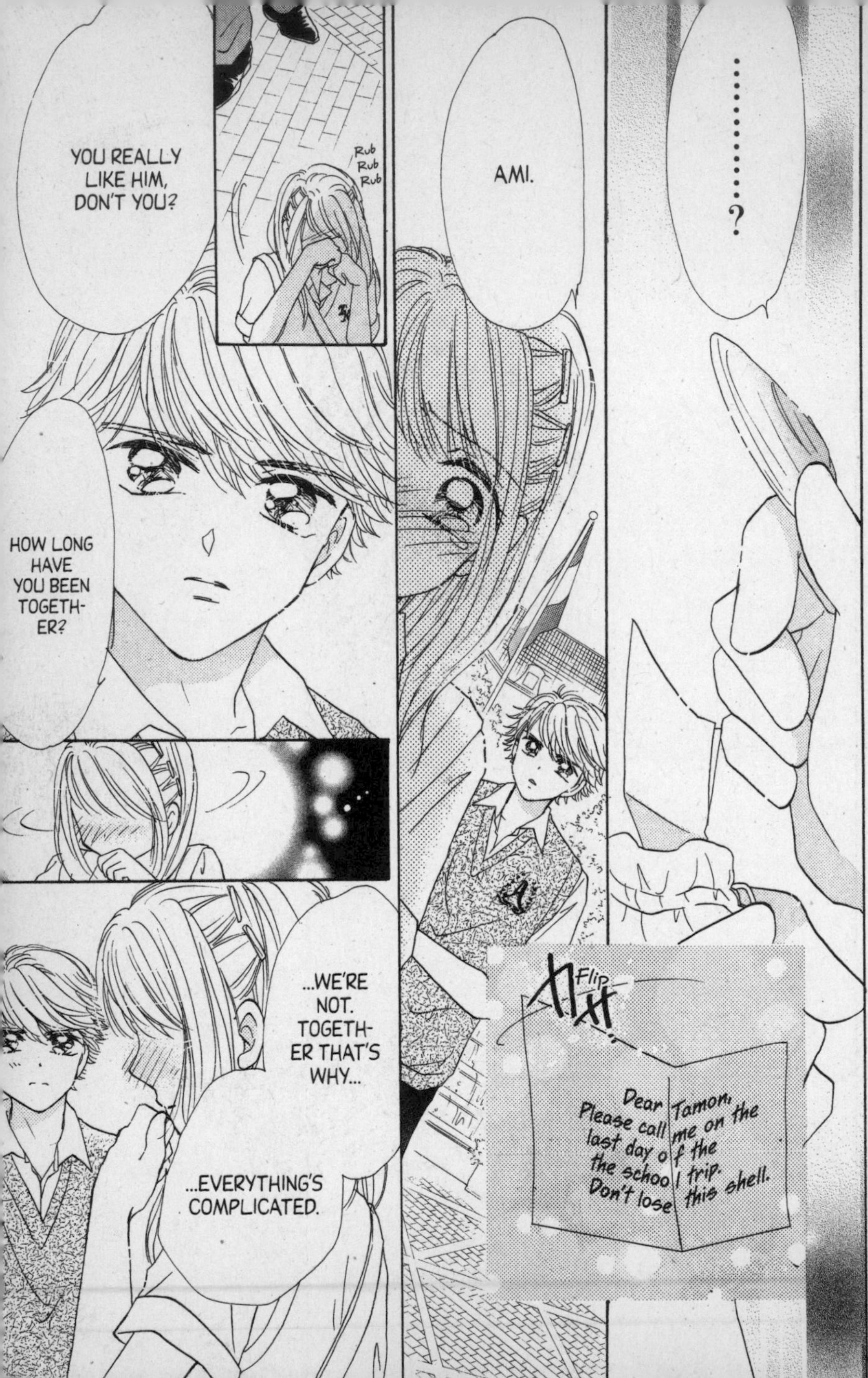
......?
Flip
Dear Tamon,
Please call me on the last day of the the school trip.
Don't lose this shell.
AMI.
Rub Rub Rub
YOU REALLY LIKE HIM, DON'T YOU?
HOW LONG HAVE YOU BEEN TOGETH-ER?
...WE'RE NOT. TOGETH-ER THAT'S WHY...
...EVERYTHING'S COMPLICATED.

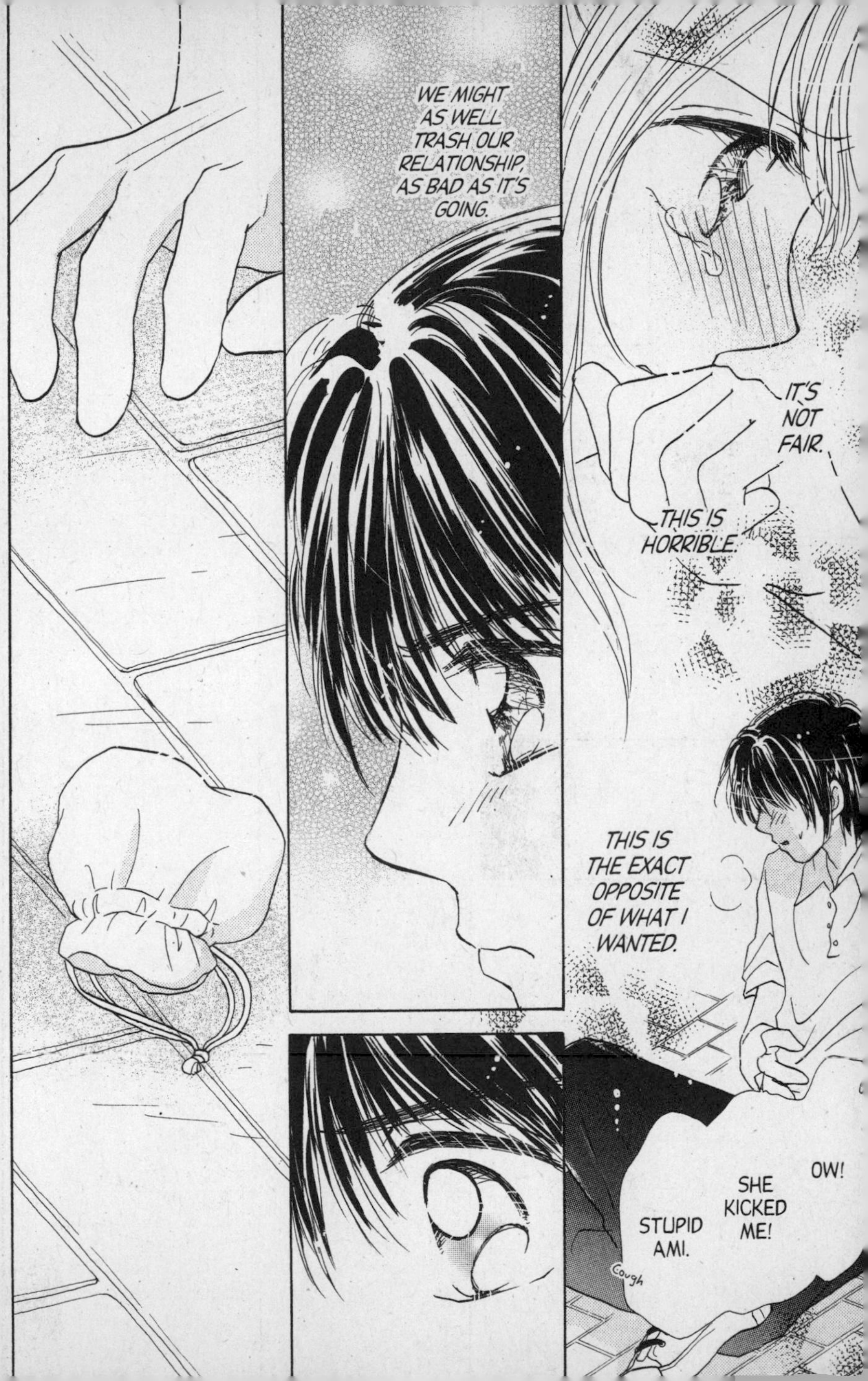
IT'S NOT FAIR.
THIS IS HORRIBLE.
THIS IS THE EXACT OPPOSITE OF WHAT I WANTED.
OW!
SHE KICKED ME!
STUPID AMI.
Cough
WE MIGHT AS WELL TRASH OUR RELATIONSHIP, AS BAD AS IT'S GOING.

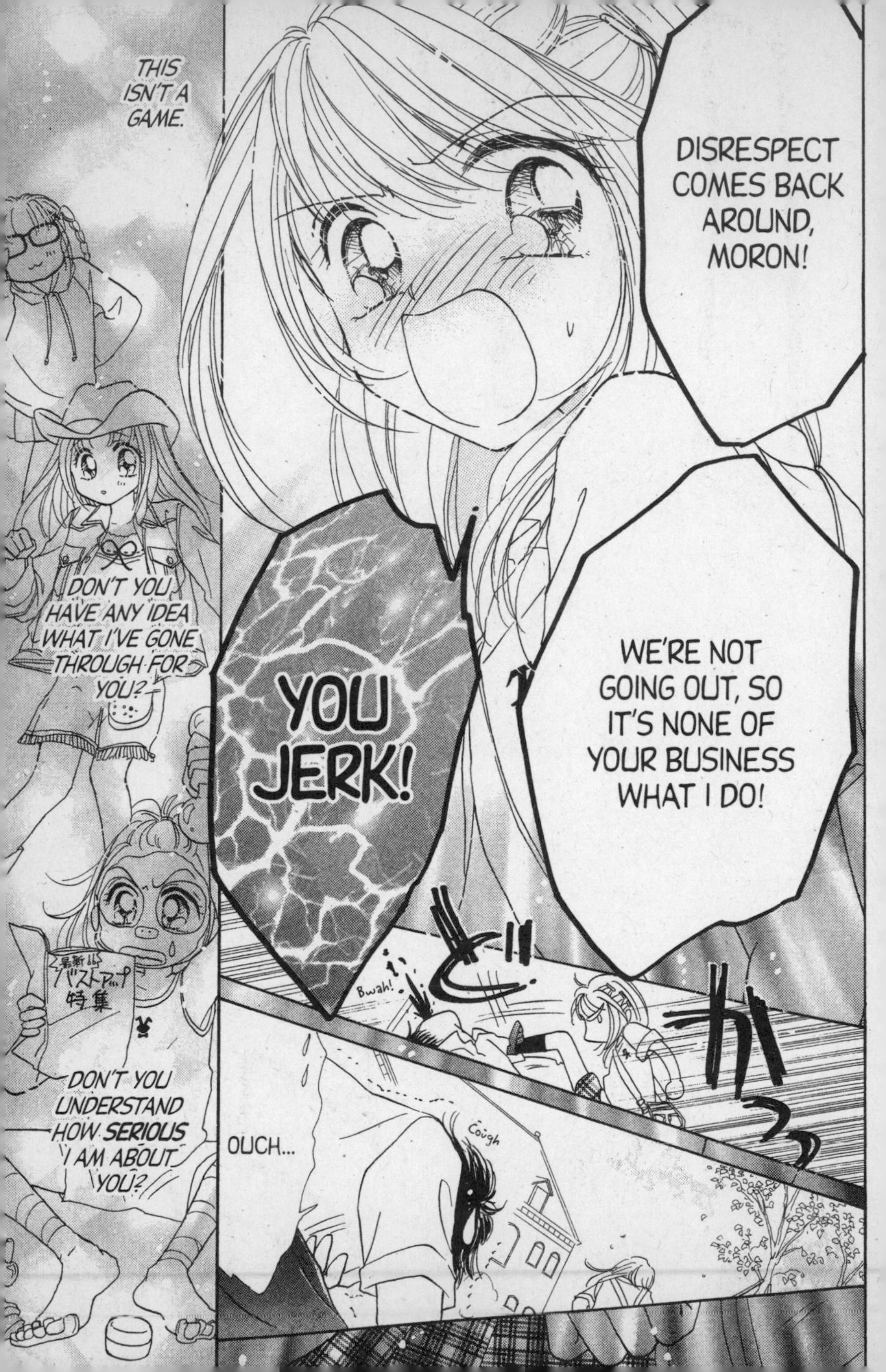
DISRESPECT COMES BACK AROUND, MORON!
WE'RE NOT GOING OUT, SO IT'S NONE OF YOUR BUSINESS WHAT I DO!
YOU JERK!
Bwah!
Cough
OUCH...
THIS ISN'T A GAME.
DON'T YOU HAVE ANY IDEA WHAT I'VE GONE THROUGH FOR YOU?
DON'T YOU UNDERSTAND HOW SERIOUS I AM ABOUT YOU?

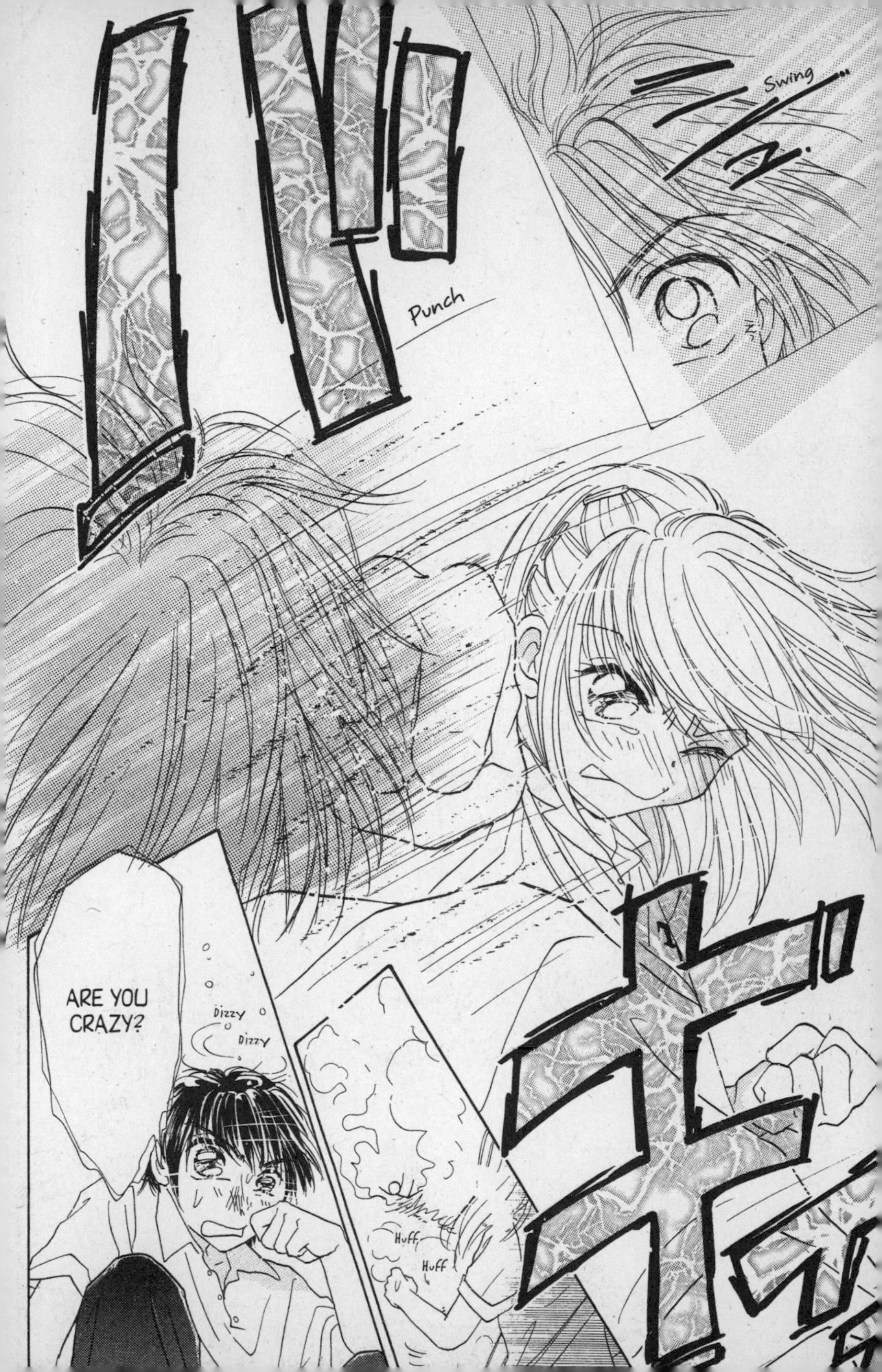
Swing...
Punch
Huff
Huff
ARE YOU CRAZY?
Dizzy
Dizzy

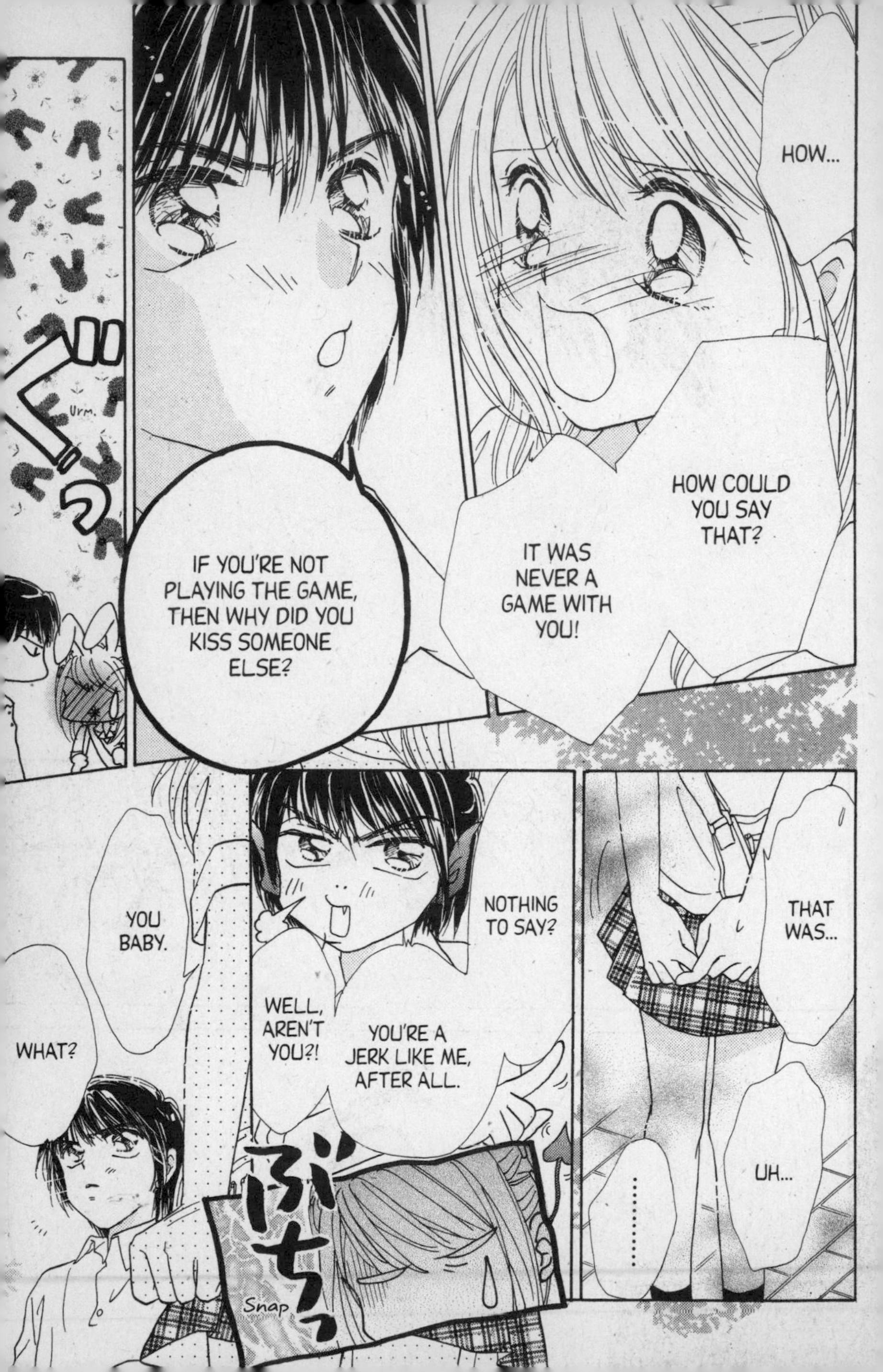
HOW...
HOW COULD YOU SAY THAT?
IT WAS NEVER A GAME WITH YOU!
IF YOU'RE NOT PLAYING THE GAME, THEN WHY DID YOU KISS SOMEONE ELSE?
Urm.
THAT WAS...
UH...
......
NOTHING TO SAY?
YOU'RE A JERK LIKE ME, AFTER ALL.
WELL, AREN'T YOU?!
Snap
YOU BABY.
WHAT?

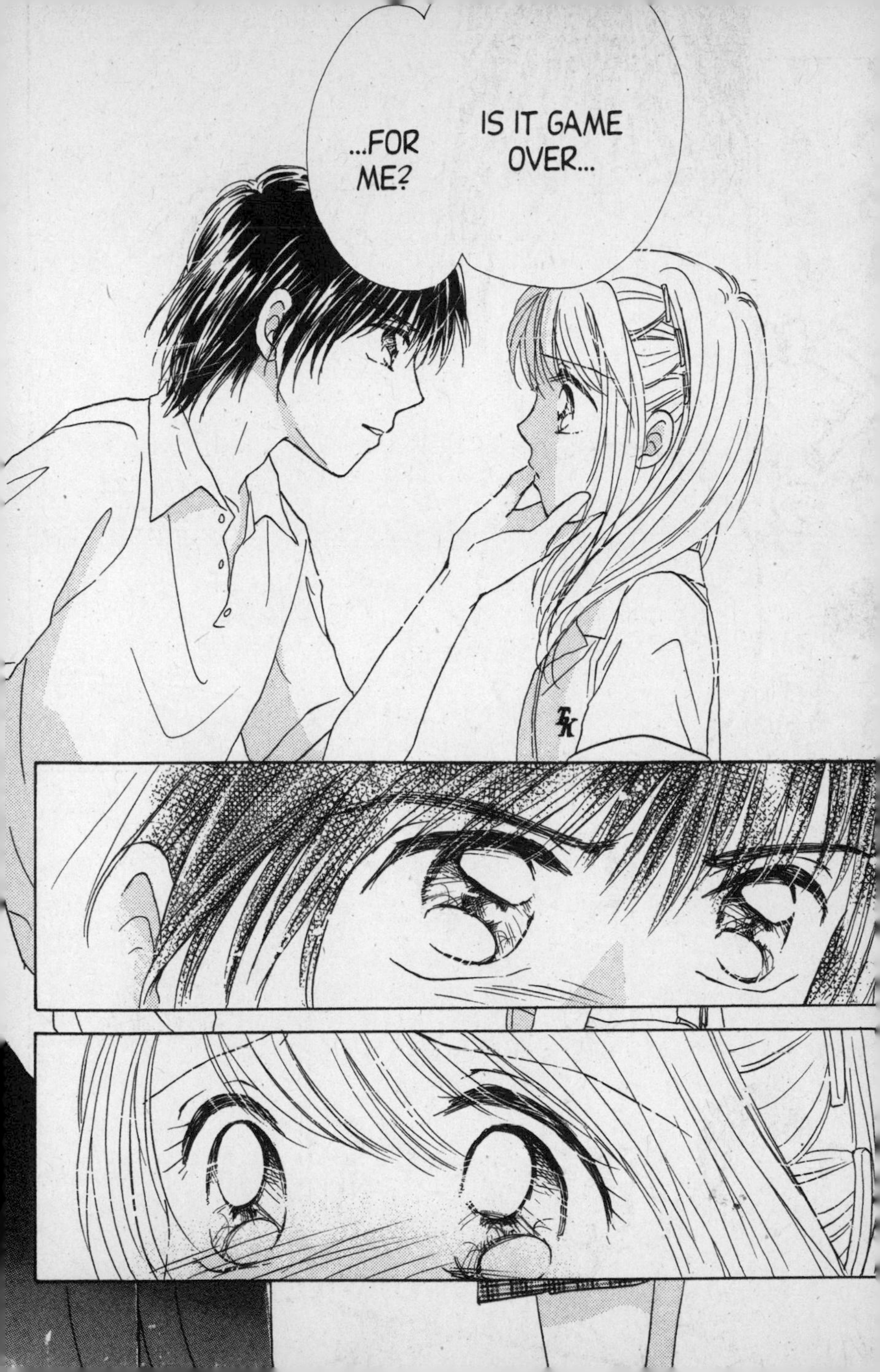
IS IT GAME OVER...
...FOR ME?

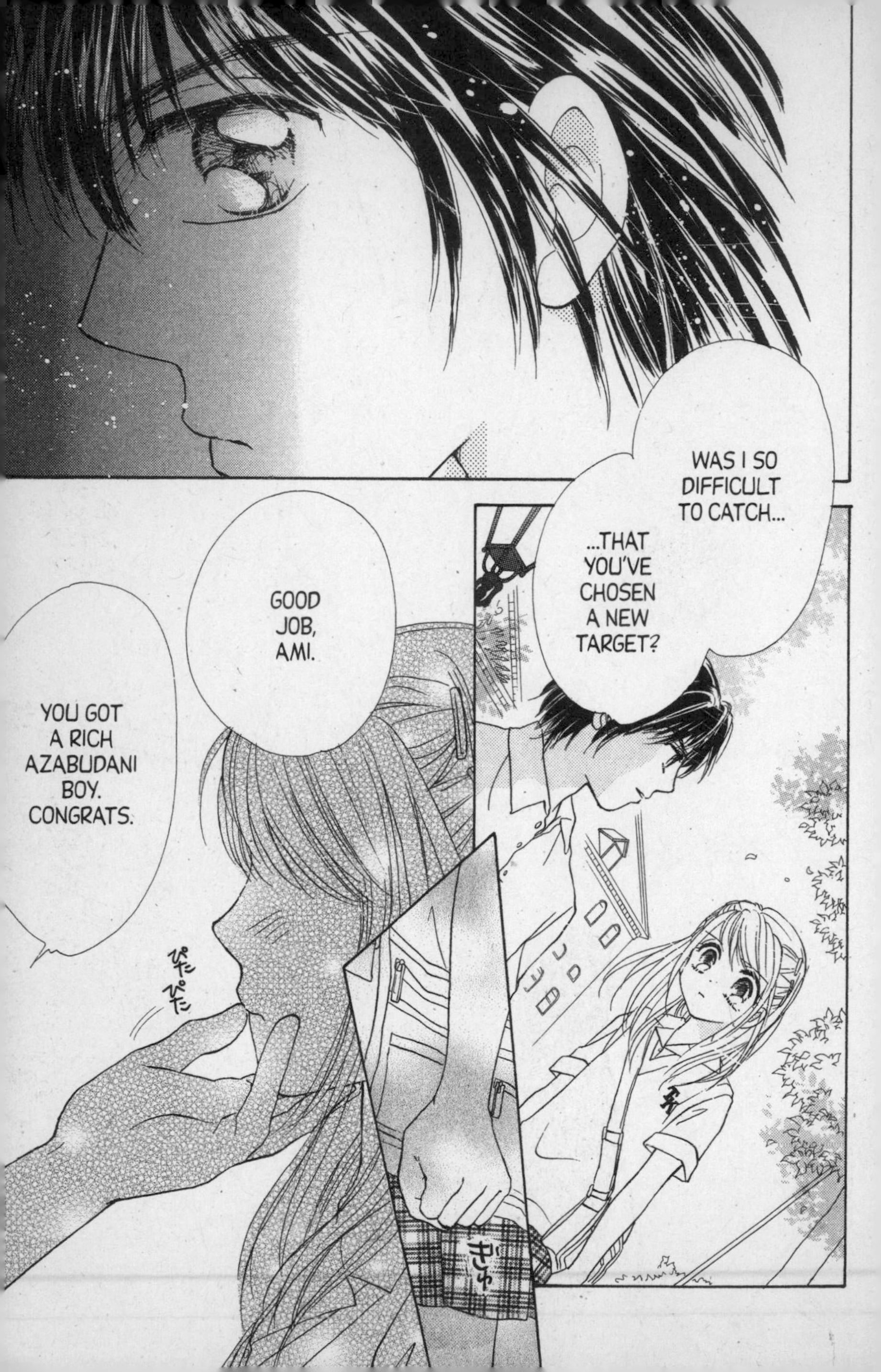
WAS I SO DIFFICULT TO CATCH...
...THAT YOU'VE CHOSEN A NEW TARGET?
GOOD JOB, AMI.
YOU GOT A RICH AZABUDANI BOY. CONGRATS.
ぴたぴた
ぎゅ

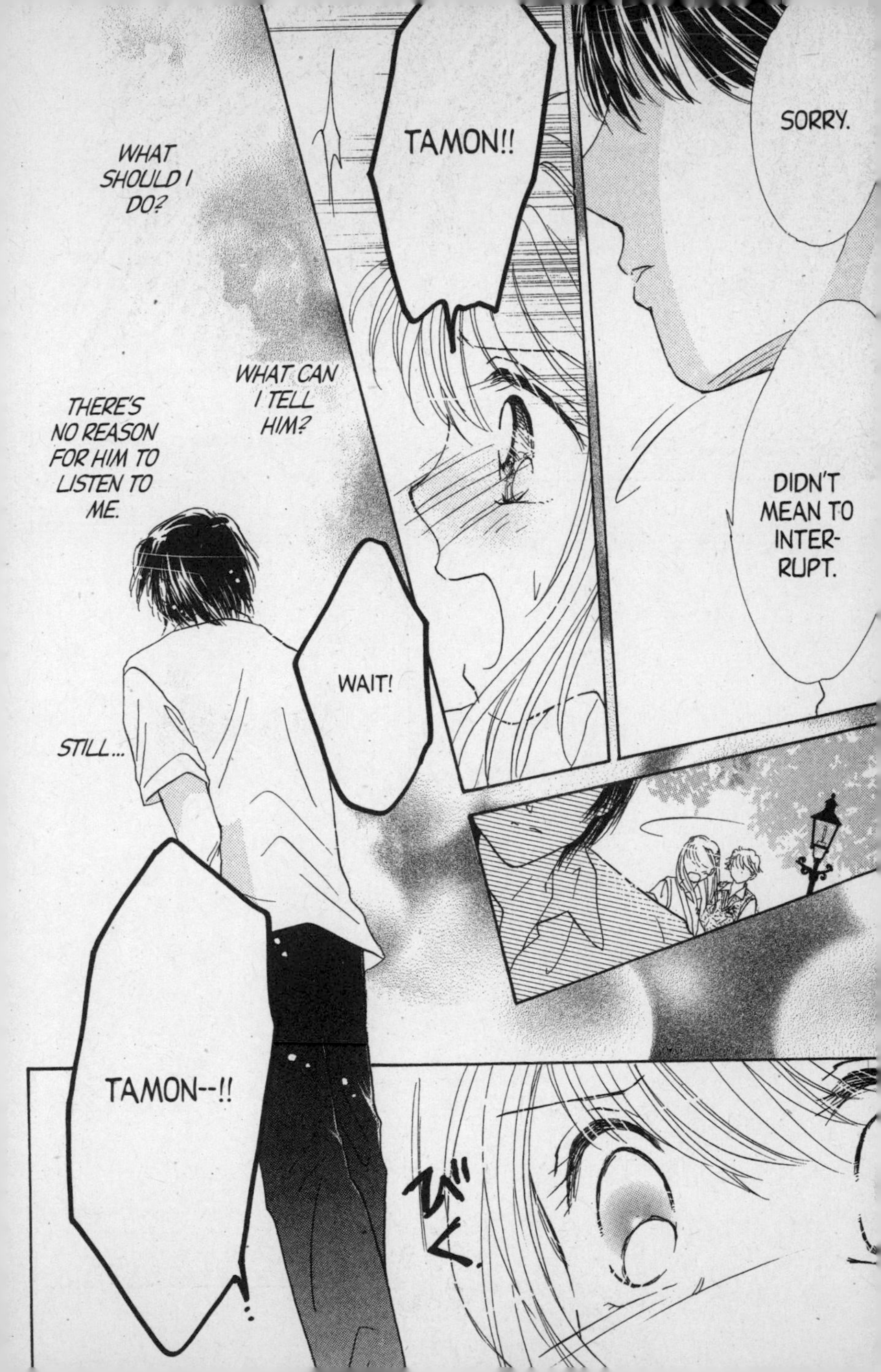
SORRY.
DIDN'T MEAN TO INTER-RUPT.
TAMON!!
WAIT!
WHAT SHOULD I DO?
WHAT CAN I TELL HIM?
THERE'S NO REASON FOR HIM TO LISTEN TO ME.
STILL...
びく
TAMON--!!

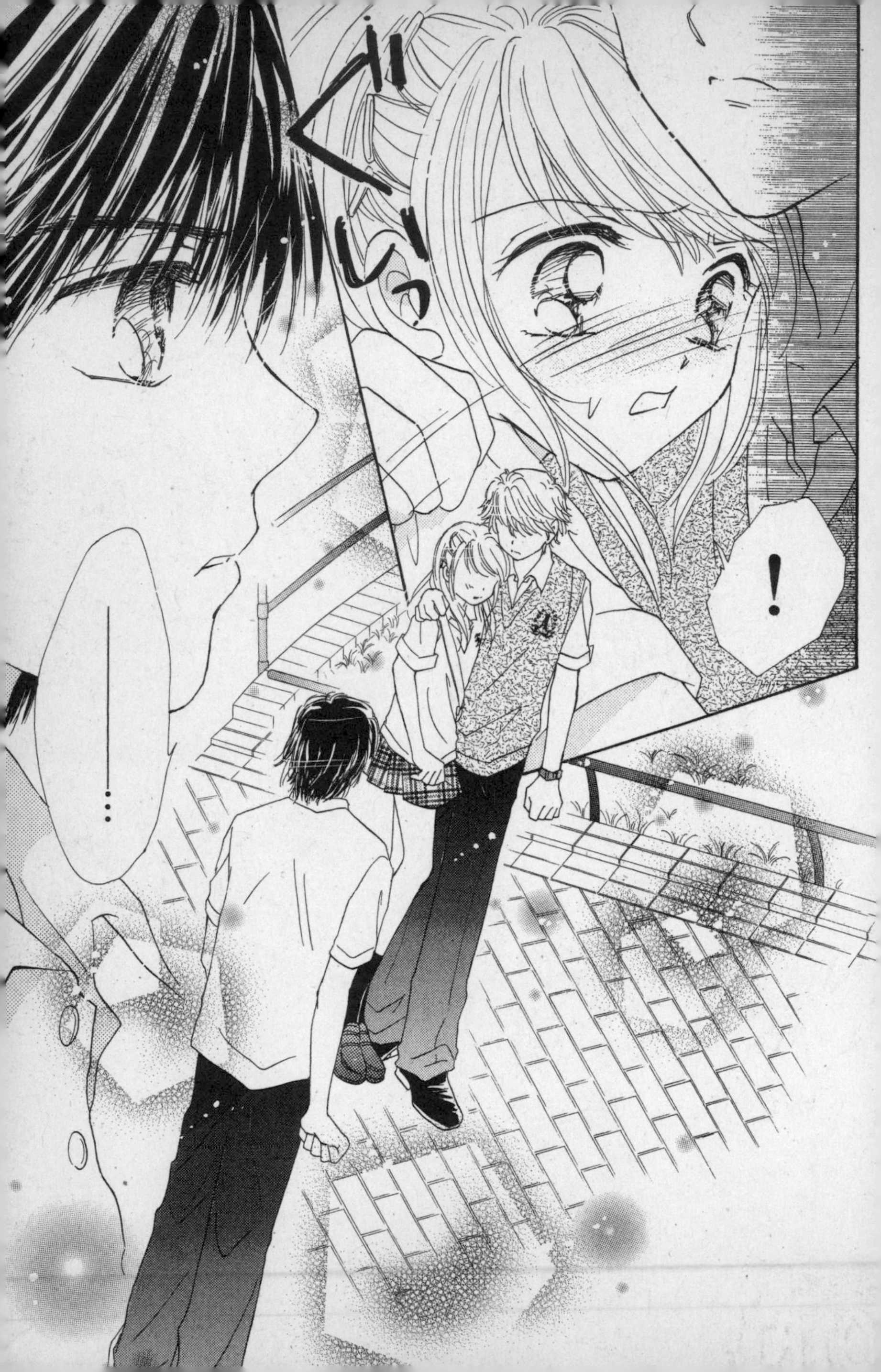
ぐいっ
!
......

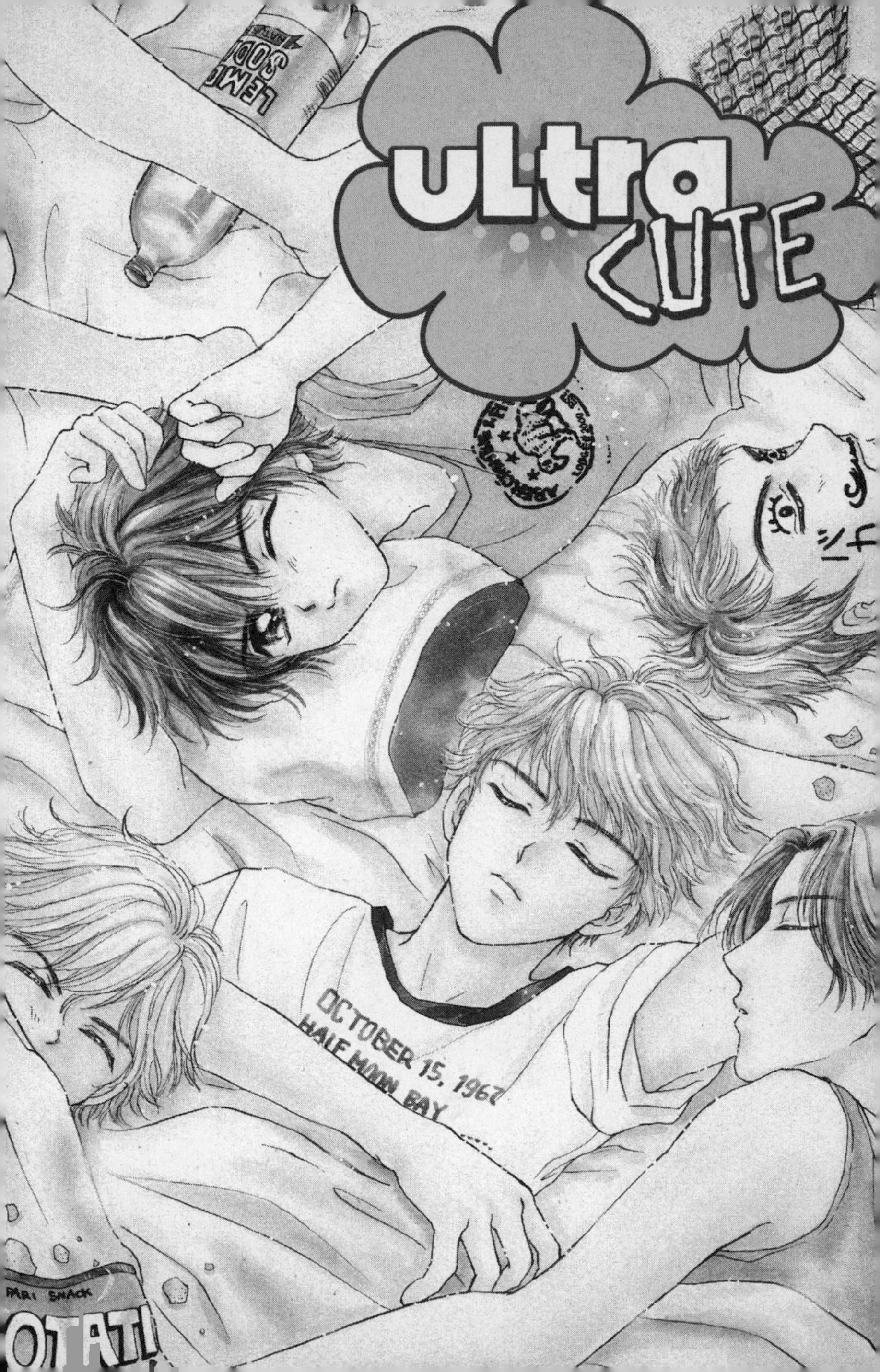
ultra
CUTE
OCTOBER 15, 1967
HALF MOON BAY
PARI SNACK

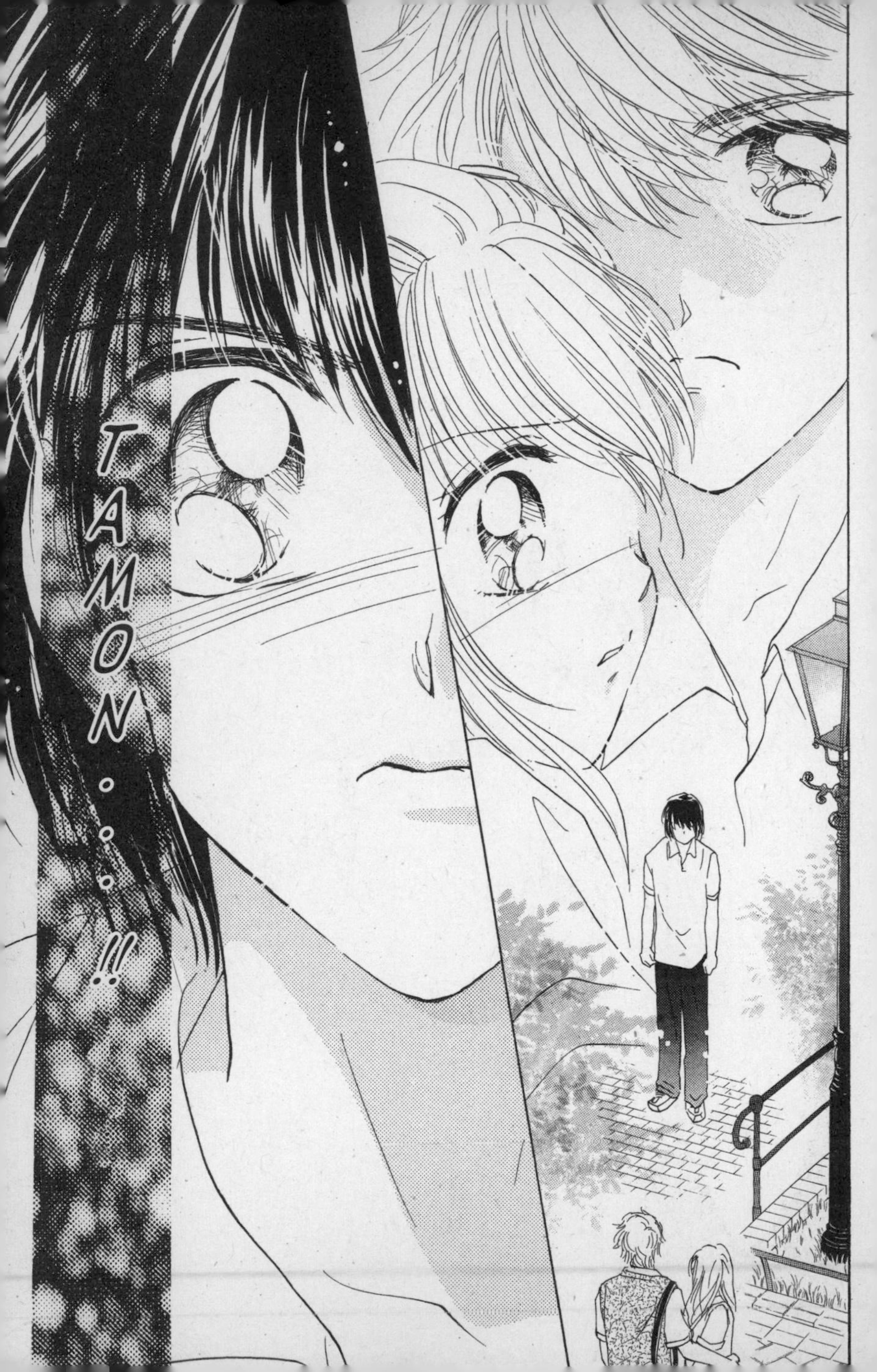
TAMON.....!!

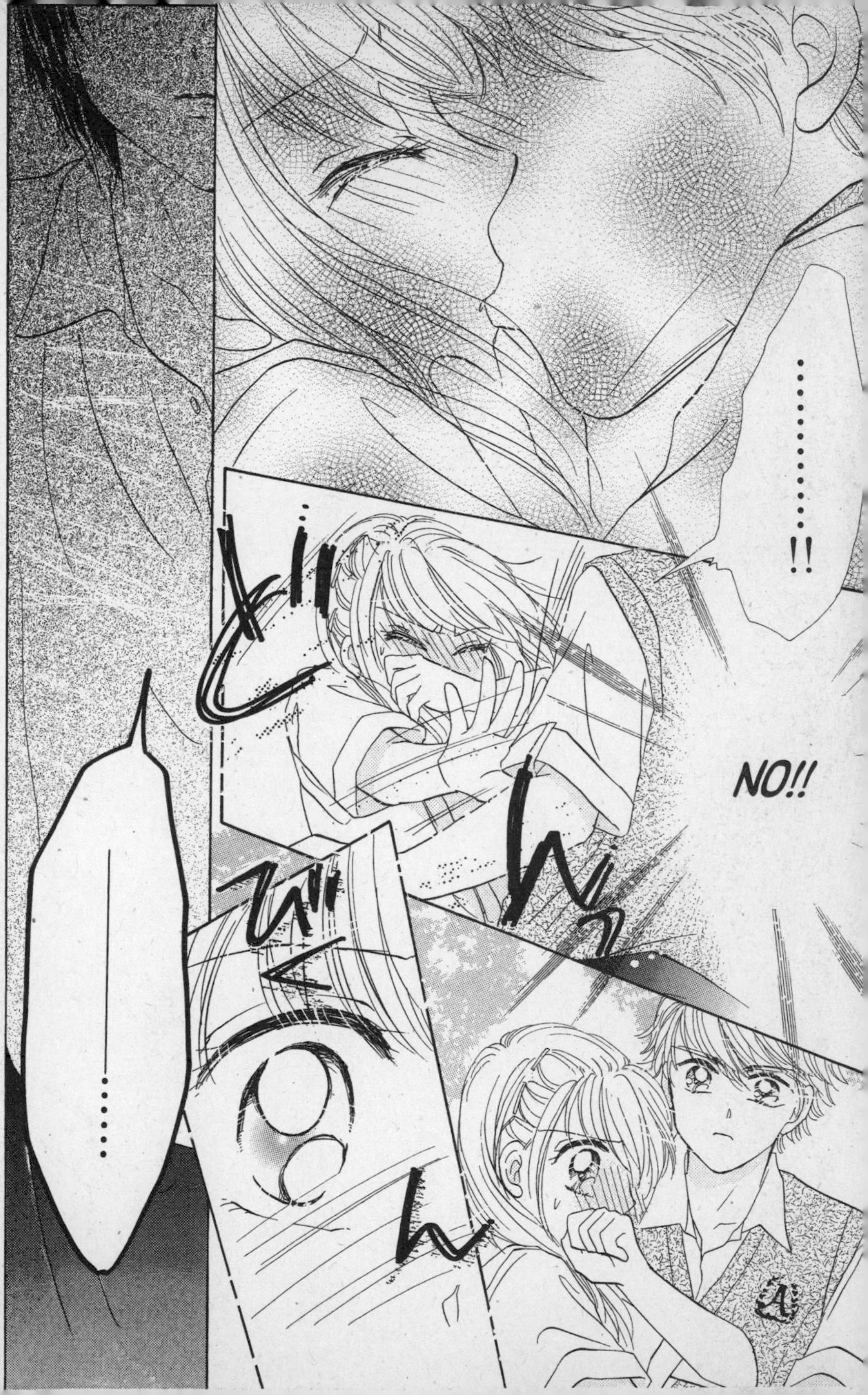

......!!
NO!!
びくん
——......

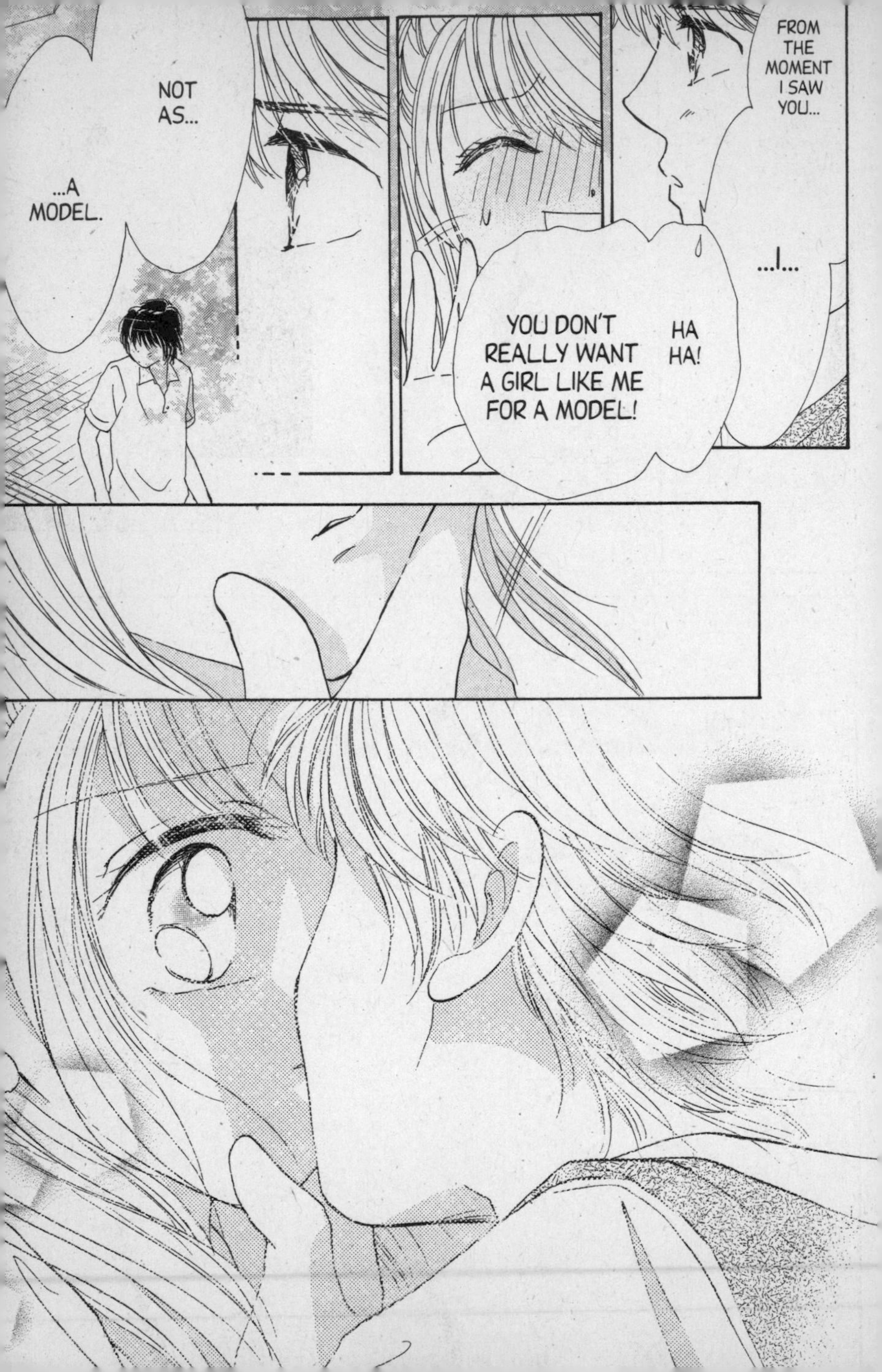
FROM THE MOMENT I SAW YOU...
...I...
HA HA!
YOU DON'T REALLY WANT A GIRL LIKE ME FOR A MODEL!
NOT AS...
...A MODEL.

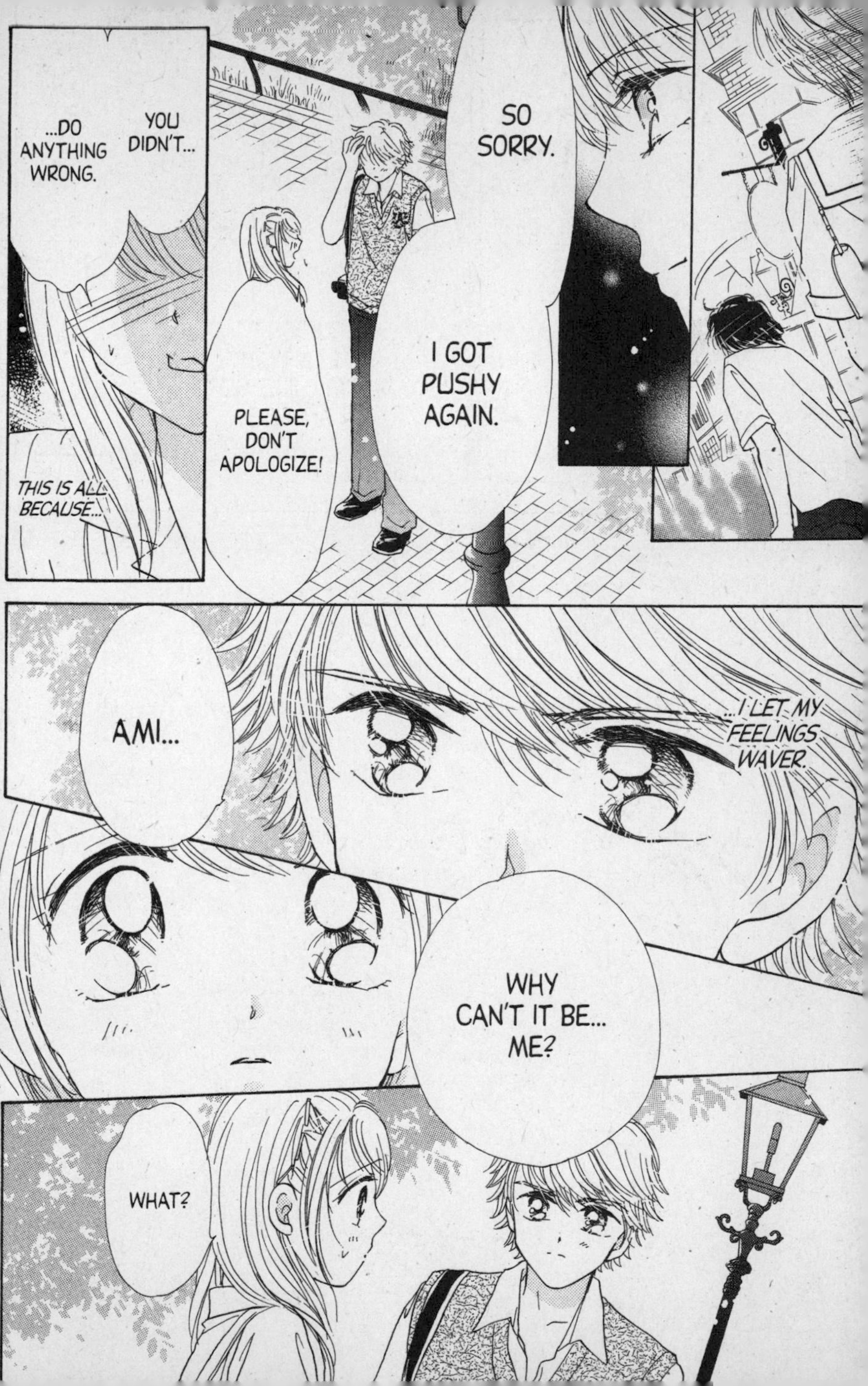
SO SORRY.
I GOT PUSHY AGAIN.
PLEASE, DON'T APOLOGIZE!
YOU DIDN'T...
...DO ANYTHING WRONG.
THIS IS ALL BECAUSE...
...I LET MY FEELINGS WAVER.
AMI...
WHY CAN'T IT BE... ME?
WHAT?

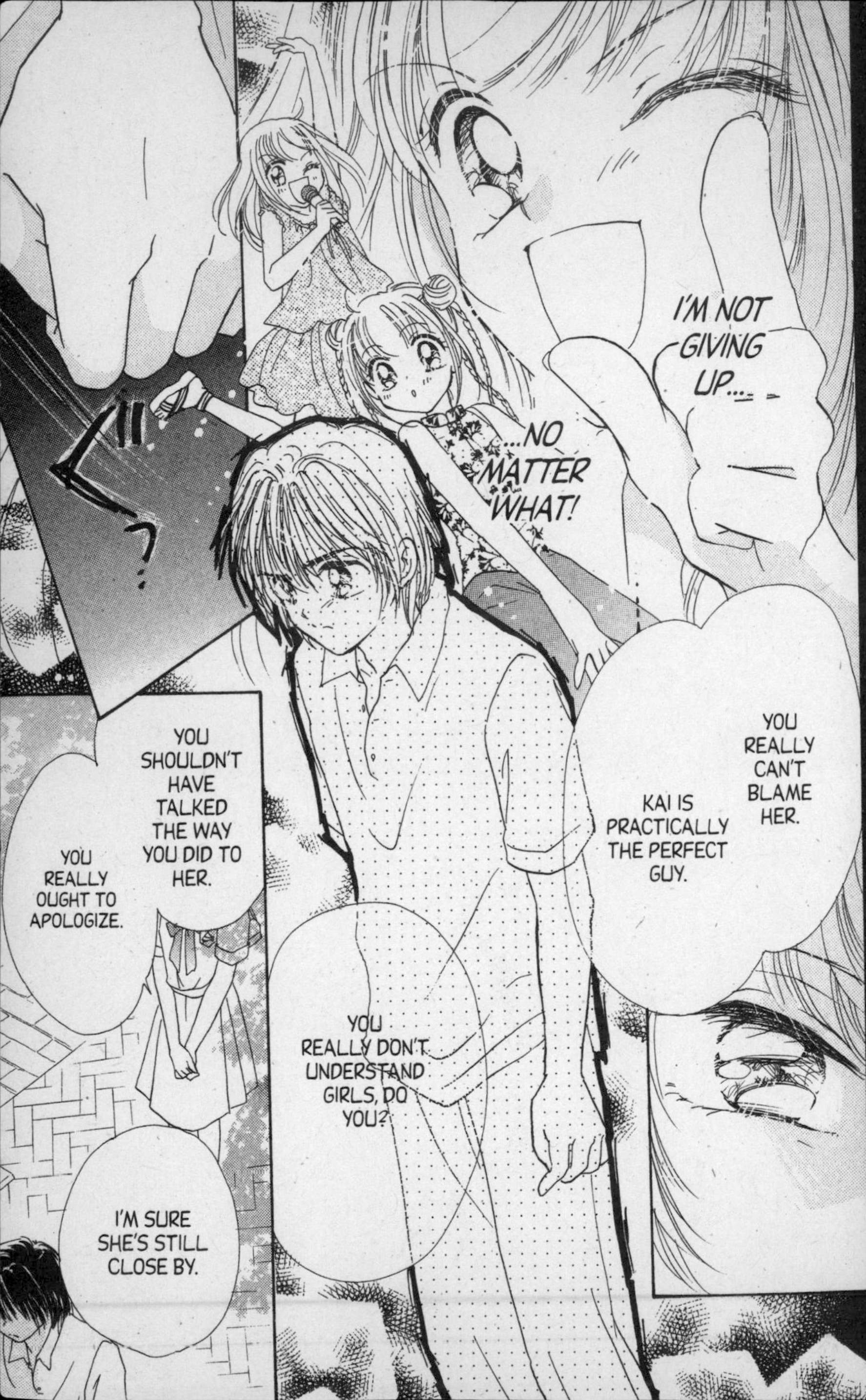
I'M NOT GIVING UP...
...NO MATTER WHAT!
YOU REALLY CAN'T BLAME HER.
KAI IS PRACTICALLY THE PERFECT GUY.
YOU REALLY DON'T UNDERSTAND GIRLS, DO YOU?
YOU SHOULDN'T HAVE TALKED THE WAY YOU DID TO HER.
YOU REALLY OUGHT TO APOLOGIZE.
I'M SURE SHE'S STILL CLOSE BY.

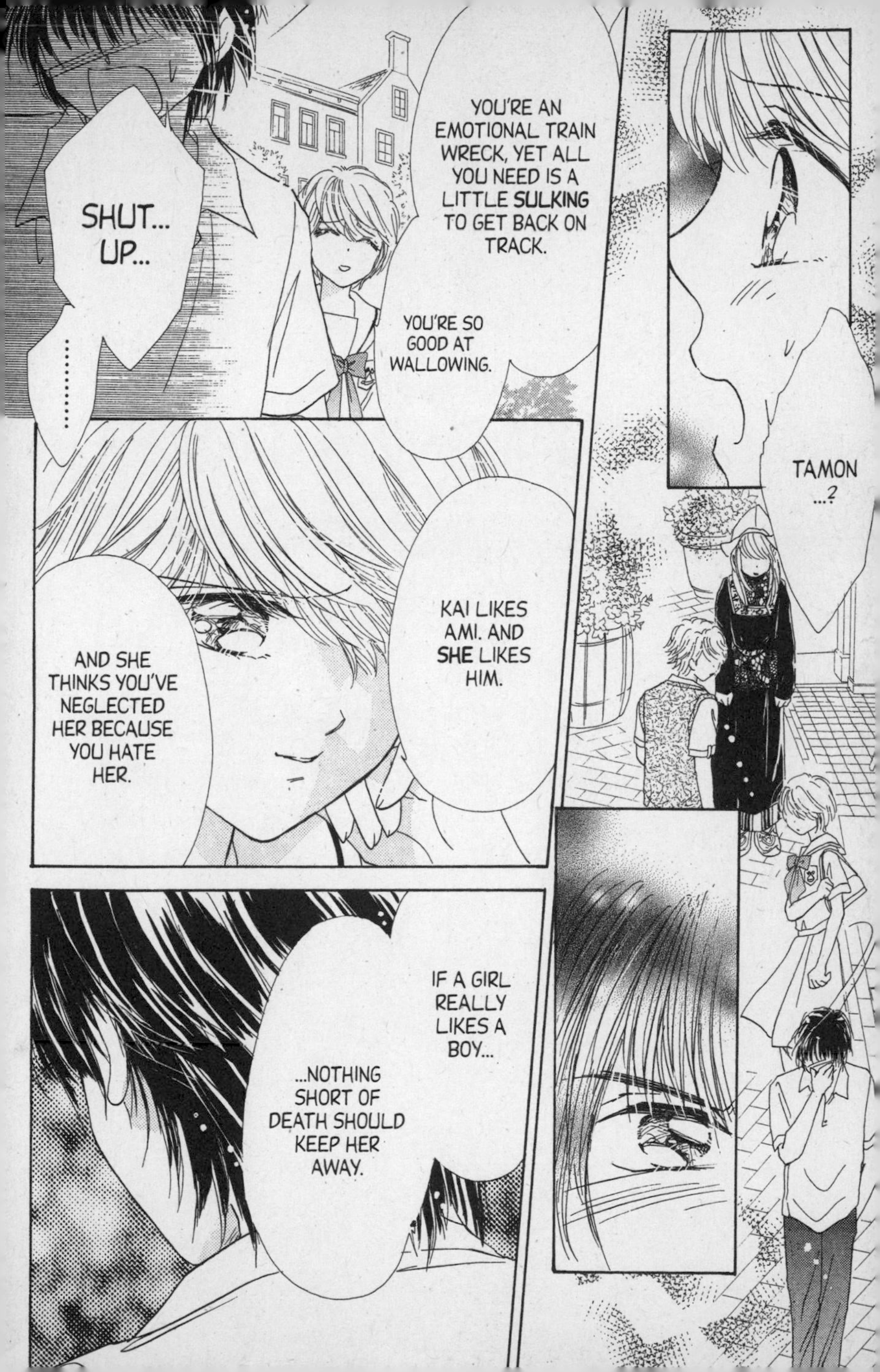
TAMON ...?
YOU'RE AN EMOTIONAL TRAIN WRECK, YET ALL YOU NEED IS A LITTLE **SULKING** TO GET BACK ON TRACK.
YOU'RE SO GOOD AT WALLOWING.
SHUT... UP...
......
KAI LIKES AMI. AND **SHE** LIKES HIM.
AND SHE THINKS YOU'VE NEGLECTED HER BECAUSE YOU HATE HER.
IF A GIRL REALLY LIKES A BOY...
...NOTHING SHORT OF DEATH SHOULD KEEP HER AWAY.

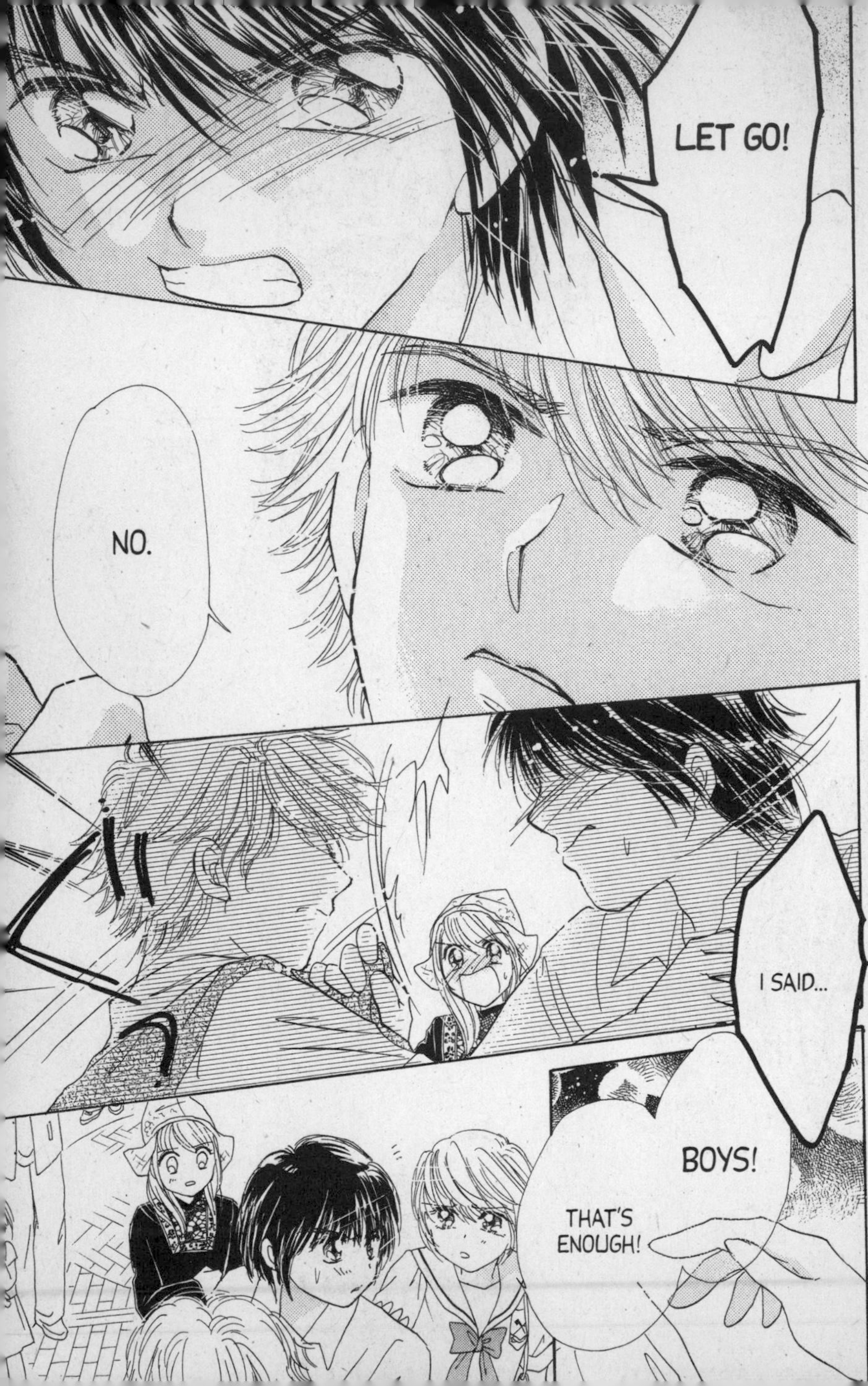
LET GO!
NO.
I SAID...
BOYS!
THAT'S ENOUGH!

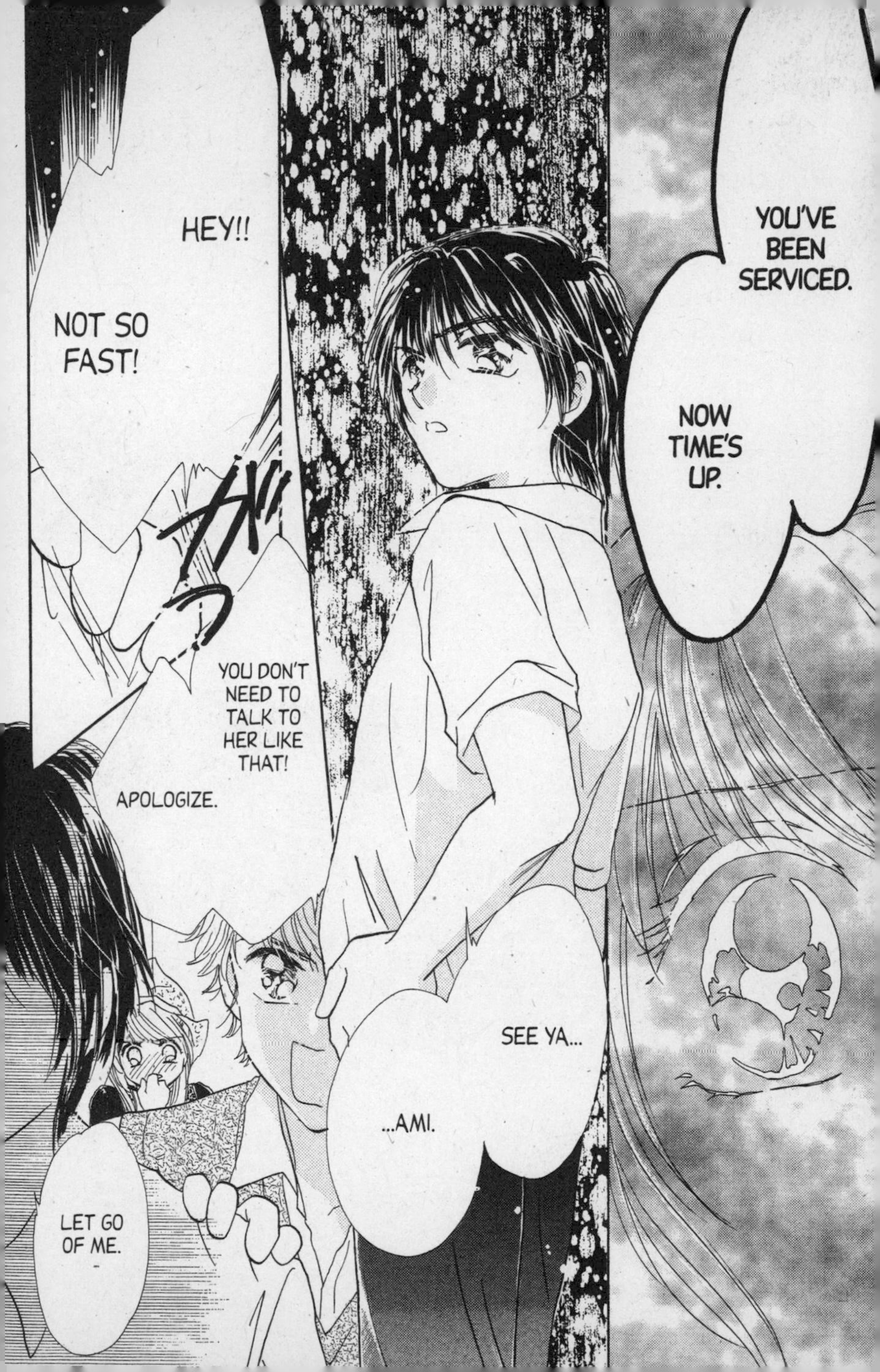
YOU'VE BEEN SERVICED.
NOW TIME'S UP.
SEE YA...
...AMI.
HEY!!
NOT SO FAST!
YOU DON'T NEED TO TALK TO HER LIKE THAT!
APOLOGIZE.
LET GO OF ME.

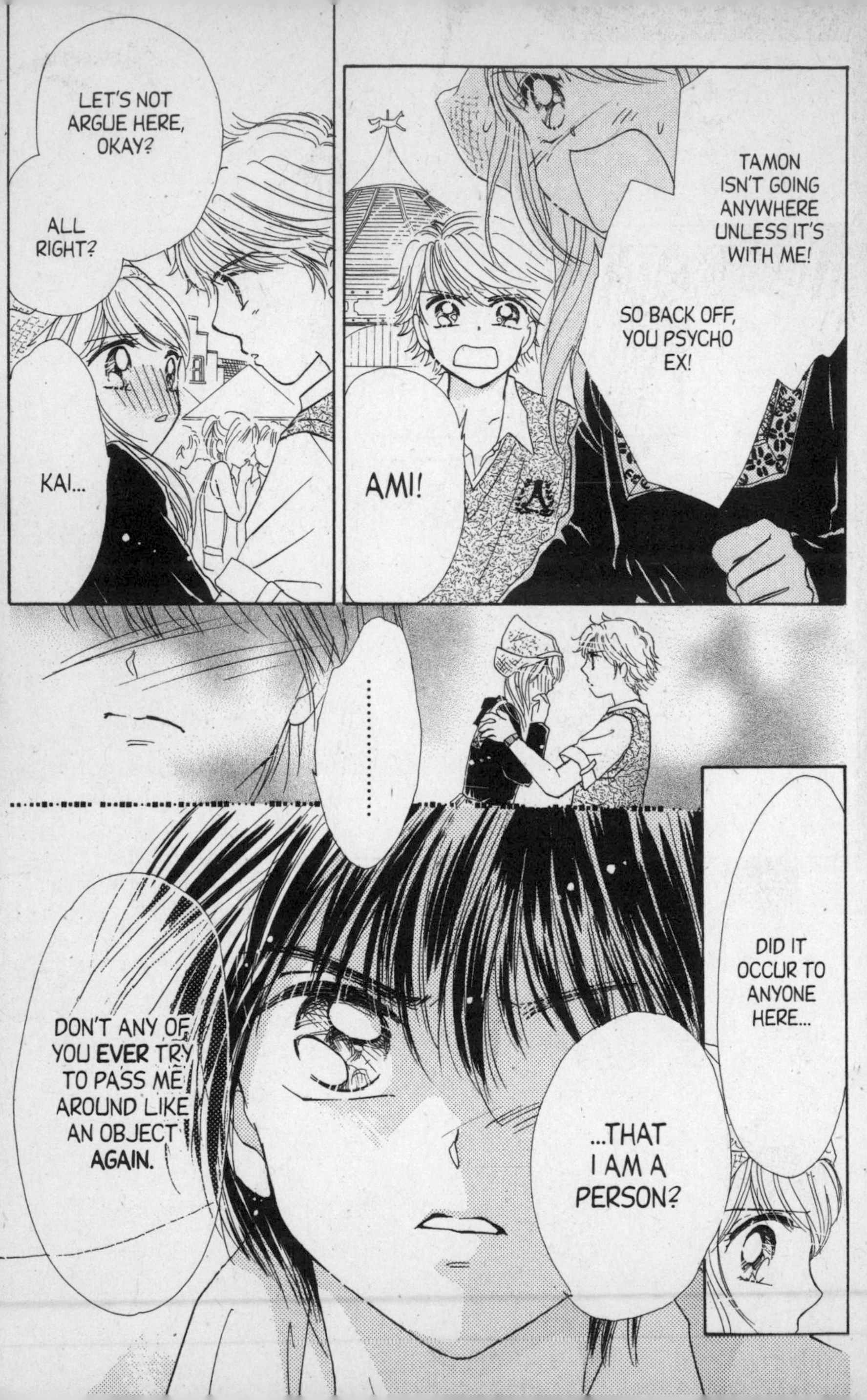
TAMON ISN'T GOING ANYWHERE UNLESS IT'S WITH ME!
SO BACK OFF, YOU PSYCHO EX!
AMI!
LET'S NOT ARGUE HERE, OKAY?
ALL RIGHT?
KAI...
......
DID IT OCCUR TO ANYONE HERE...
...THAT I AM A PERSON?
DON'T ANY OF YOU **EVER** TRY TO PASS ME AROUND LIKE AN OBJECT **AGAIN.**

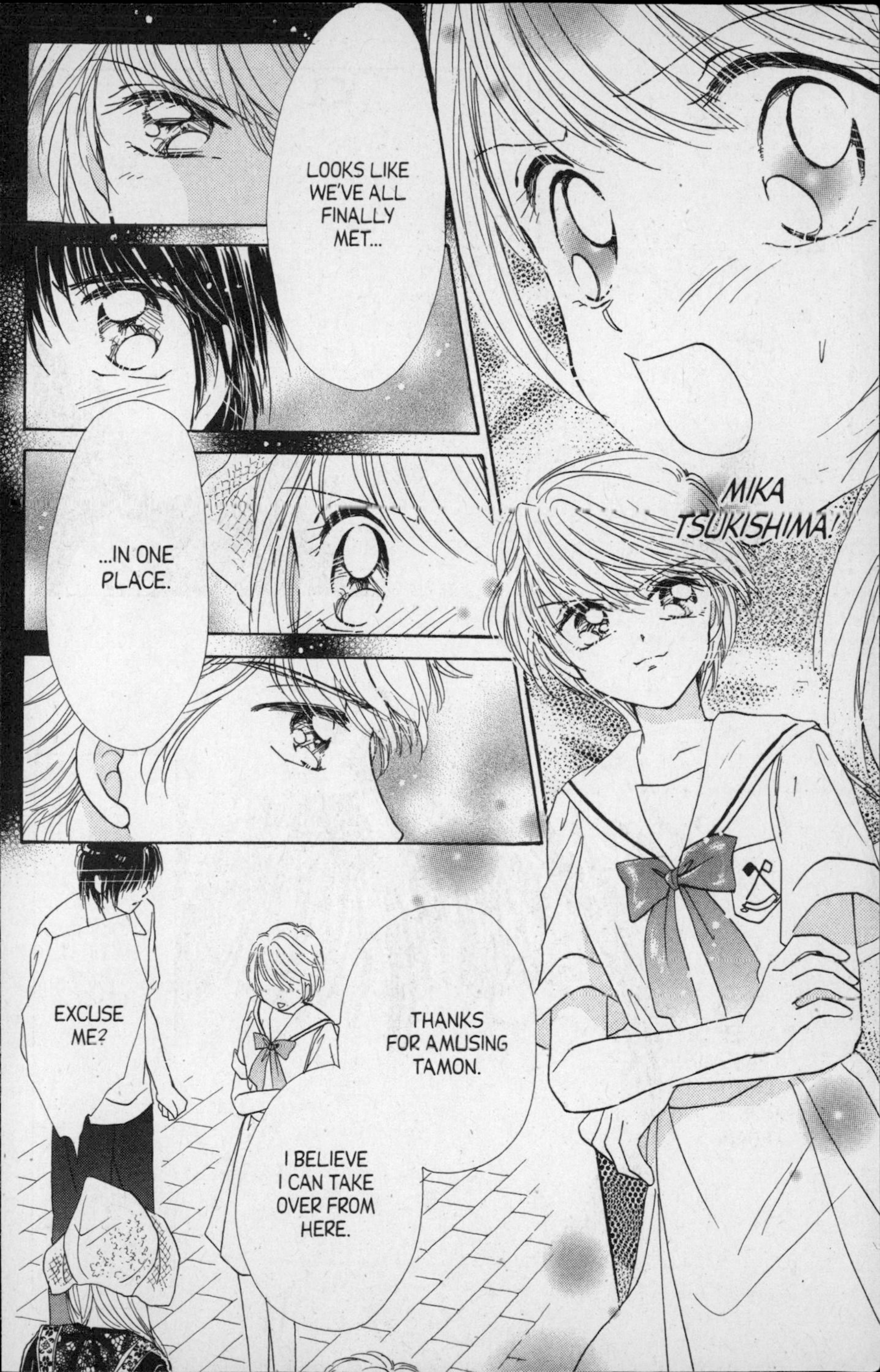
LOOKS LIKE WE'VE ALL FINALLY MET...
...IN ONE PLACE.
MIKA TSUKISHIMA!
THANKS FOR AMUSING TAMON.
I BELIEVE I CAN TAKE OVER FROM HERE.
EXCUSE ME?

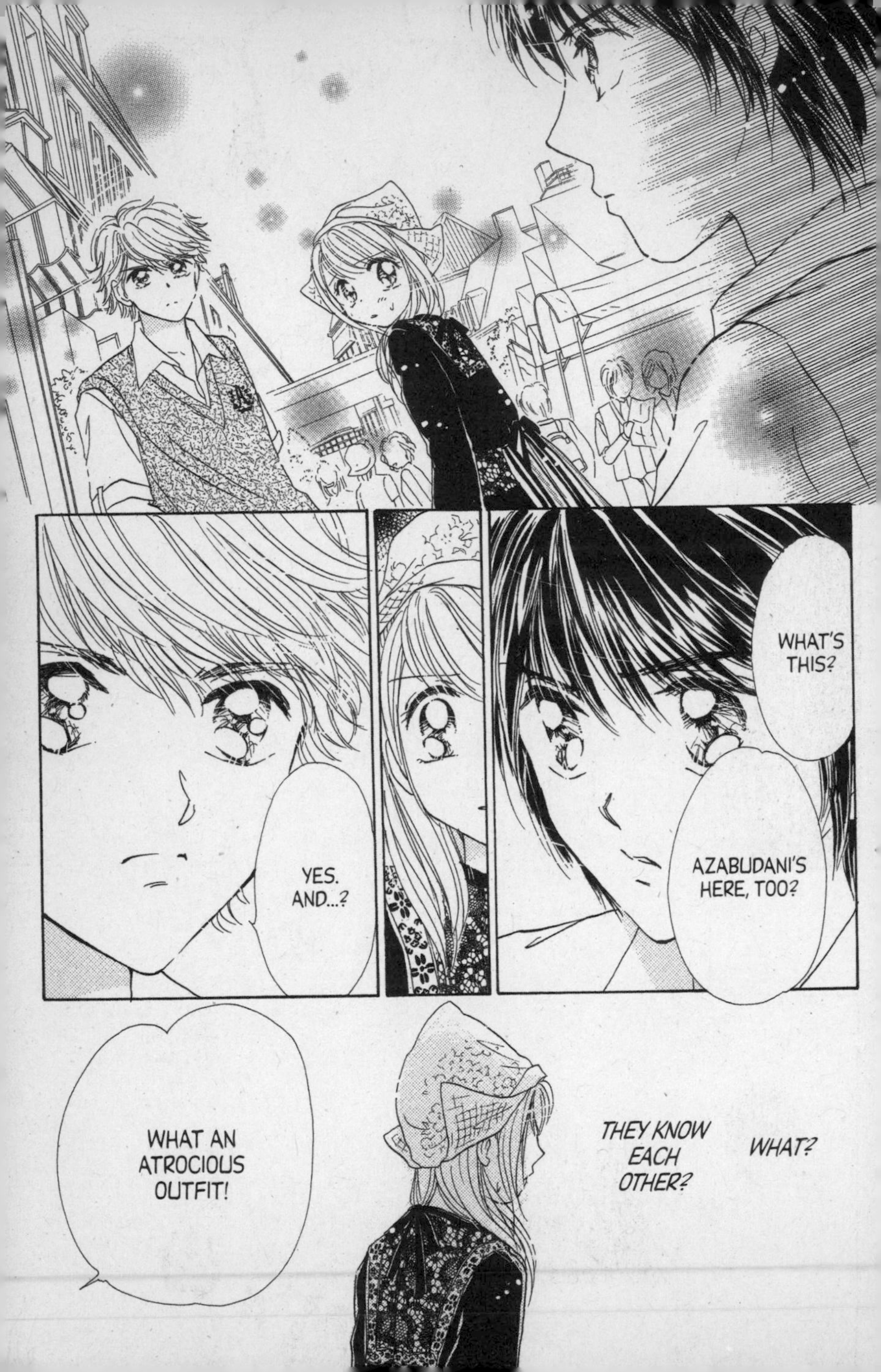
WHAT'S THIS?
AZABUDANI'S HERE, TOO?
YES. AND...?
WHAT?
THEY KNOW EACH OTHER?
WHAT AN ATROCIOUS OUTFIT!

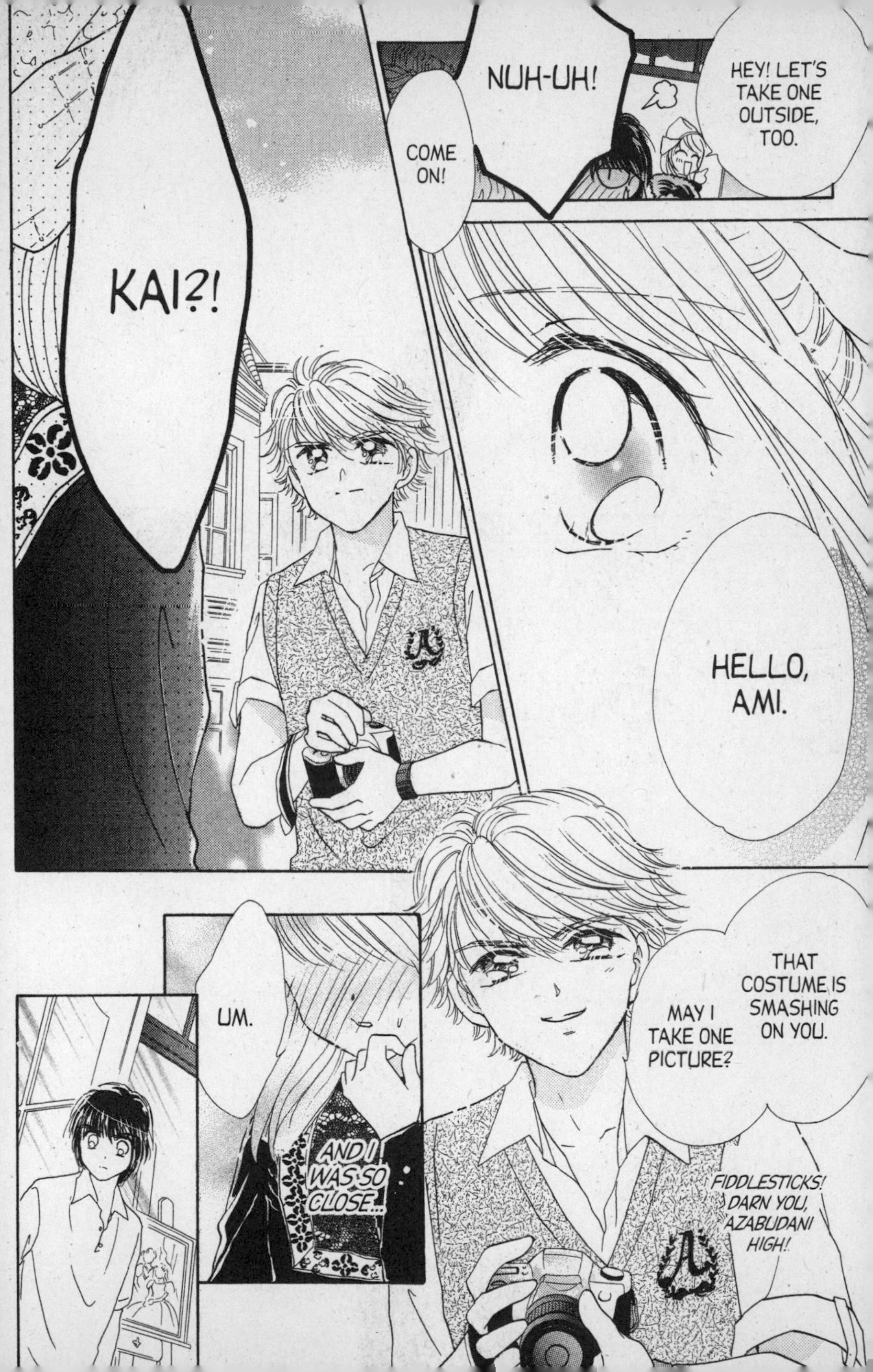
HEY! LET'S TAKE ONE OUTSIDE, TOO.
NUH-UH!
COME ON!
HELLO, AMI.
KAI?!
THAT COSTUME IS SMASHING ON YOU.
MAY I TAKE ONE PICTURE?
FIDDLESTICKS! DARN YOU, AZABUDANI HIGH!
UM.
AND I WAS SO CLOSE...

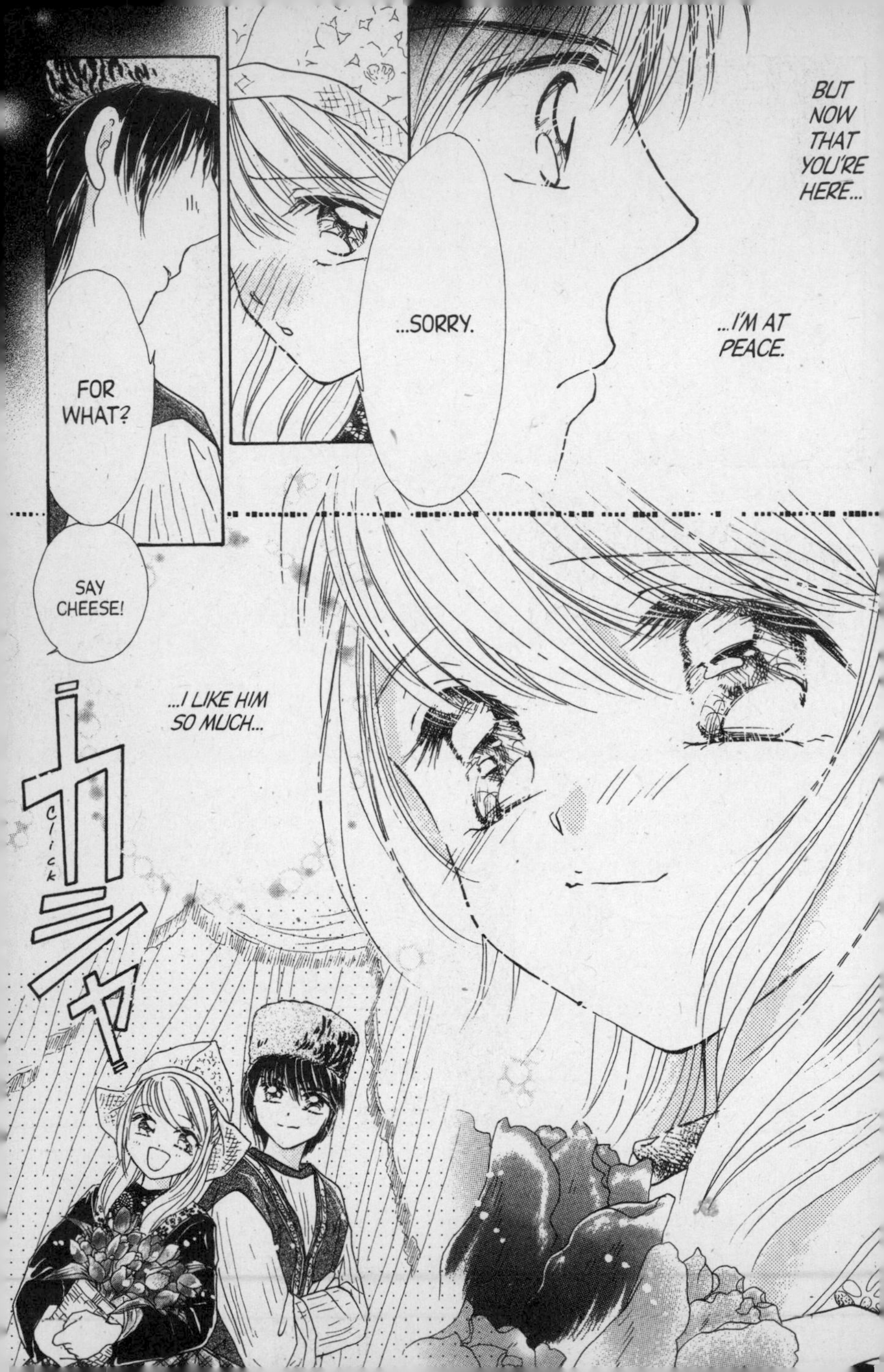

BUT NOW THAT YOU'RE HERE...
...I'M AT PEACE.
...SORRY.
FOR WHAT?
SAY CHEESE!
...I LIKE HIM SO MUCH...
カシャ
Click

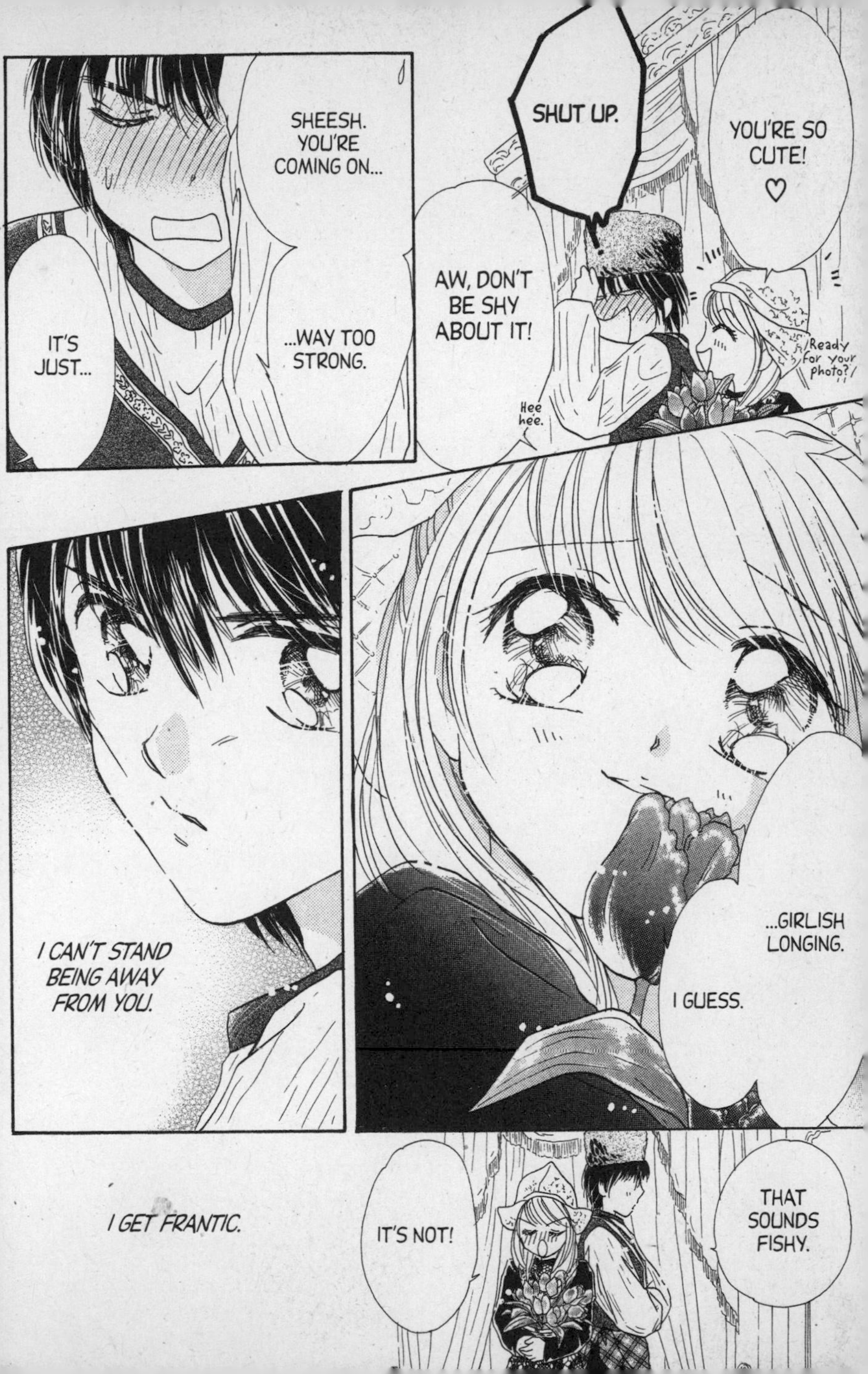
YOU'RE SO CUTE! ♡
SHUT UP.
Ready for your photo?
AW, DON'T BE SHY ABOUT IT!
Hee hee.
SHEESH. YOU'RE COMING ON...
...WAY TOO STRONG.
IT'S JUST...
...GIRLISH LONGING.
I GUESS.
I CAN'T STAND BEING AWAY FROM YOU.
THAT SOUNDS FISHY.
IT'S NOT!
I GET FRANTIC.

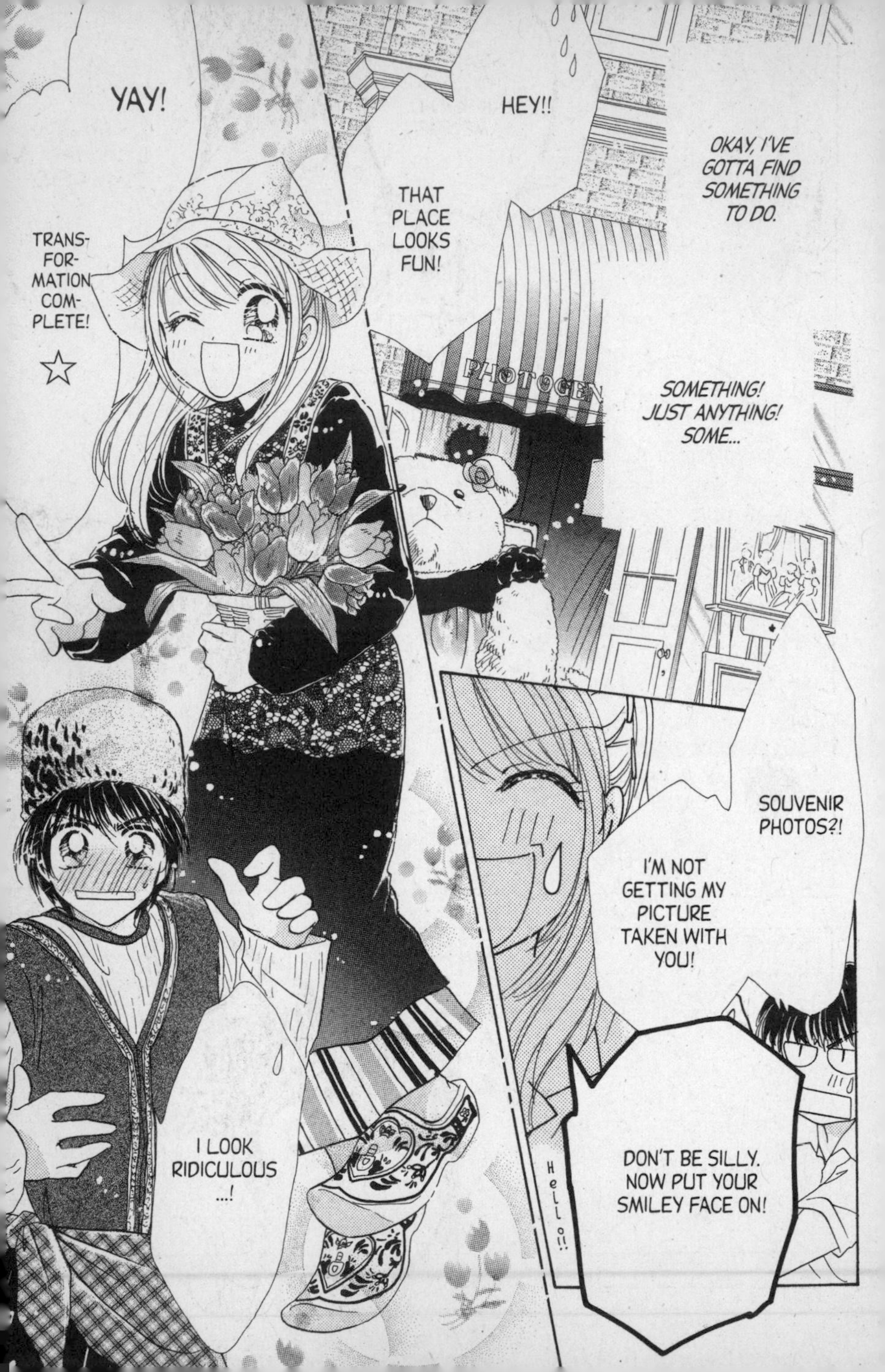
OKAY, I'VE GOTTA FIND SOMETHING TO DO.
SOMETHING! JUST ANYTHING! SOME...
HEY!!
THAT PLACE LOOKS FUN!
PHOTOGEN
SOUVENIR PHOTOS?!
I'M NOT GETTING MY PICTURE TAKEN WITH YOU!
DON'T BE SILLY. NOW PUT YOUR SMILEY FACE ON!
Hello!!
YAY!
TRANS-FORMATION COM-PLETE! ☆
I LOOK RIDICULOUS ...!

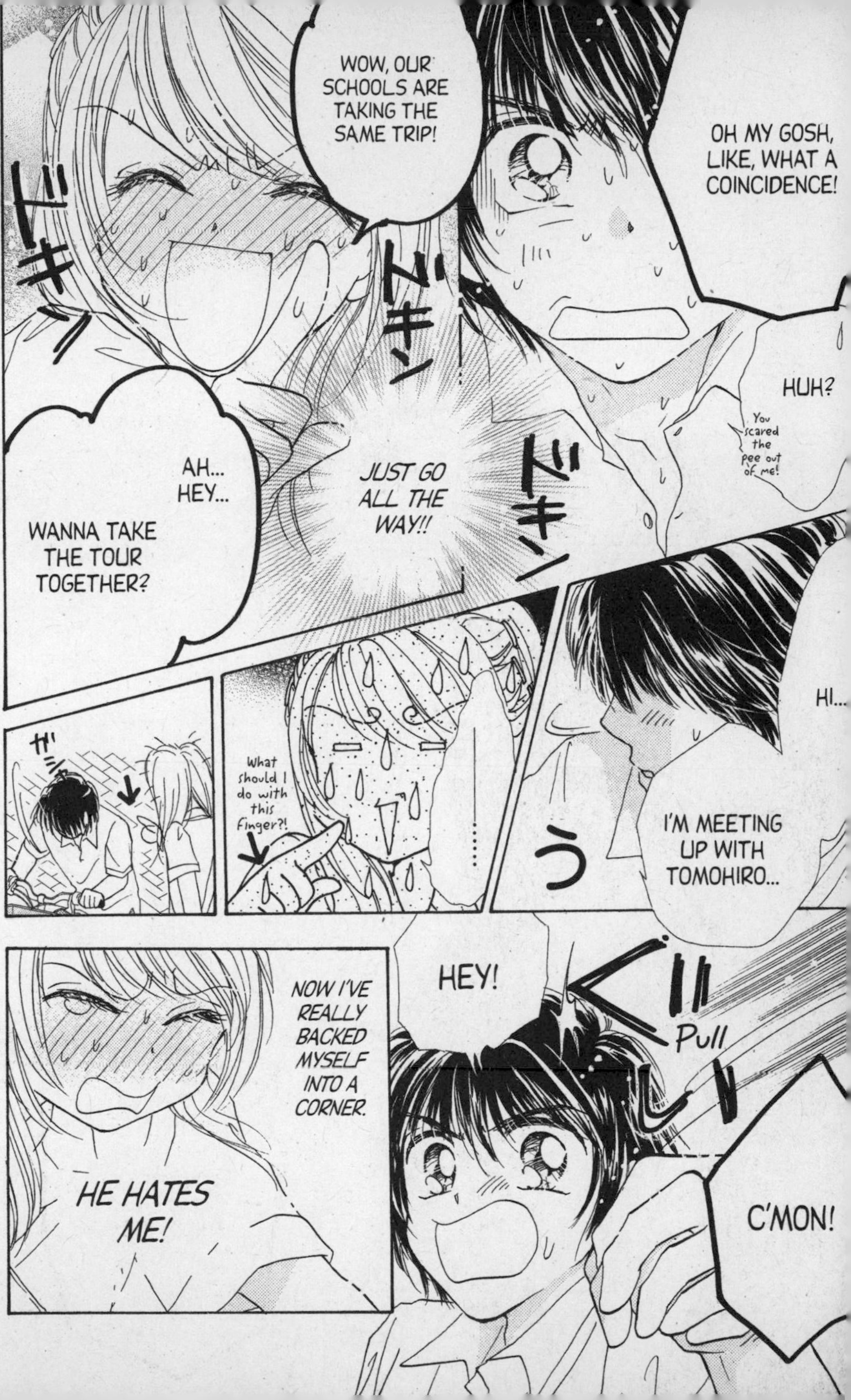
OH MY GOSH, LIKE, WHAT A COINCIDENCE!
WOW, OUR SCHOOLS ARE TAKING THE SAME TRIP!
HUH?
You scared the pee out of me!
ドキン
ドキン
ドキン
JUST GO ALL THE WAY!!
AH... HEY...
WANNA TAKE THE TOUR TOGETHER?
HI...
I'M MEETING UP WITH TOMOHIRO...
う
What should I do with this finger?!
HEY!
Pull
C'MON!
NOW I'VE REALLY BACKED MYSELF INTO A CORNER.
HE HATES ME!

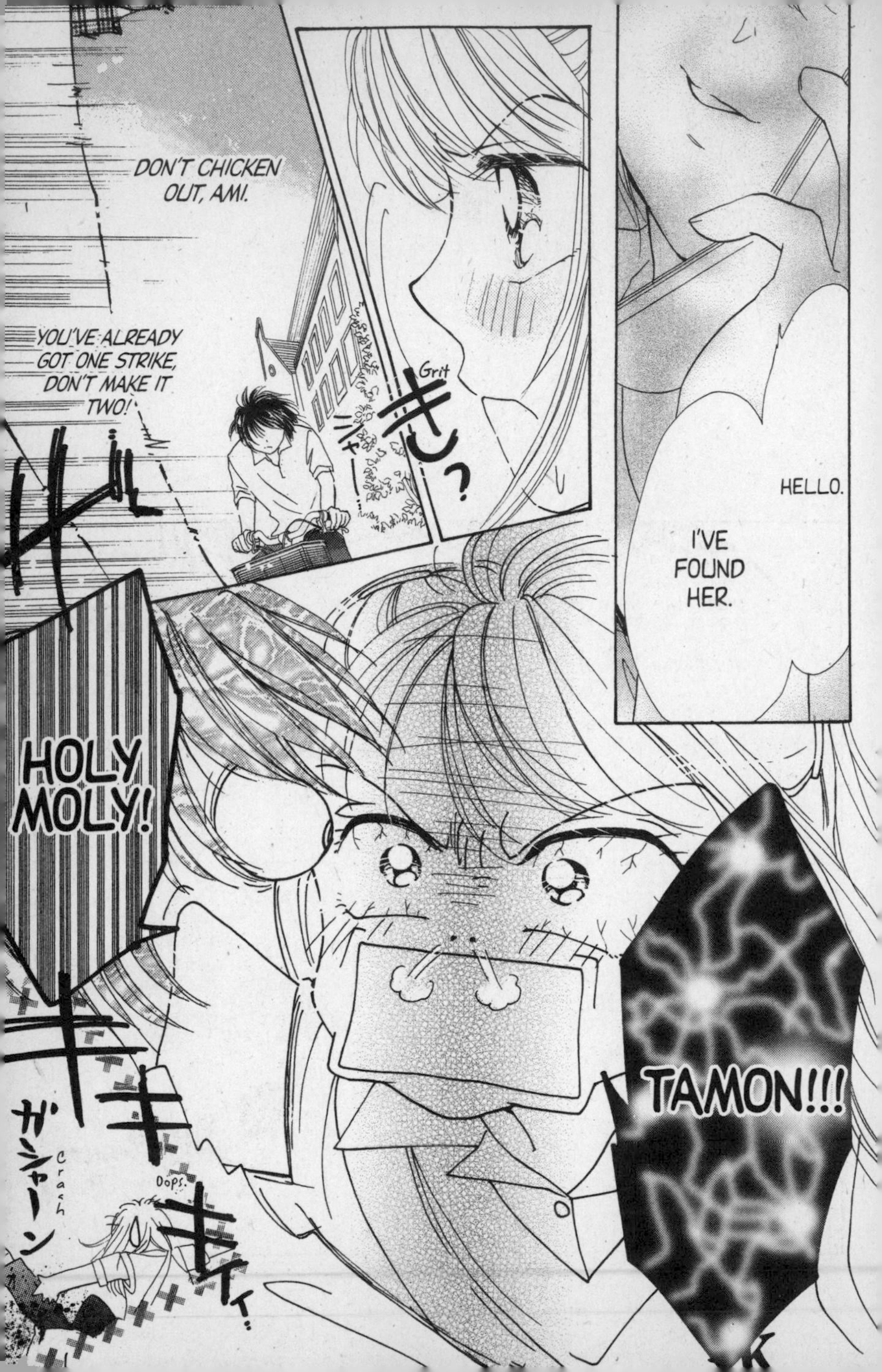
HELLO.
I'VE FOUND HER.
Grit
シャー…
DON'T CHICKEN OUT, AMI.
YOU'VE ALREADY GOT ONE STRIKE, DON'T MAKE IT TWO!
TAMON!!!
HOLY MOLY!
ガシャーン
Crash
Oops.

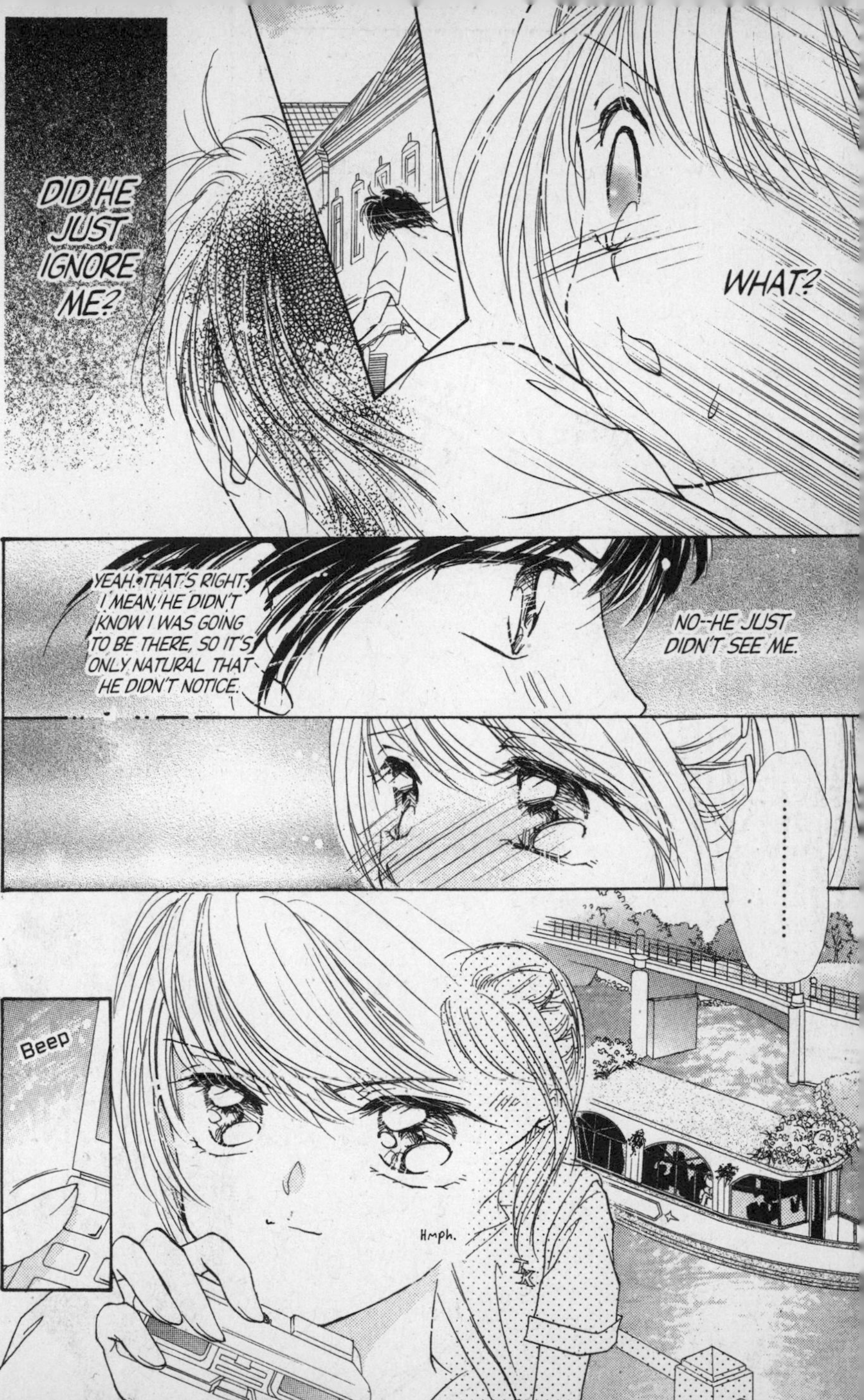
WHAT?
DID HE JUST IGNORE ME?
NO--HE JUST DIDN'T SEE ME.
YEAH. THAT'S RIGHT. I MEAN, HE DIDN'T KNOW I WAS GOING TO BE THERE, SO IT'S ONLY NATURAL THAT HE DIDN'T NOTICE.
......
Hmph.
Beep

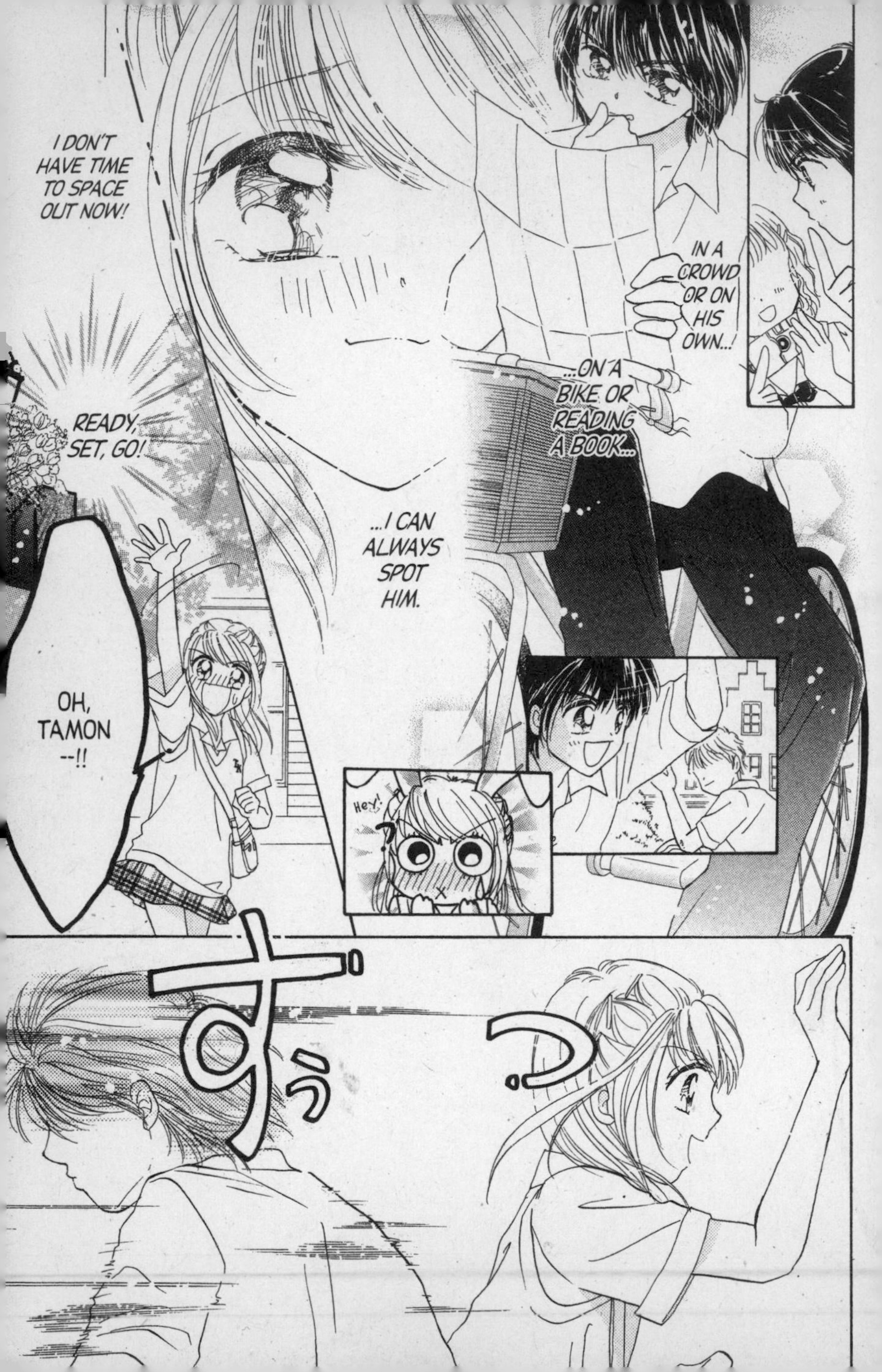
IN A CROWD OR ON HIS OWN...
...ON A BIKE OR READING A BOOK...
...I CAN ALWAYS SPOT HIM.
I DON'T HAVE TIME TO SPACE OUT NOW!
READY, SET, GO!
OH, TAMON--!!
Hey!
すぅっ

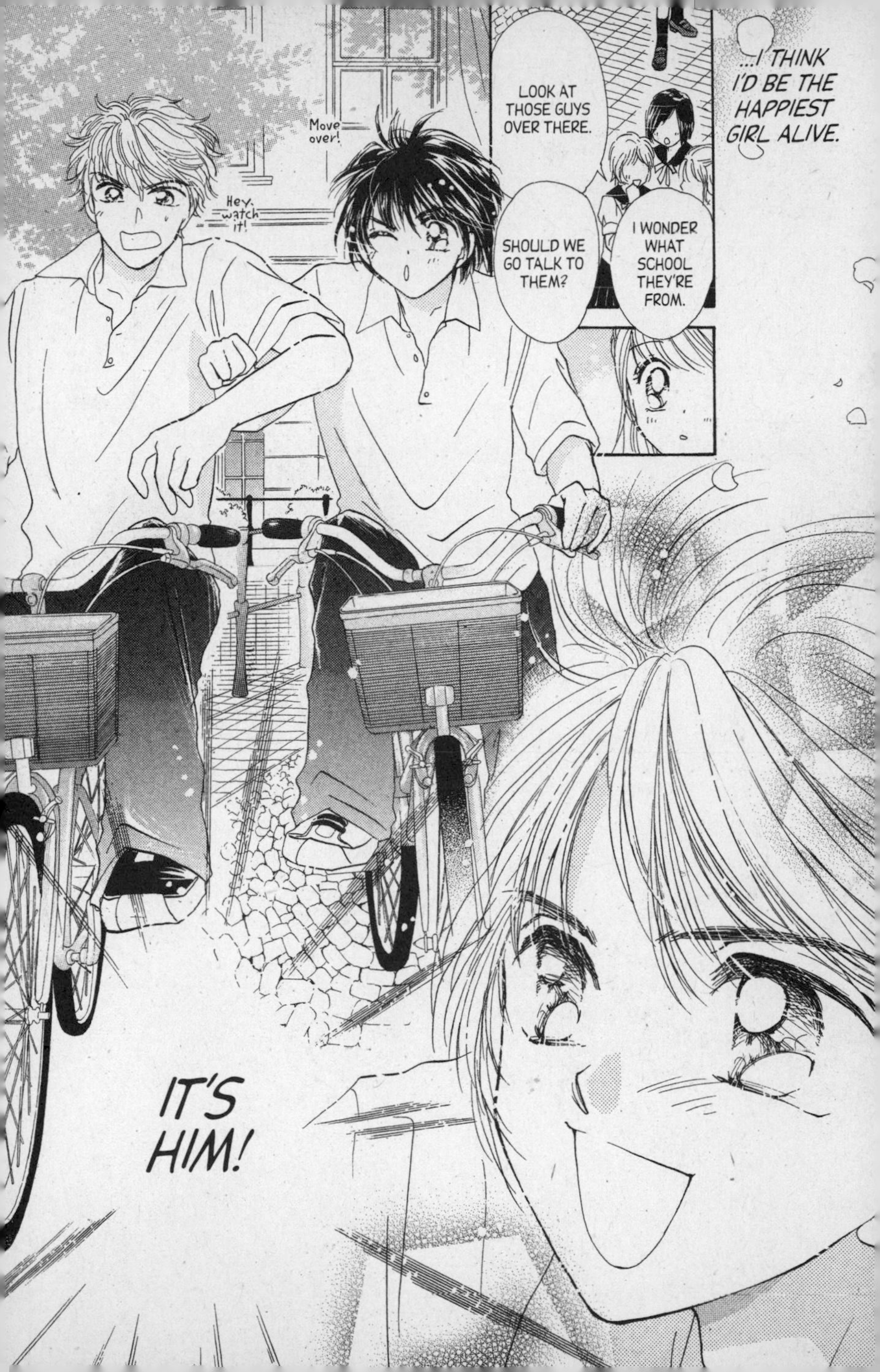
...I THINK I'D BE THE HAPPIEST GIRL ALIVE.
LOOK AT THOSE GUYS OVER THERE.
I WONDER WHAT SCHOOL THEY'RE FROM.
SHOULD WE GO TALK TO THEM?
Move over!
Hey, watch it!
IT'S HIM!

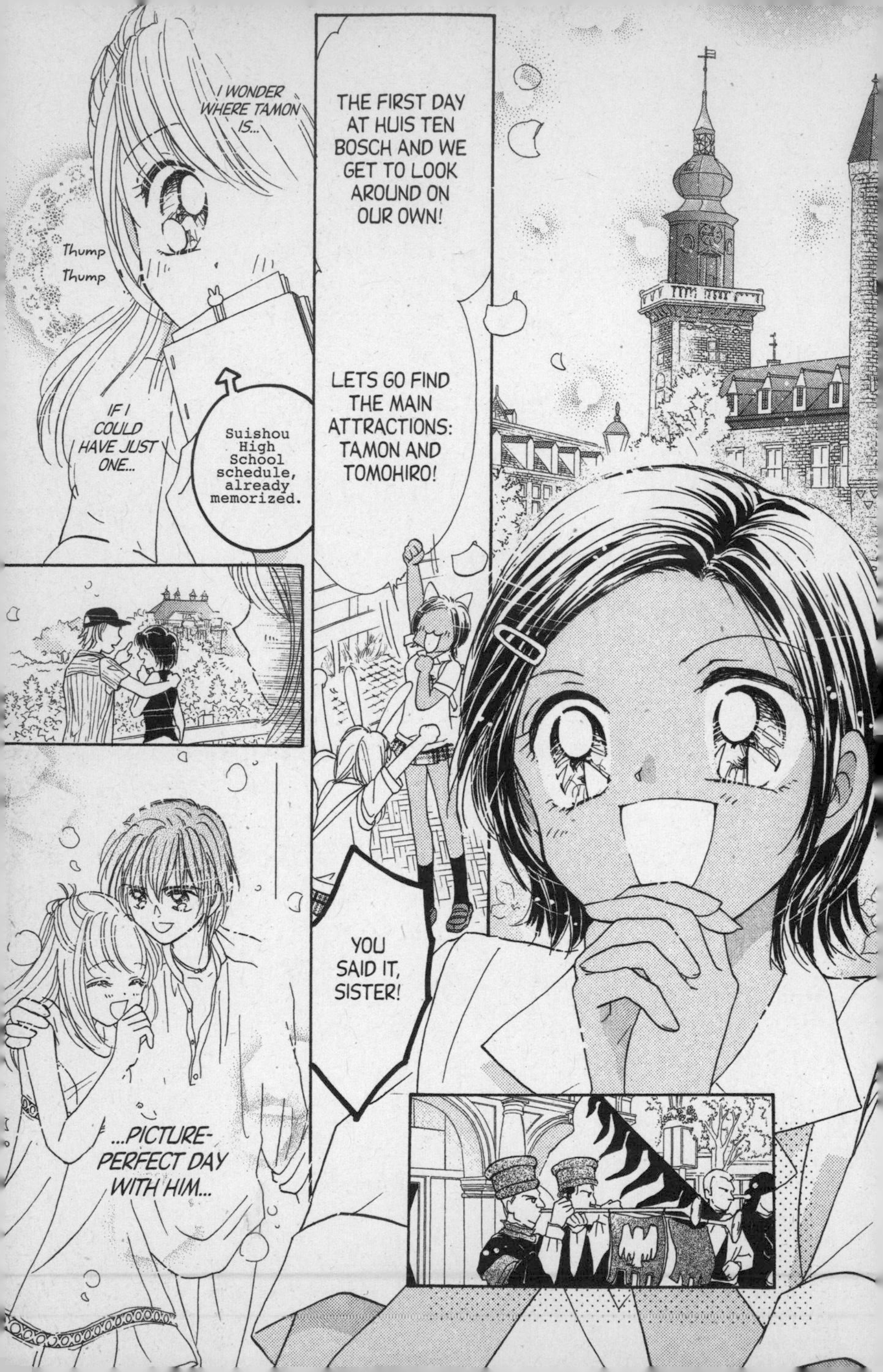
THE FIRST DAY AT HUIS TEN BOSCH AND WE GET TO LOOK AROUND ON OUR OWN!
LETS GO FIND THE MAIN ATTRACTIONS: TAMON AND TOMOHIRO!
YOU SAID IT, SISTER!
I WONDER WHERE TAMON IS...
Thump
Thump
Suishou High School schedule, already memorized.
IF I COULD HAVE JUST ONE...
...PICTURE-PERFECT DAY WITH HIM...

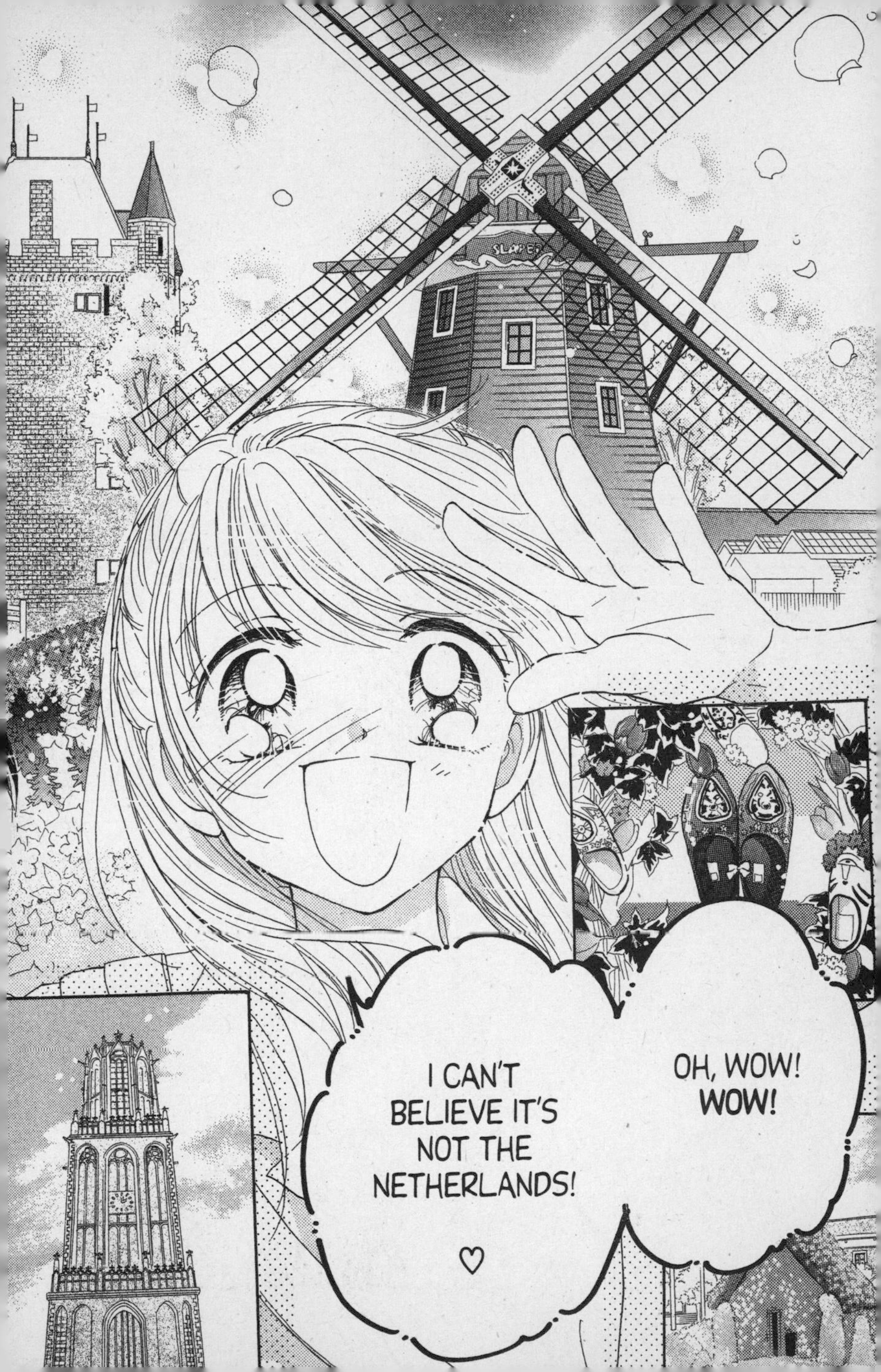
OH, WOW! WOW!
I CAN'T BELIEVE IT'S NOT THE NETHERLANDS! ♡

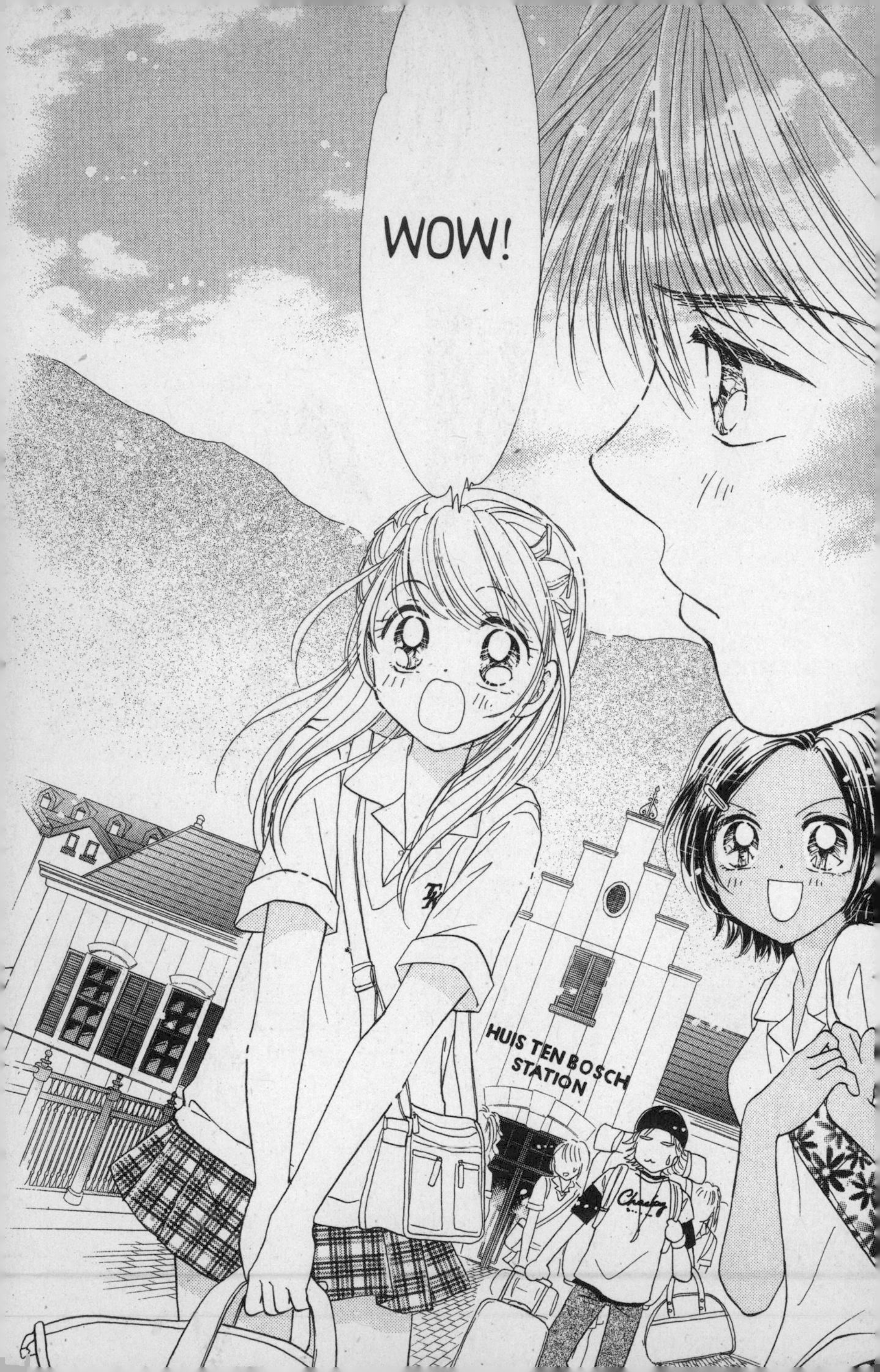
WOW!
HUIS TEN BOSCH STATION
Cheeky

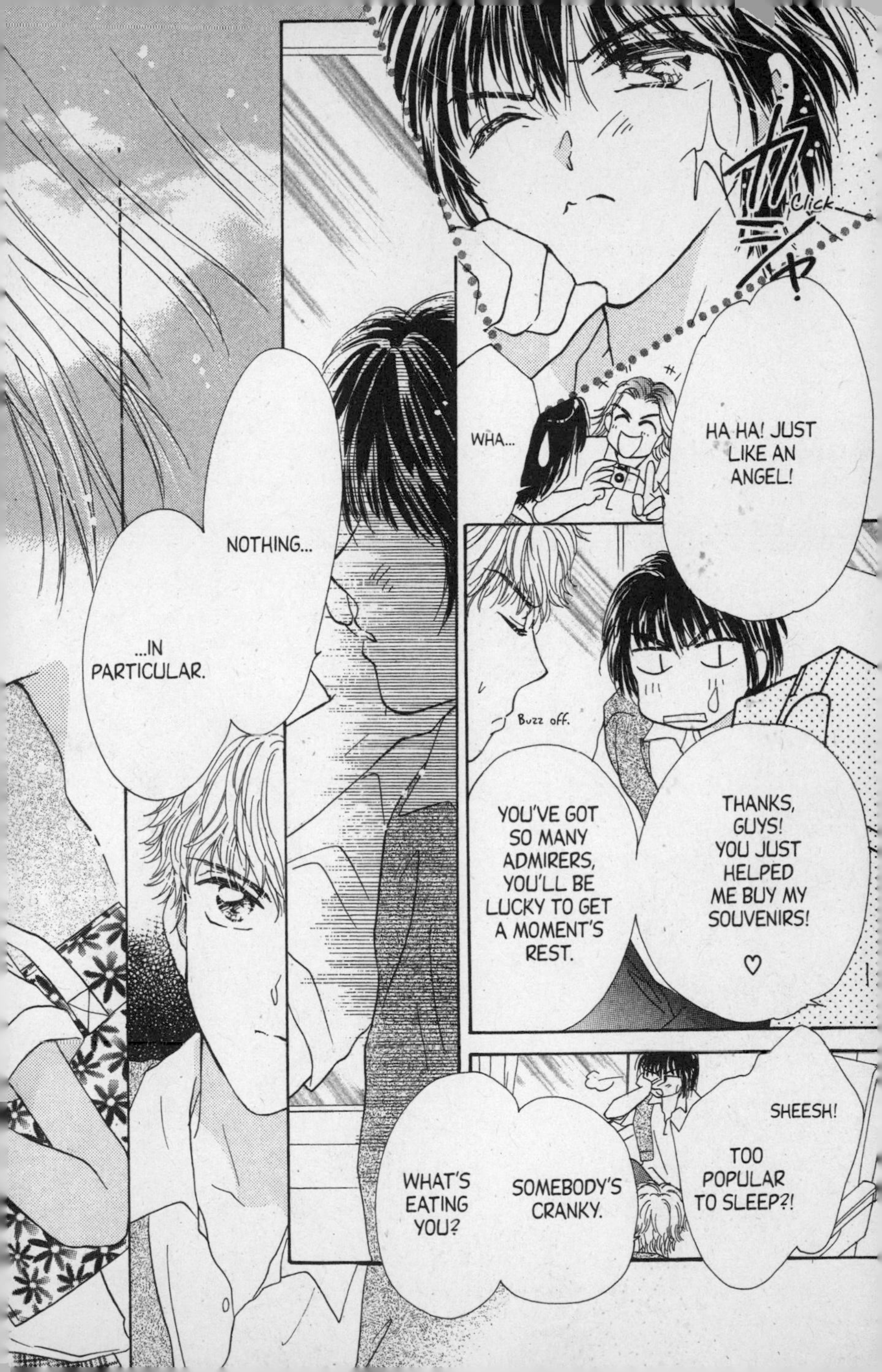
Click
HA HA! JUST LIKE AN ANGEL!
WHA...
THANKS, GUYS! YOU JUST HELPED ME BUY MY SOUVENIRS! ♡
YOU'VE GOT SO MANY ADMIRERS, YOU'LL BE LUCKY TO GET A MOMENT'S REST.
Buzz off.
SHEESH!
TOO POPULAR TO SLEEP?!
SOMEBODY'S CRANKY.
WHAT'S EATING YOU?
NOTHING...
...IN PARTICULAR.

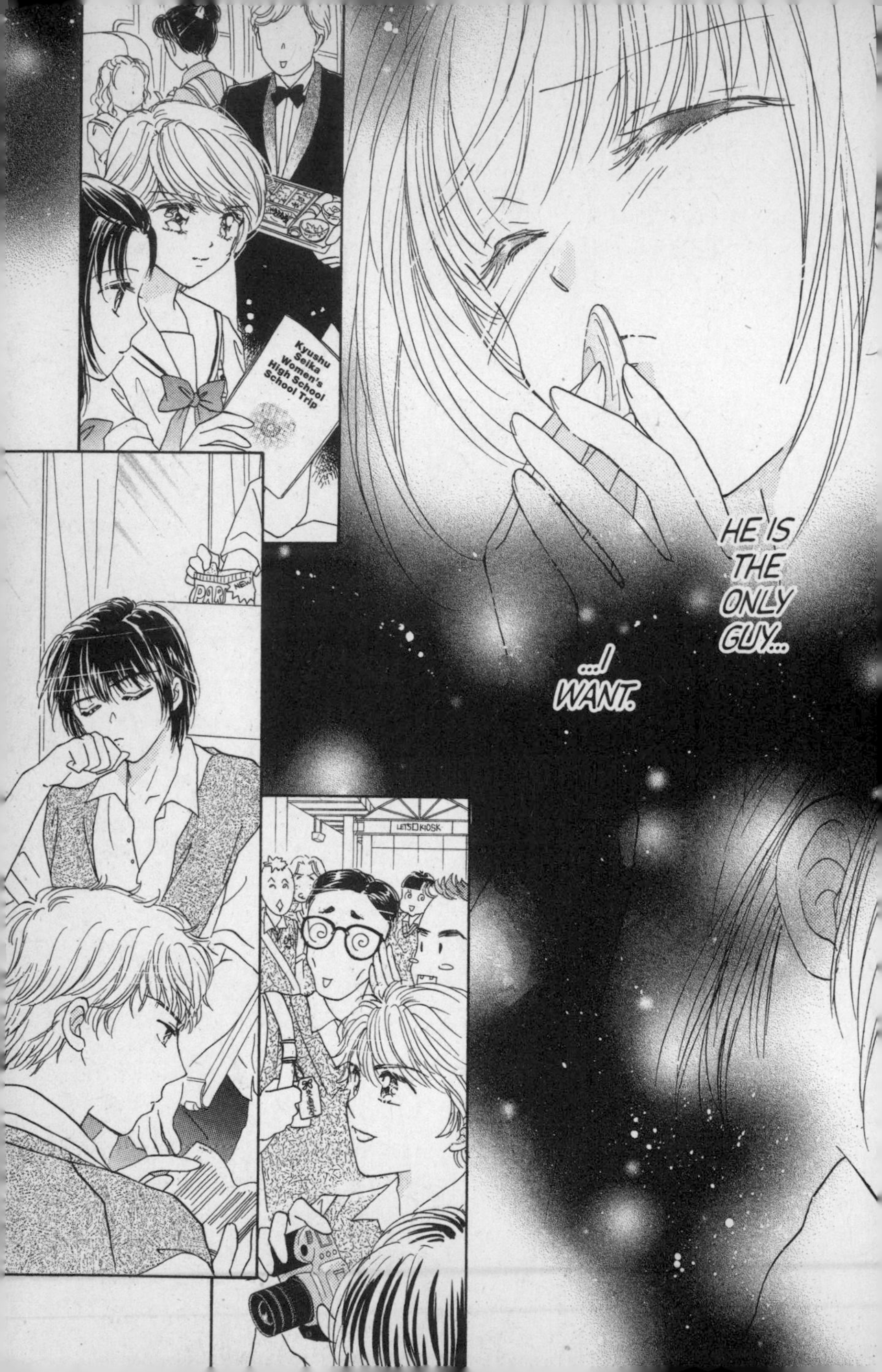
HE IS THE ONLY GUY...
...I WANT.
Kyushu Seika Women's High School School Trip
LETS KIOSK

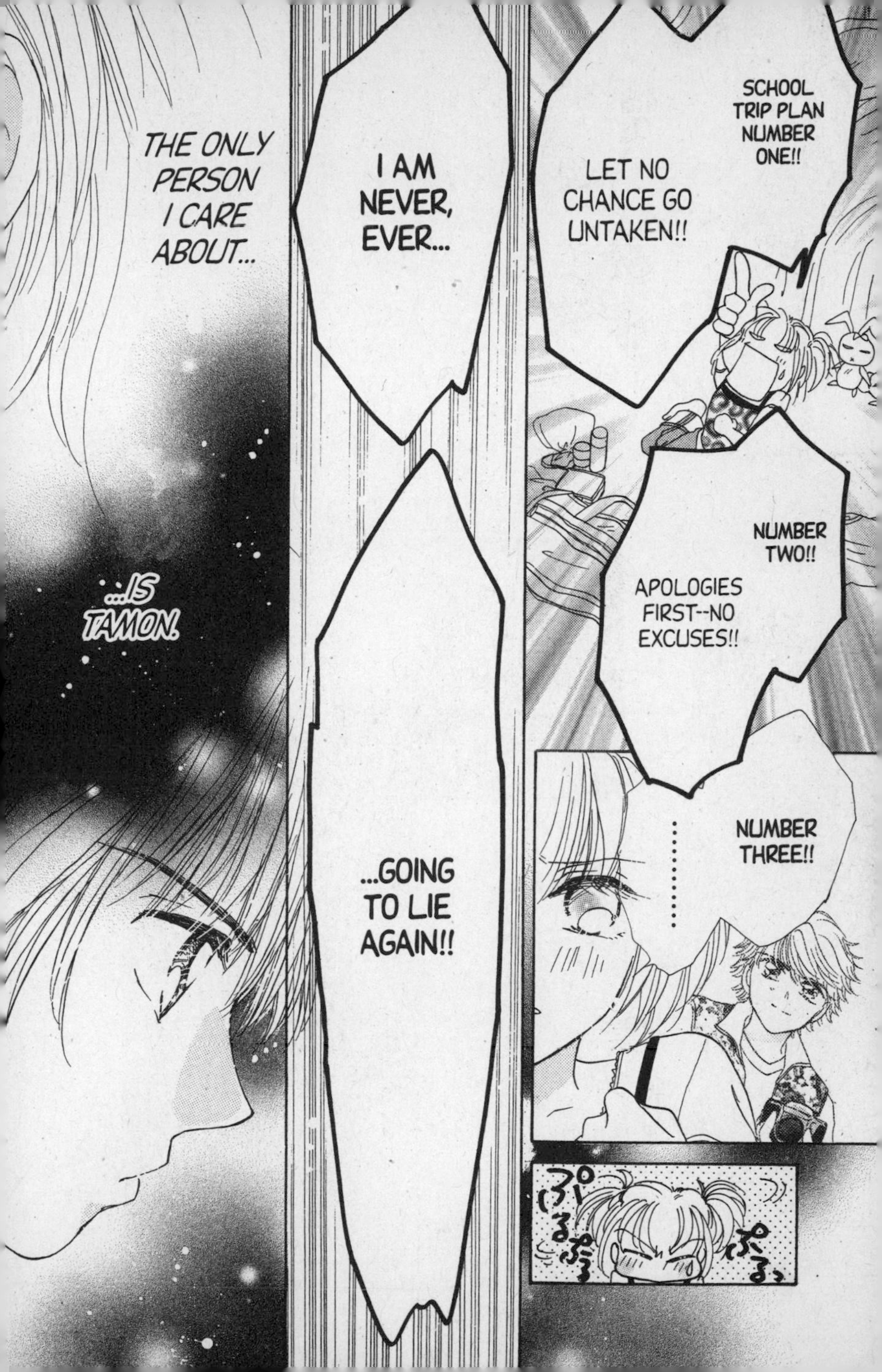
SCHOOL TRIP PLAN NUMBER ONE!!
LET NO CHANCE GO UNTAKEN!!
NUMBER TWO!!
APOLOGIES FIRST--NO EXCUSES!!
NUMBER THREE!!
......
ぷるっ
ぷるぷる
I AM NEVER, EVER...
...GOING TO LIE AGAIN!!
THE ONLY PERSON I CARE ABOUT...
...IS TAMON.

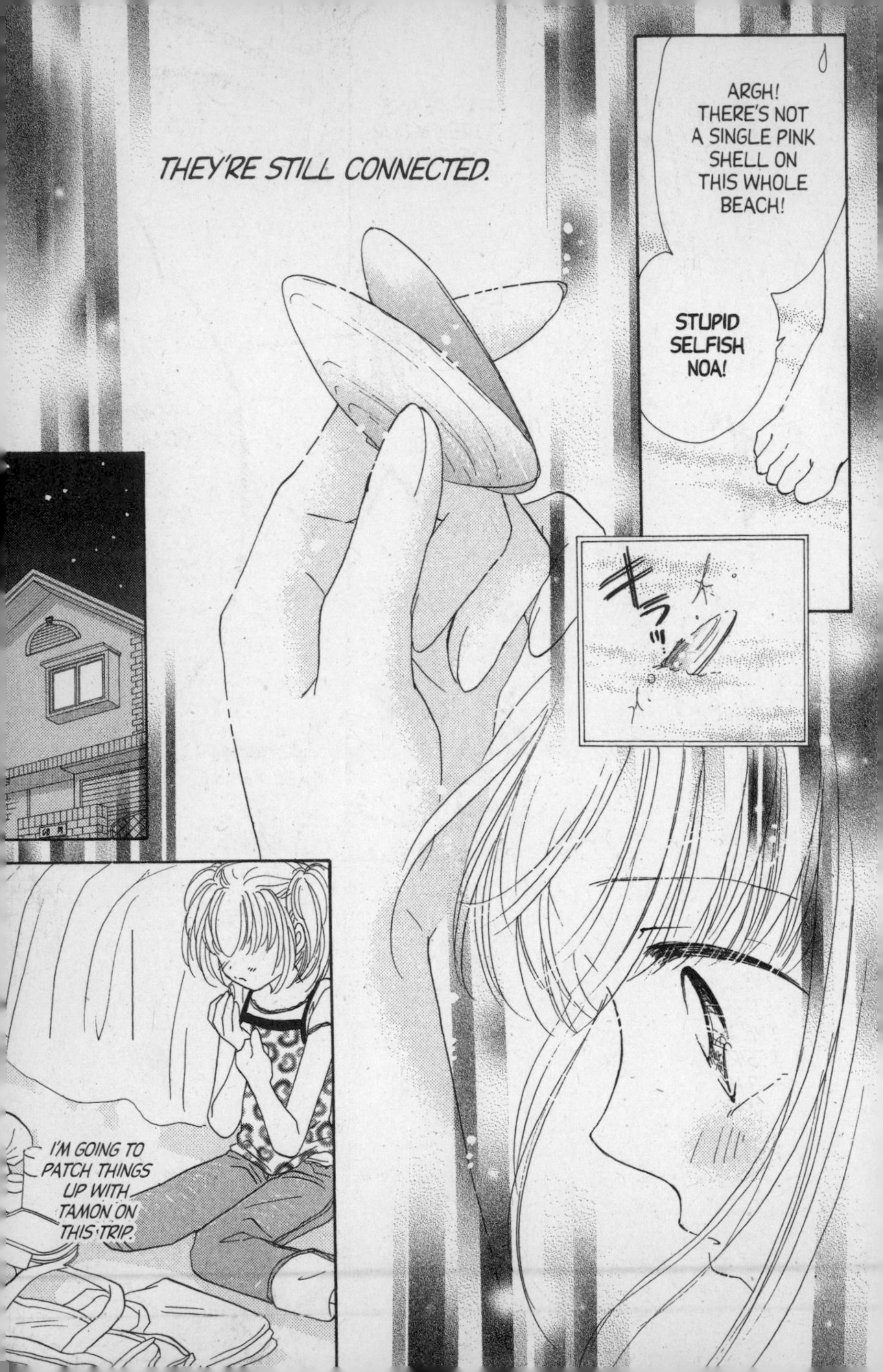
ARGH! THERE'S NOT A SINGLE PINK SHELL ON THIS WHOLE BEACH!
STUPID SELFISH NOA!
キラッ
THEY'RE STILL CONNECTED.
I'M GOING TO PATCH THINGS UP WITH TAMON ON THIS TRIP.

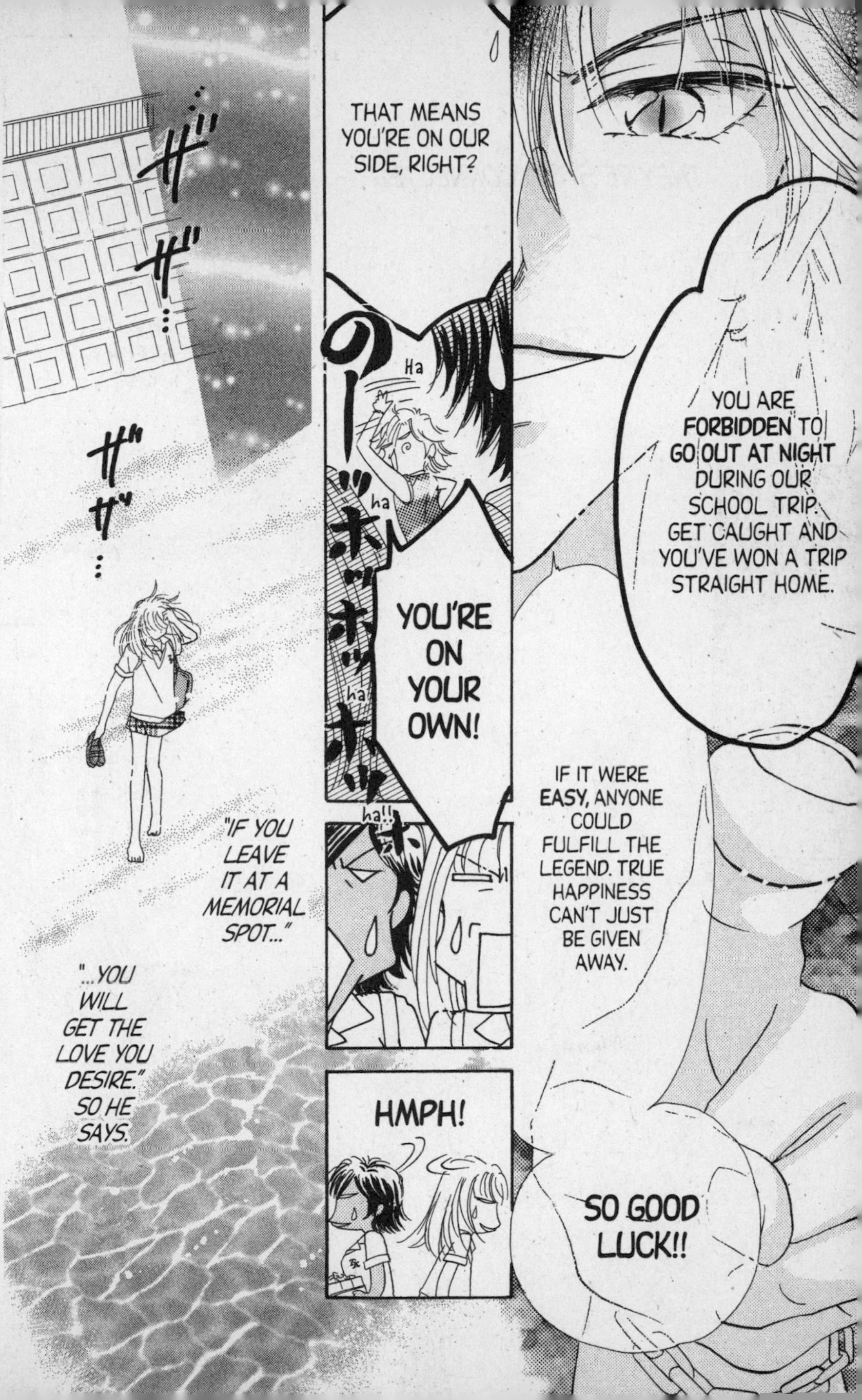

YOU ARE FORBIDDEN TO GO OUT AT NIGHT DURING OUR SCHOOL TRIP. GET CAUGHT AND YOU'VE WON A TRIP STRAIGHT HOME.
IF IT WERE EASY, ANYONE COULD FULFILL THE LEGEND. TRUE HAPPINESS CAN'T JUST BE GIVEN AWAY.
SO GOOD LUCK!!
THAT MEANS YOU'RE ON OUR SIDE, RIGHT?
Ha
ha
ha
ha!!
YOU'RE ON YOUR OWN!
HMPH!
"IF YOU LEAVE IT AT A MEMORIAL SPOT..."
"...YOU WILL GET THE LOVE YOU DESIRE." SO HE SAYS.

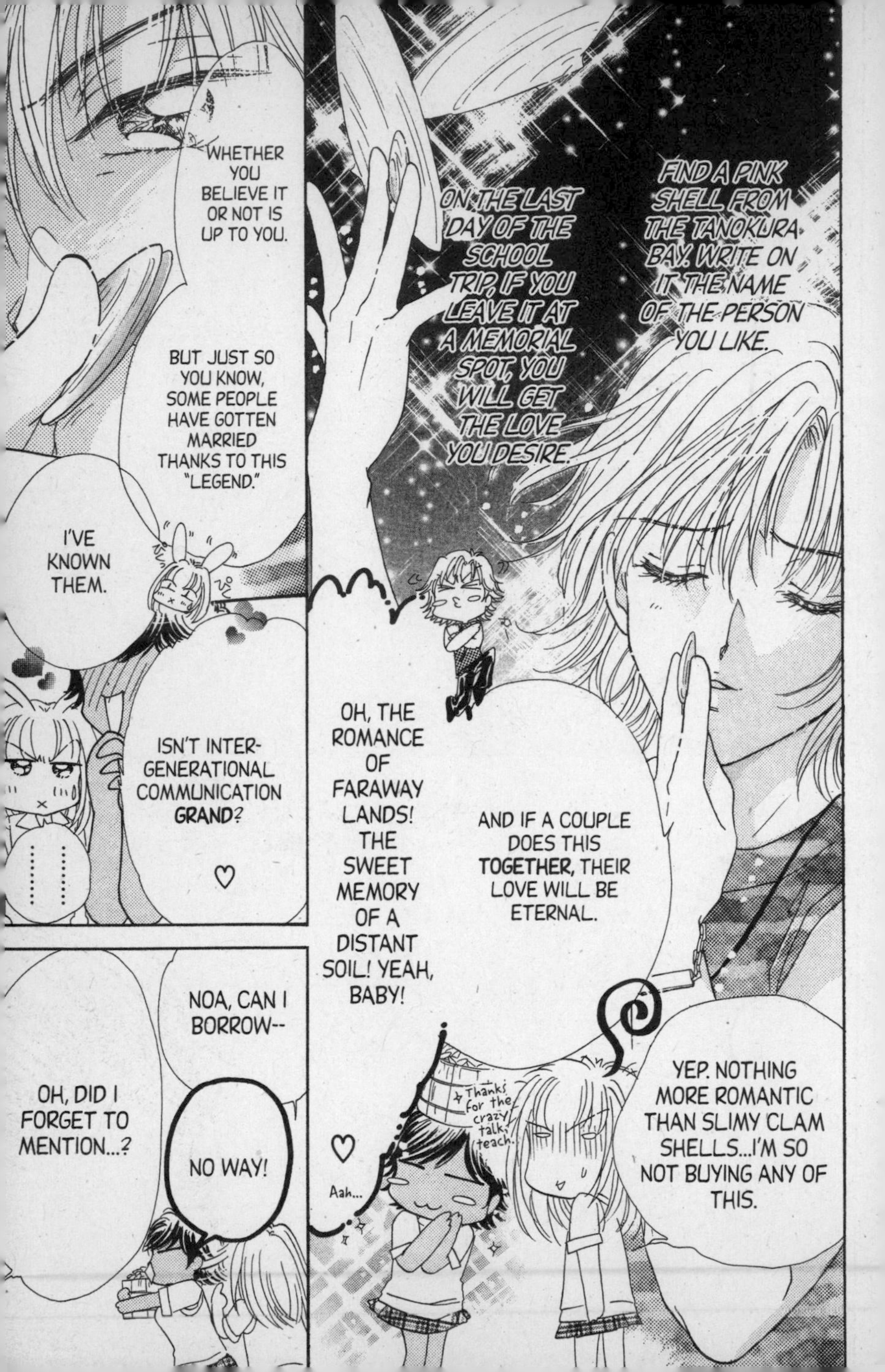
FIND A PINK SHELL FROM THE TANOKURA BAY. WRITE ON IT THE NAME OF THE PERSON YOU LIKE.
ON THE LAST DAY OF THE SCHOOL TRIP, IF YOU LEAVE IT AT A MEMORIAL SPOT, YOU WILL GET THE LOVE YOU DESIRE.
AND IF A COUPLE DOES THIS TOGETHER, THEIR LOVE WILL BE ETERNAL.
OH, THE ROMANCE OF FARAWAY LANDS! THE SWEET MEMORY OF A DISTANT SOIL! YEAH, BABY!
YEP. NOTHING MORE ROMANTIC THAN SLIMY CLAM SHELLS...I'M SO NOT BUYING ANY OF THIS.
Thanks for the crazy talk, teach.
Aah...
WHETHER YOU BELIEVE IT OR NOT IS UP TO YOU.
BUT JUST SO YOU KNOW, SOME PEOPLE HAVE GOTTEN MARRIED THANKS TO THIS "LEGEND."
I'VE KNOWN THEM.
ISN'T INTER-GENERATIONAL COMMUNICATION GRAND? ♡
......
NOA, CAN I BORROW--
NO WAY!
OH, DID I FORGET TO MENTION...?

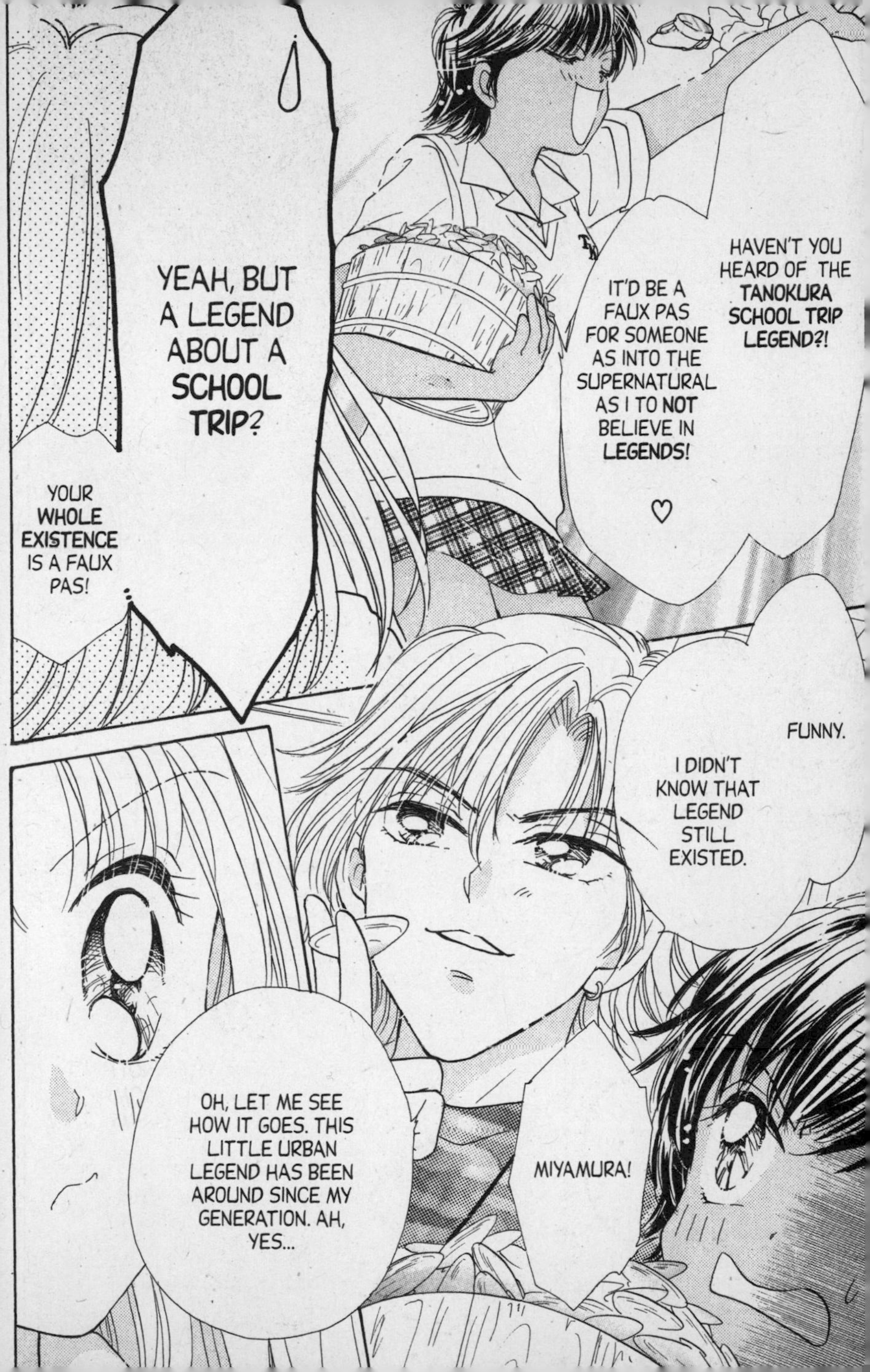
HAVEN'T YOU HEARD OF THE TANOKURA SCHOOL TRIP LEGEND?!
IT'D BE A FAUX PAS FOR SOMEONE AS INTO THE SUPERNATURAL AS I TO NOT BELIEVE IN LEGENDS! ♡
YEAH, BUT A LEGEND ABOUT A SCHOOL TRIP?
YOUR WHOLE EXISTENCE IS A FAUX PAS!
FUNNY.
I DIDN'T KNOW THAT LEGEND STILL EXISTED.
MIYAMURA!
OH, LET ME SEE HOW IT GOES. THIS LITTLE URBAN LEGEND HAS BEEN AROUND SINCE MY GENERATION. AH, YES...

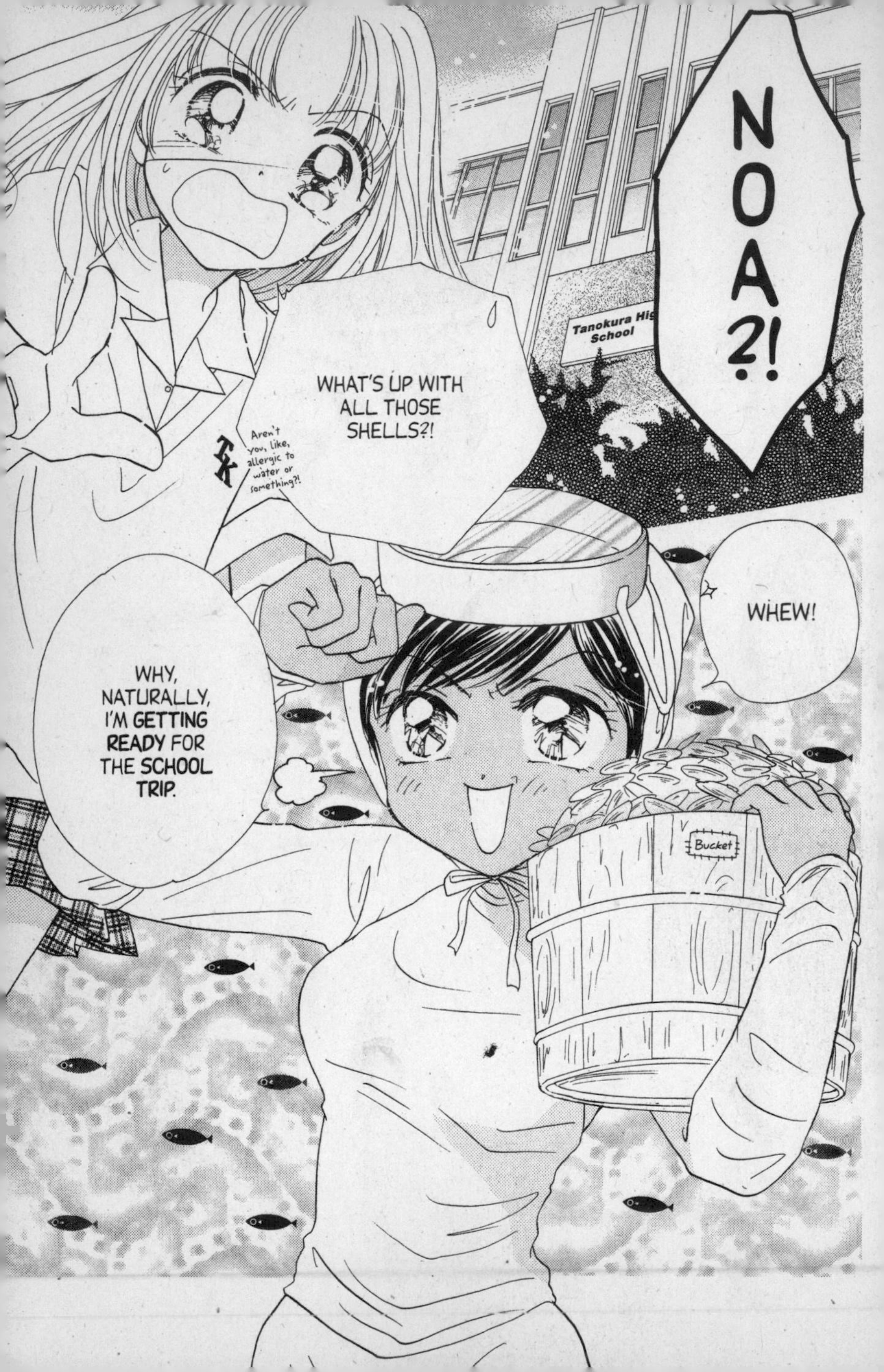
NOA?!
Tanokura Hig
School
WHAT'S UP WITH ALL THOSE SHELLS?!
Aren't you, like, allergic to water or something?!
WHEW!
WHY, NATURALLY, I'M GETTING READY FOR THE SCHOOL TRIP.
Bucket

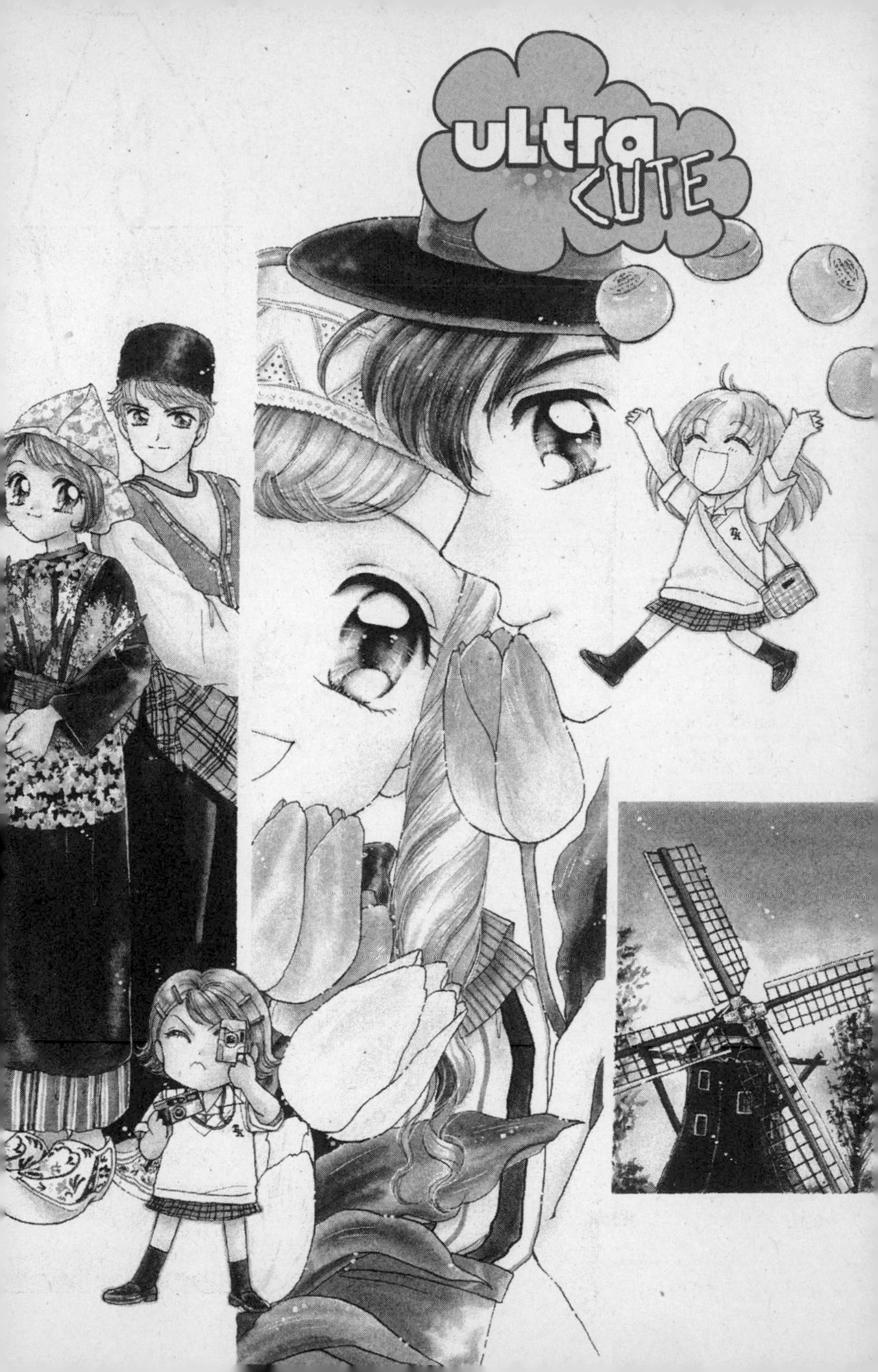
Ultra
CUTE

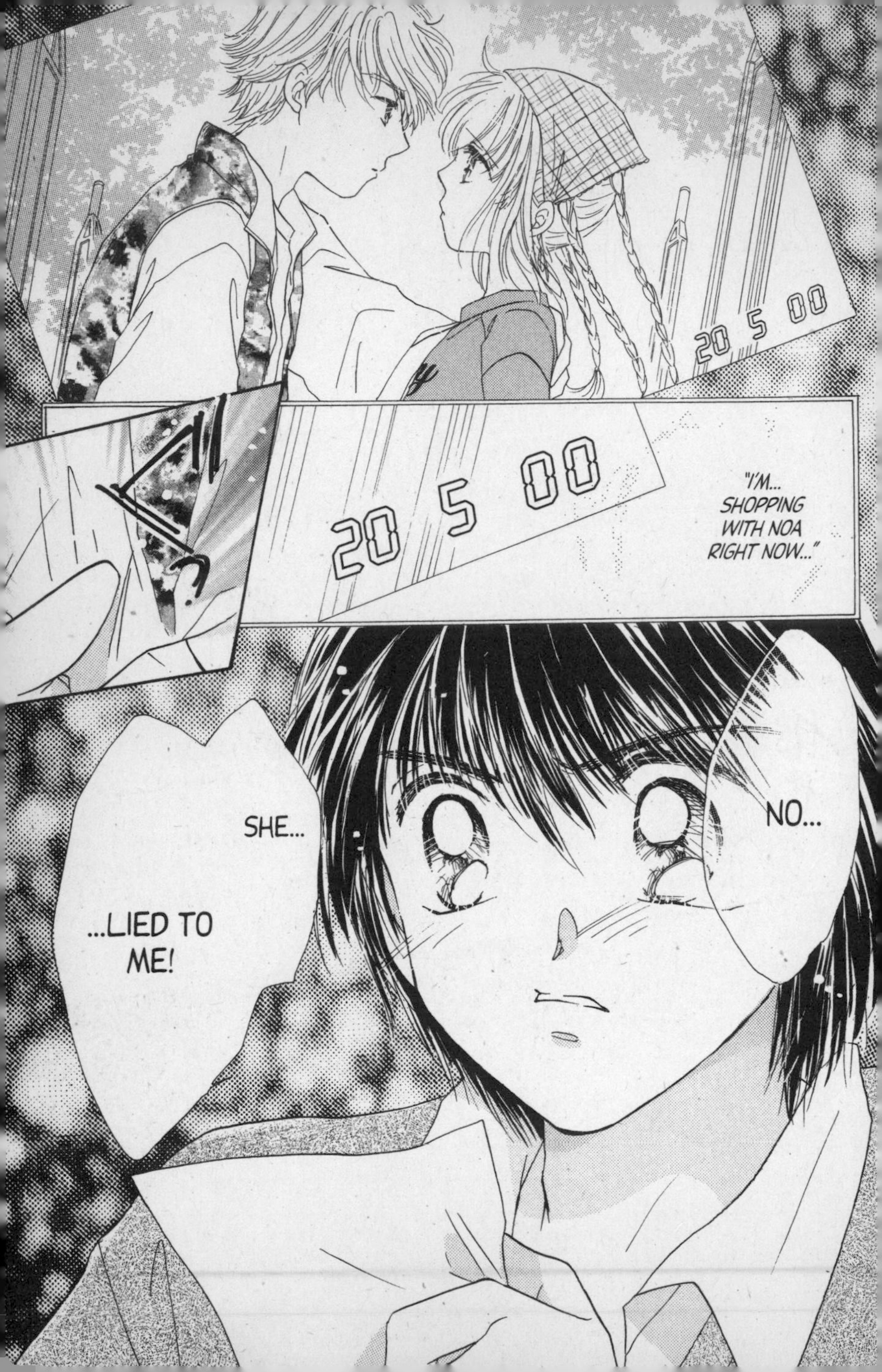
20 5 00
"I'M... SHOPPING WITH NOA RIGHT NOW..."
20 5 00
NO...
SHE...
...LIED TO ME!

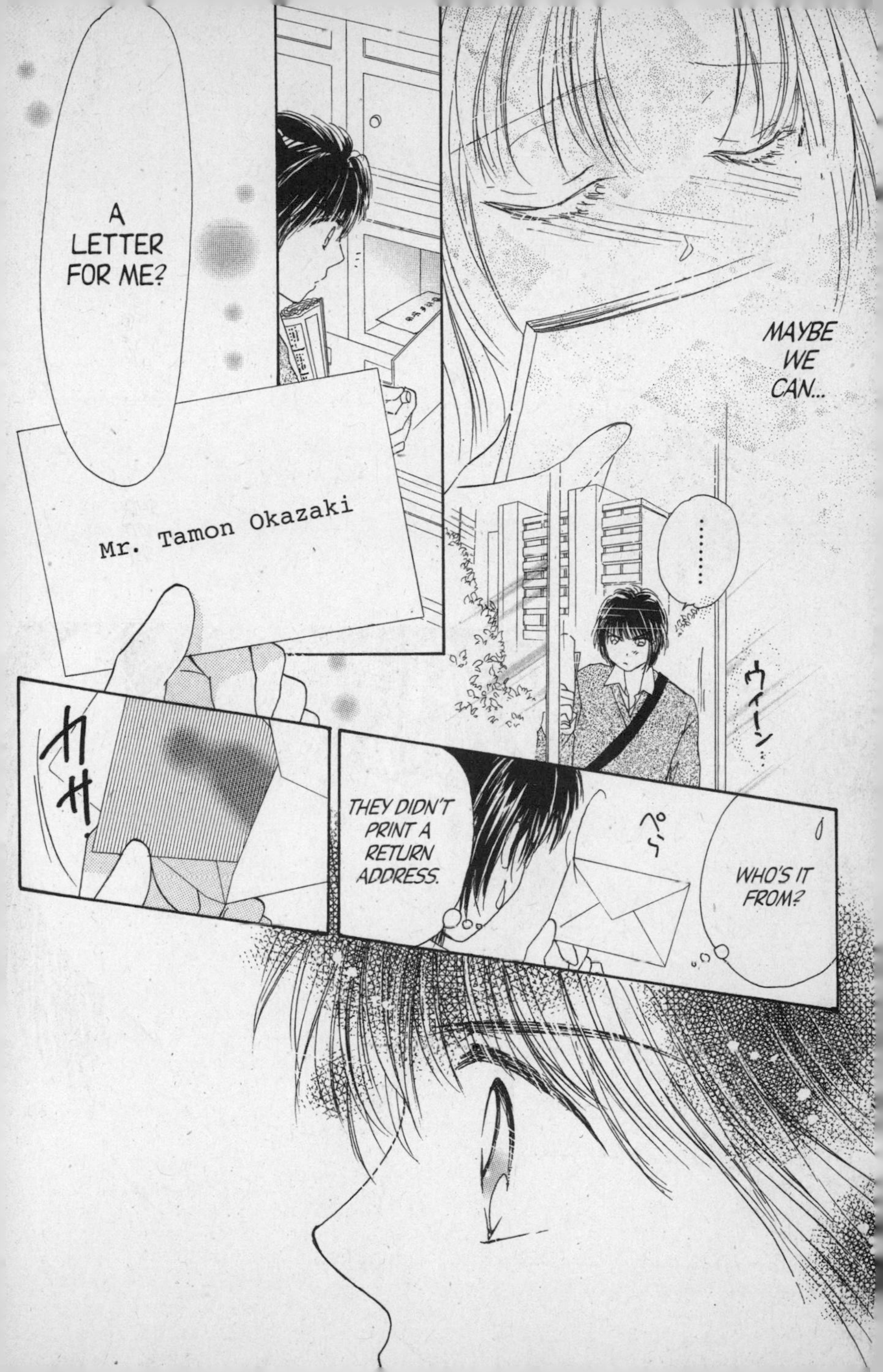
MAYBE WE CAN...
......
ウイーン...
A LETTER FOR ME?
Mr. Tamon Okazaki
WHO'S IT FROM?
ぺら
THEY DIDN'T PRINT A RETURN ADDRESS.
カサ!

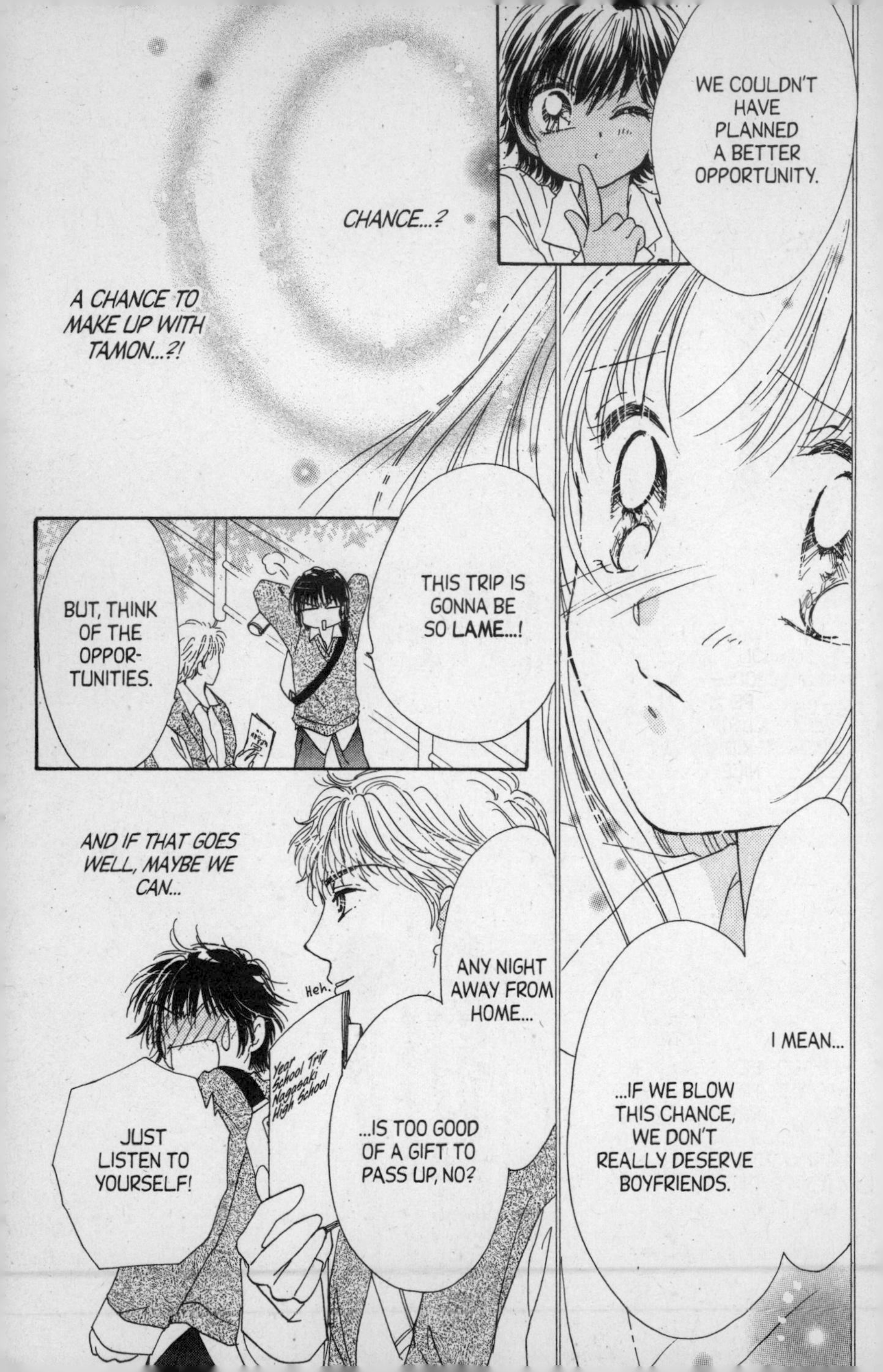
WE COULDN'T HAVE PLANNED A BETTER OPPORTUNITY.
I MEAN...
...IF WE BLOW THIS CHANCE, WE DON'T REALLY DESERVE BOYFRIENDS.
CHANCE...?
A CHANCE TO MAKE UP WITH TAMON...?!
THIS TRIP IS GONNA BE SO LAME...!
BUT, THINK OF THE OPPORTUNITIES.
AND IF THAT GOES WELL, MAYBE WE CAN...
ANY NIGHT AWAY FROM HOME...
...IS TOO GOOD OF A GIFT TO PASS UP, NO?
Heh.
Year School Trip Nagasaki High School
JUST LISTEN TO YOURSELF!

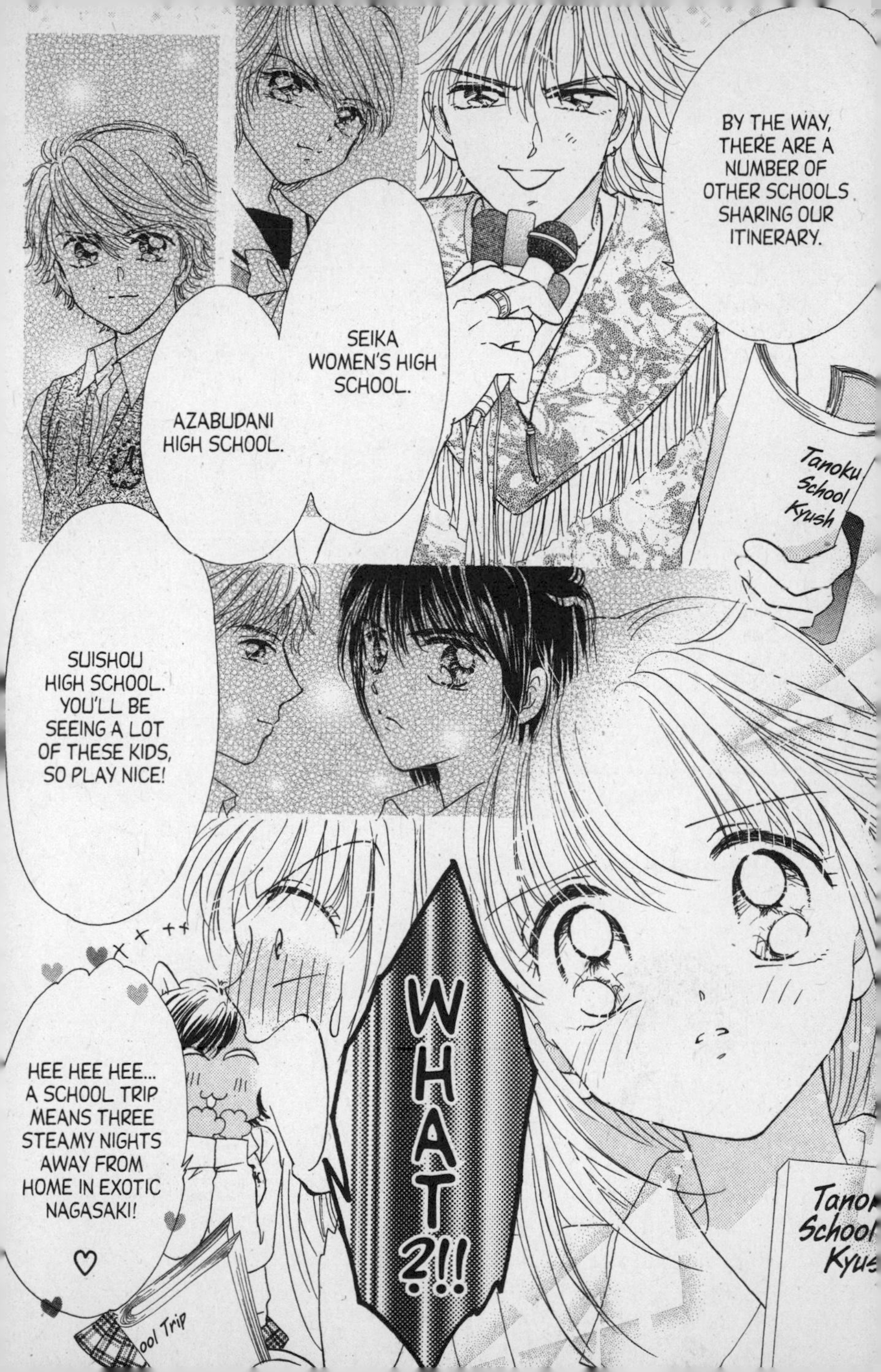
BY THE WAY, THERE ARE A NUMBER OF OTHER SCHOOLS SHARING OUR ITINERARY.
Tanoku School Kyush
SEIKA WOMEN'S HIGH SCHOOL.
AZABUDANI HIGH SCHOOL.
SUISHOU HIGH SCHOOL. YOU'LL BE SEEING A LOT OF THESE KIDS, SO PLAY NICE!
WHAT?!!
HEE HEE HEE... A SCHOOL TRIP MEANS THREE STEAMY NIGHTS AWAY FROM HOME IN EXOTIC NAGASAKI!

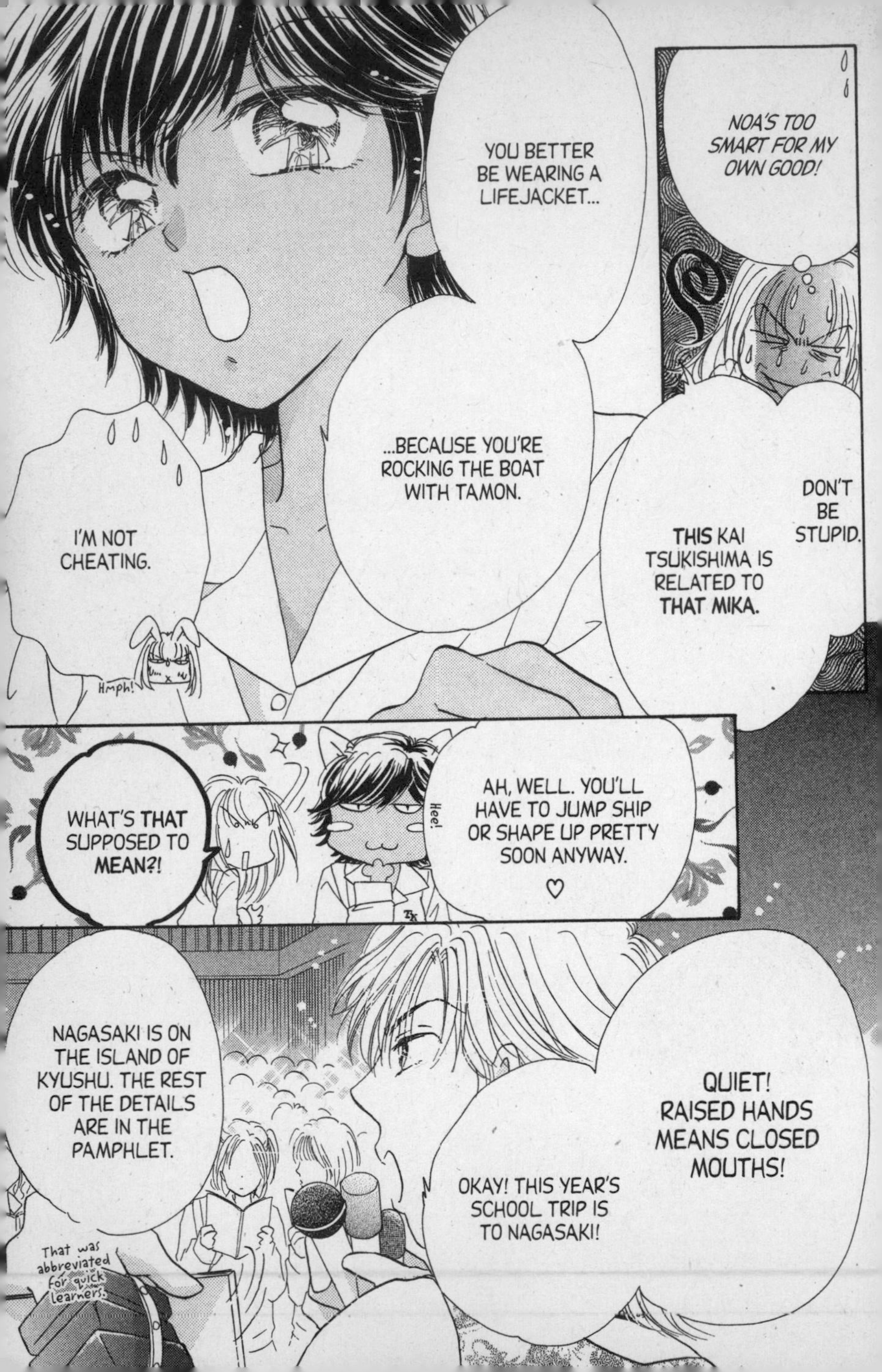
NOA'S TOO SMART FOR MY OWN GOOD!
YOU BETTER BE WEARING A LIFEJACKET...
...BECAUSE YOU'RE ROCKING THE BOAT WITH TAMON.
I'M NOT CHEATING.
Hmph!
DON'T BE STUPID.
THIS KAI TSUKISHIMA IS RELATED TO THAT MIKA.
AH, WELL. YOU'LL HAVE TO JUMP SHIP OR SHAPE UP PRETTY SOON ANYWAY. ♡
Hee!
WHAT'S THAT SUPPOSED TO MEAN?!
QUIET! RAISED HANDS MEANS CLOSED MOUTHS!
OKAY! THIS YEAR'S SCHOOL TRIP IS TO NAGASAKI!
NAGASAKI IS ON THE ISLAND OF KYUSHU. THE REST OF THE DETAILS ARE IN THE PAMPHLET.
That was abbreviated for quick learners.

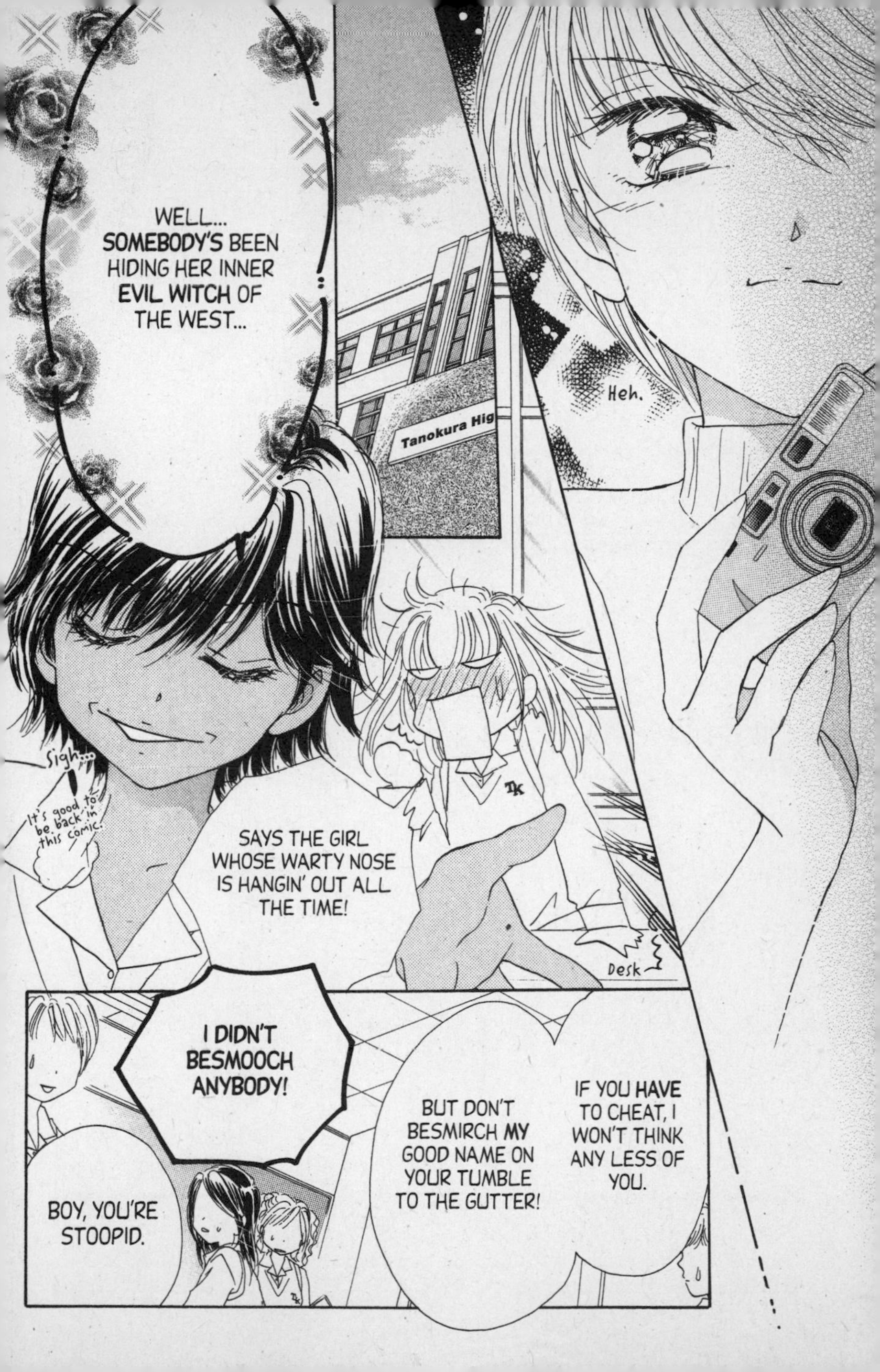
Heh.
Tanokura Hig
WELL... SOMEBODY'S BEEN HIDING HER INNER EVIL WITCH OF THE WEST...
Sigh...
It's good to be back in this comic.
SAYS THE GIRL WHOSE WARTY NOSE IS HANGIN' OUT ALL THE TIME!
Desk
IF YOU HAVE TO CHEAT, I WON'T THINK ANY LESS OF YOU.
BUT DON'T BESMIRCH MY GOOD NAME ON YOUR TUMBLE TO THE GUTTER!
I DIDN'T BESMOOCH ANYBODY!
BOY, YOU'RE STOOPID.

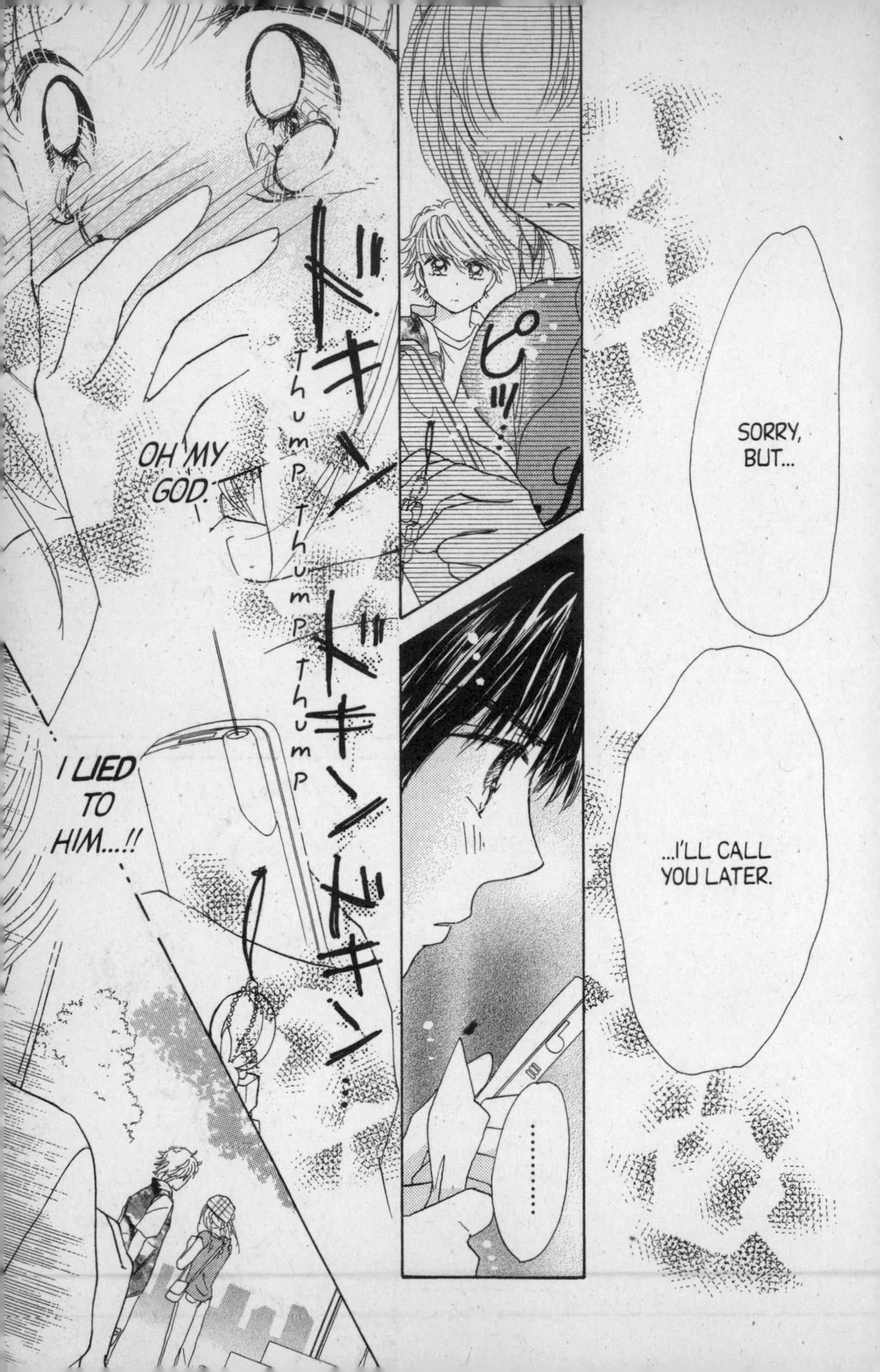
SORRY, BUT...
...I'LL CALL YOU LATER.
ピッ
......
OH MY GOD.
ドキン ドキン ドキン...
Thump thump thump thump
I LIED TO HIM...!!

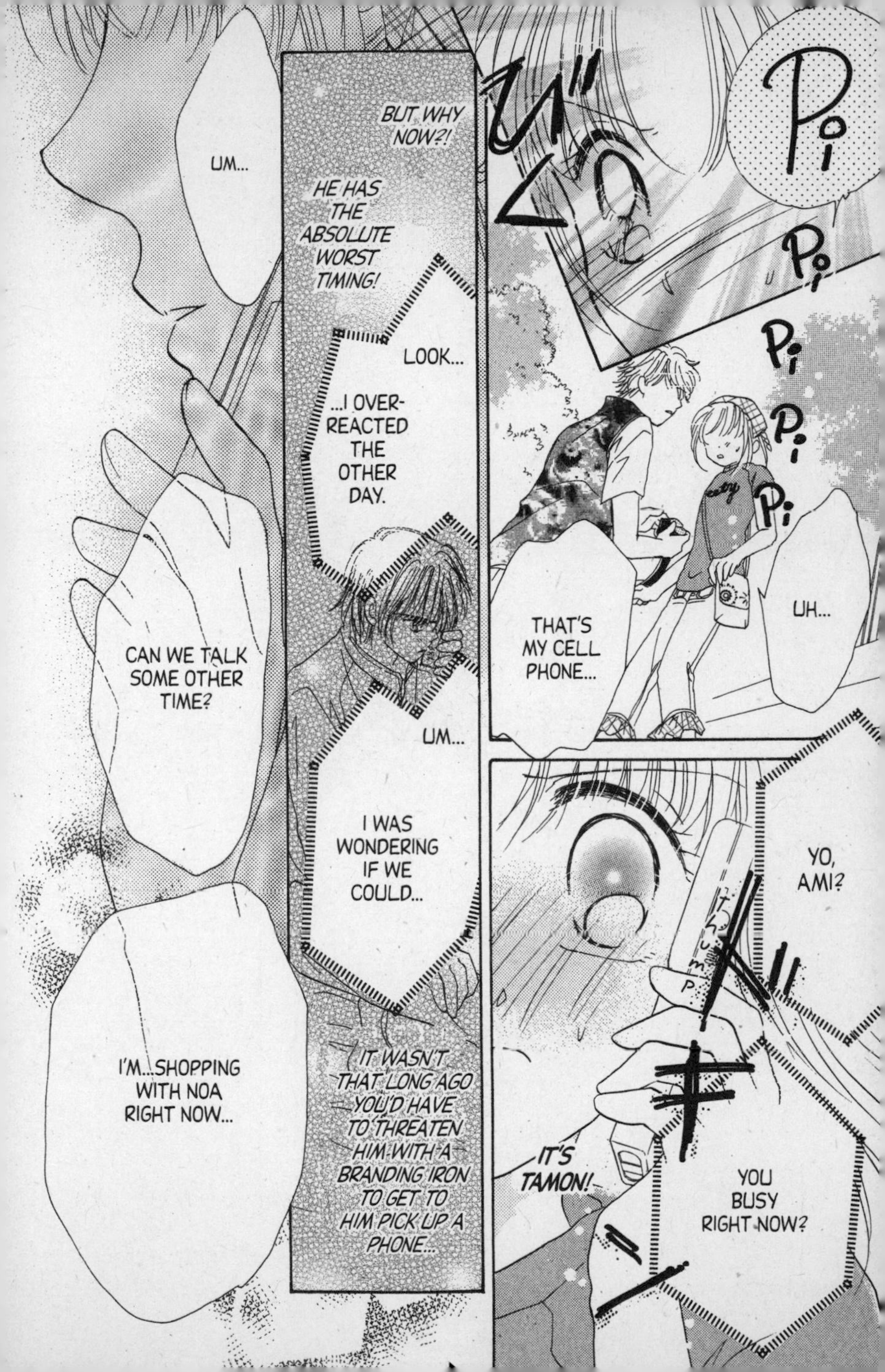
Pi
Pi
Pi
Pi
Pi
UH...
THAT'S MY CELL PHONE...
YO, AMI?
thump
IT'S TAMON!
YOU BUSY RIGHT NOW?
BUT WHY NOW?!
HE HAS THE ABSOLUTE WORST TIMING!
LOOK...
...I OVER-REACTED THE OTHER DAY.
UM...
I WAS WONDERING IF WE COULD...
IT WASN'T THAT LONG AGO YOU'D HAVE TO THREATEN HIM WITH A BRANDING IRON TO GET TO HIM PICK UP A PHONE...
UM...
CAN WE TALK SOME OTHER TIME?
I'M...SHOPPING WITH NOA RIGHT NOW...

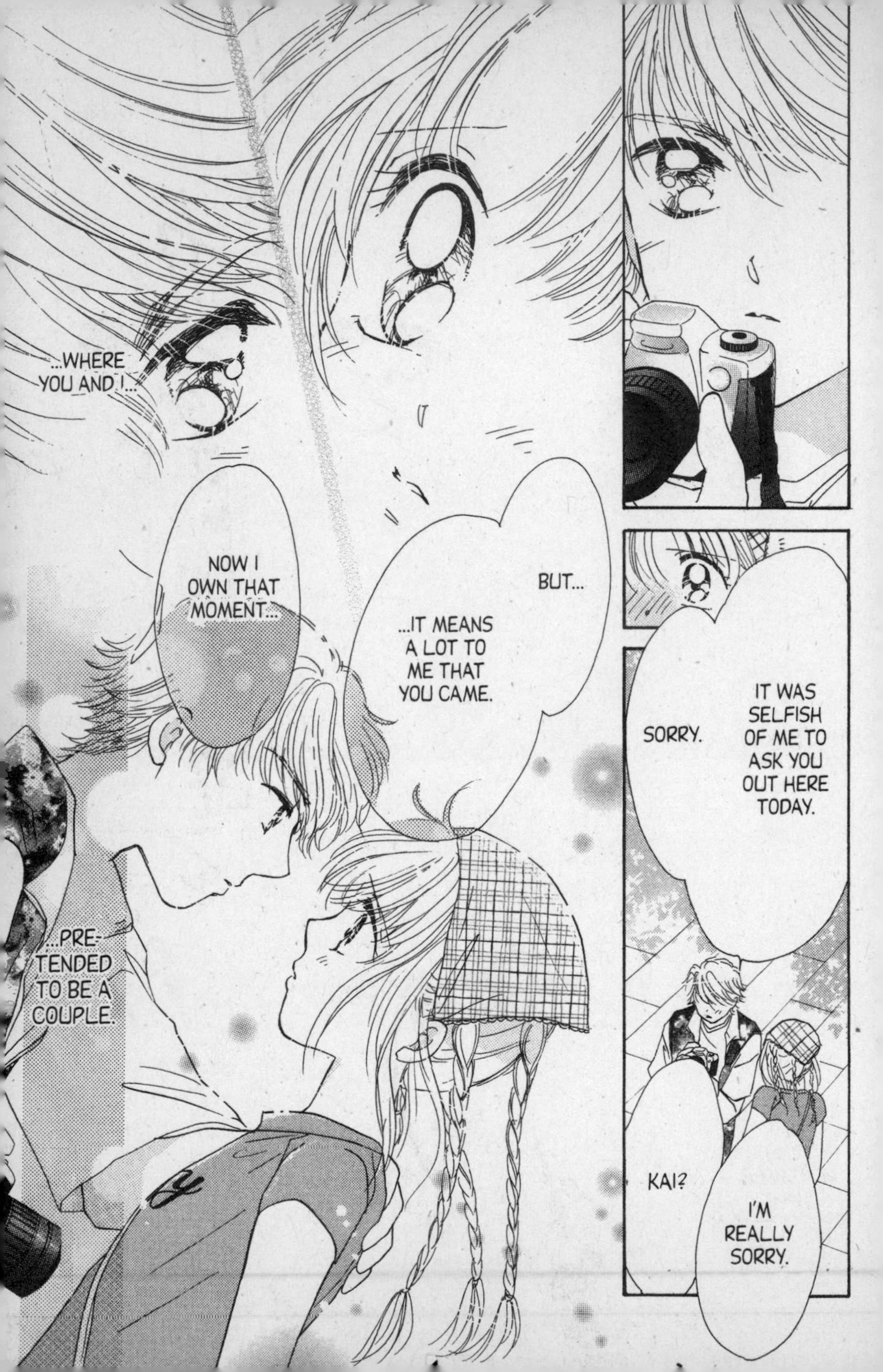
IT WAS SELFISH OF ME TO ASK YOU OUT HERE TODAY.
SORRY.
I'M REALLY SORRY.
KAI?
BUT...
...IT MEANS A LOT TO ME THAT YOU CAME.
NOW I OWN THAT MOMENT...
...WHERE YOU AND I...
...PRE-TENDED TO BE A COUPLE.

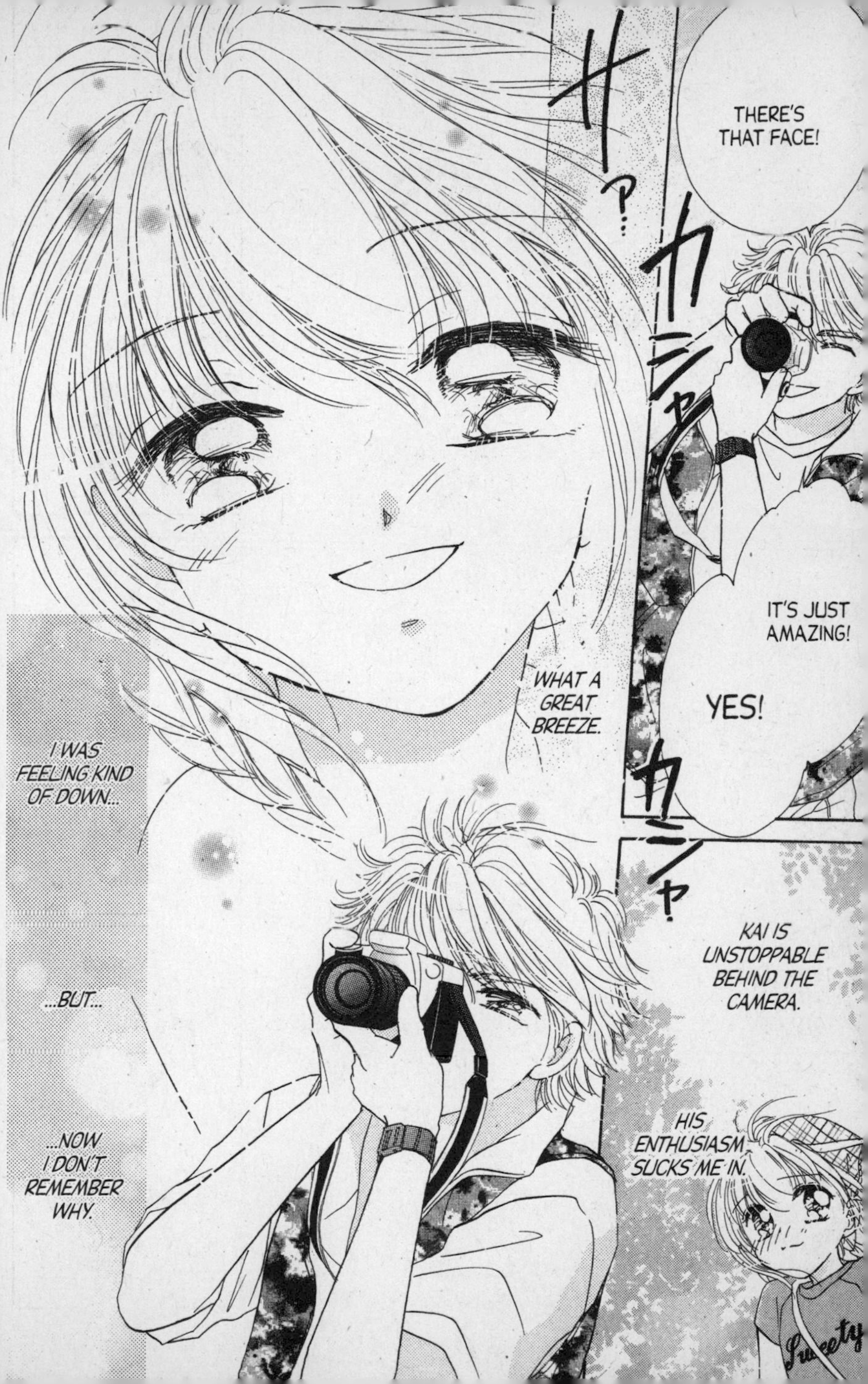
THERE'S THAT FACE!
カシャ
IT'S JUST AMAZING!
YES!
カシャ
KAI IS UNSTOPPABLE BEHIND THE CAMERA.
HIS ENTHUSIASM SUCKS ME IN.
Sweety
サァ…
WHAT A GREAT BREEZE.
I WAS FEELING KIND OF DOWN...
...BUT...
...NOW I DON'T REMEMBER WHY.

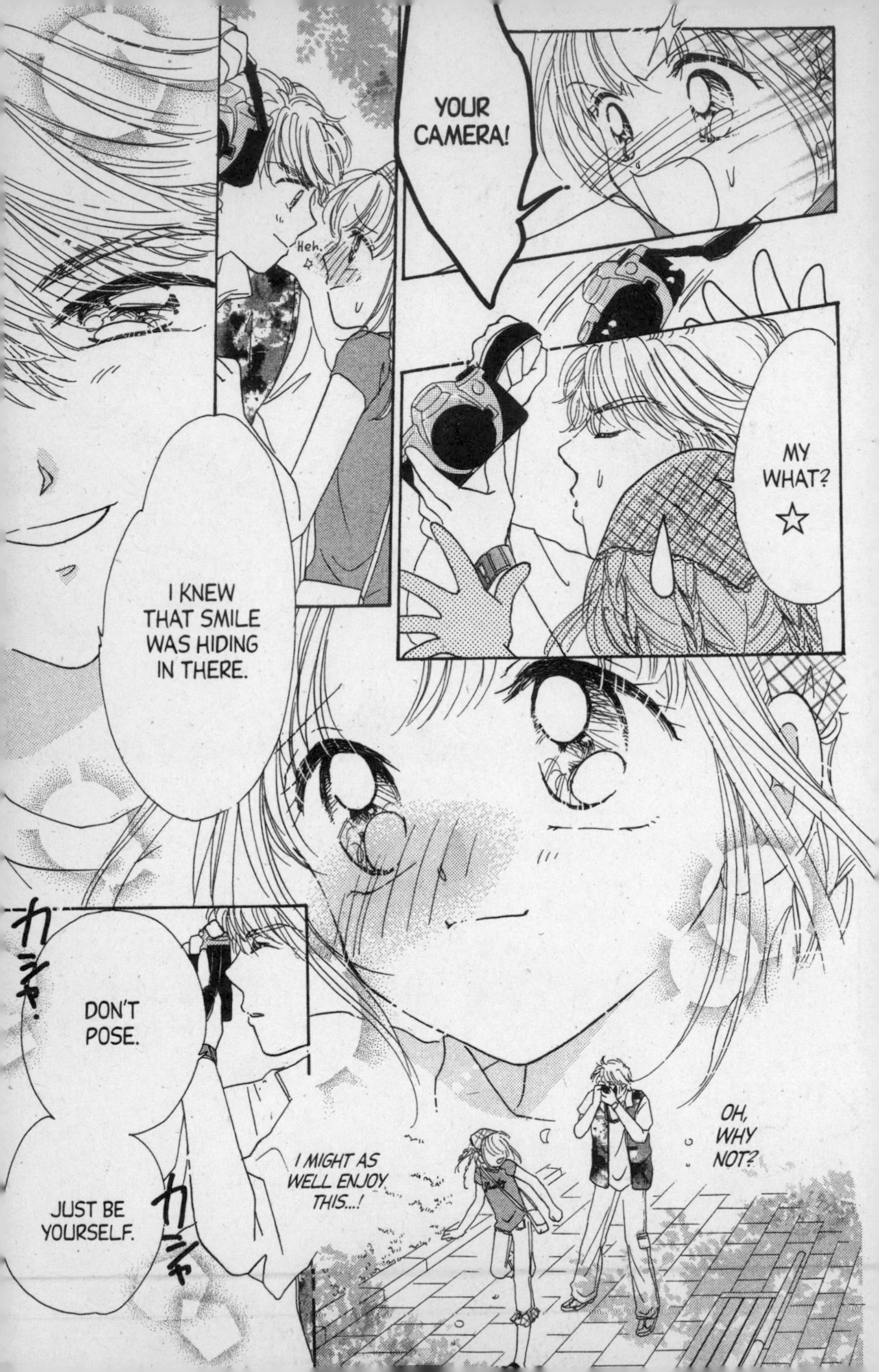
YOUR CAMERA!
MY WHAT? ☆
Heh.
I KNEW THAT SMILE WAS HIDING IN THERE.
OH, WHY NOT?
I MIGHT AS WELL ENJOY THIS...!
カシャ
DON'T POSE.
カシャ
JUST BE YOURSELF.

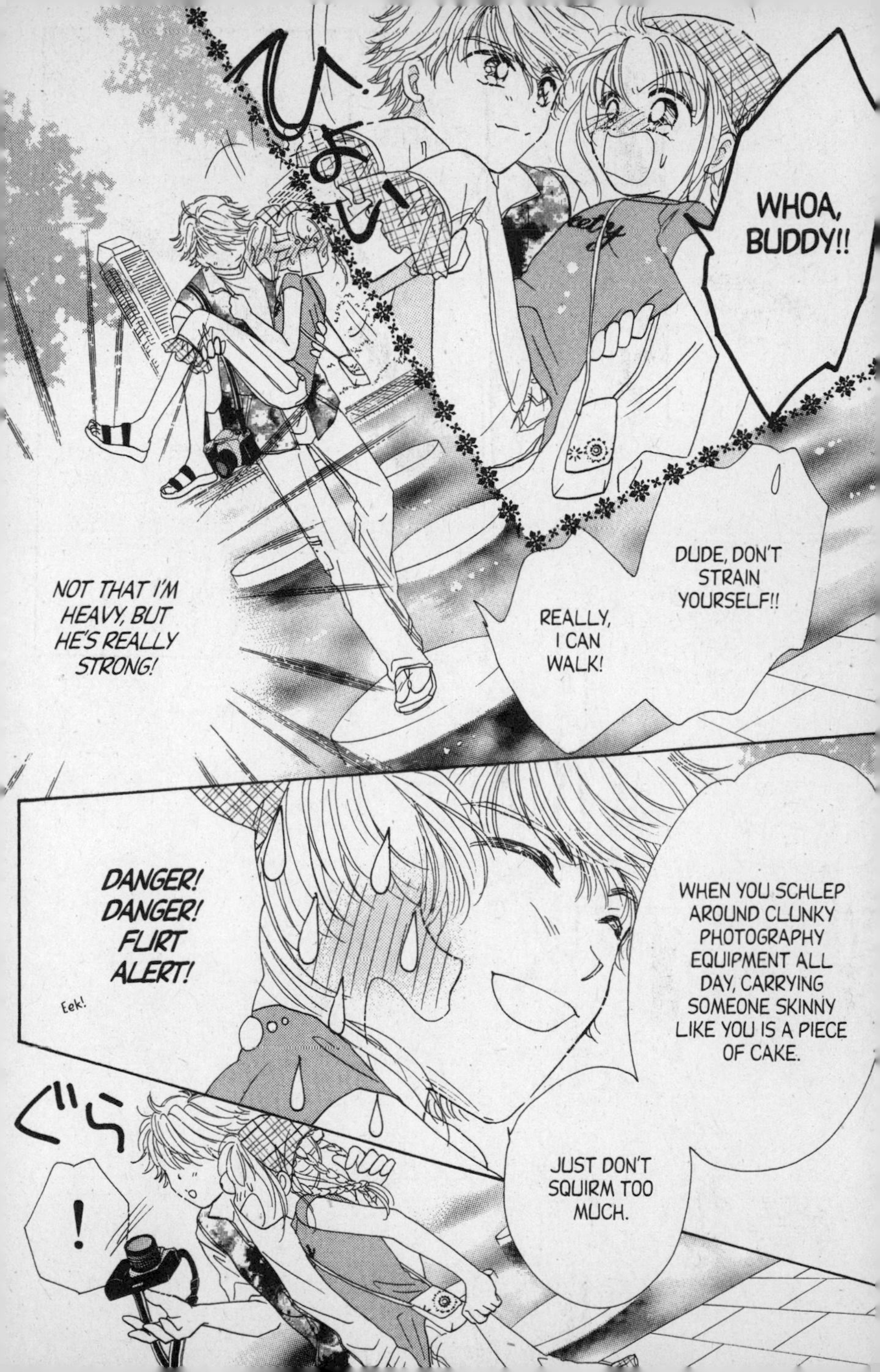
WHOA, BUDDY!!
ひょい
DUDE, DON'T STRAIN YOURSELF!!
REALLY, I CAN WALK!
NOT THAT I'M HEAVY, BUT HE'S REALLY STRONG!
WHEN YOU SCHLEP AROUND CLUNKY PHOTOGRAPHY EQUIPMENT ALL DAY, CARRYING SOMEONE SKINNY LIKE YOU IS A PIECE OF CAKE.
DANGER! DANGER! FLIRT ALERT!
Eek!
JUST DON'T SQUIRM TOO MUCH.
ぐら
!

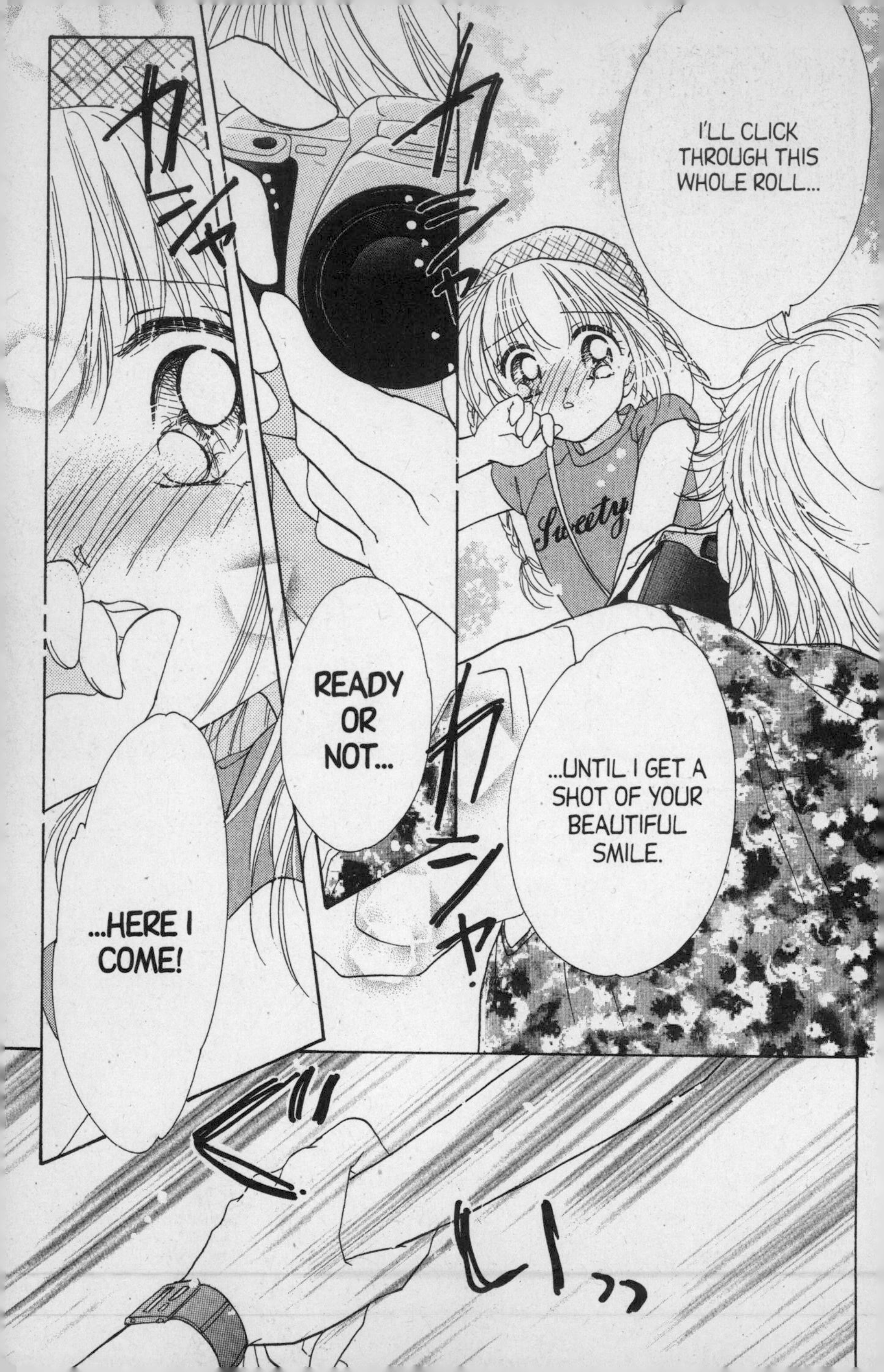
I'LL CLICK THROUGH THIS WHOLE ROLL...
...UNTIL I GET A SHOT OF YOUR BEAUTIFUL SMILE.
READY OR NOT...
...HERE I COME!

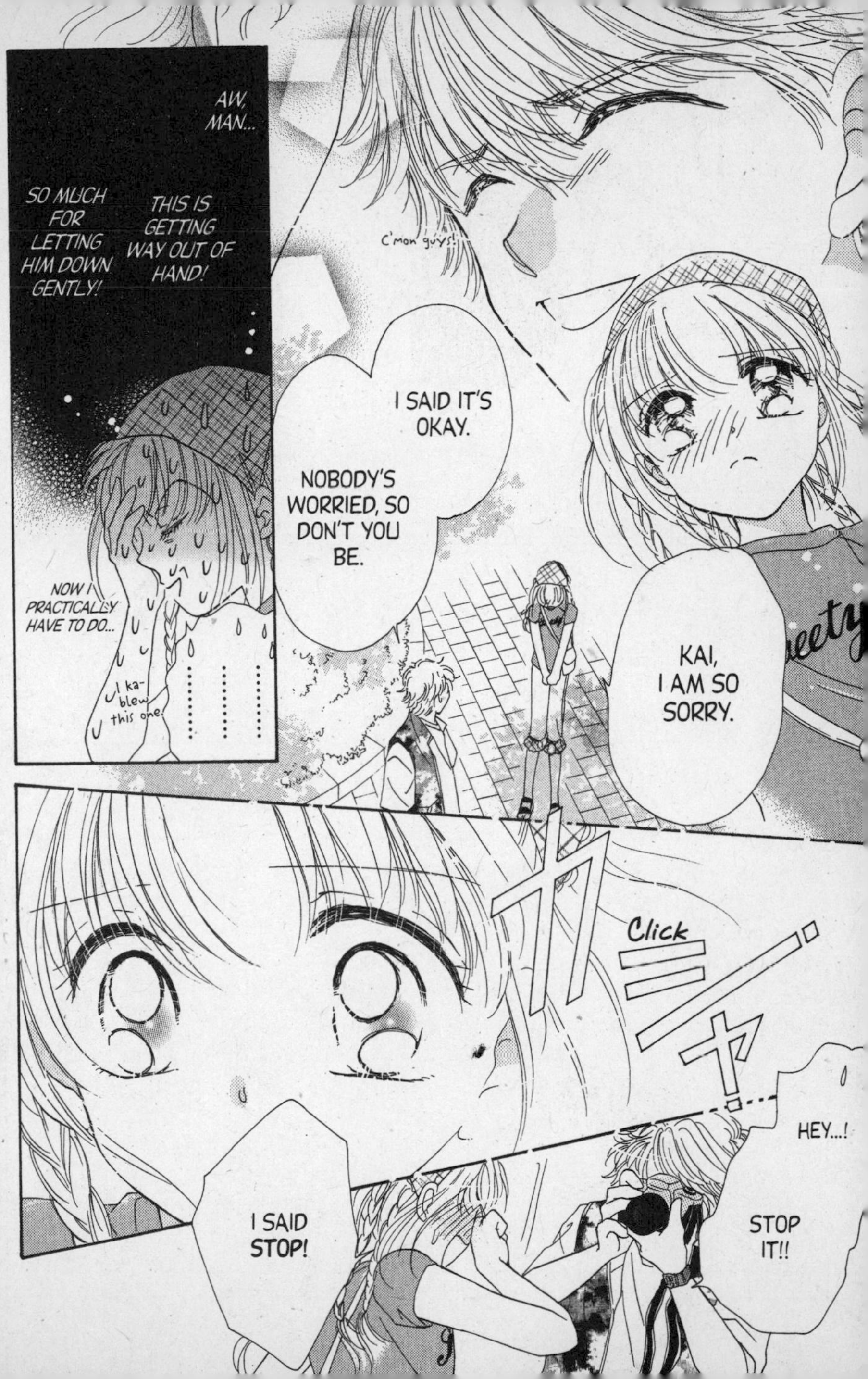
KAI, I AM SO SORRY.
I SAID IT'S OKAY.
NOBODY'S WORRIED, SO DON'T YOU BE.
C'mon guys!
AW, MAN...
THIS IS GETTING WAY OUT OF HAND!
SO MUCH FOR LETTING HIM DOWN GENTLY!
NOW I PRACTICALLY HAVE TO DO...
I ka-blew this one!
......
Click
HEY...!
STOP IT!!
I SAID STOP!

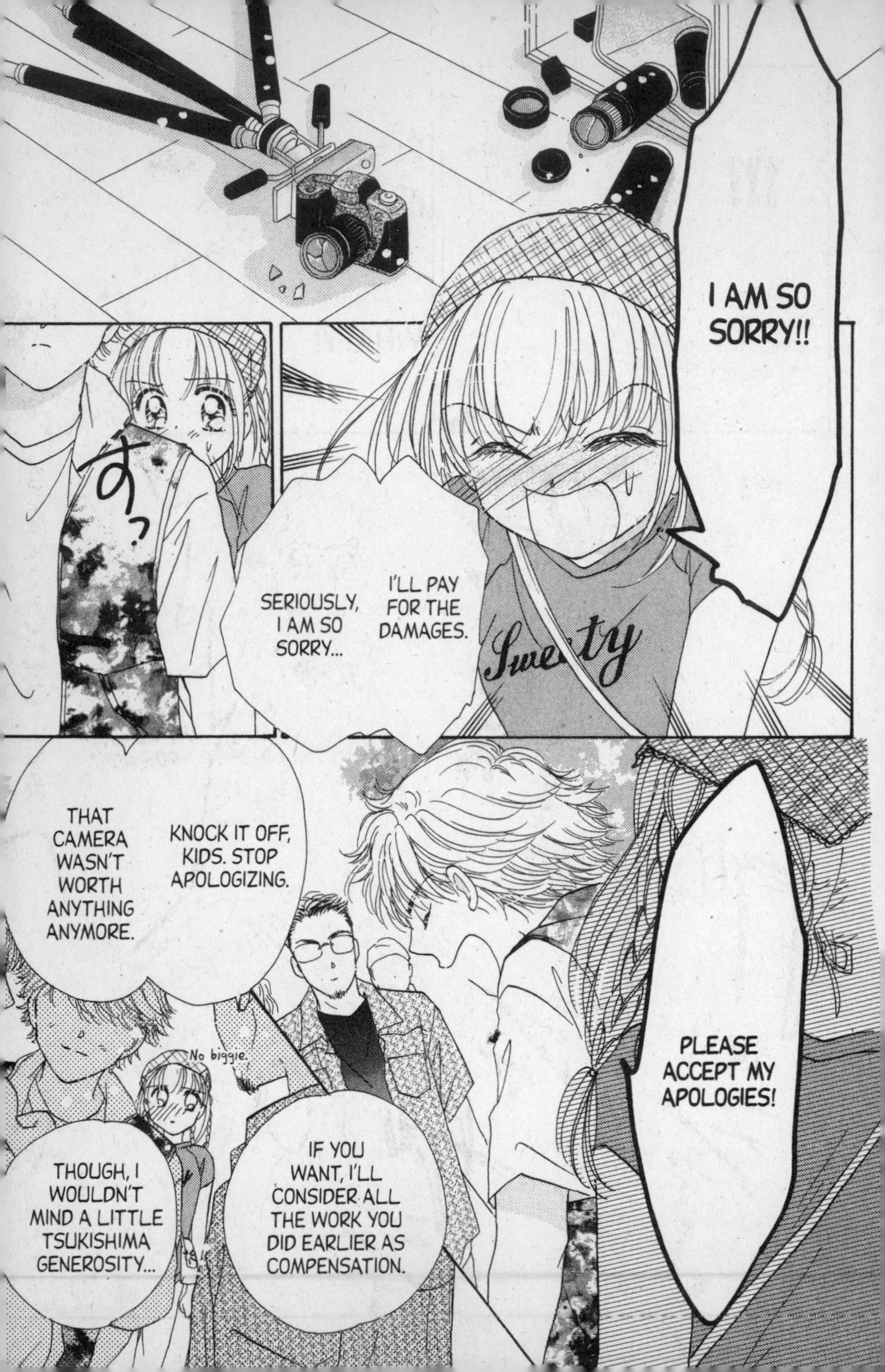
I AM SO SORRY!!
I'LL PAY FOR THE DAMAGES.
SERIOUSLY, I AM SO SORRY...
すっ
PLEASE ACCEPT MY APOLOGIES!
KNOCK IT OFF, KIDS. STOP APOLOGIZING.
THAT CAMERA WASN'T WORTH ANYTHING ANYMORE.
IF YOU WANT, I'LL CONSIDER ALL THE WORK YOU DID EARLIER AS COMPENSATION.
No biggie.
THOUGH, I WOULDN'T MIND A LITTLE TSUKISHIMA GENEROSITY...

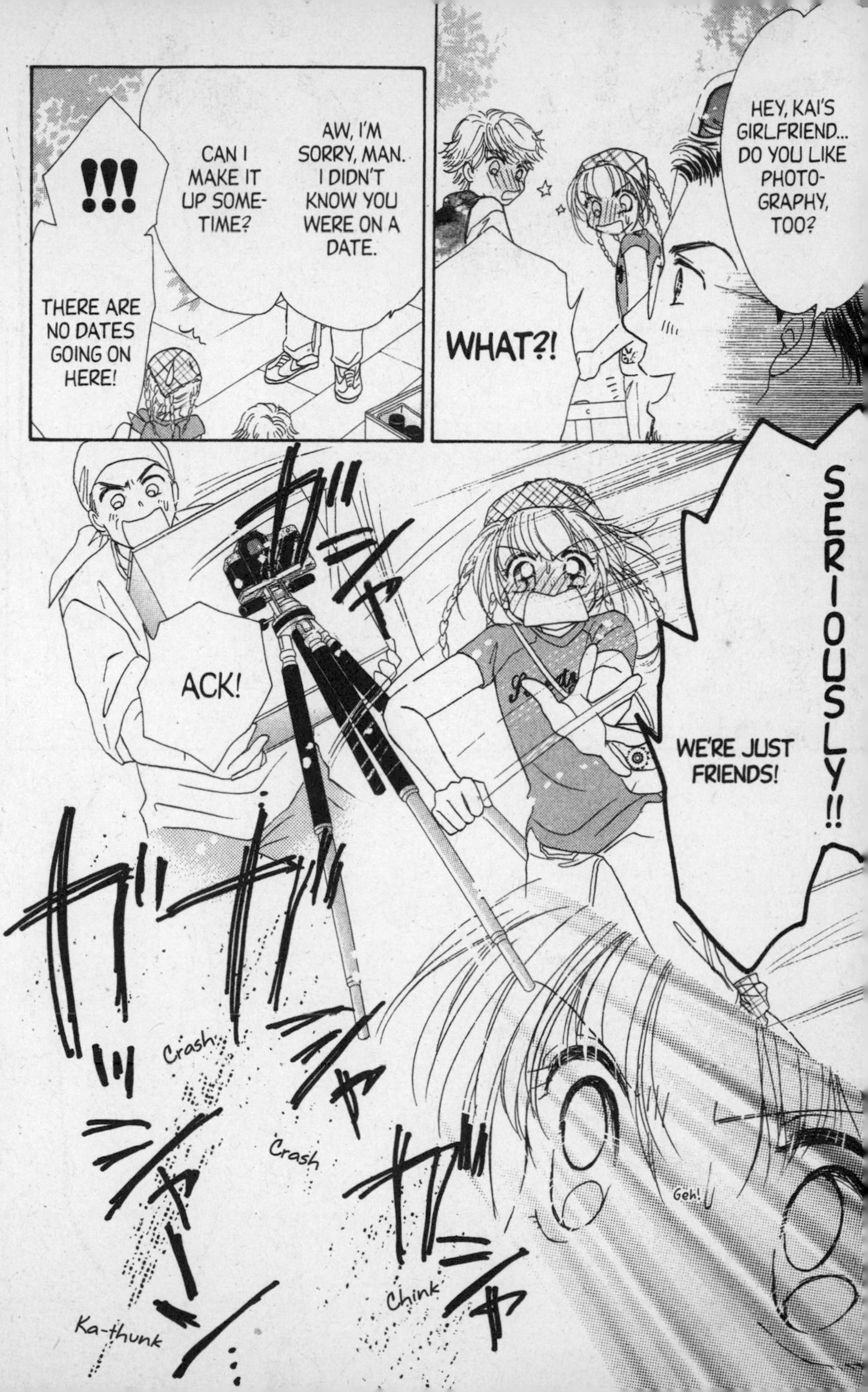
HEY, KAI'S GIRLFRIEND... DO YOU LIKE PHOTOGRAPHY, TOO?
WHAT?!
AW, I'M SORRY, MAN. I DIDN'T KNOW YOU WERE ON A DATE.
CAN I MAKE IT UP SOMETIME?
!!!
THERE ARE NO DATES GOING ON HERE!
SERIOUSLY!!
WE'RE JUST FRIENDS!
ACK!
Geh!
Crash
Crash
Chink
Ka-thunk

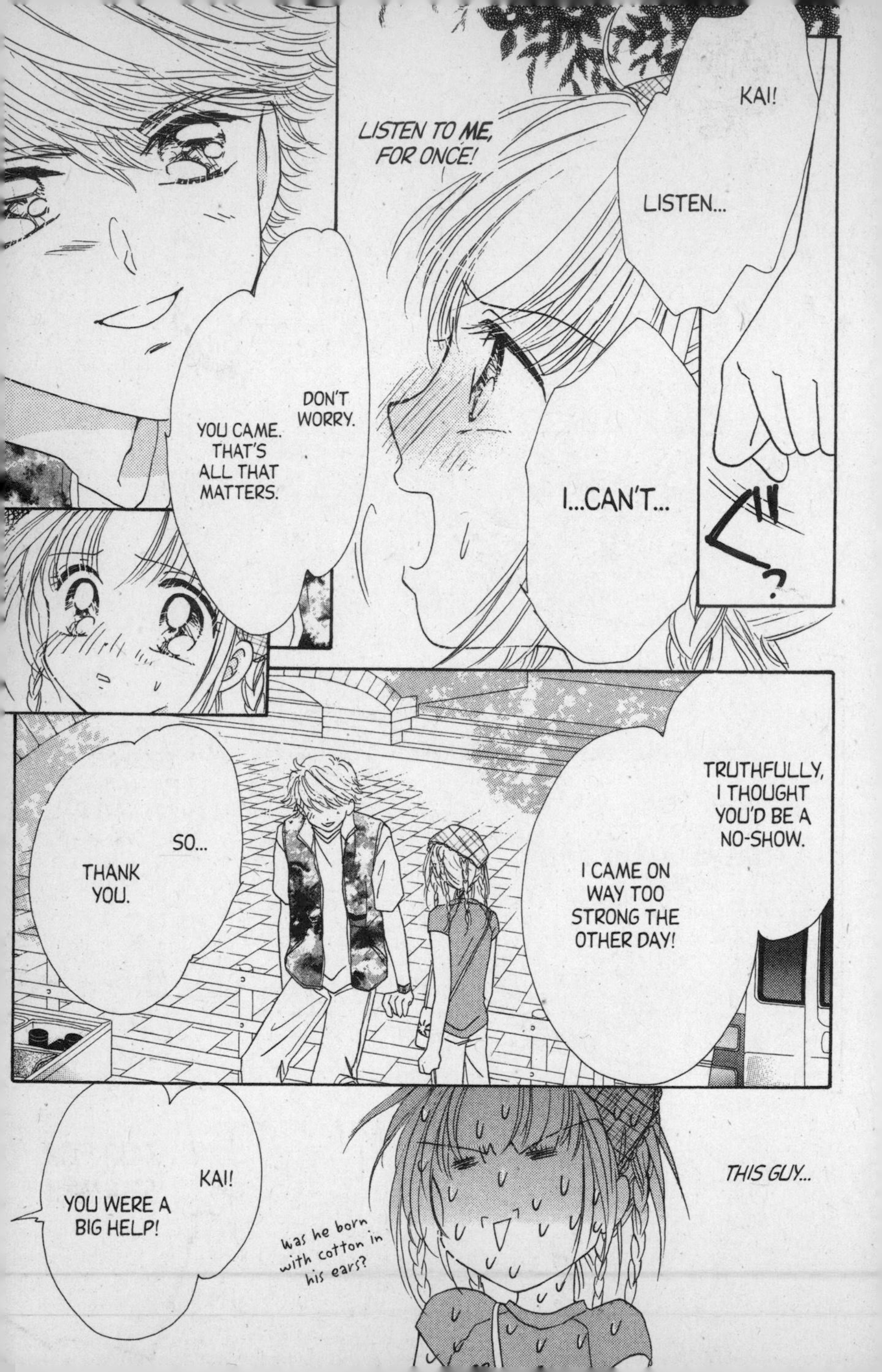
KAI!
LISTEN...
LISTEN TO ME, FOR ONCE!
I...CAN'T...
DON'T WORRY.
YOU CAME. THAT'S ALL THAT MATTERS.
TRUTHFULLY, I THOUGHT YOU'D BE A NO-SHOW.
I CAME ON WAY TOO STRONG THE OTHER DAY!
SO...
THANK YOU.
THIS GUY...
Was he born with cotton in his ears?
KAI!
YOU WERE A BIG HELP!

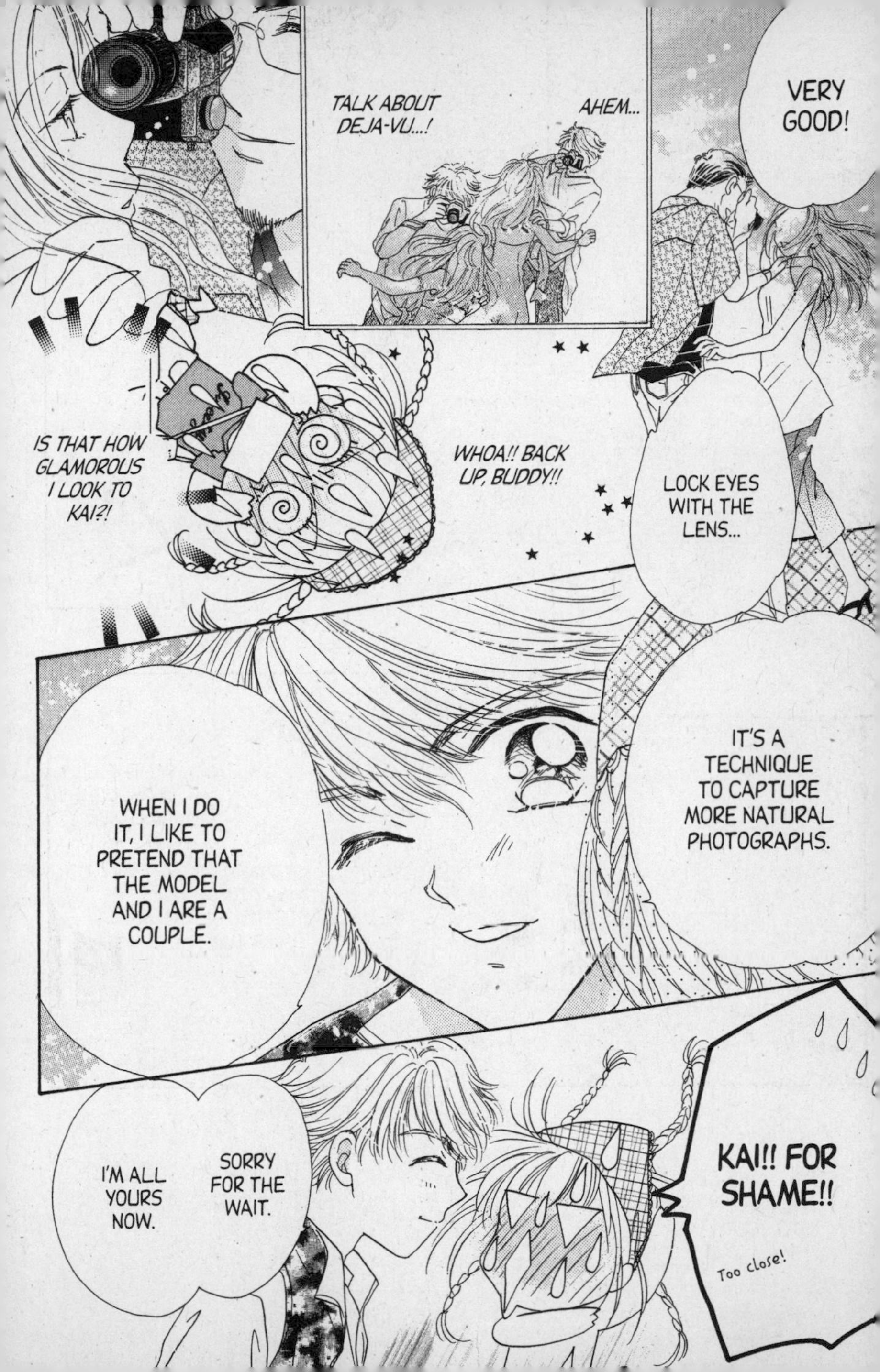
VERY GOOD!
LOCK EYES WITH THE LENS...
AHEM...
TALK ABOUT DEJA-VU...!
WHOA!! BACK UP, BUDDY!!
IS THAT HOW GLAMOROUS I LOOK TO KAI?!
IT'S A TECHNIQUE TO CAPTURE MORE NATURAL PHOTOGRAPHS.
WHEN I DO IT, I LIKE TO PRETEND THAT THE MODEL AND I ARE A COUPLE.
KAI!! FOR SHAME!!
Too close!
SORRY FOR THE WAIT.
I'M ALL YOURS NOW.

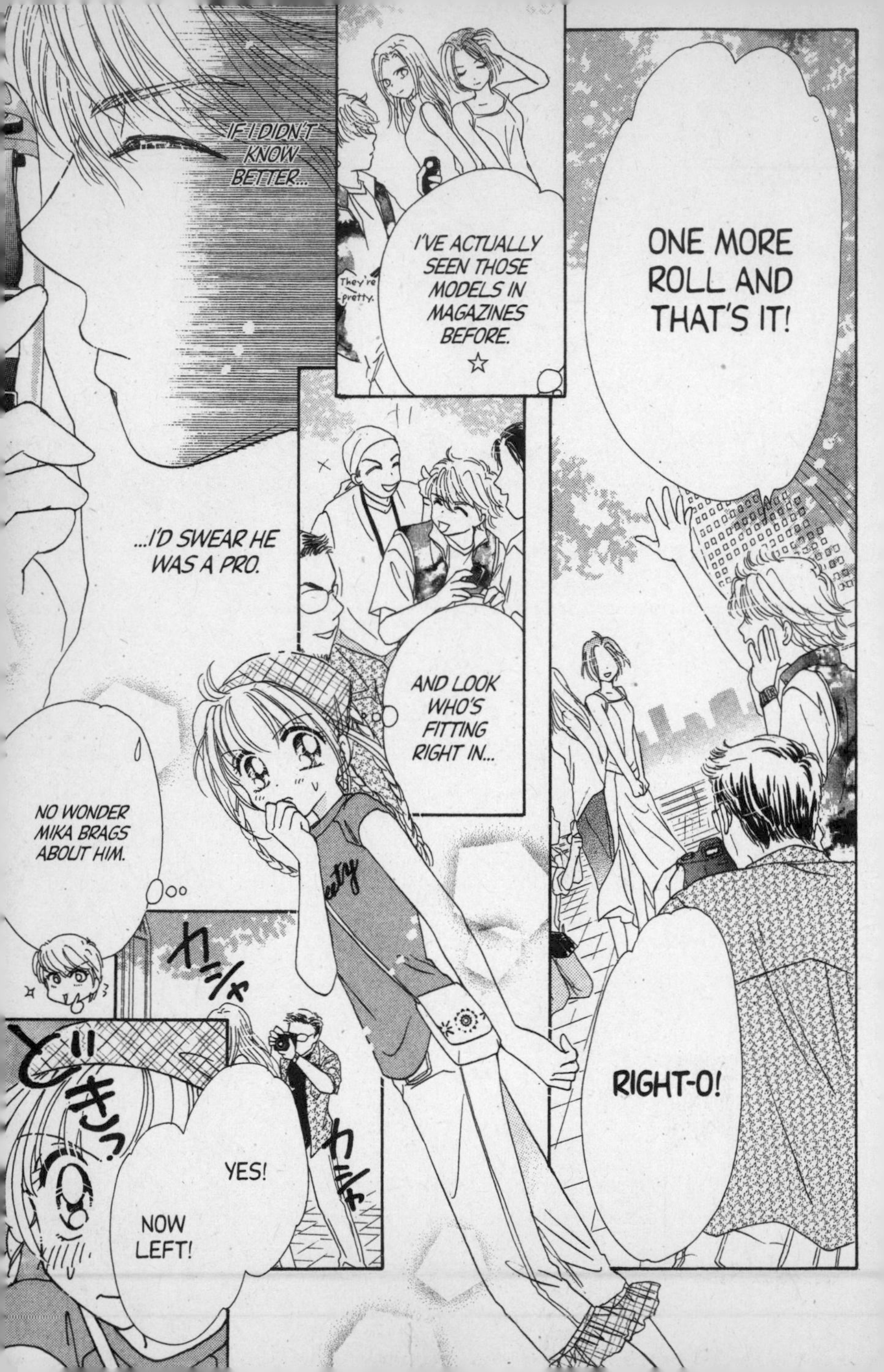

ONE MORE ROLL AND THAT'S IT!
RIGHT-O!
I'VE ACTUALLY SEEN THOSE MODELS IN MAGAZINES BEFORE. ☆
They're pretty.
IF I DIDN'T KNOW BETTER...
...I'D SWEAR HE WAS A PRO.
AND LOOK WHO'S FITTING RIGHT IN...
NO WONDER MIKA BRAGS ABOUT HIM.
YES!
NOW LEFT!

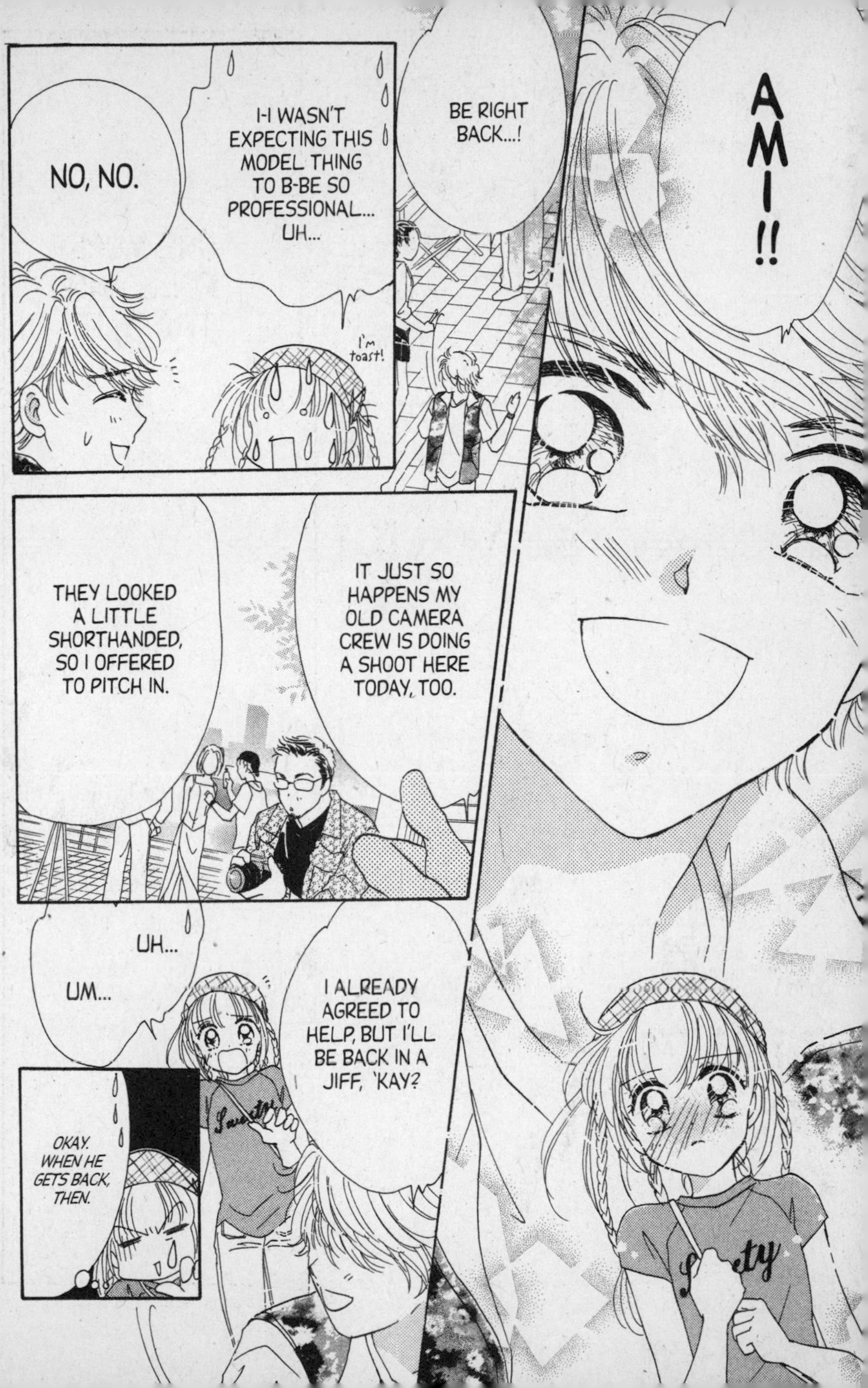
AMI!!
BE RIGHT BACK...!
NO, NO.
I-I WASN'T EXPECTING THIS MODEL THING TO B-BE SO PROFESSIONAL... UH...
I'm toast!
IT JUST SO HAPPENS MY OLD CAMERA CREW IS DOING A SHOOT HERE TODAY, TOO.
THEY LOOKED A LITTLE SHORTHANDED, SO I OFFERED TO PITCH IN.
I ALREADY AGREED TO HELP, BUT I'LL BE BACK IN A JIFF, 'KAY?
UH...
UM...
OKAY. WHEN HE GETS BACK, THEN.

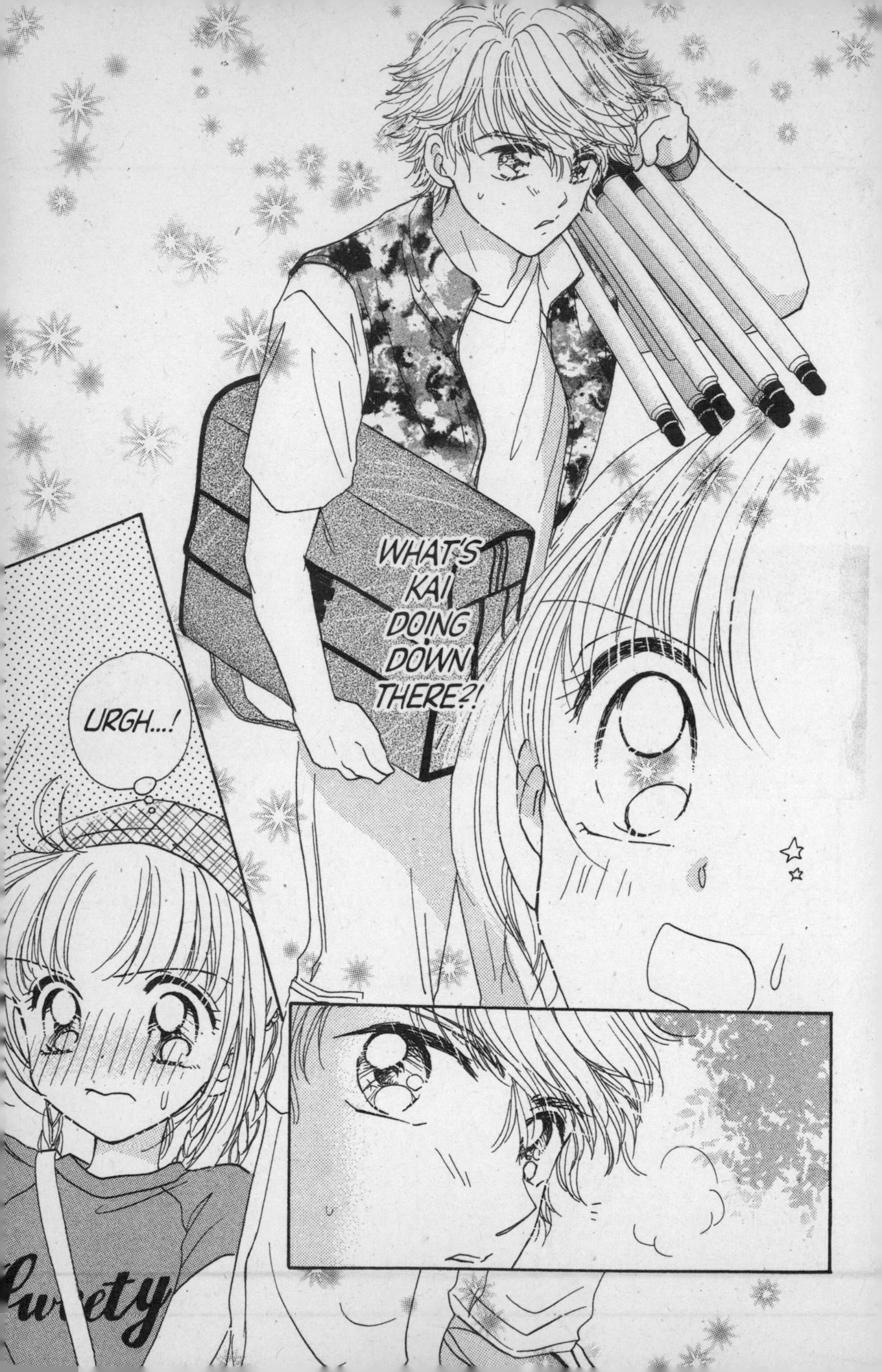
WHAT'S KAI DOING DOWN THERE?!
URGH...!

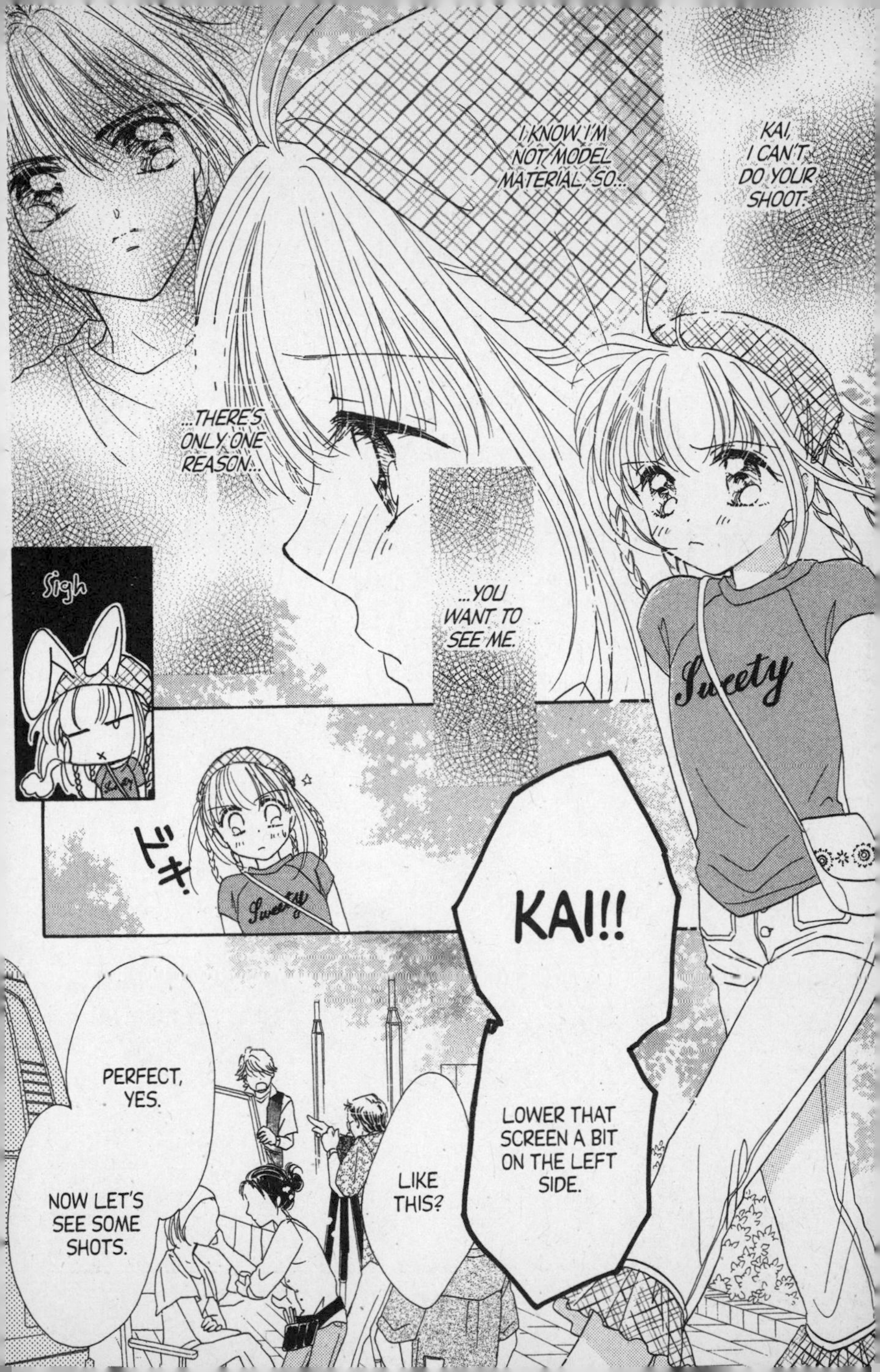
KAI, I CAN'T DO YOUR SHOOT.
I KNOW I'M NOT MODEL MATERIAL, SO...
...THERE'S ONLY ONE REASON...
...YOU WANT TO SEE ME.
Sigh
ドキ
KAI!!
LOWER THAT SCREEN A BIT ON THE LEFT SIDE.
LIKE THIS?
PERFECT, YES.
NOW LET'S SEE SOME SHOTS.

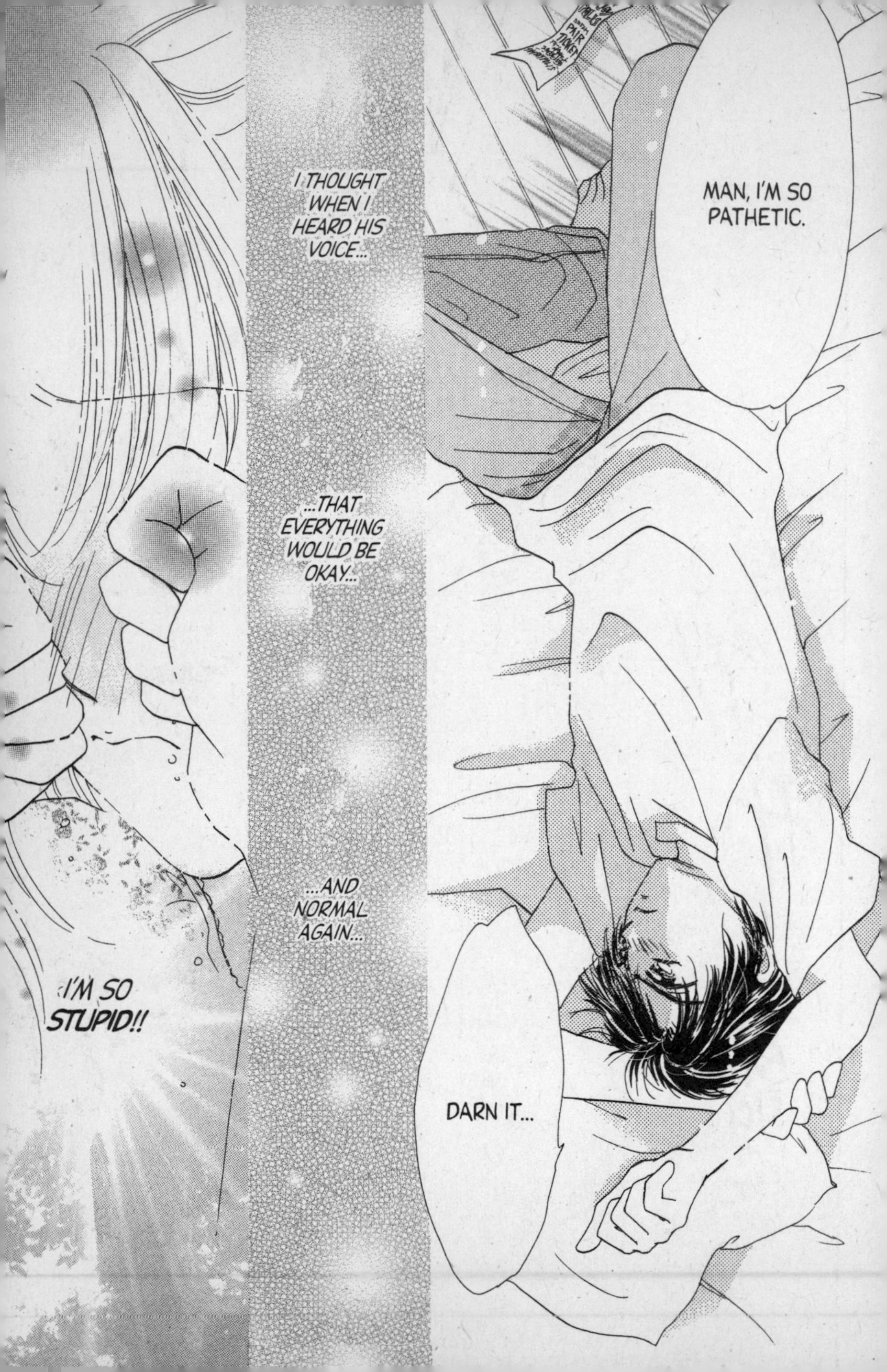
MAN, I'M SO PATHETIC.
DARN IT...
I THOUGHT WHEN I HEARD HIS VOICE...
...THAT EVERYTHING WOULD BE OKAY...
...AND NORMAL AGAIN...
I'M SO STUPID!!

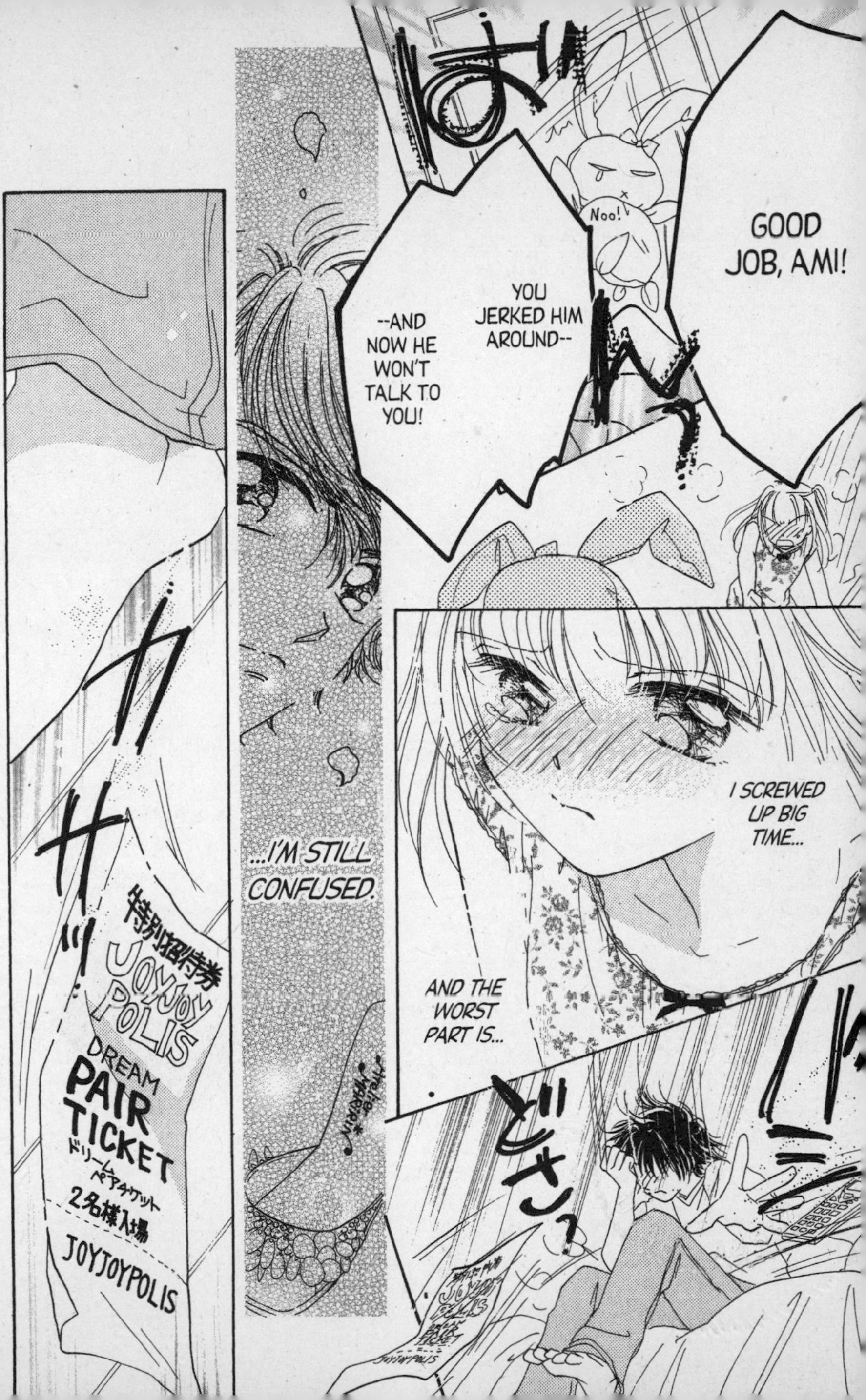
GOOD JOB, AMI!
YOU JERKED HIM AROUND--
--AND NOW HE WON'T TALK TO YOU!
Noo!
...I'M STILL CONFUSED.
I SCREWED UP BIG TIME...
AND THE WORST PART IS...
どさっ
特別招待券
JOYJOY POLIS
DREAM
PAIR TICKET
ドリームペアチケット
2名様入場
JOYJOYPOLIS

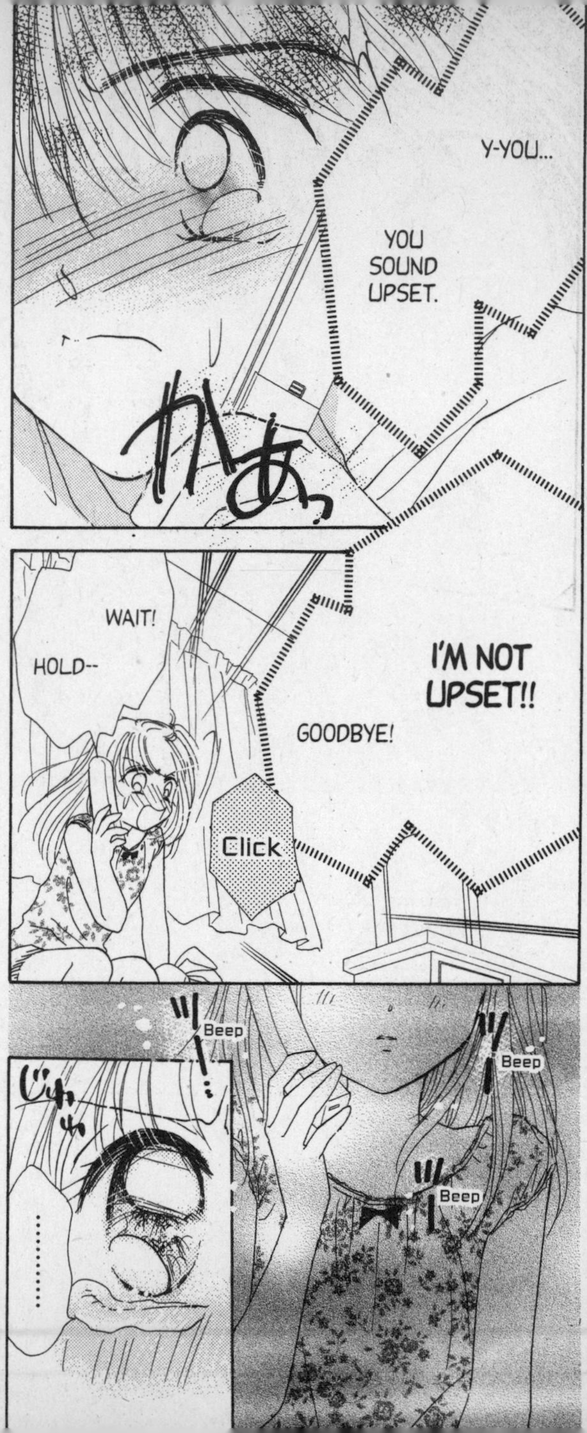
Y-YOU...
YOU SOUND UPSET.
かあっ
I'M NOT UPSET!!
GOODBYE!
Click
WAIT!
HOLD--
Beep
Beep
Beep
......

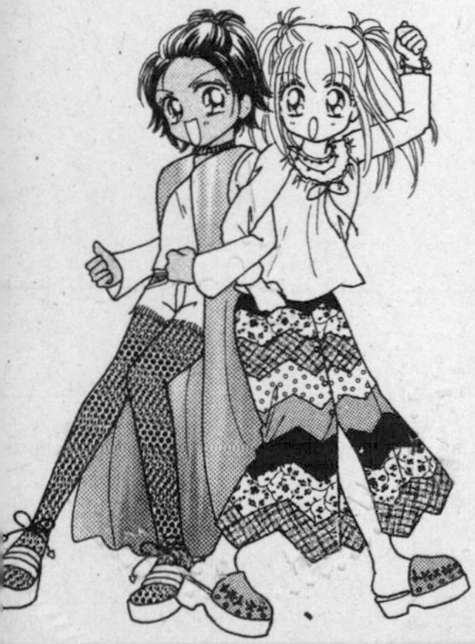

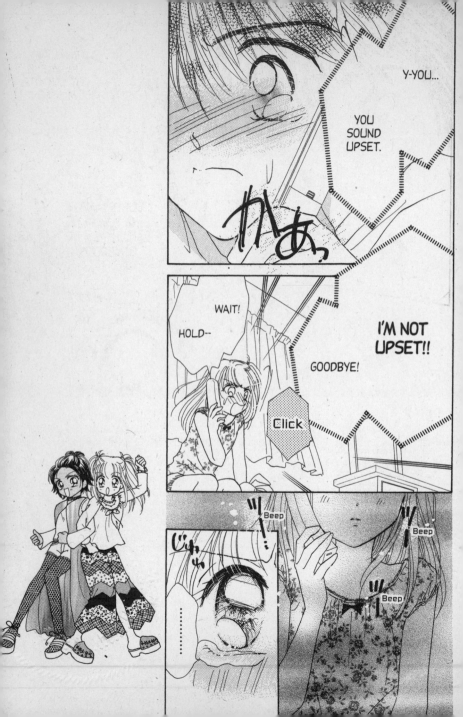

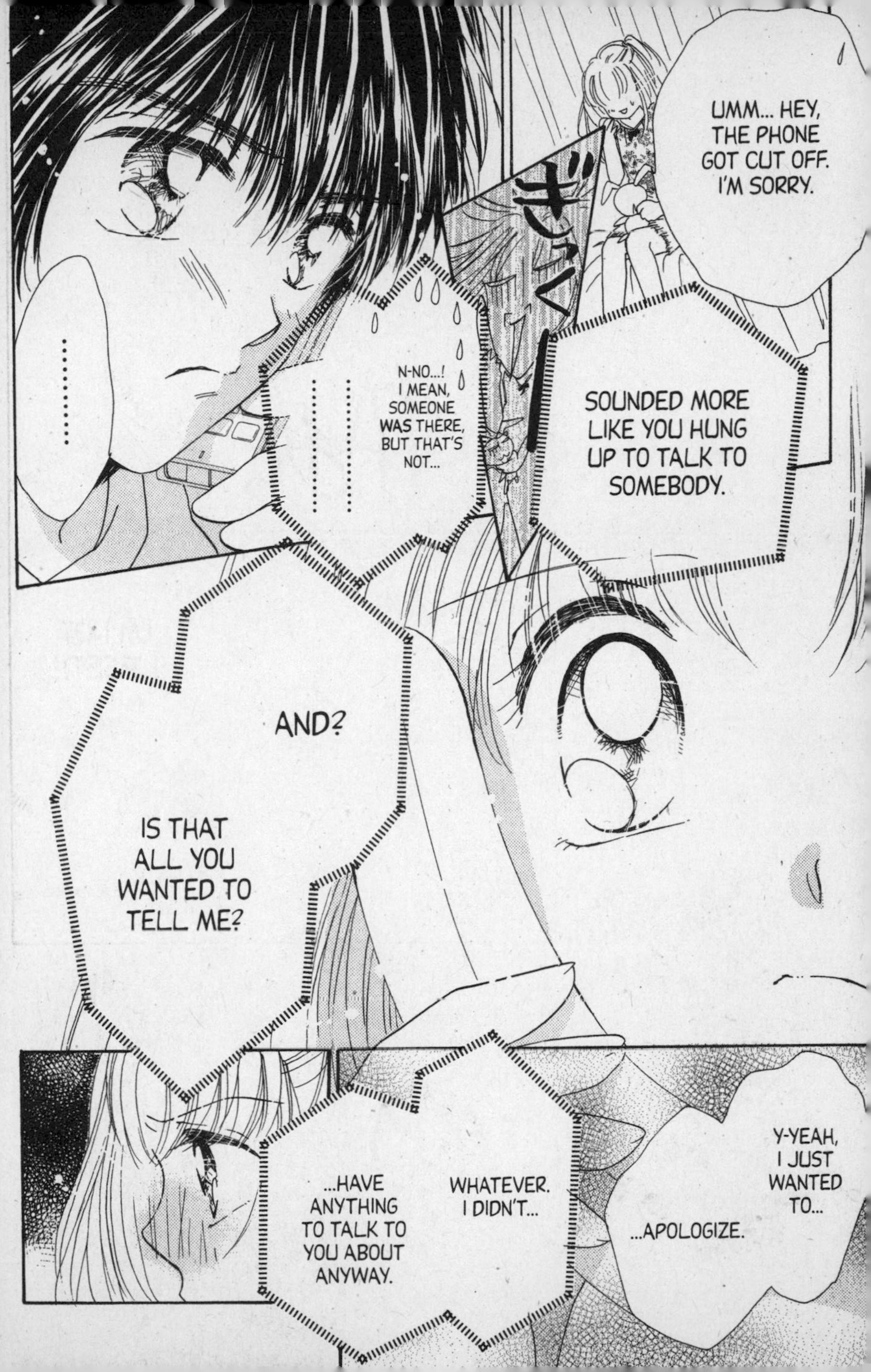
UMM... HEY, THE PHONE GOT CUT OFF. I'M SORRY.
ぎっくー
SOUNDED MORE LIKE YOU HUNG UP TO TALK TO SOMEBODY.
N-NO...! I MEAN, SOMEONE WAS THERE, BUT THAT'S NOT...
......
......
......
AND?
IS THAT ALL YOU WANTED TO TELL ME?
Y-YEAH, I JUST WANTED TO...
...APOLOGIZE.
WHATEVER. I DIDN'T...
...HAVE ANYTHING TO TALK TO YOU ABOUT ANYWAY.

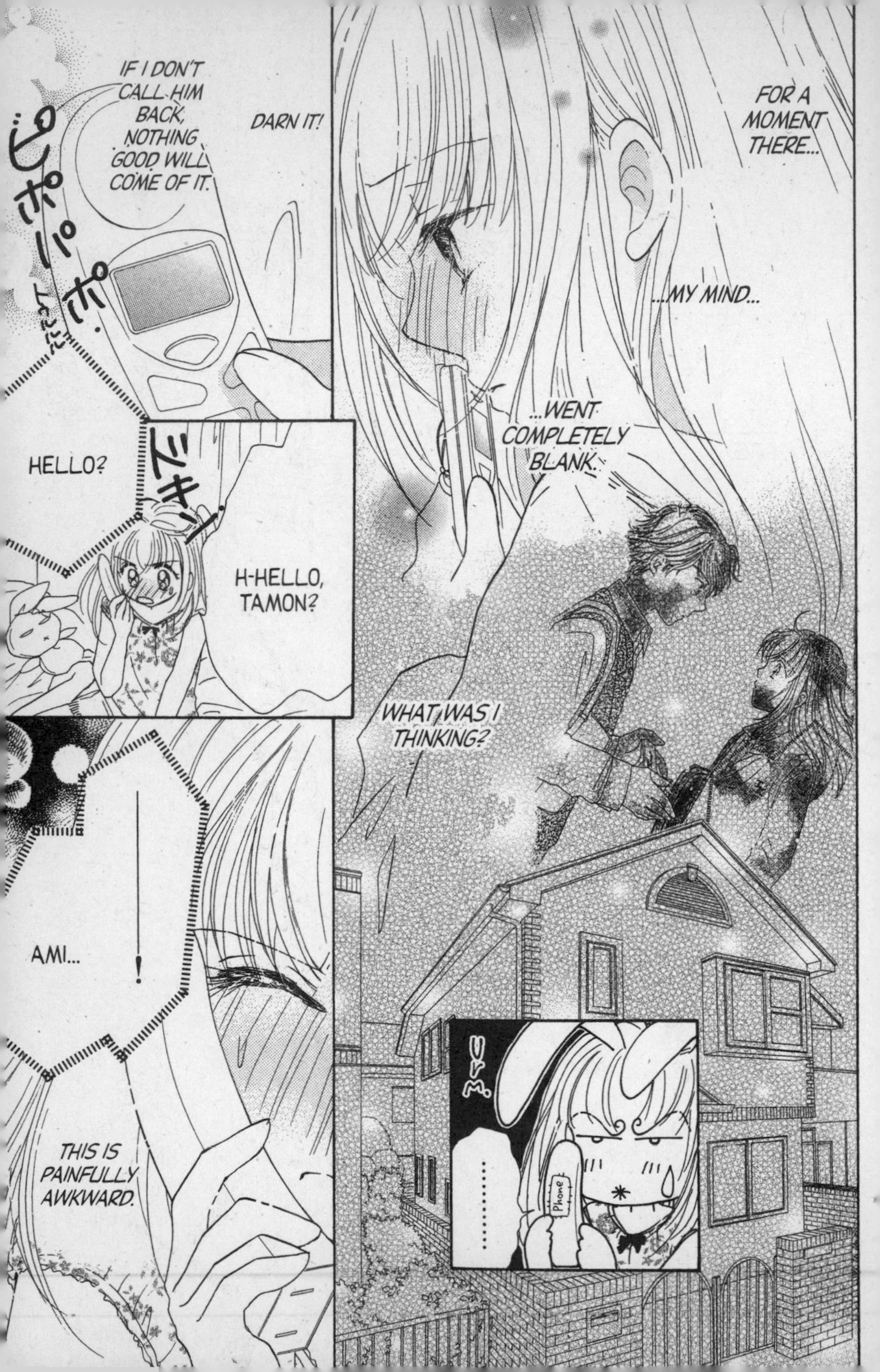
FOR A MOMENT THERE...
...MY MIND...
...WENT COMPLETELY BLANK.
WHAT WAS I THINKING?
UM.
......
Phone
DARN IT!
IF I DON'T CALL HIM BACK, NOTHING GOOD WILL COME OF IT.
ピポパポ
ドキッ
H-HELLO, TAMON?
HELLO?
!
AMI...
THIS IS PAINFULLY AWKWARD.

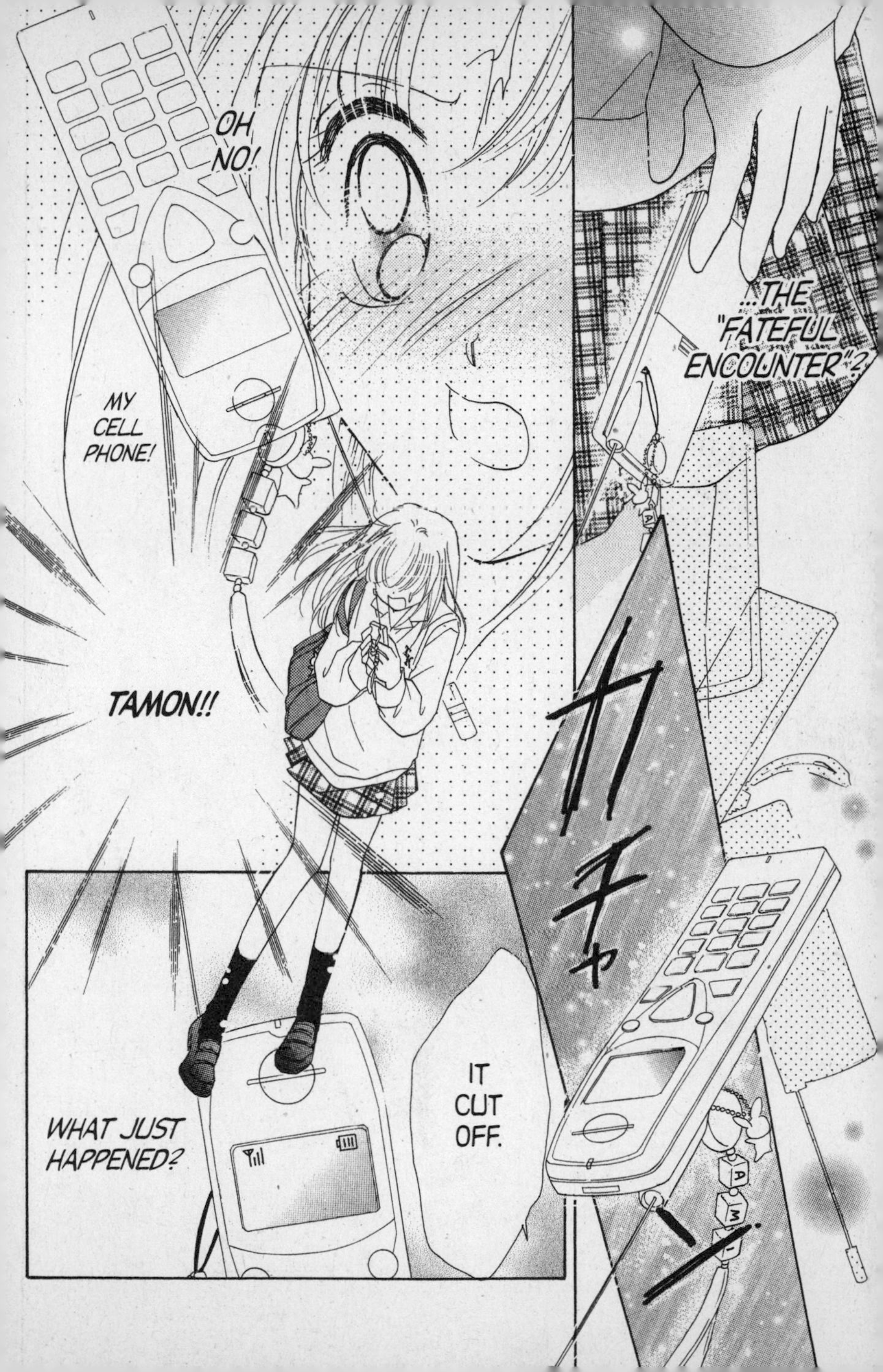
...THE "FATEFUL ENCOUNTER"?
カチャ
OH NO!
MY CELL PHONE!
TAMON!!
IT CUT OFF.
WHAT JUST HAPPENED?

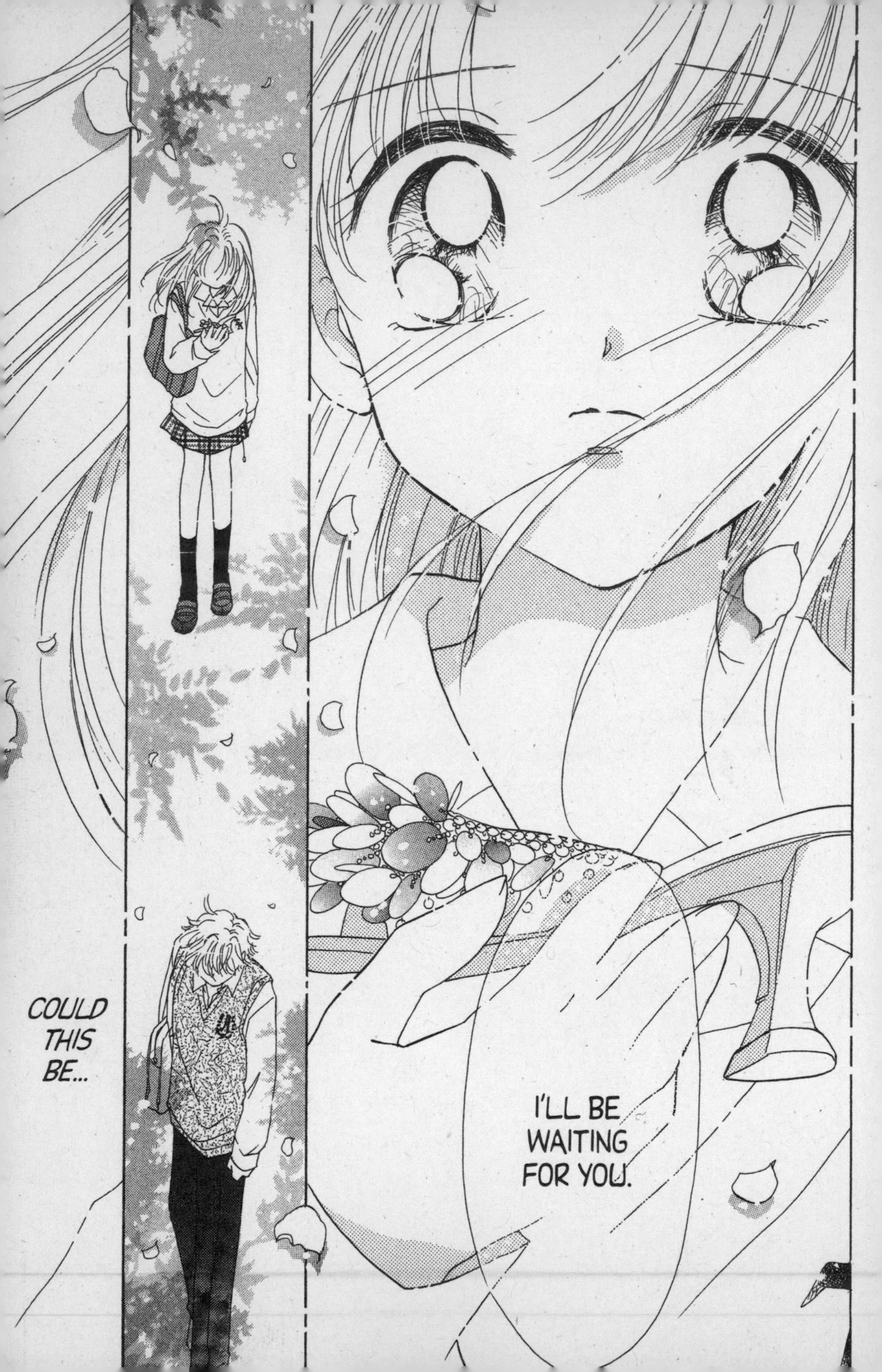
I'LL BE WAITING FOR YOU.
COULD THIS BE...

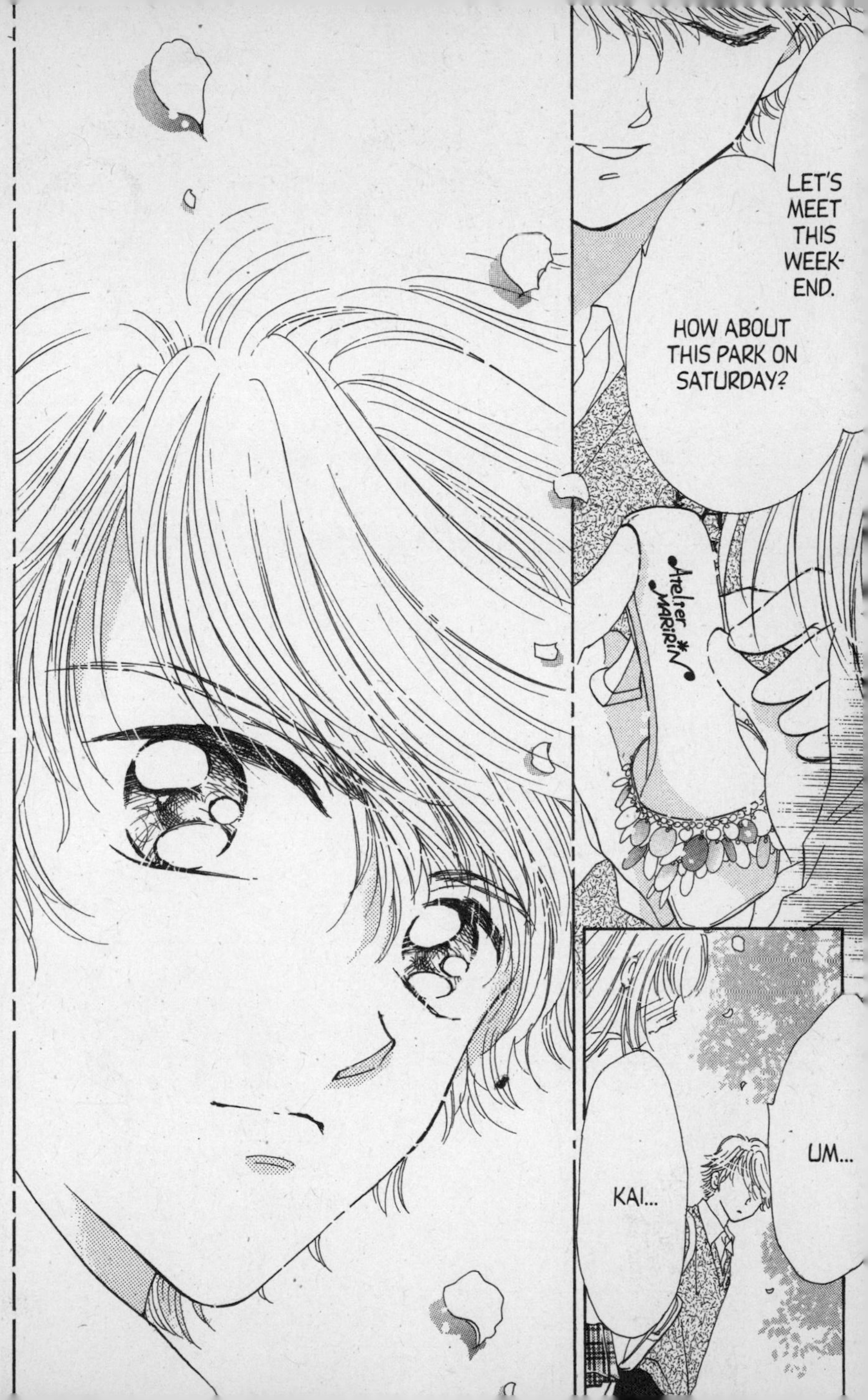
LET'S MEET THIS WEEK-END.
HOW ABOUT THIS PARK ON SATURDAY?
Atelier * MARIRIN
UM...
KAI...

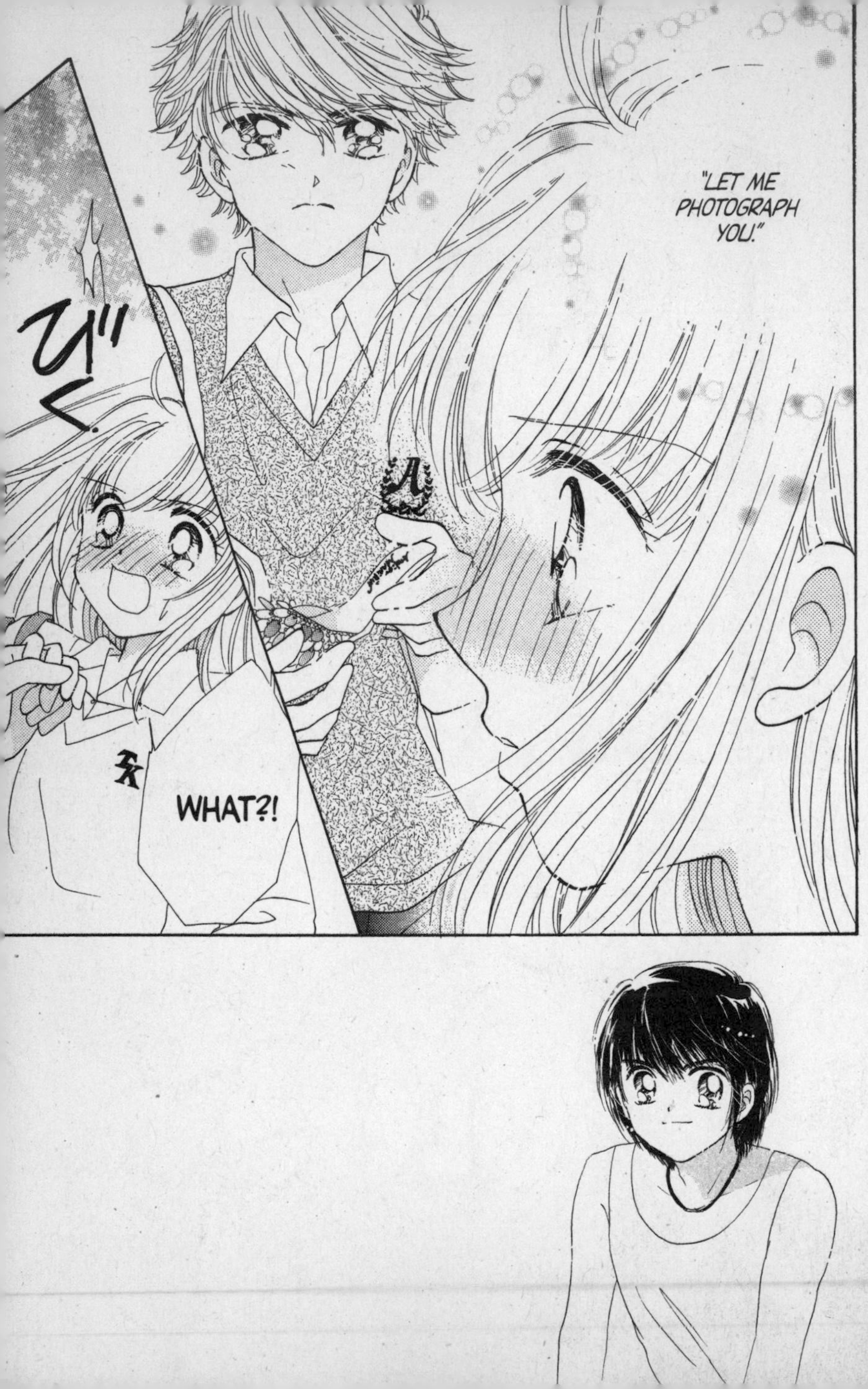
"LET ME PHOTOGRAPH YOU."
びく
WHAT?!

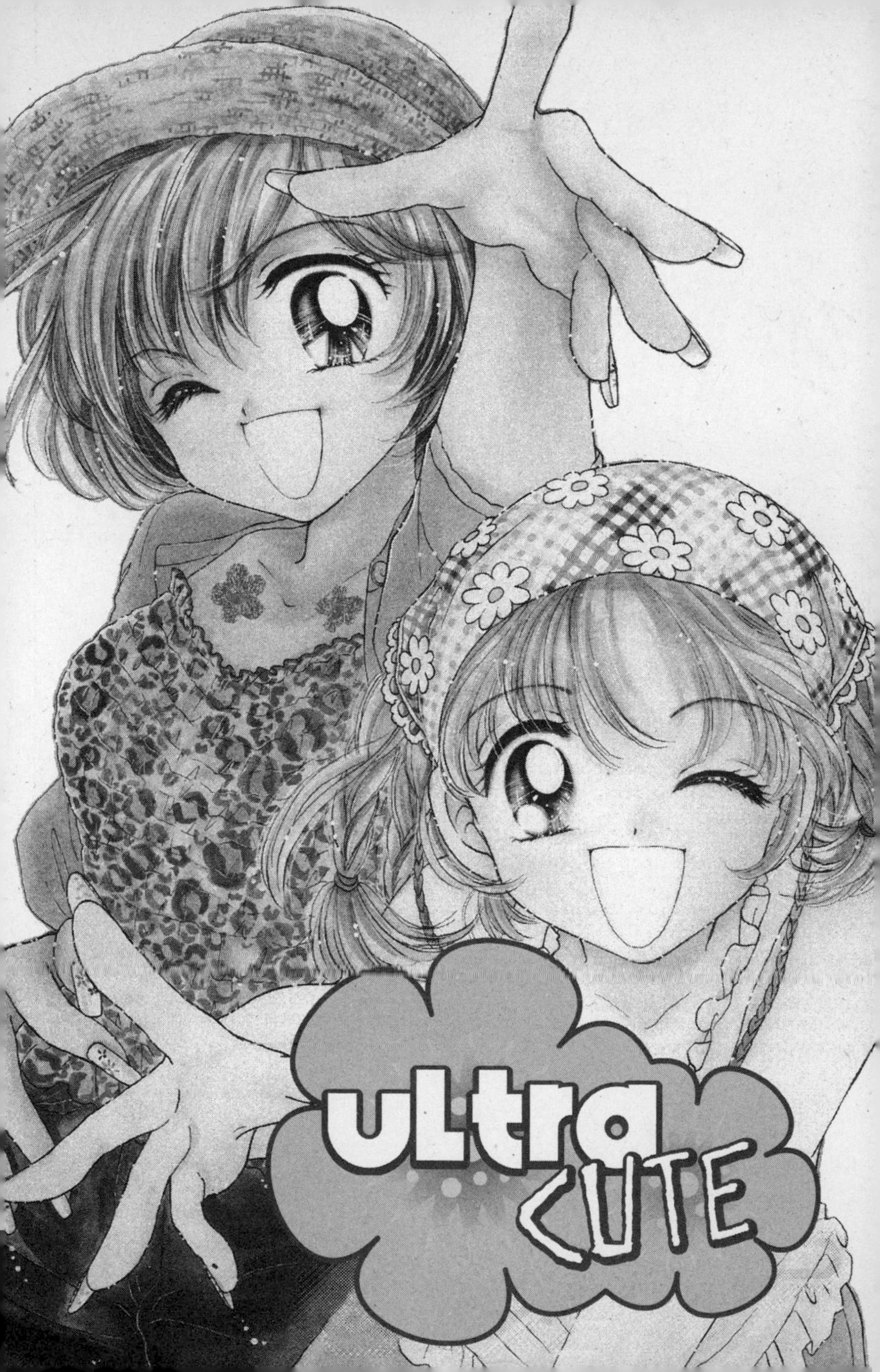
ultra
CUTE

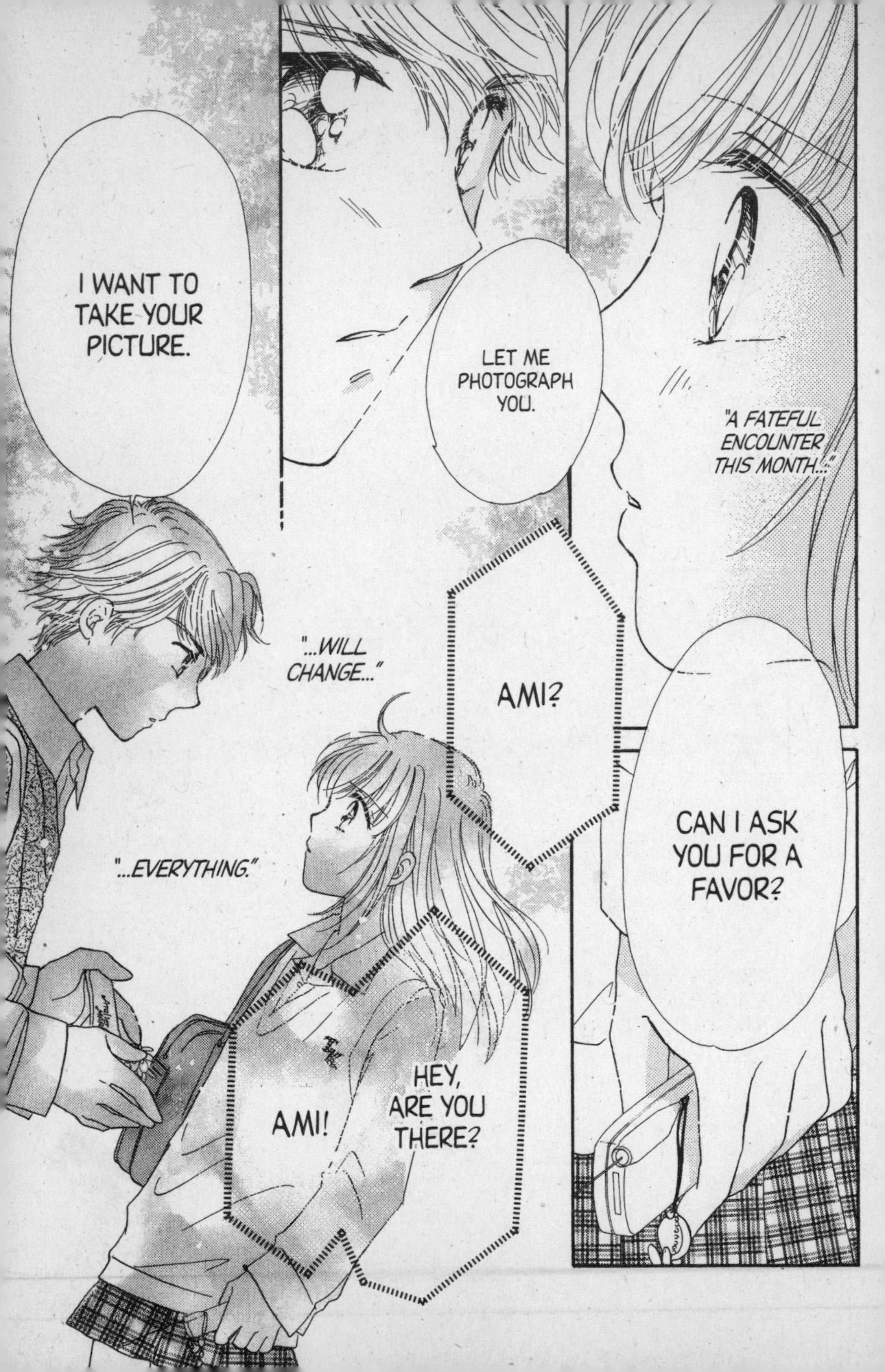
"A FATEFUL ENCOUNTER THIS MONTH..."
LET ME PHOTOGRAPH YOU.
CAN I ASK YOU FOR A FAVOR?
AMI?
I WANT TO TAKE YOUR PICTURE.
"...WILL CHANGE..."
"...EVERYTHING."
HEY, ARE YOU THERE?
AMI!

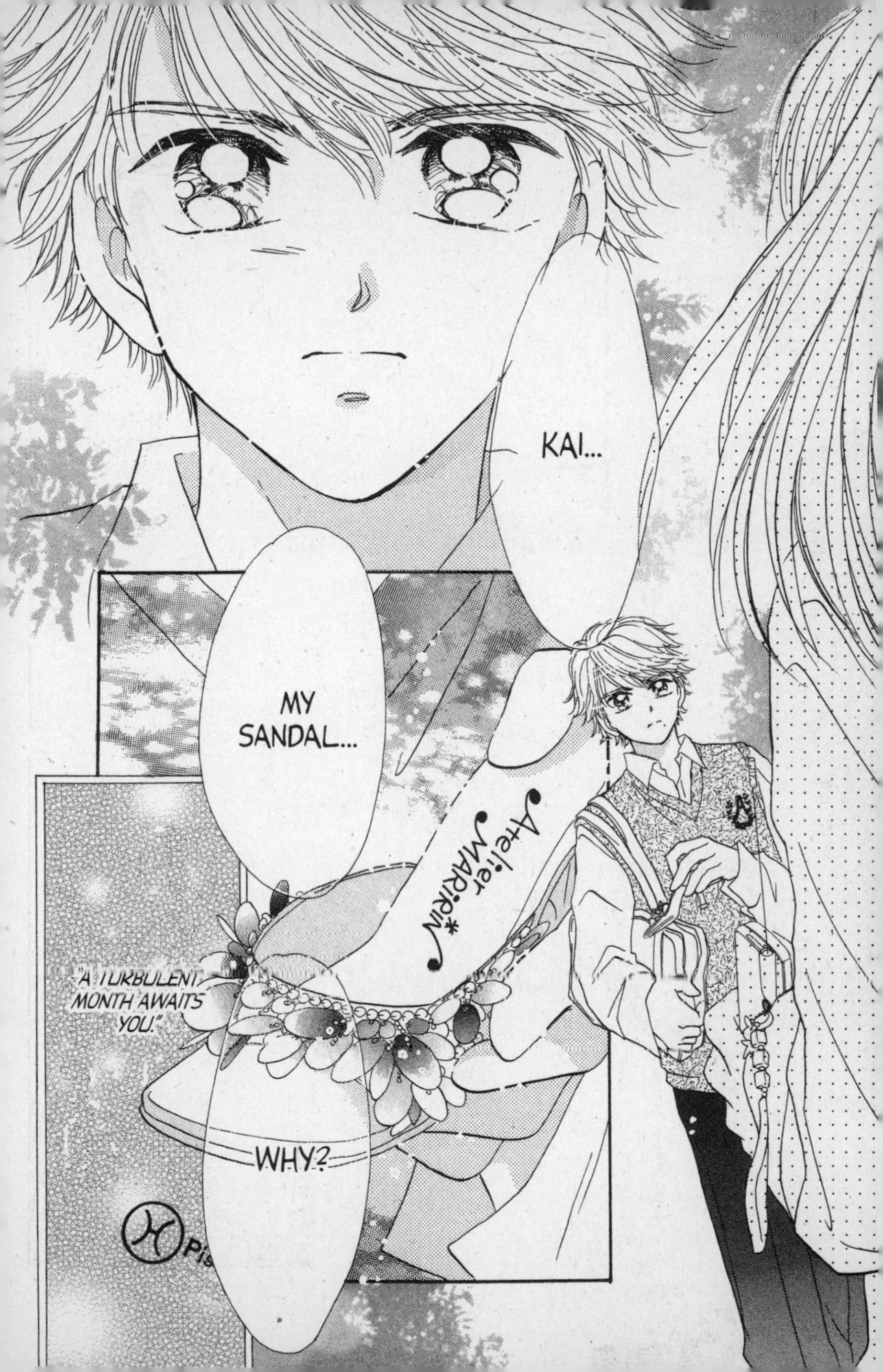
KAI...
MY SANDAL...
Atelier MARIRIN*
WHY?
"A TURBULENT MONTH AWAITS YOU."

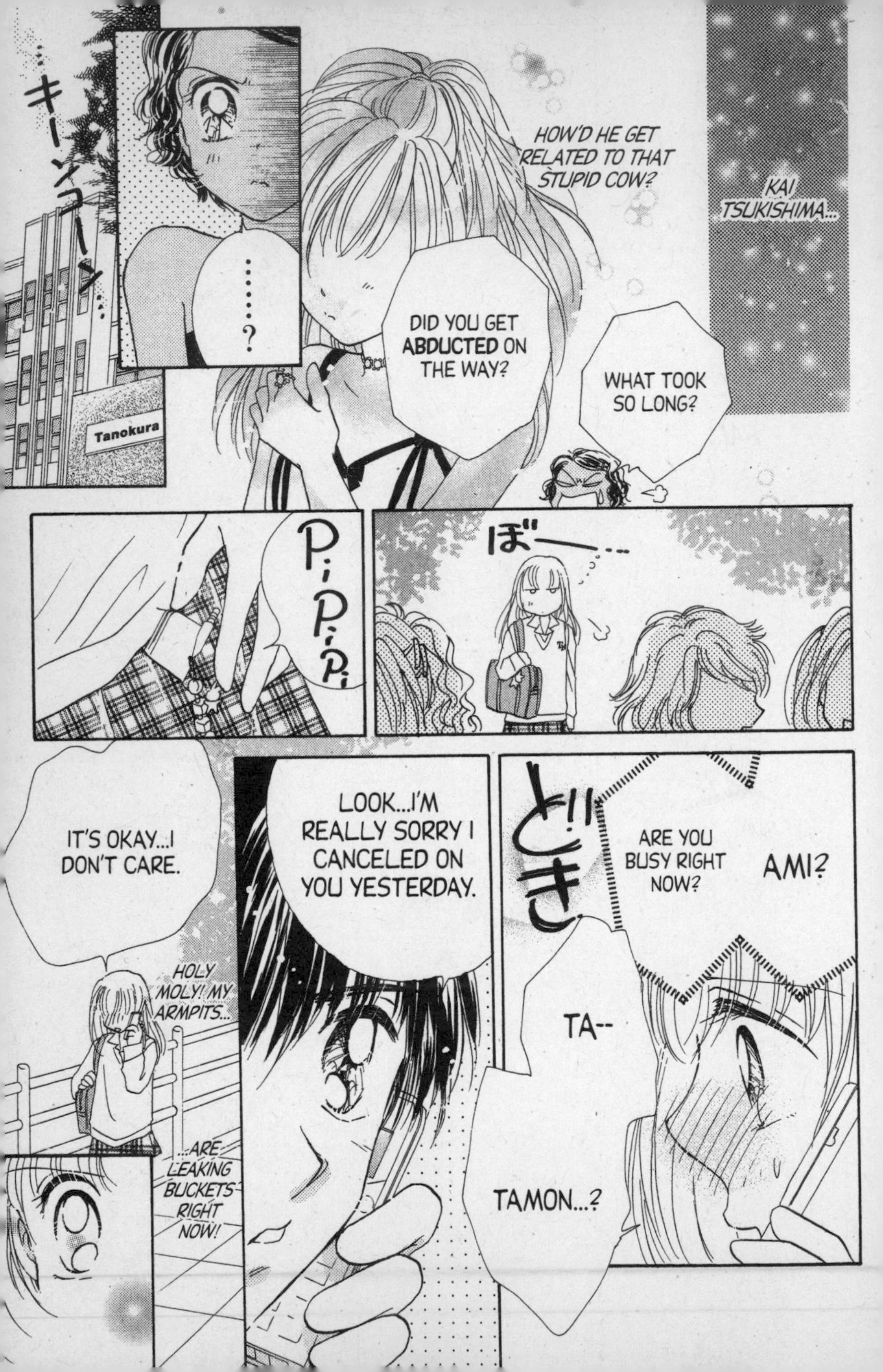
KAI TSUKISHIMA...
HOW'D HE GET RELATED TO THAT STUPID COW?
WHAT TOOK SO LONG?
DID YOU GET ABDUCTED ON THE WAY?
……?
キーンコーン
Tanokura
ぼー
Pi Pi Pi
AMI?
ARE YOU BUSY RIGHT NOW?
どき!!
TA--
TAMON...?
LOOK...I'M REALLY SORRY I CANCELED ON YOU YESTERDAY.
IT'S OKAY...I DON'T CARE.
HOLY MOLY! MY ARMPITS...
...ARE LEAKING BUCKETS RIGHT NOW!

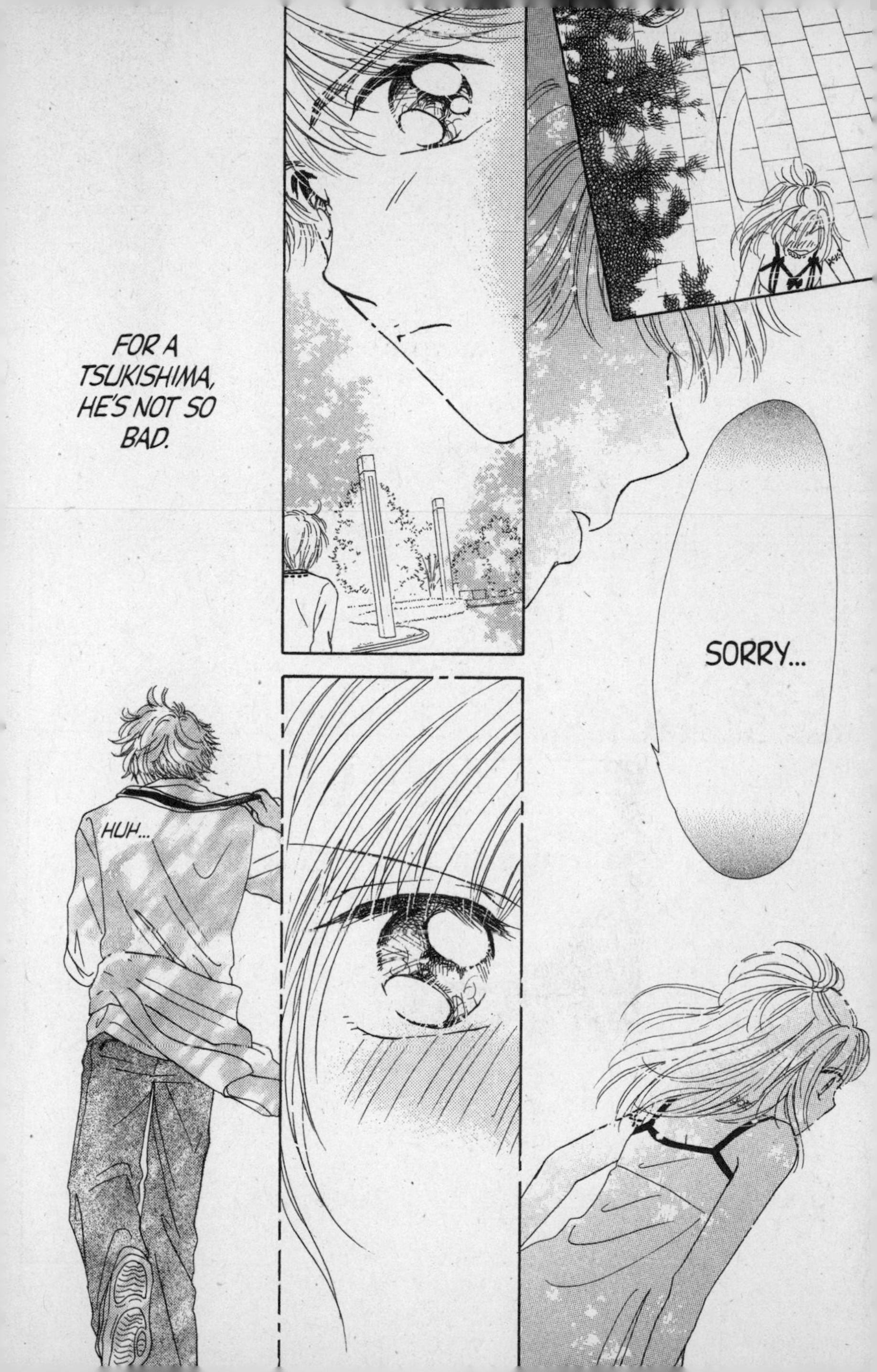
SORRY...
FOR A TSUKISHIMA, HE'S NOT SO BAD.
HUH...

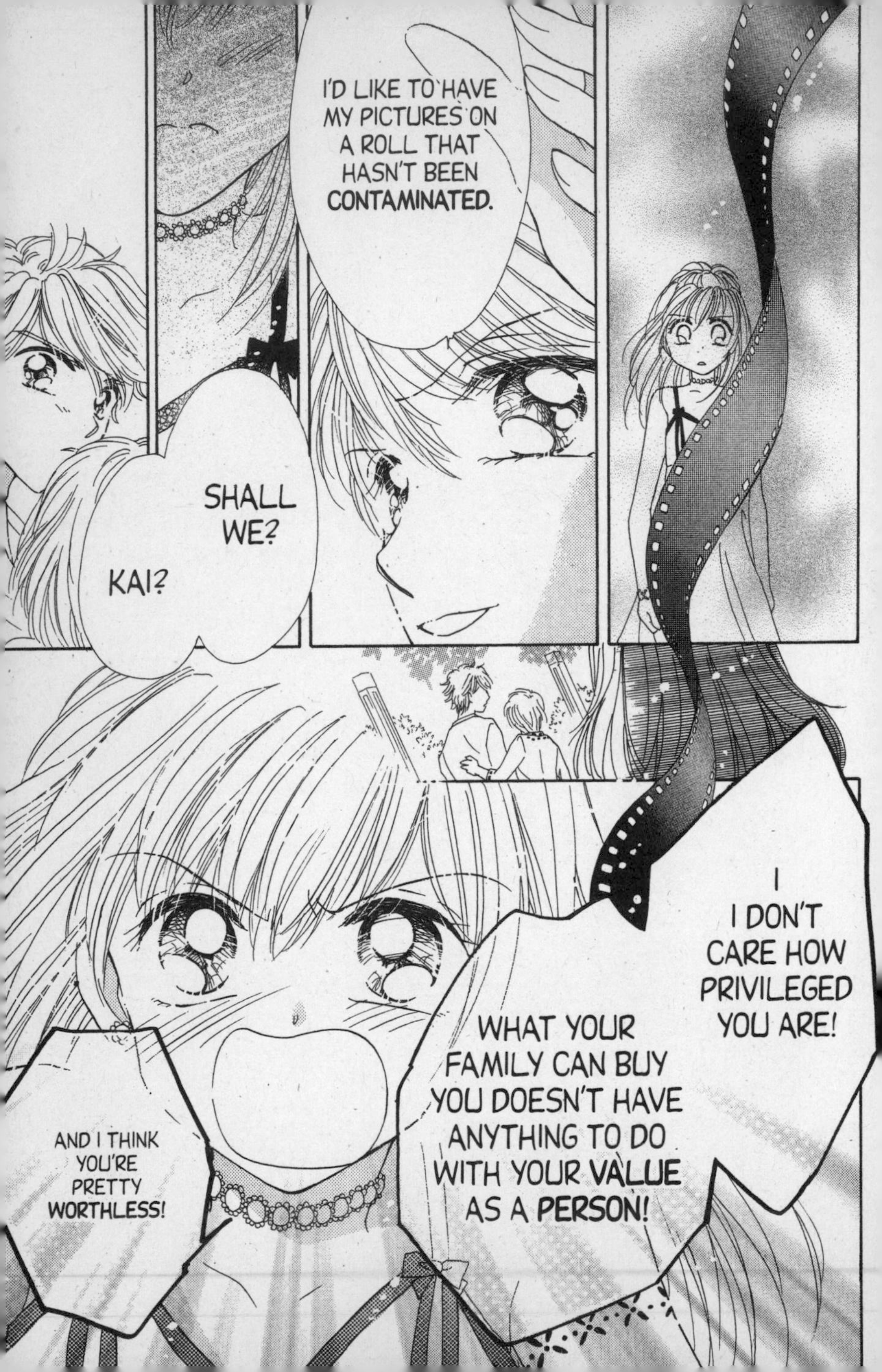

I'D LIKE TO HAVE MY PICTURES ON A ROLL THAT HASN'T BEEN **CONTAMINATED.**
SHALL WE?
KAI?
I
I DON'T CARE HOW PRIVILEGED YOU ARE!
WHAT YOUR FAMILY CAN BUY YOU DOESN'T HAVE ANYTHING TO DO WITH YOUR **VALUE** AS A **PERSON!**
AND I THINK YOU'RE PRETTY **WORTHLESS!**

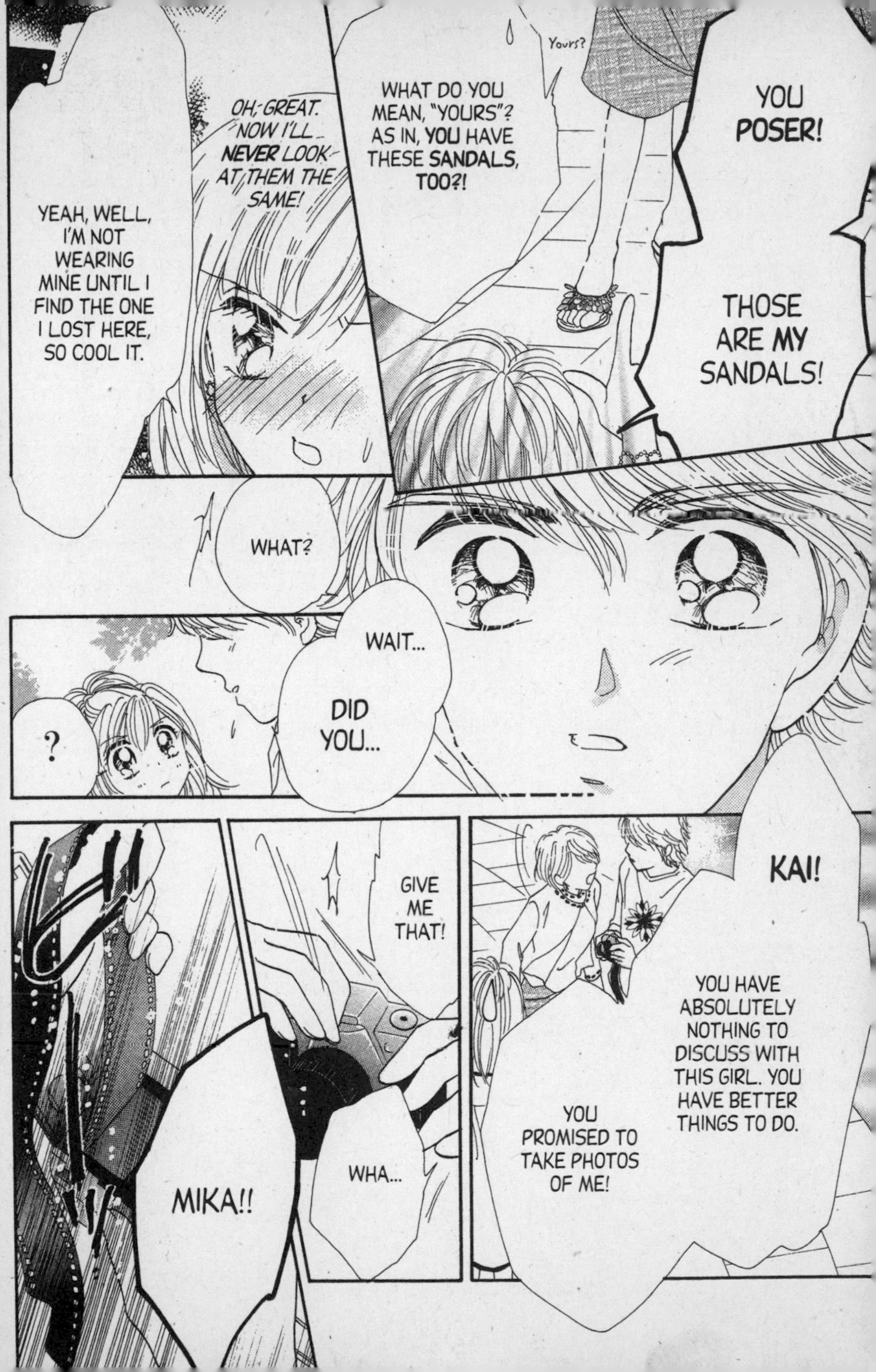
YOU POSER!
THOSE ARE MY SANDALS!
Yours?
WHAT DO YOU MEAN, "YOURS"? AS IN, YOU HAVE THESE SANDALS, TOO?!
OH, GREAT. NOW I'LL NEVER LOOK AT THEM THE SAME!
YEAH, WELL, I'M NOT WEARING MINE UNTIL I FIND THE ONE I LOST HERE, SO COOL IT.
WHAT?
WAIT...
DID YOU...
?
KAI!
YOU HAVE ABSOLUTELY NOTHING TO DISCUSS WITH THIS GIRL. YOU HAVE BETTER THINGS TO DO.
YOU PROMISED TO TAKE PHOTOS OF ME!
GIVE ME THAT!
WHA...
MIKA!!

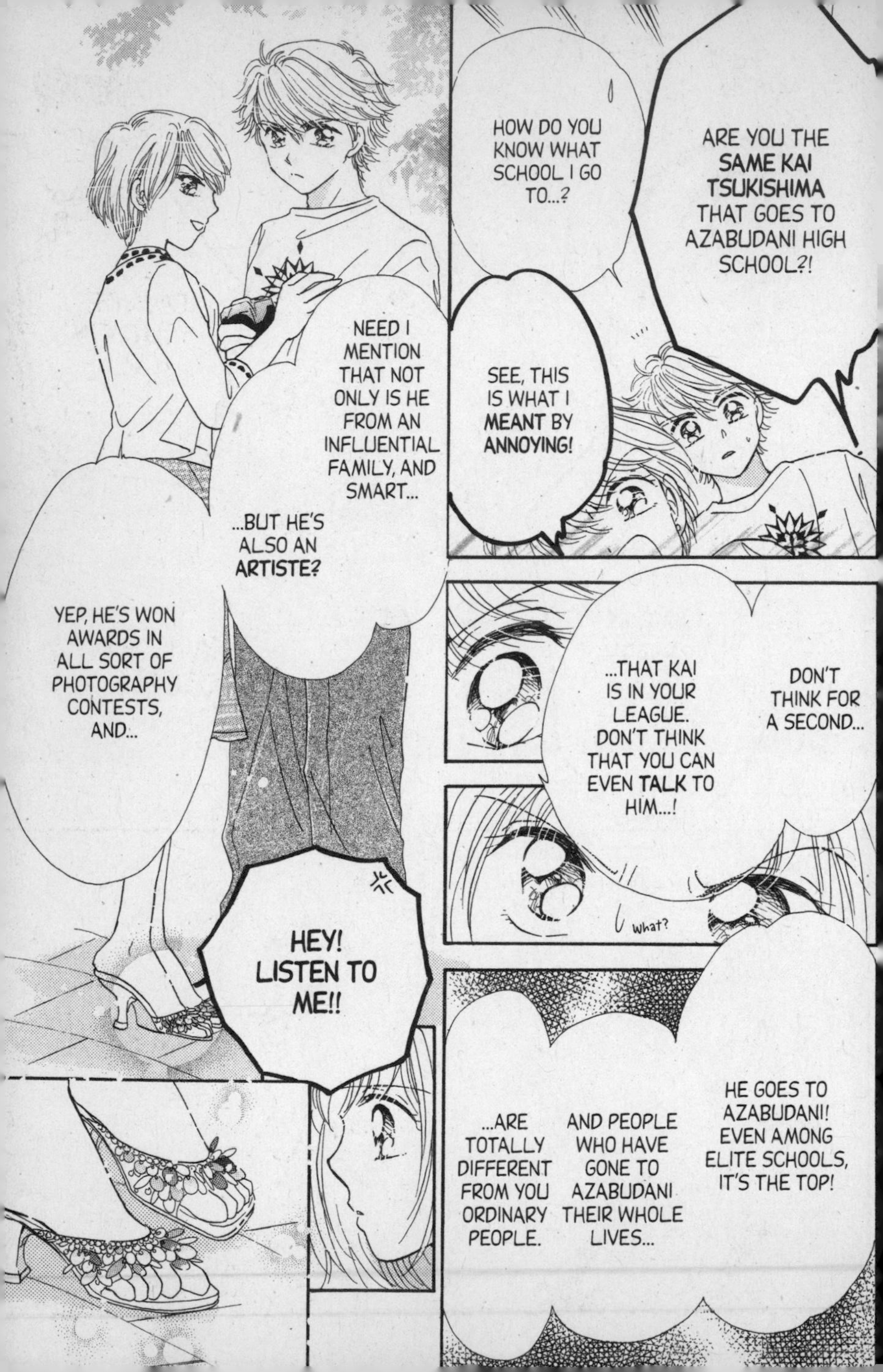
ARE YOU THE SAME KAI TSUKISHIMA THAT GOES TO AZABUDANI HIGH SCHOOL?!
HOW DO YOU KNOW WHAT SCHOOL I GO TO...?
SEE, THIS IS WHAT I MEANT BY ANNOYING!
NEED I MENTION THAT NOT ONLY IS HE FROM AN INFLUENTIAL FAMILY, AND SMART...
...BUT HE'S ALSO AN ARTISTE?
YEP, HE'S WON AWARDS IN ALL SORT OF PHOTOGRAPHY CONTESTS, AND...
HEY! LISTEN TO ME!!
DON'T THINK FOR A SECOND...
...THAT KAI IS IN YOUR LEAGUE. DON'T THINK THAT YOU CAN EVEN TALK TO HIM...!
what?
HE GOES TO AZABUDANI! EVEN AMONG ELITE SCHOOLS, IT'S THE TOP!
AND PEOPLE WHO HAVE GONE TO AZABUDANI THEIR WHOLE LIVES...
...ARE TOTALLY DIFFERENT FROM YOU ORDINARY PEOPLE.

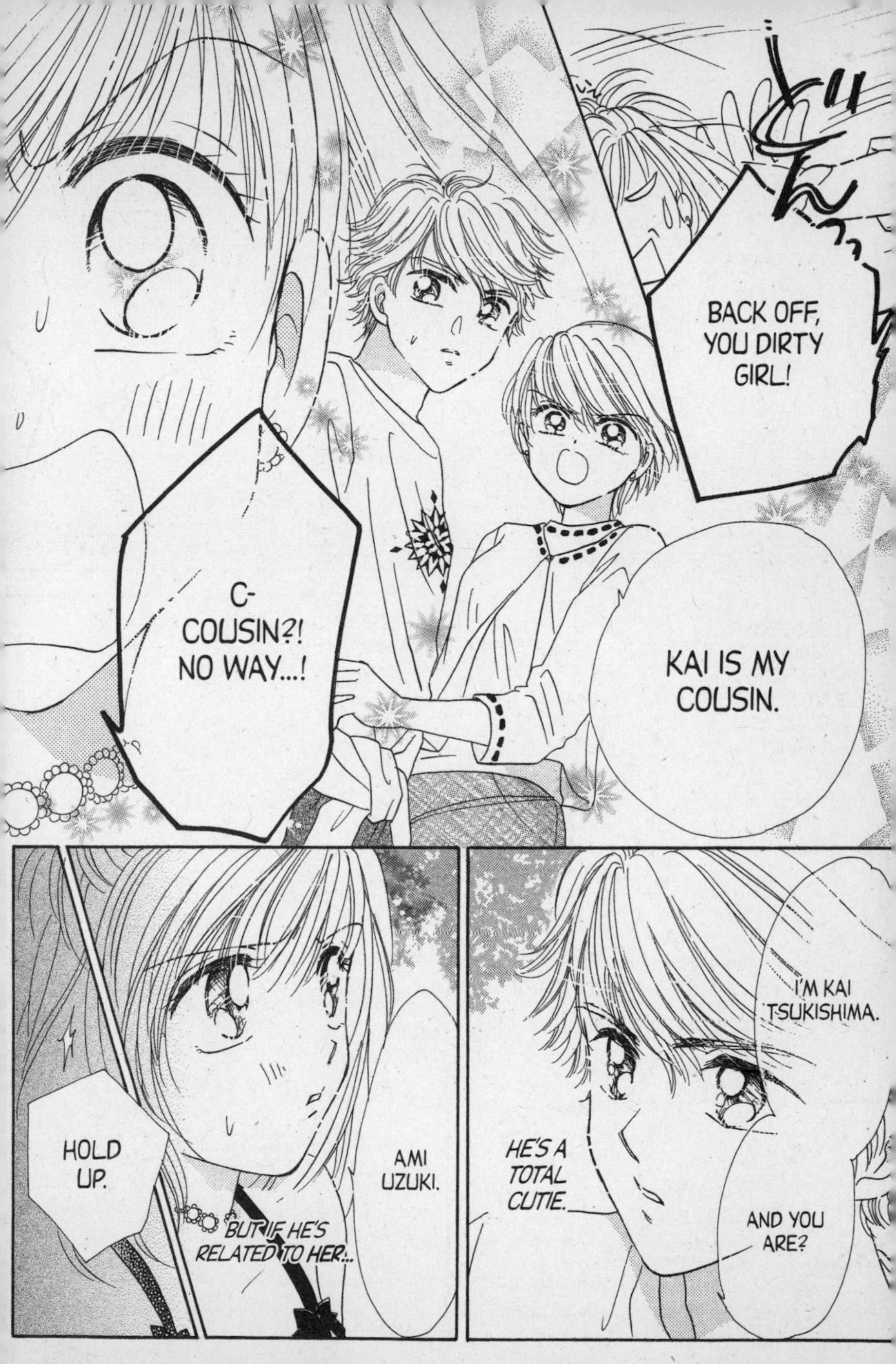
BACK OFF, YOU DIRTY GIRL!
KAI IS MY COUSIN.
C-COUSIN?! NO WAY...!
I'M KAI TSUKISHIMA.
AND YOU ARE?
HE'S A TOTAL CUTIE.
AMI UZUKI.
BUT IF HE'S RELATED TO HER...
HOLD UP.

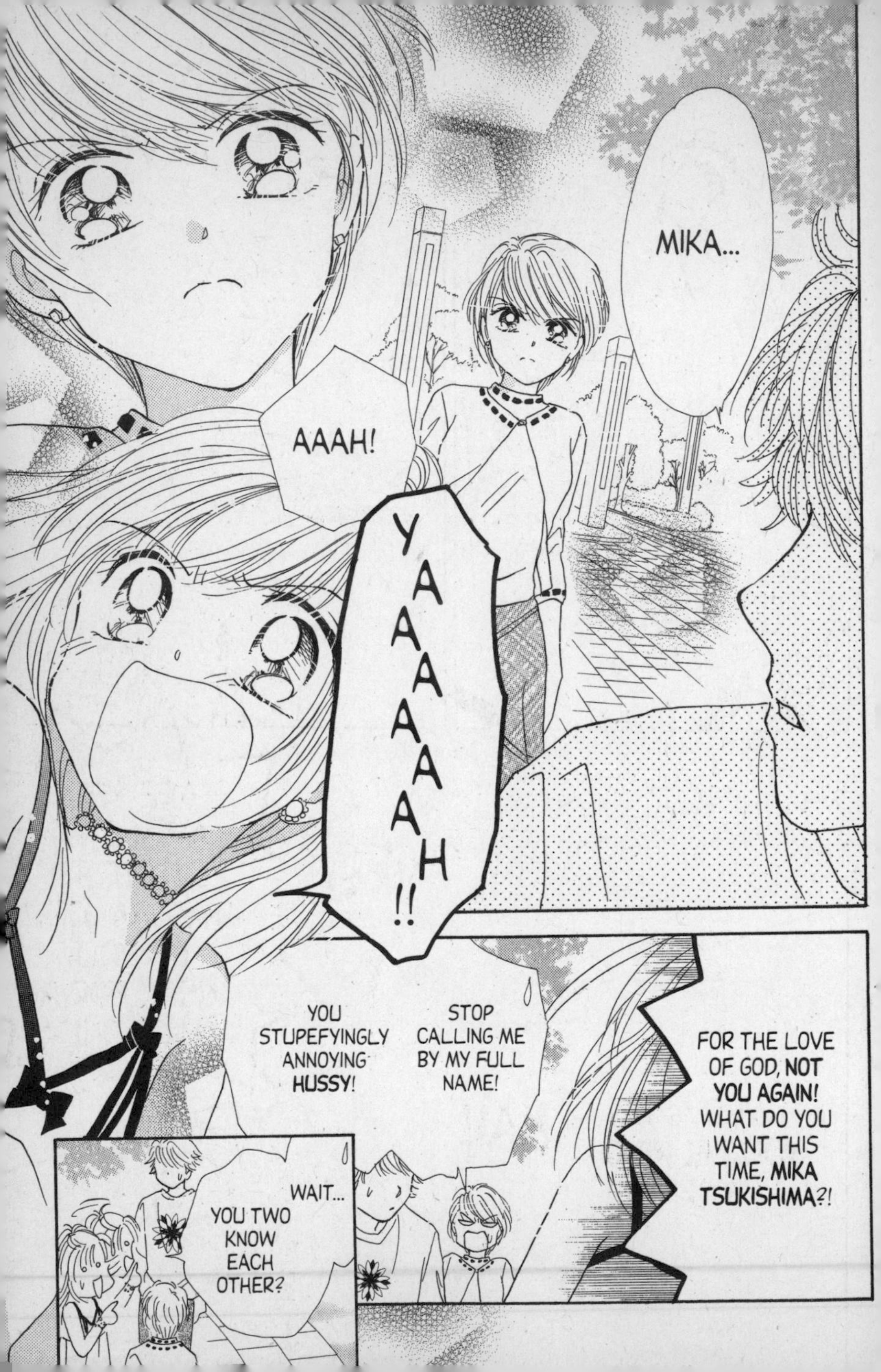
MIKA...
AAAH!
YAAAAAAH!!
FOR THE LOVE OF GOD, NOT YOU AGAIN! WHAT DO YOU WANT THIS TIME, MIKA TSUKISHIMA?!
STOP CALLING ME BY MY FULL NAME!
YOU STUPEFYINGLY ANNOYING HUSSY!
WAIT... YOU TWO KNOW EACH OTHER?

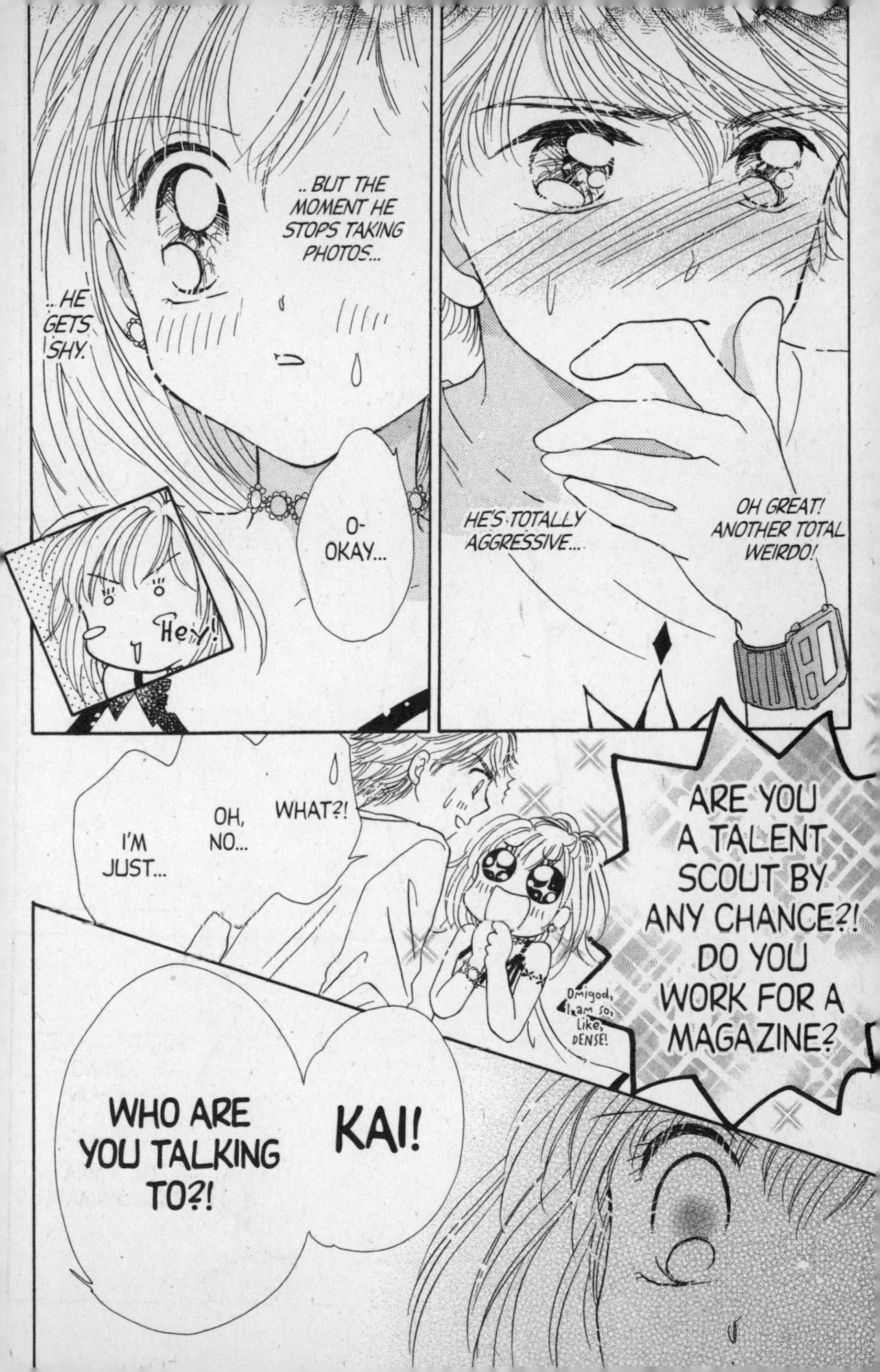
OH GREAT! ANOTHER TOTAL WEIRDO!
HE'S TOTALLY AGGRESSIVE...
..BUT THE MOMENT HE STOPS TAKING PHOTOS...
..HE GETS SHY.
O-OKAY...
Hey!
ARE YOU A TALENT SCOUT BY ANY CHANCE?! DO YOU WORK FOR A MAGAZINE?
Omigod, I am so, like, DENSE!
WHAT?!
OH, NO...
I'M JUST...
KAI!
WHO ARE YOU TALKING TO?!

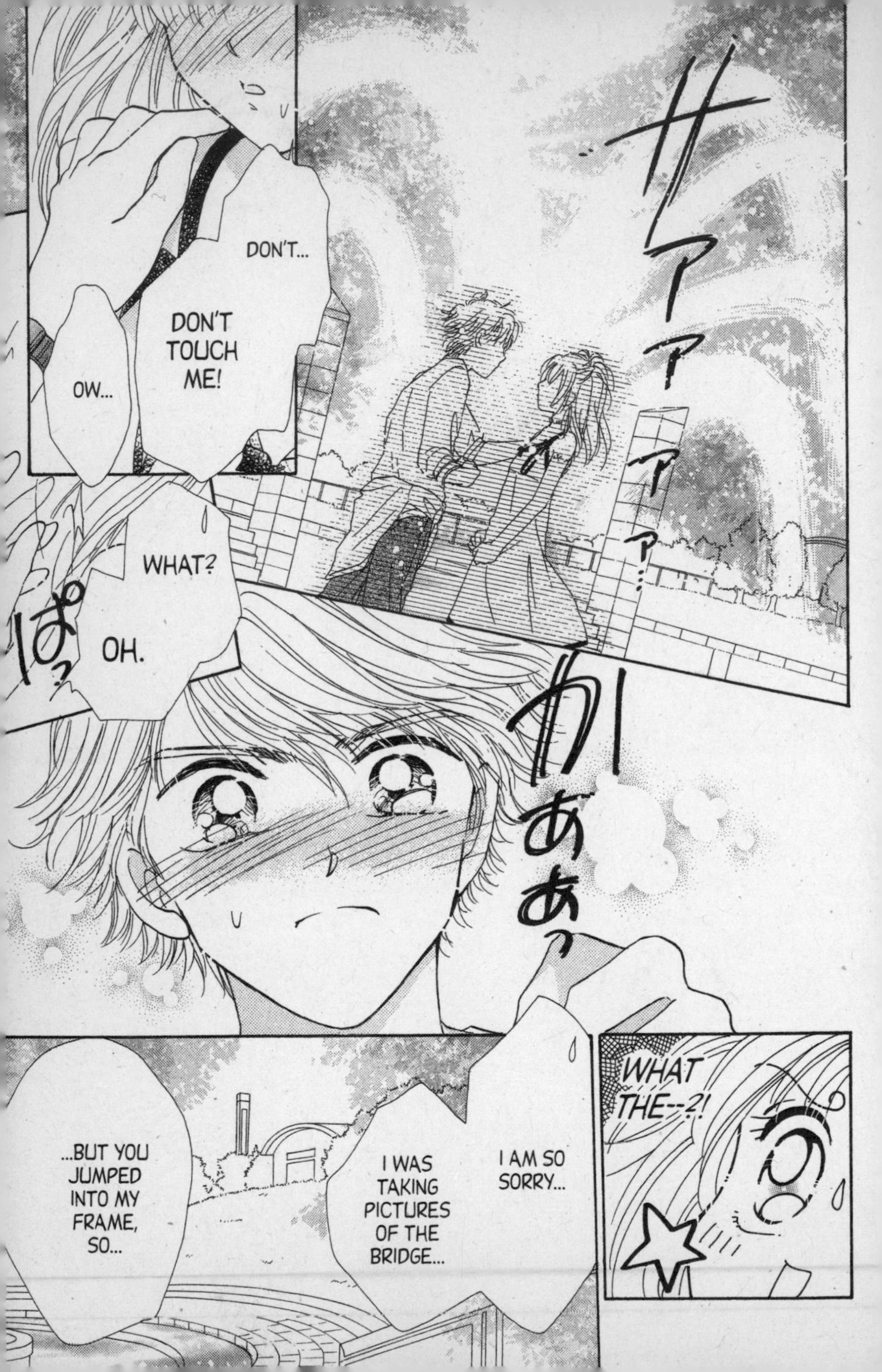
DON'T...
DON'T TOUCH ME!
OW...
WHAT?
OH.
WHAT THE--?!
I AM SO SORRY...
I WAS TAKING PICTURES OF THE BRIDGE...
...BUT YOU JUMPED INTO MY FRAME, SO...

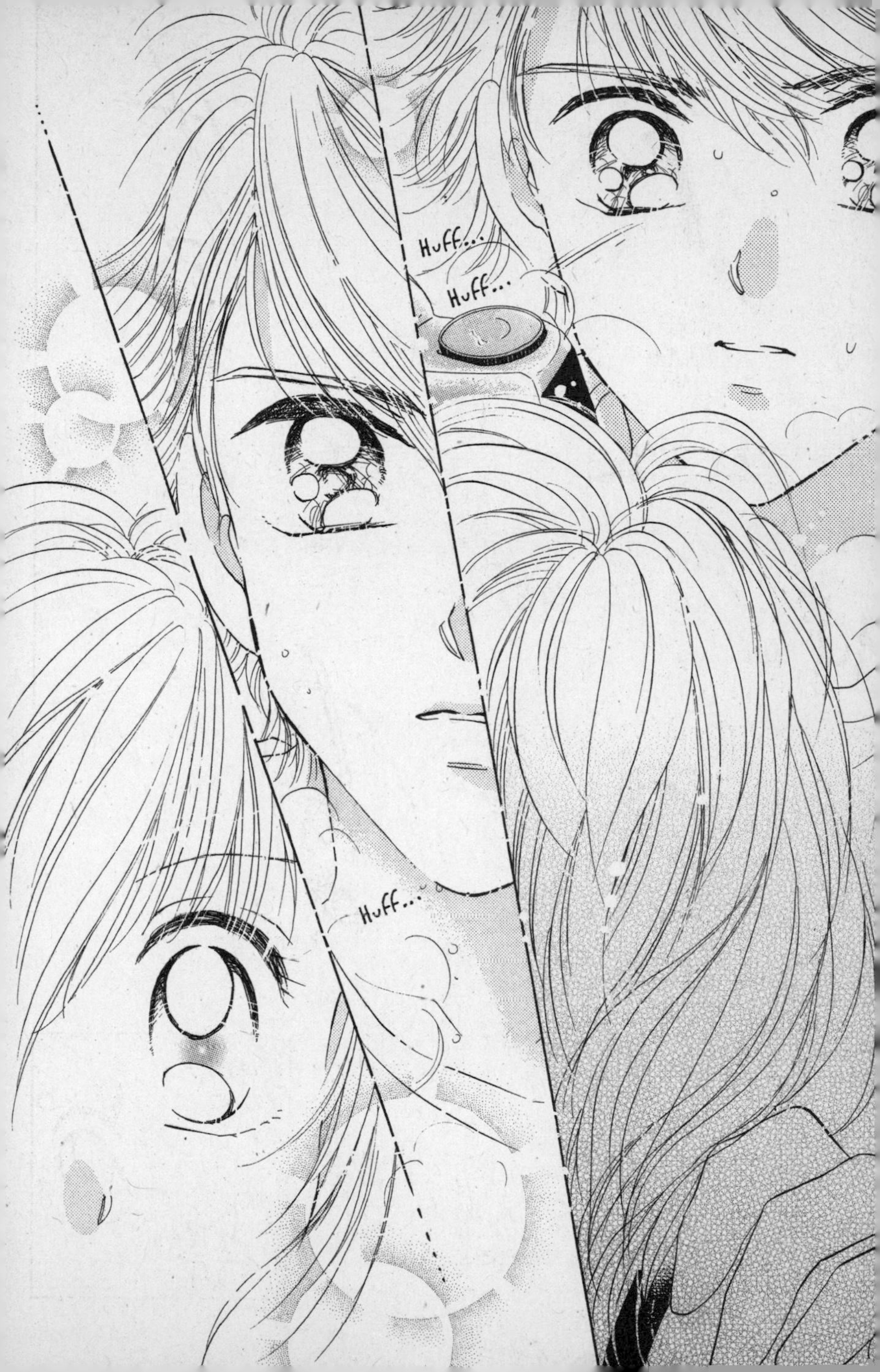
Huff...
Huff...
Huff...

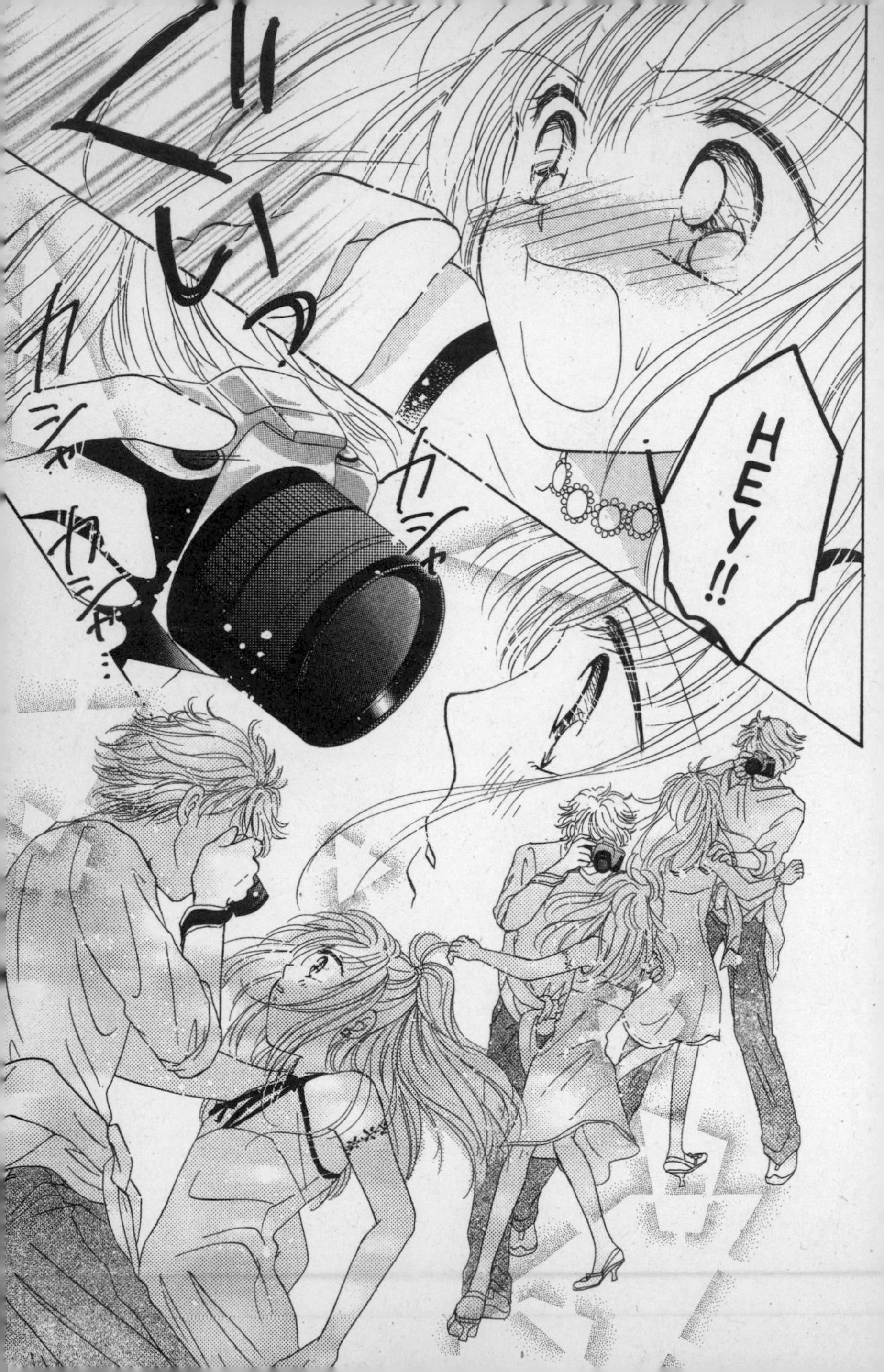
HEY!!
カシャ
カシャ
カシャ…

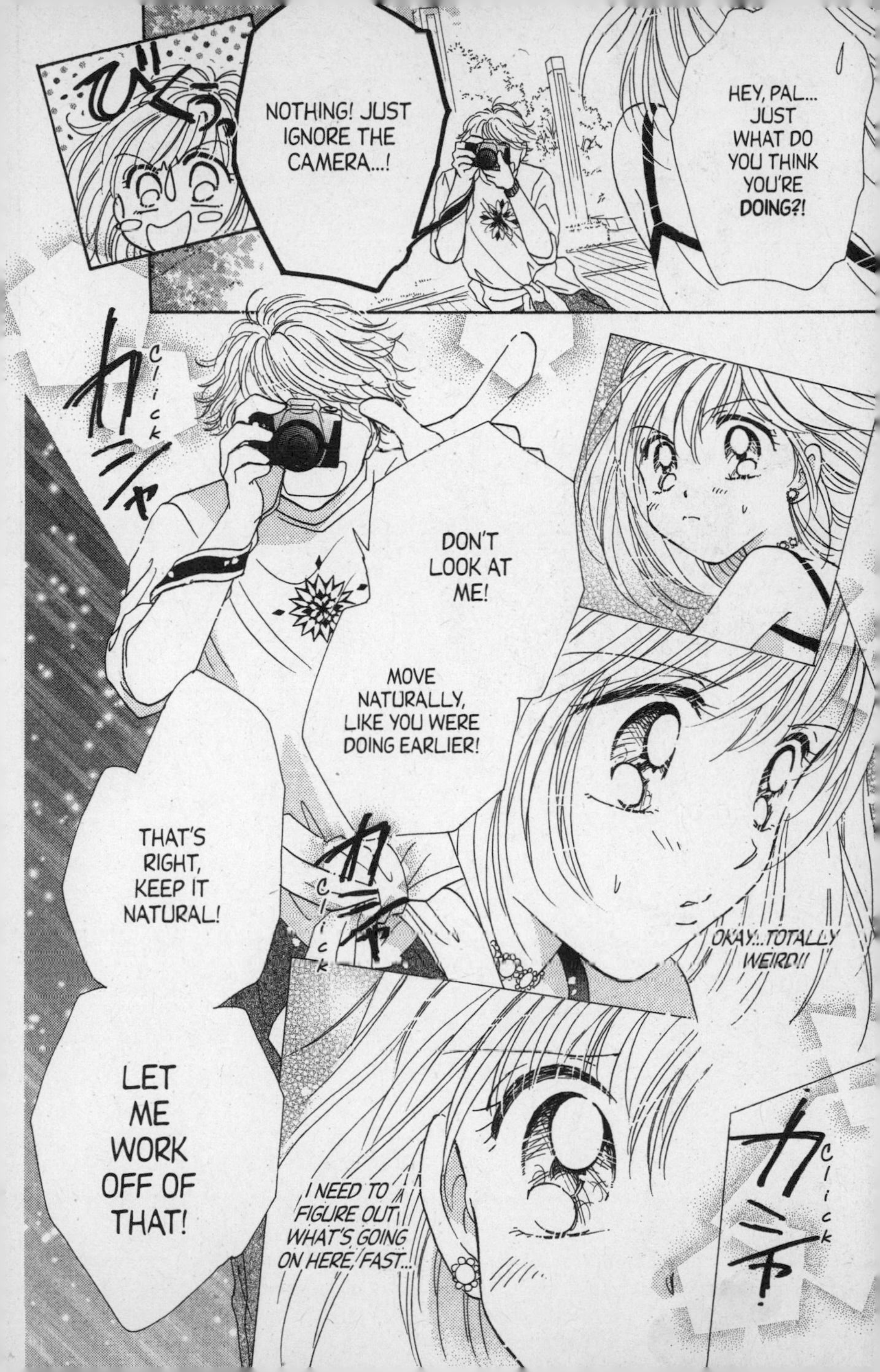

HEY, PAL... JUST WHAT DO YOU THINK YOU'RE DOING?!
NOTHING! JUST IGNORE THE CAMERA...!
びくっ
OKAY!...TOTALLY WEIRD!!
I NEED TO FIGURE OUT WHAT'S GOING ON HERE, FAST...
カシャ
click
カシャ
click
DON'T LOOK AT ME!
MOVE NATURALLY, LIKE YOU WERE DOING EARLIER!
カシャ
click
THAT'S RIGHT, KEEP IT NATURAL!
LET ME WORK OFF OF THAT!

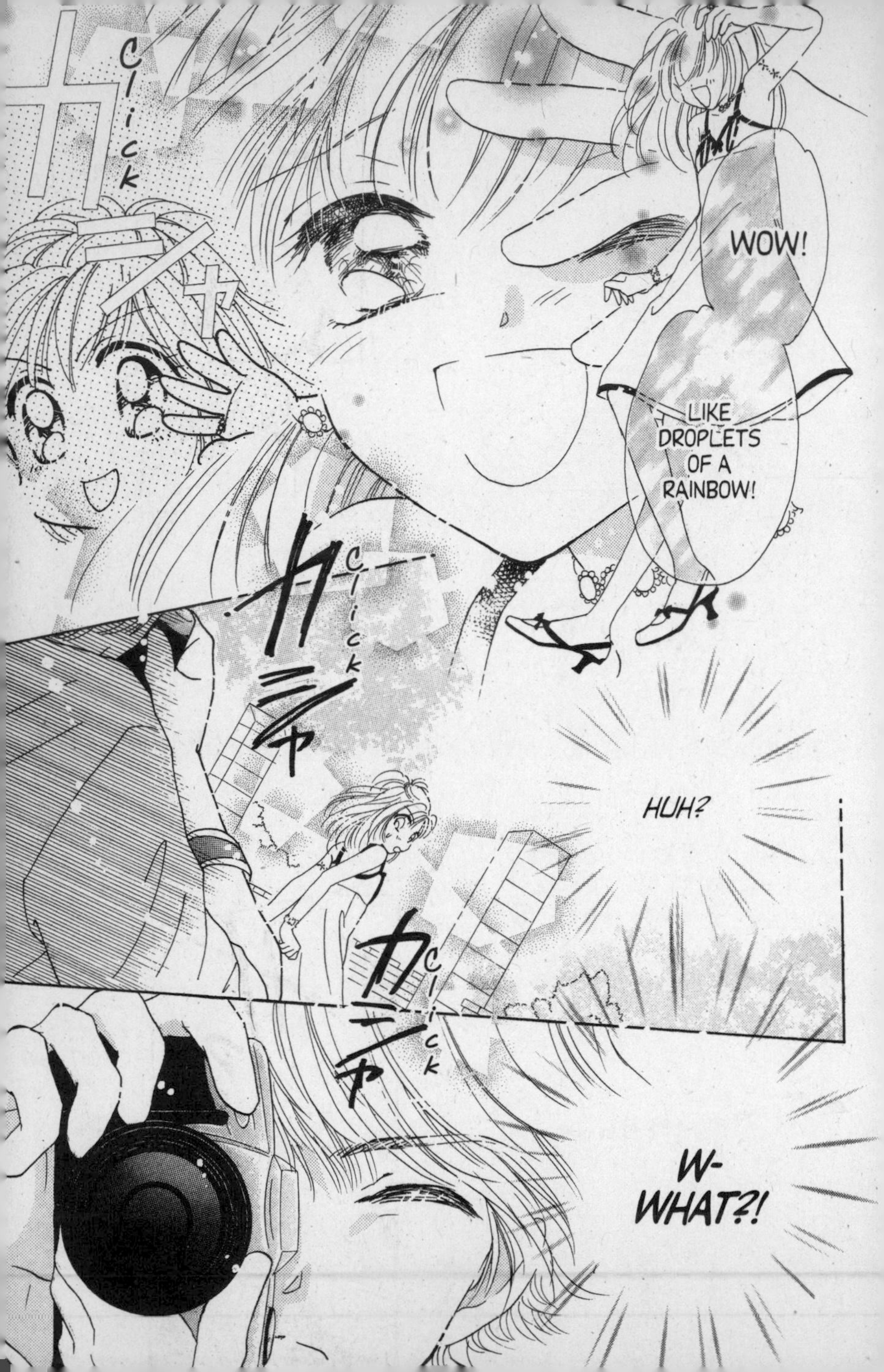
WOW!
LIKE DROPLETS OF A RAINBOW!
Click
Click
HUH?
Click
W-WHAT?!

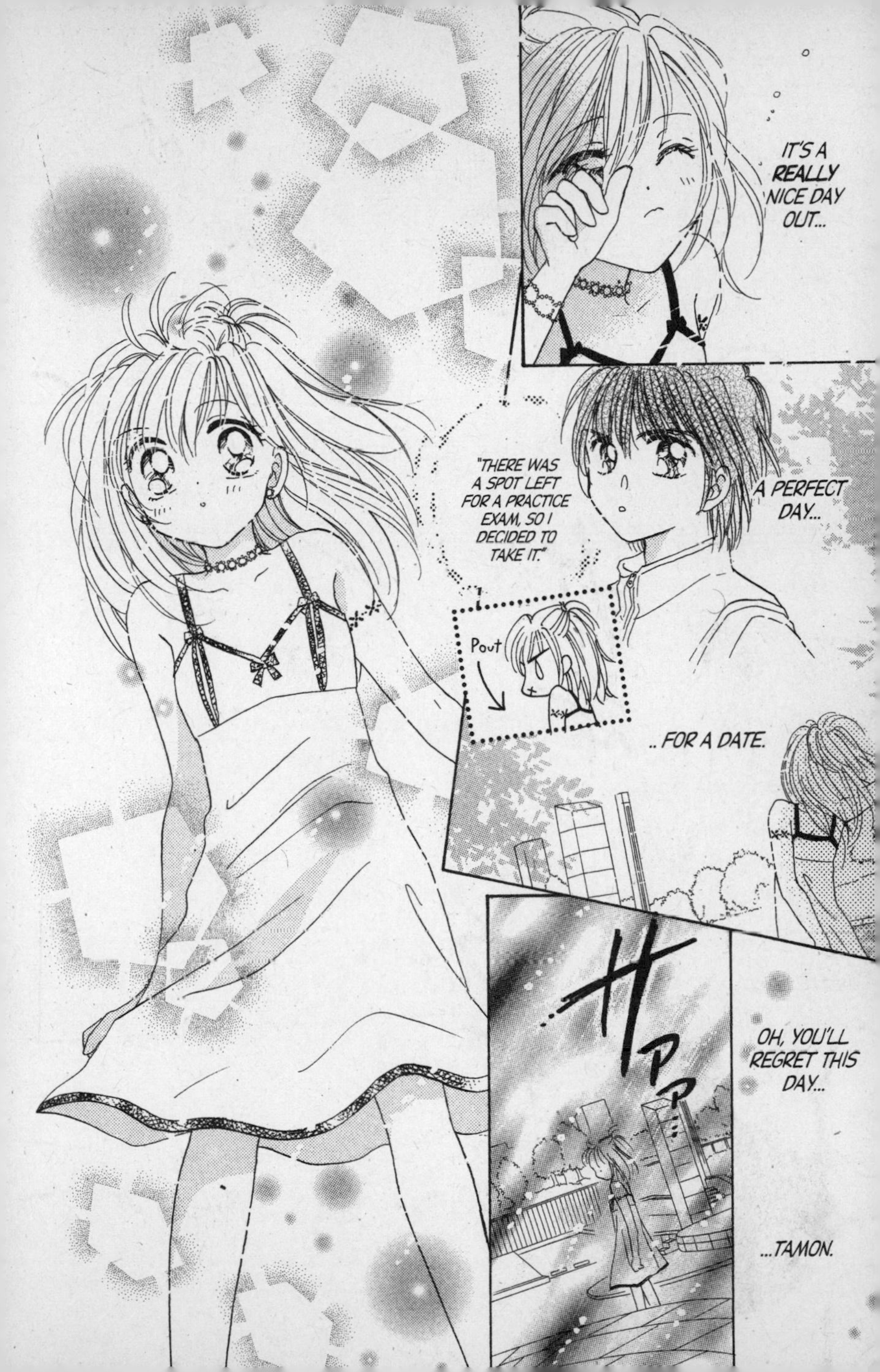
IT'S A REALLY NICE DAY OUT...
A PERFECT DAY...
"THERE WAS A SPOT LEFT FOR A PRACTICE EXAM, SO I DECIDED TO TAKE IT."
Pout
.. FOR A DATE.
HPP
OH, YOU'LL REGRET THIS DAY...
...TAMON.

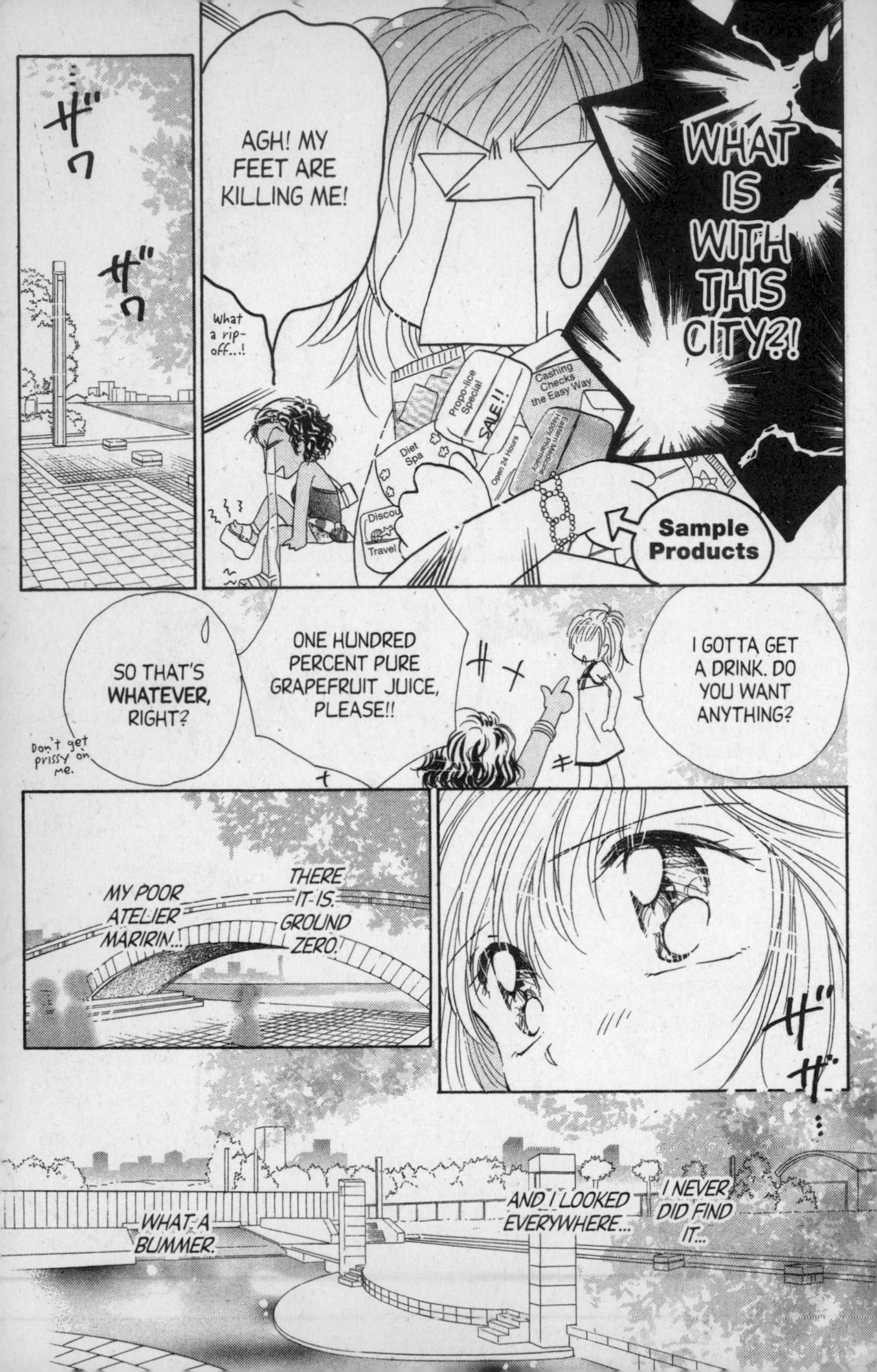
WHAT IS WITH THIS CITY?!
AGH! MY FEET ARE KILLING ME!
What a rip-off...!
Propo-lice Special
SALE!!
Cashing Checks the Easy Way
Eastern Medicine Happy Pharmacy
Open 24 Hours
Diet Spa
Travel
Sample Products
ザワ
ザワ
I GOTTA GET A DRINK. DO YOU WANT ANYTHING?
ONE HUNDRED PERCENT PURE GRAPEFRUIT JUICE, PLEASE!!
SO THAT'S WHATEVER, RIGHT?
Don't get prissy on me.
ザ
ザ
THERE IT IS. GROUND ZERO.
MY POOR ATELIER MARIRIN...
I NEVER DID FIND IT...
AND I LOOKED EVERYWHERE...
WHAT A BUMMER.

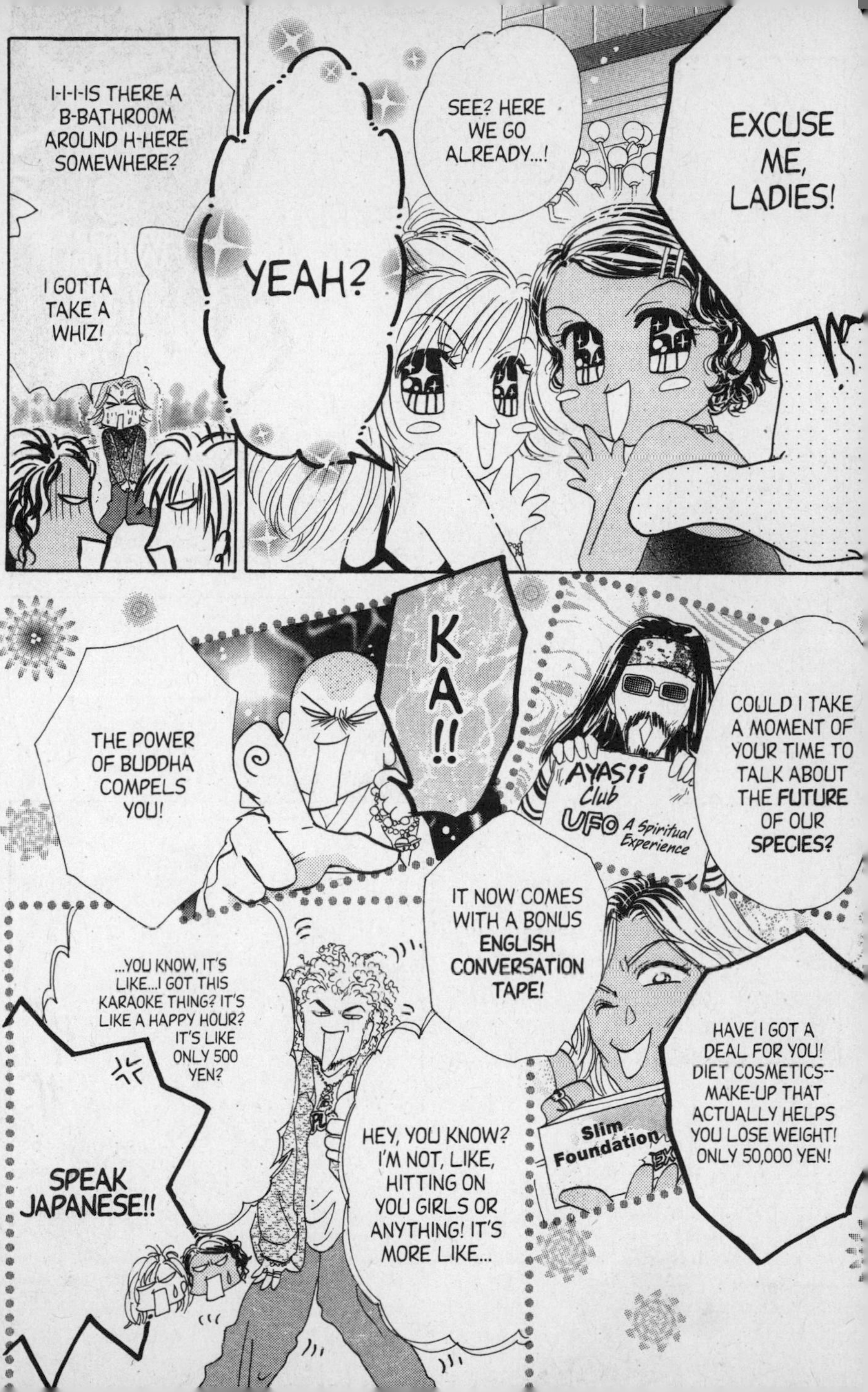
EXCUSE ME, LADIES!
SEE? HERE WE GO ALREADY...!
YEAH?
I-I-I-IS THERE A B-BATHROOM AROUND H-HERE SOMEWHERE?
I GOTTA TAKE A WHIZ!
COULD I TAKE A MOMENT OF YOUR TIME TO TALK ABOUT THE FUTURE OF OUR SPECIES?
AYASii Club UFO A Spiritual Experience
KA!!
THE POWER OF BUDDHA COMPELS YOU!
HAVE I GOT A DEAL FOR YOU! DIET COSMETICS--MAKE-UP THAT ACTUALLY HELPS YOU LOSE WEIGHT! ONLY 50,000 YEN!
Slim Foundation
IT NOW COMES WITH A BONUS ENGLISH CONVERSATION TAPE!
HEY, YOU KNOW? I'M NOT, LIKE, HITTING ON YOU GIRLS OR ANYTHING! IT'S MORE LIKE...
...YOU KNOW, IT'S LIKE...I GOT THIS KARAOKE THING? IT'S LIKE A HAPPY HOUR? IT'S LIKE ONLY 500 YEN?
SPEAK JAPANESE!!

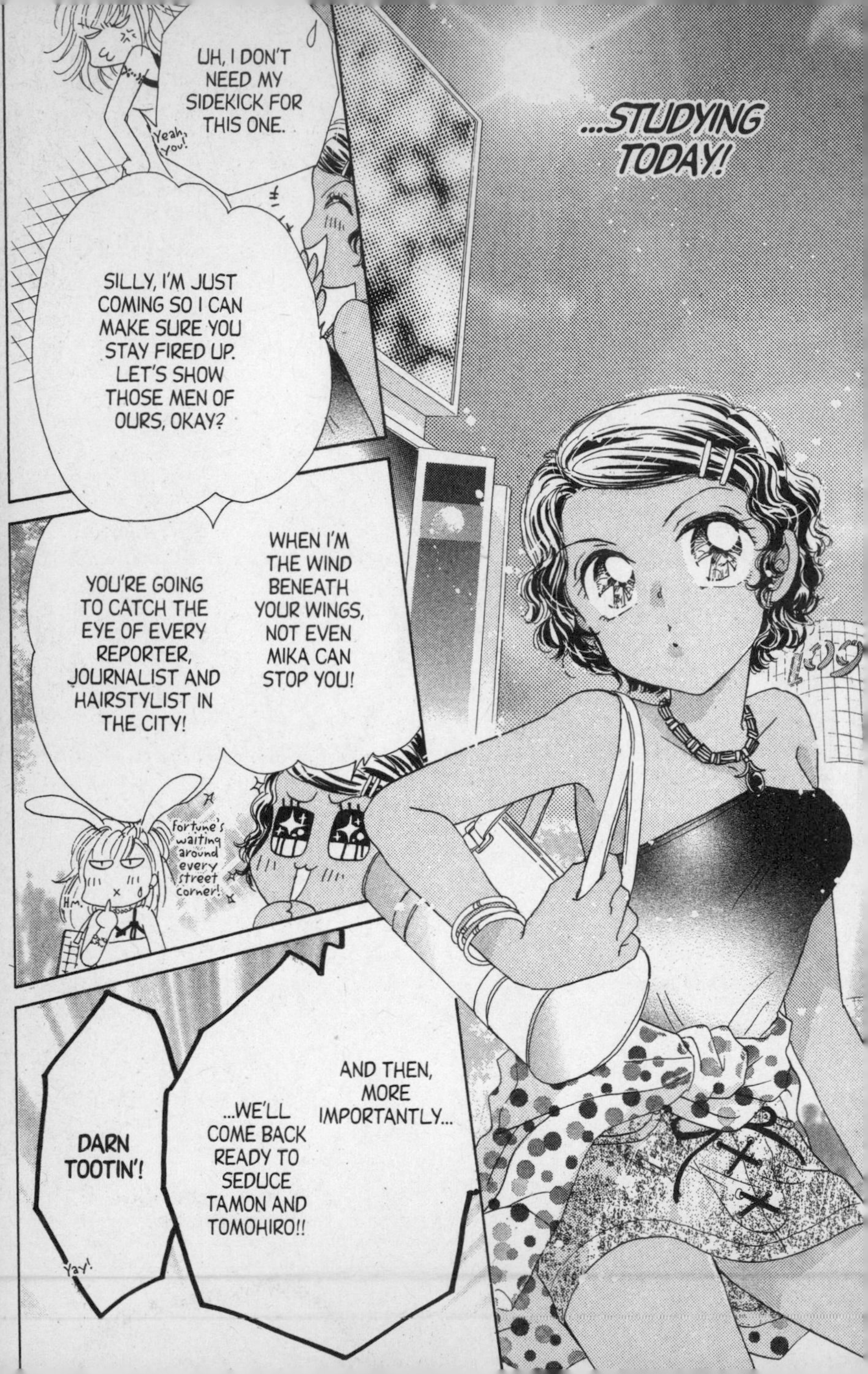
...STUDYING TODAY!
UH, I DON'T NEED MY SIDEKICK FOR THIS ONE.
Yeah, you!
SILLY, I'M JUST COMING SO I CAN MAKE SURE YOU STAY FIRED UP. LET'S SHOW THOSE MEN OF OURS, OKAY?
WHEN I'M THE WIND BENEATH YOUR WINGS, NOT EVEN MIKA CAN STOP YOU!
YOU'RE GOING TO CATCH THE EYE OF EVERY REPORTER, JOURNALIST AND HAIRSTYLIST IN THE CITY!
Fortune's waiting around every street corner!
Hm.
AND THEN, MORE IMPORTANTLY...
...WE'LL COME BACK READY TO SEDUCE TAMON AND TOMOHIRO!!
DARN TOOTIN'!
Yay!

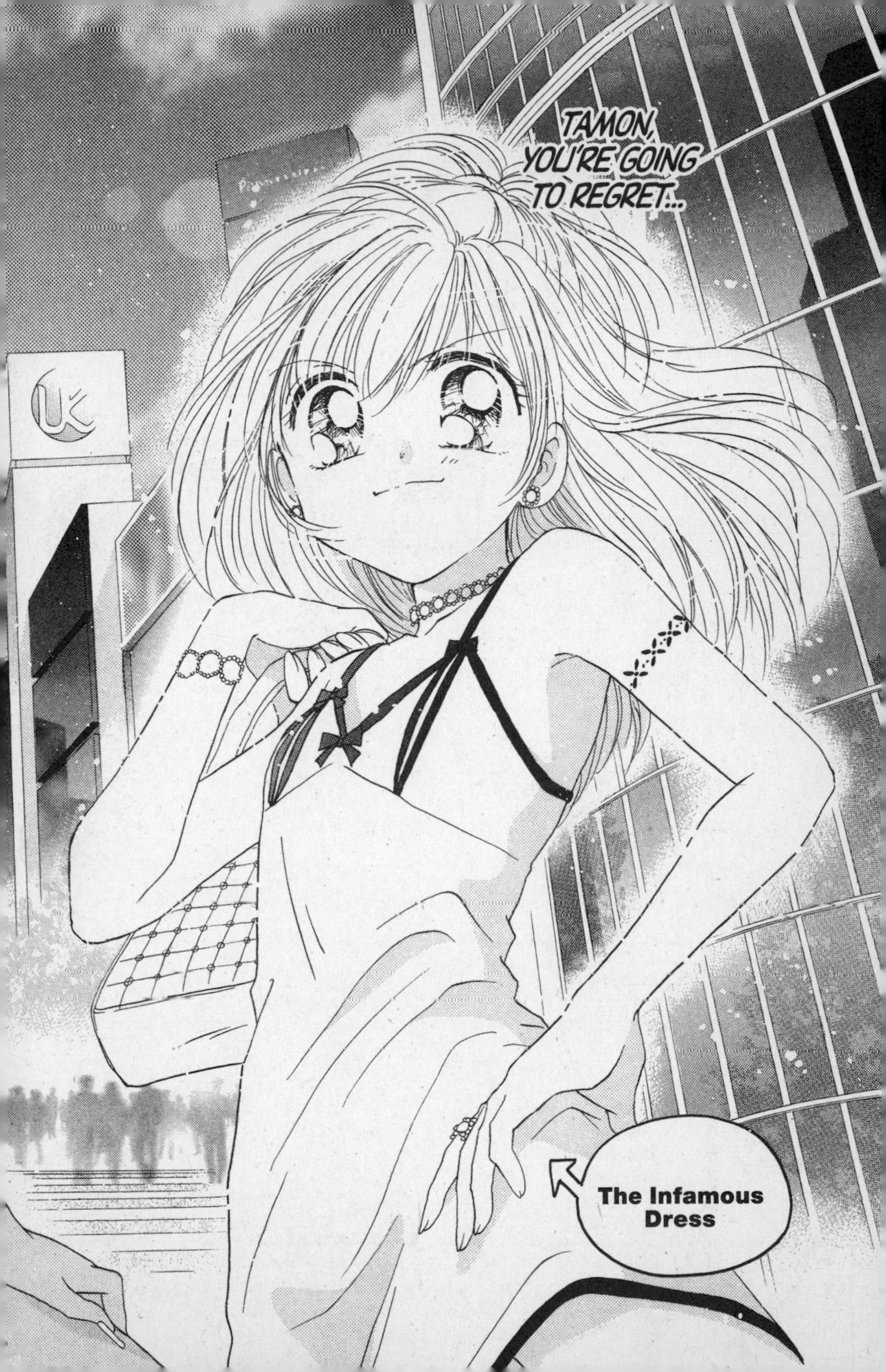
TAMON, YOU'RE GOING TO REGRET...
The Infamous Dress

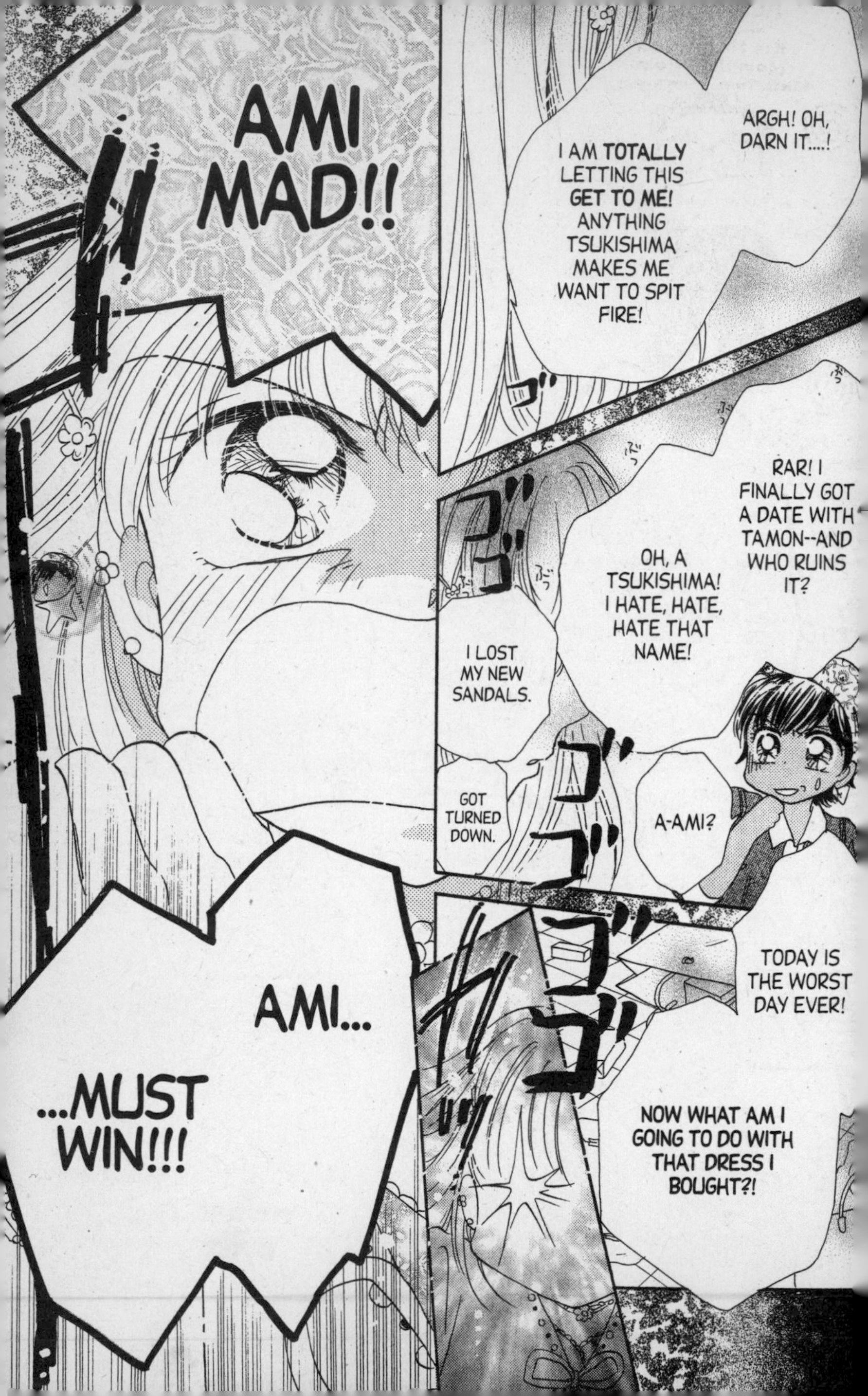
ARGH! OH, DARN IT....!
I AM TOTALLY LETTING THIS GET TO ME! ANYTHING TSUKISHIMA MAKES ME WANT TO SPIT FIRE!
RAR! I FINALLY GOT A DATE WITH TAMON--AND WHO RUINS IT?
OH, A TSUKISHIMA! I HATE, HATE, HATE THAT NAME!
I LOST MY NEW SANDALS.
A-AMI?
GOT TURNED DOWN.
TODAY IS THE WORST DAY EVER!
NOW WHAT AM I GOING TO DO WITH THAT DRESS I BOUGHT?!
AMI MAD!!
AMI...
...MUST WIN!!!

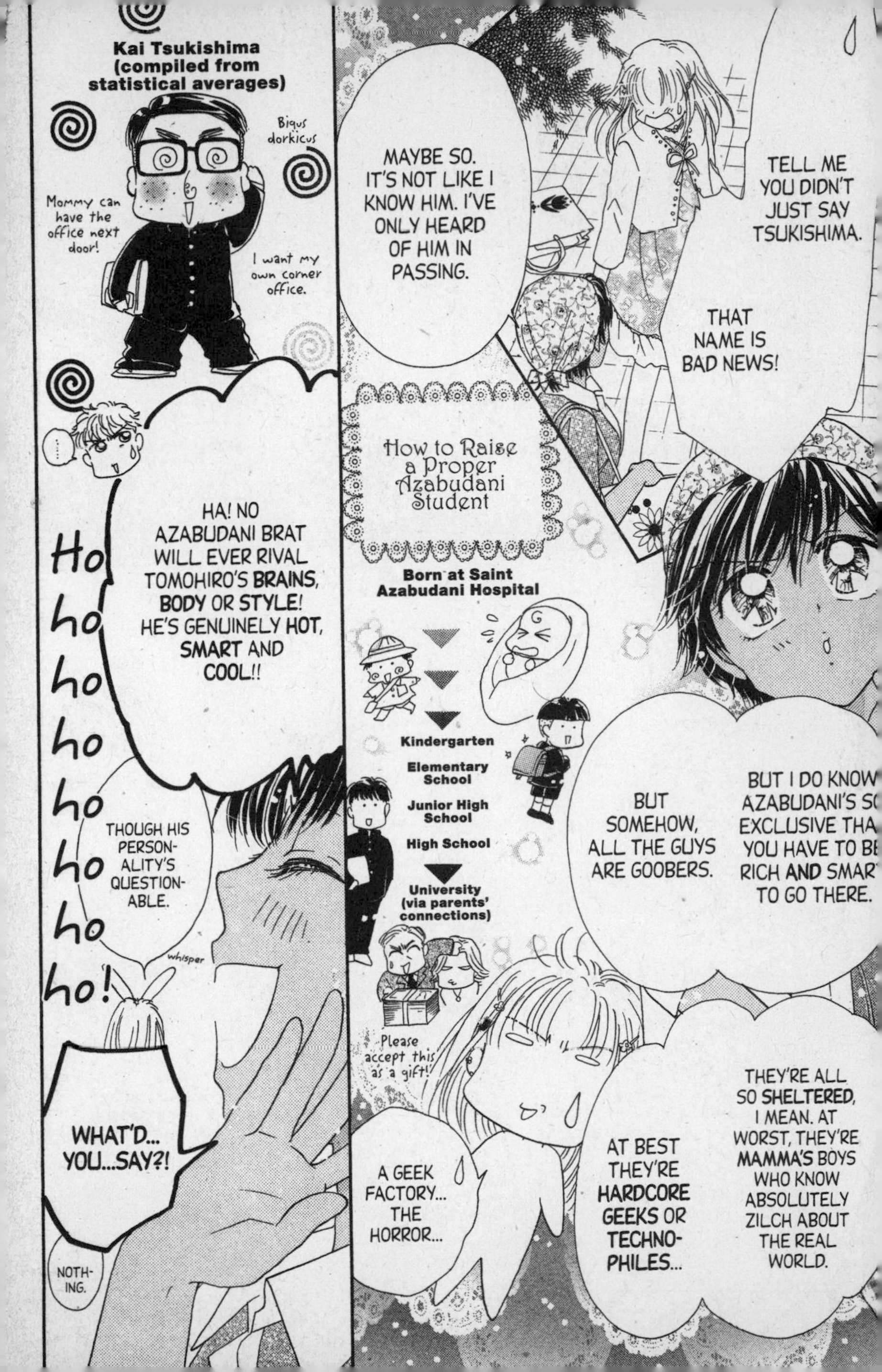

TELL ME YOU DIDN'T JUST SAY TSUKISHIMA.
THAT NAME IS BAD NEWS!
MAYBE SO. IT'S NOT LIKE I KNOW HIM. I'VE ONLY HEARD OF HIM IN PASSING.
How to Raise a Proper Azabudani Student
Born at Saint Azabudani Hospital
Kindergarten
Elementary School
Junior High School
High School
University (via parents' connections)
Please accept this as a gift!
BUT I DO KNOW AZABUDANI'S SC EXCLUSIVE THA YOU HAVE TO BE RICH AND SMAR TO GO THERE.
BUT SOMEHOW, ALL THE GUYS ARE GOOBERS.
THEY'RE ALL SO SHELTERED, I MEAN. AT WORST, THEY'RE MAMMA'S BOYS WHO KNOW ABSOLUTELY ZILCH ABOUT THE REAL WORLD.
AT BEST THEY'RE HARDCORE GEEKS OR TECHNO-PHILES...
A GEEK FACTORY... THE HORROR...
Kai Tsukishima (compiled from statistical averages)
Biqus dorkicus
Mommy can have the office next door!
I want my own corner office.
...
HA! NO AZABUDANI BRAT WILL EVER RIVAL TOMOHIRO'S BRAINS, BODY OR STYLE! HE'S GENUINELY HOT, SMART AND COOL!!
Ho ho ho ho ho ho ho ho!
THOUGH HIS PERSON-ALITY'S QUESTION-ABLE.
whisper
WHAT'D... YOU...SAY?!
NOTH-ING.

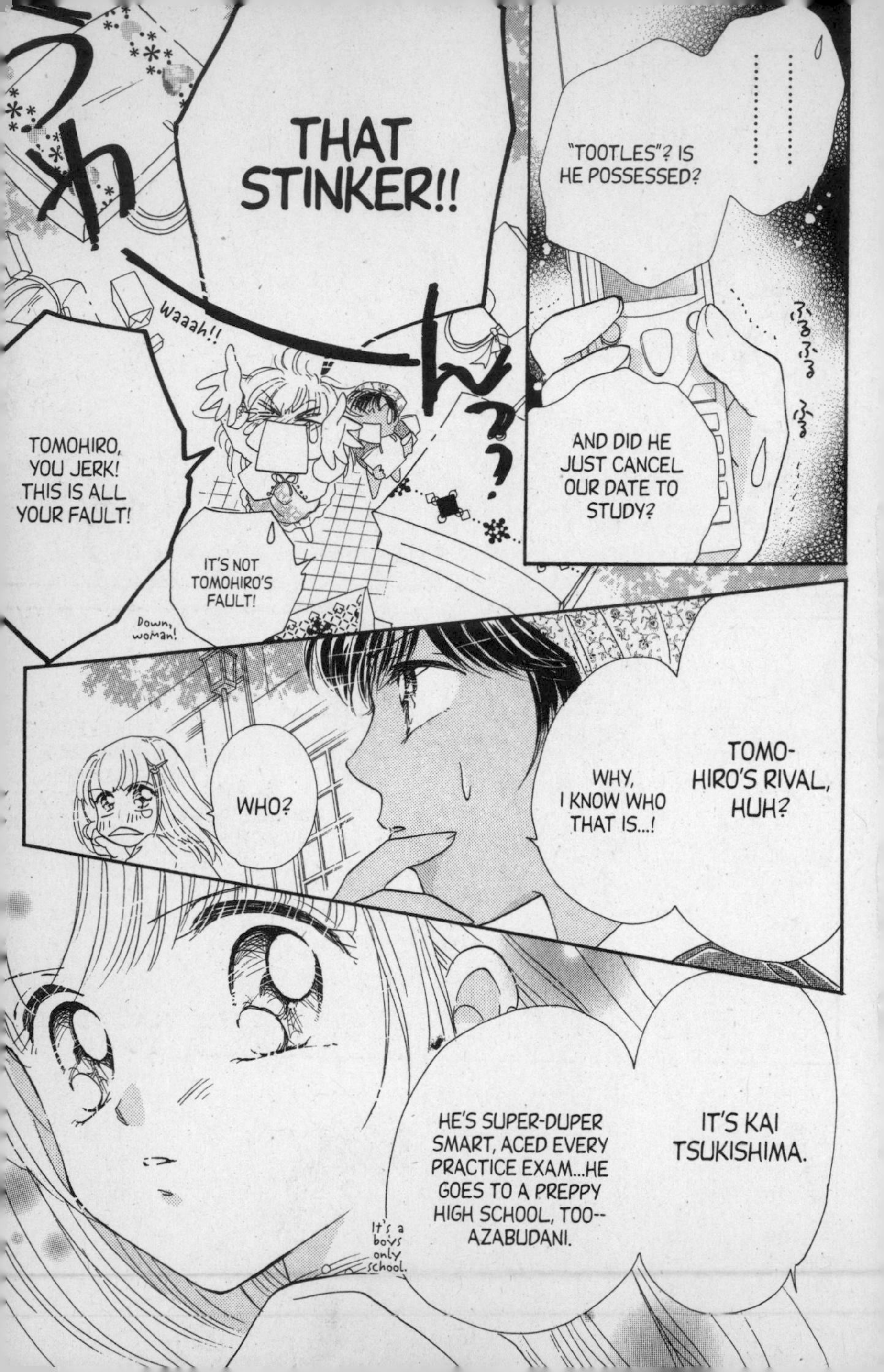
......
"TOOTLES"? IS HE POSSESSED?
AND DID HE JUST CANCEL OUR DATE TO STUDY?
THAT STINKER!!
うわーんっ??
Waaah!!
TOMOHIRO, YOU JERK! THIS IS ALL YOUR FAULT!
IT'S NOT TOMOHIRO'S FAULT!
Down, woman!
TOMO-HIRO'S RIVAL, HUH?
WHY, I KNOW WHO THAT IS...!
WHO?
IT'S KAI TSUKISHIMA.
HE'S SUPER-DUPER SMART, ACED EVERY PRACTICE EXAM...HE GOES TO A PREPPY HIGH SCHOOL, TOO--AZABUDANI.
It's a boys only school.

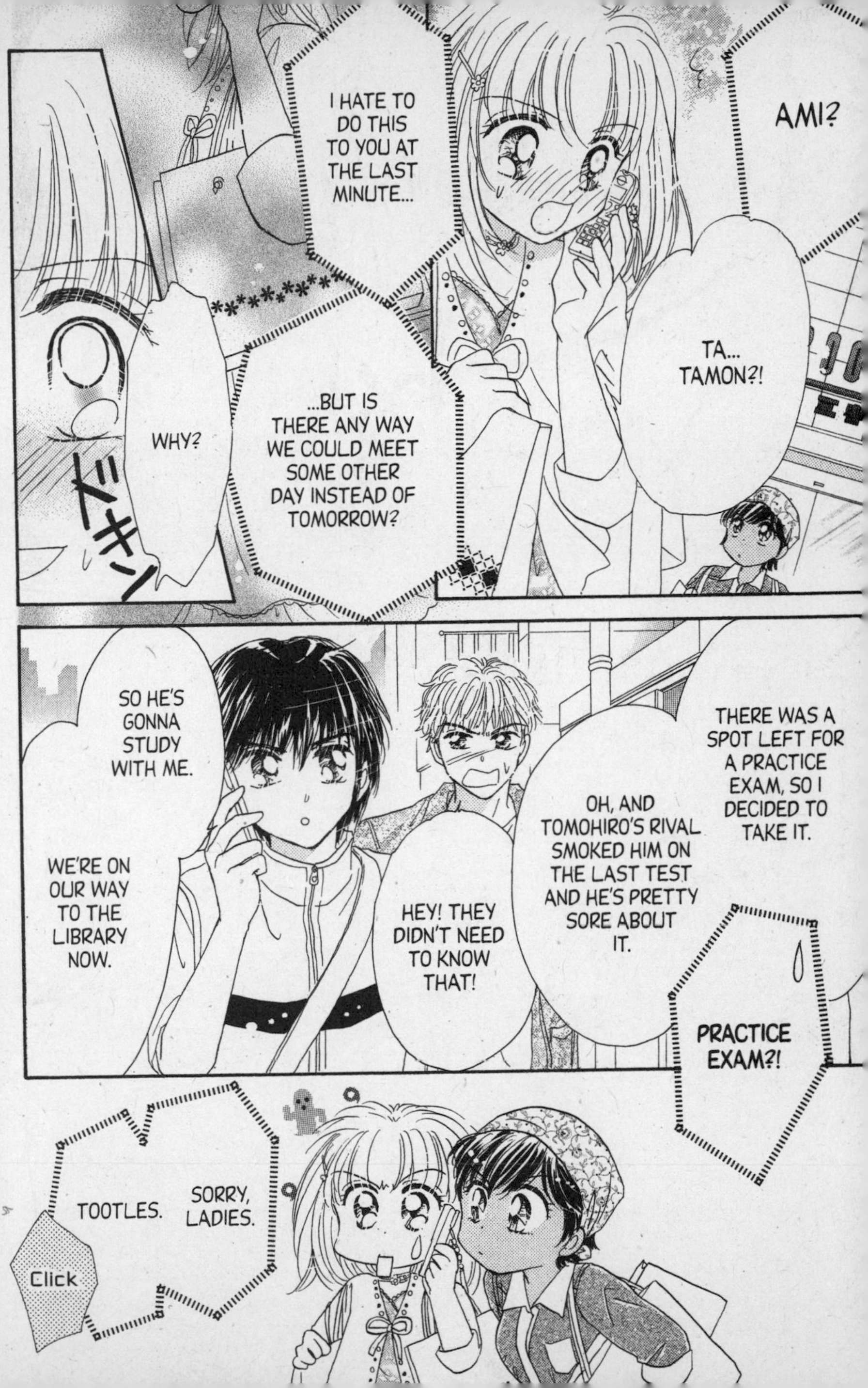
AMI?
TA... TAMON?!
I HATE TO DO THIS TO YOU AT THE LAST MINUTE...
...BUT IS THERE ANY WAY WE COULD MEET SOME OTHER DAY INSTEAD OF TOMORROW?
WHY?
ドキン
THERE WAS A SPOT LEFT FOR A PRACTICE EXAM, SO I DECIDED TO TAKE IT.
OH, AND TOMOHIRO'S RIVAL SMOKED HIM ON THE LAST TEST AND HE'S PRETTY SORE ABOUT IT.
HEY! THEY DIDN'T NEED TO KNOW THAT!
SO HE'S GONNA STUDY WITH ME.
WE'RE ON OUR WAY TO THE LIBRARY NOW.
PRACTICE EXAM?!
SORRY, LADIES.
TOOTLES.
Click

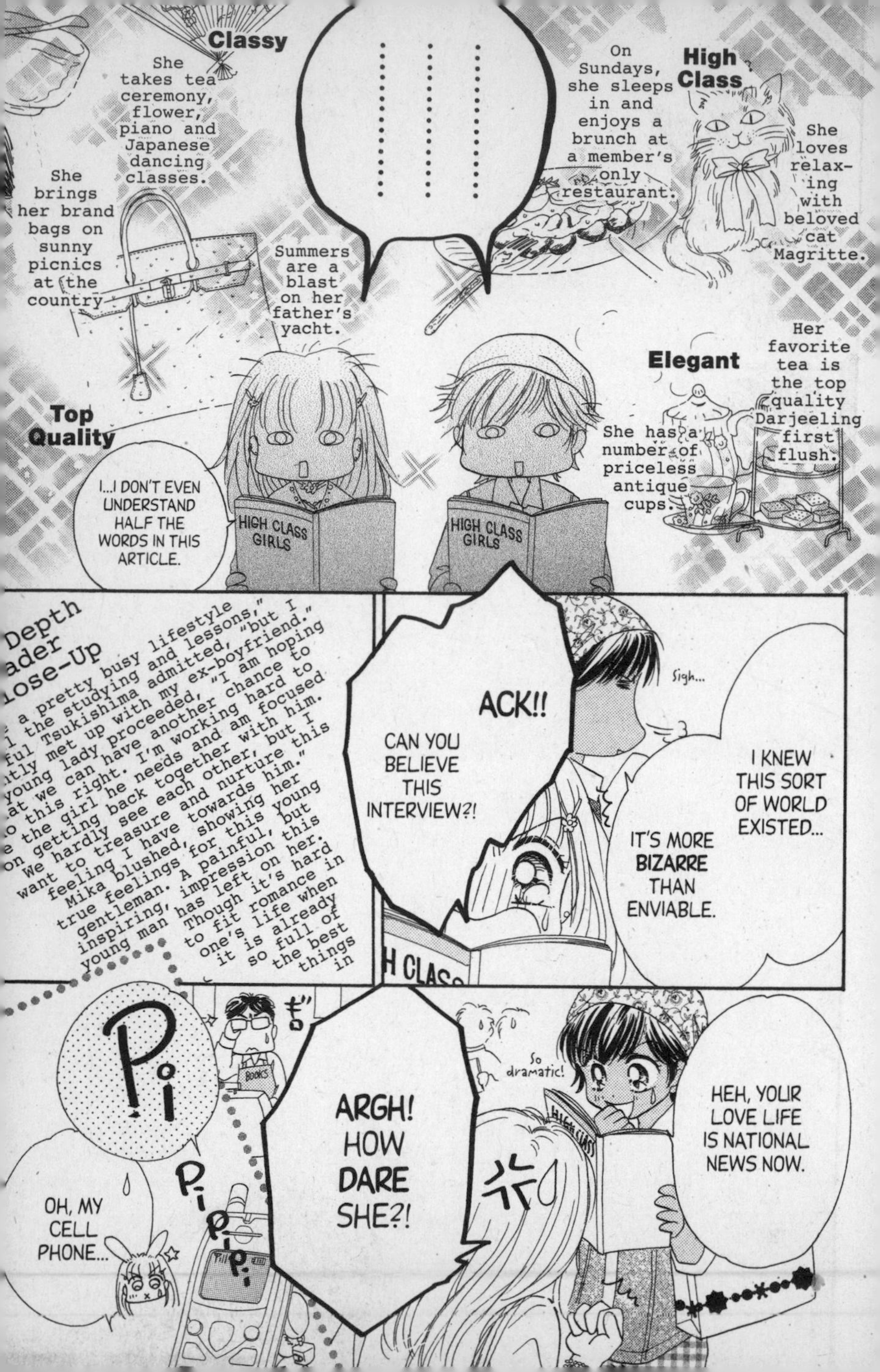
......
High Class
On Sundays, she sleeps in and enjoys a brunch at a member's only restaurant.
She loves relaxing with beloved cat Magritte.
Classy
She takes tea ceremony, flower, piano and Japanese dancing classes.
She brings her brand bags on sunny picnics at the country
Summers are a blast on her father's yacht.
Elegant
Her favorite tea is the top quality Darjeeling first flush.
She has a number of priceless antique cups.
Top Quality
HIGH CLASS GIRLS
HIGH CLASS GIRLS
I...I DON'T EVEN UNDERSTAND HALF THE WORDS IN THIS ARTICLE.
Sigh...
I KNEW THIS SORT OF WORLD EXISTED...
IT'S MORE BIZARRE THAN ENVIABLE.
ACK!!
CAN YOU BELIEVE THIS INTERVIEW?!
H CLASS
Depth
ader
lose-Up
a pretty busy lifestyle
l the studying and lessons,"
ful Tsukishima admitted, "but I
ntly met up with my ex-boyfriend."
young lady proceeded, "I am hoping
at we can have another chance to
o this right. I'm working hard to
o the girl he needs and am focused
e on getting back together with him.
on We hardly see each other, but I
want to treasure and nurture this
feeling I have towards him."
Mika blushed, showing her
true feelings for this young
gentleman. A painful, but
inspiring impression this
young man has left on her.
Though it's hard
to fit romance in
one's life when
it is already
so full of
the best
things
in
HEH, YOUR LOVE LIFE IS NATIONAL NEWS NOW.
HIGH CLASS
So dramatic!
ARGH! HOW DARE SHE?!
BOOKS
Pi
Pi-pi-pi
OH, MY CELL PHONE...

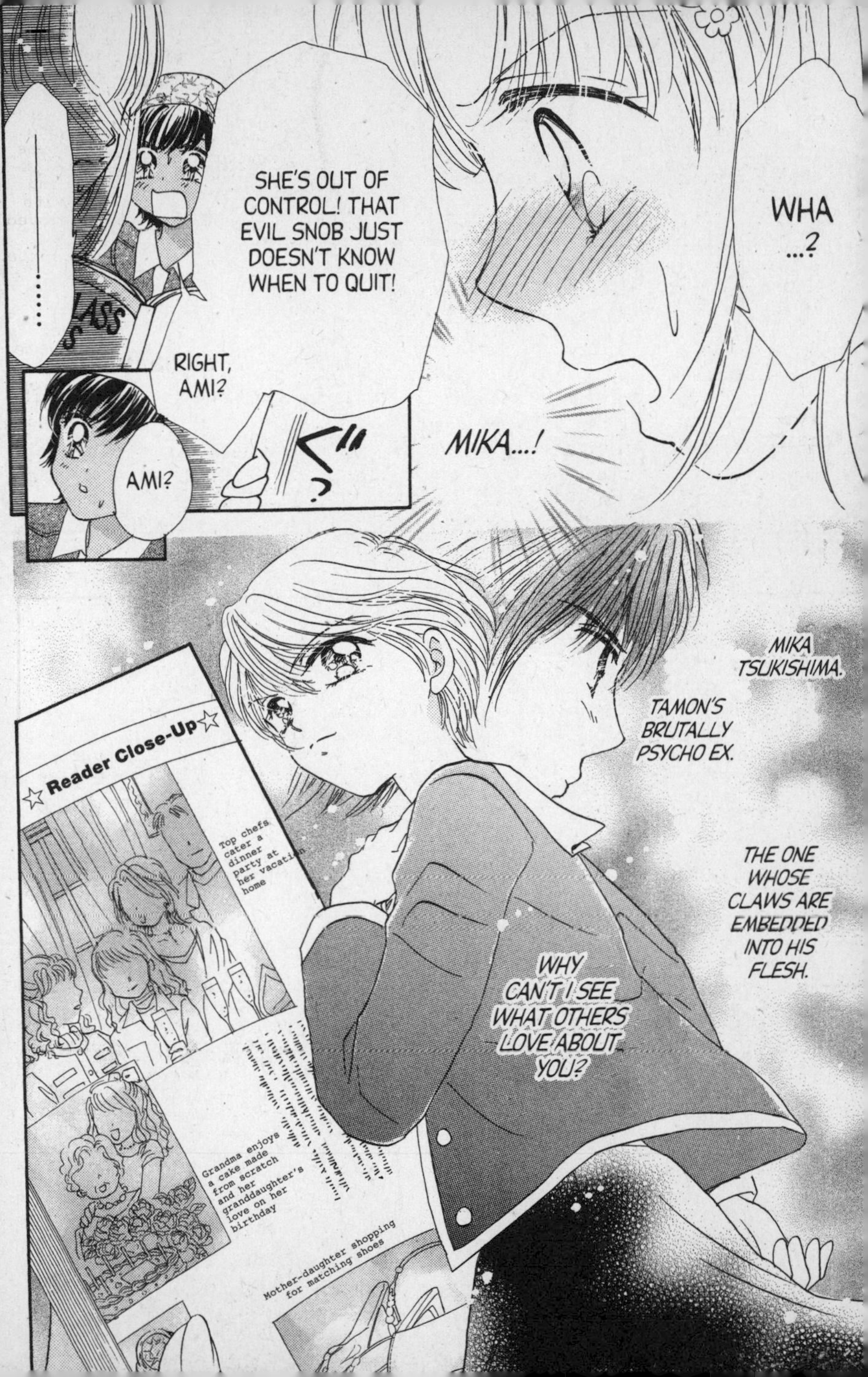
WHA ...?
MIKA...!
SHE'S OUT OF CONTROL! THAT EVIL SNOB JUST DOESN'T KNOW WHEN TO QUIT!
......
RIGHT, AMI?
AMI?
MIKA TSUKISHIMA.
TAMON'S BRUTALLY PSYCHO EX.
THE ONE WHOSE CLAWS ARE EMBEDDED INTO HIS FLESH.
WHY CAN'T I SEE WHAT OTHERS LOVE ABOUT YOU?
Reader Close-Up
Top chefs cater a dinner party at her vacation home
Grandma enjoys a cake made from scratch and her granddaughter's love on her birthday
Mother-daughter shopping for matching shoes

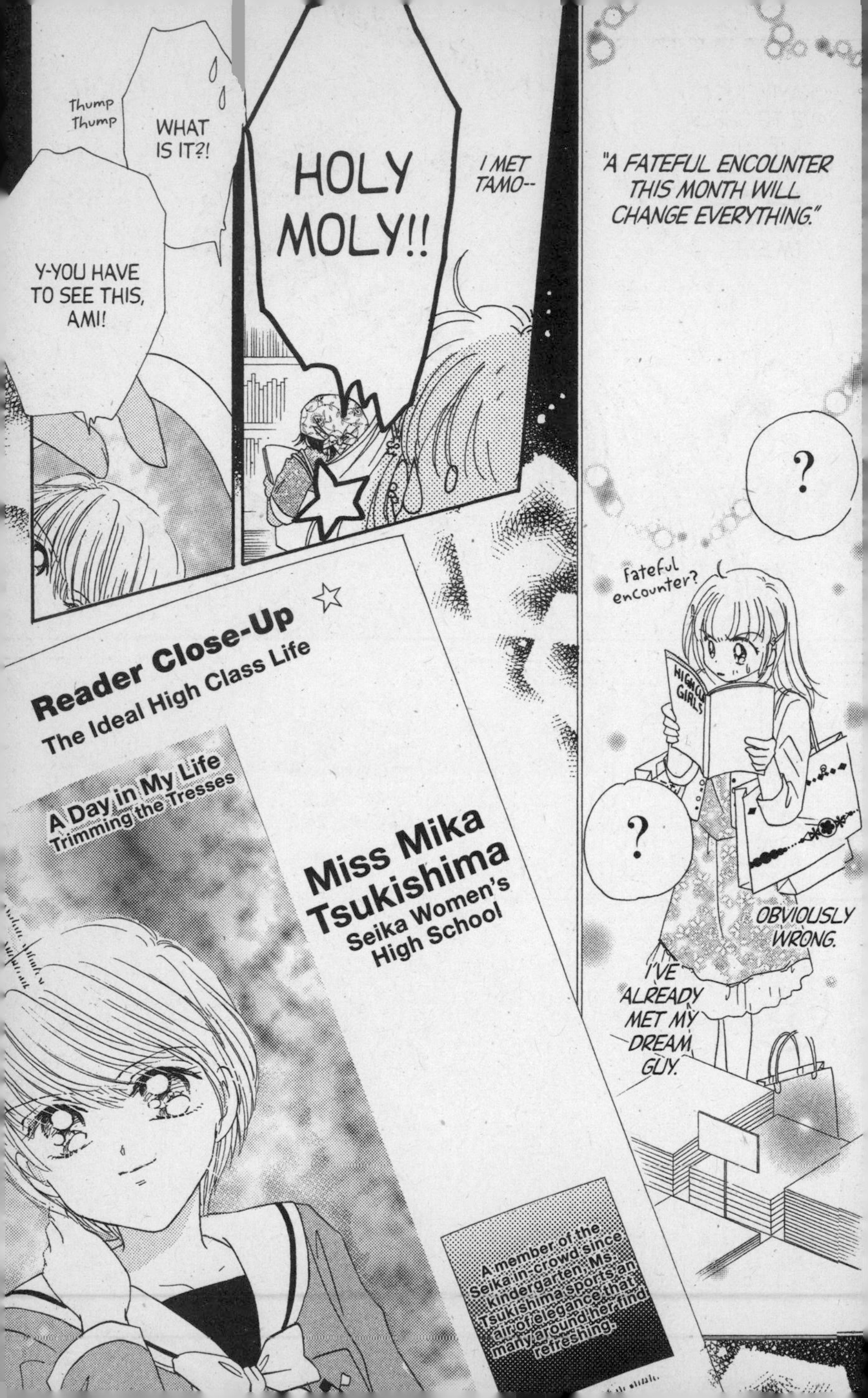
"A FATEFUL ENCOUNTER THIS MONTH WILL CHANGE EVERYTHING."
?
fateful encounter?
HIGH GIRLS
?
OBVIOUSLY WRONG.
I'VE ALREADY MET MY DREAM GUY.
I MET TAMO--
HOLY MOLY!!
WHAT IS IT?!
Thump Thump
Y-YOU HAVE TO SEE THIS, AMI!
Reader Close-Up
The Ideal High Class Life
A Day in My Life
Trimming the Tresses
Miss Mika Tsukishima
Seika Women's High School
A member of the Seika in-crowd since kindergarten, Ms. Tsukishima sports an air of elegance that many around her find refreshing.

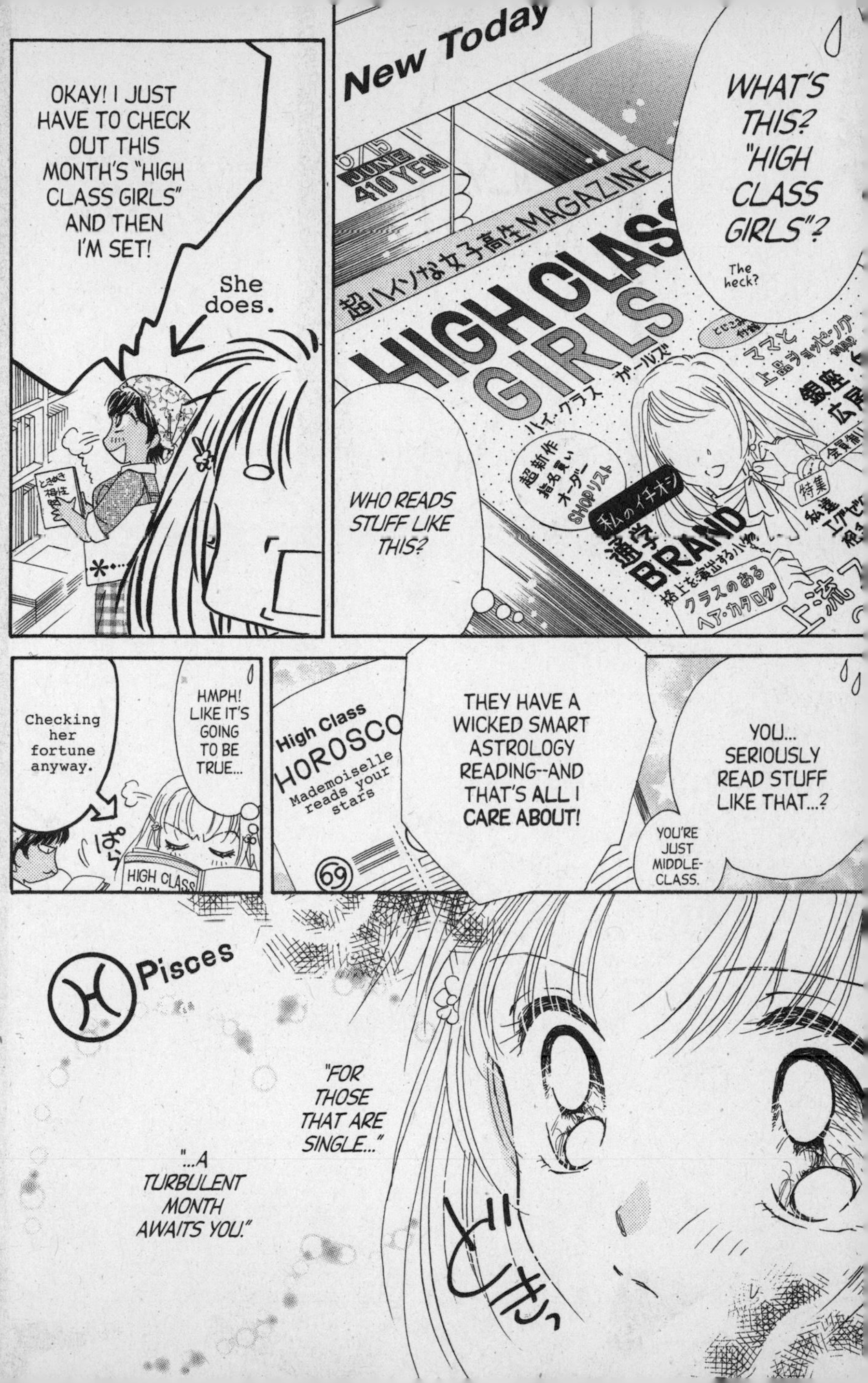
New Today
JUNE 410 YEN
超ハイソな女子高生MAGAZINE
HIGH CLASS GIRLS
WHAT'S THIS? "HIGH CLASS GIRLS"?
The heck?
WHO READS STUFF LIKE THIS?
OKAY! I JUST HAVE TO CHECK OUT THIS MONTH'S "HIGH CLASS GIRLS" AND THEN I'M SET!
She does.
YOU... SERIOUSLY READ STUFF LIKE THAT...?
YOU'RE JUST MIDDLE-CLASS.
THEY HAVE A WICKED SMART ASTROLOGY READING--AND THAT'S ALL I CARE ABOUT!
High Class HOROSCO
Mademoiselle reads your stars
HMPH! LIKE IT'S GOING TO BE TRUE...
Checking her fortune anyway.
HIGH CLASS
Pisces
"FOR THOSE THAT ARE SINGLE..."
"...A TURBULENT MONTH AWAITS YOU."

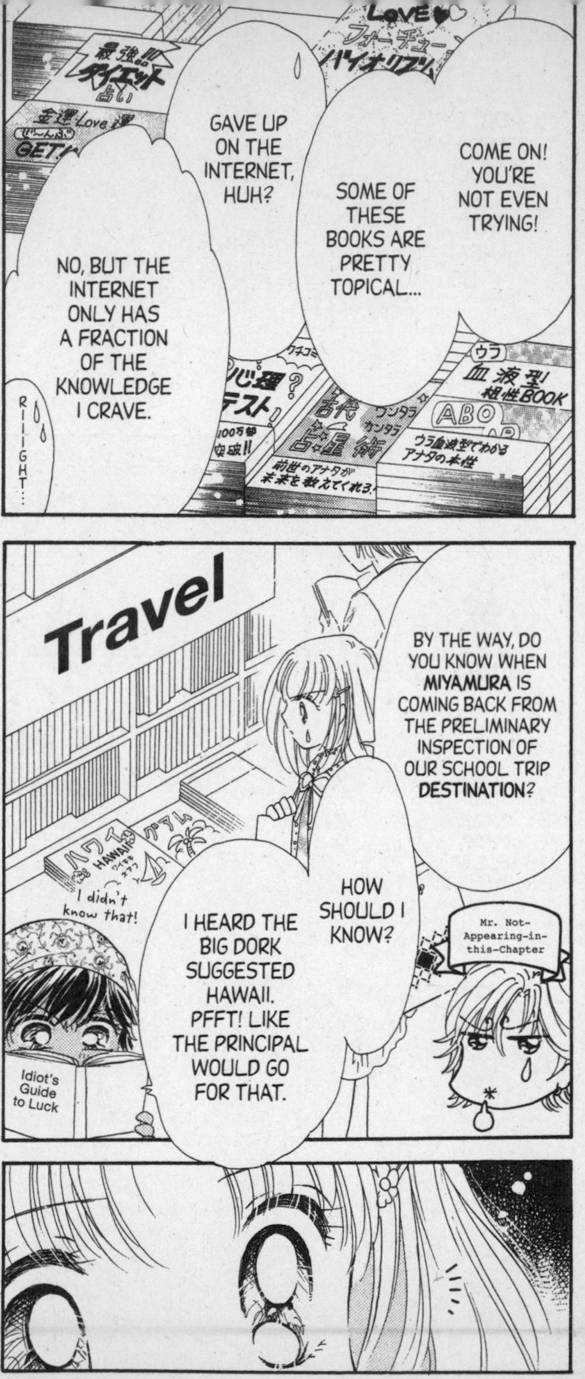
COME ON! YOU'RE NOT EVEN TRYING!
SOME OF THESE BOOKS ARE PRETTY TOPICAL...
GAVE UP ON THE INTERNET, HUH?
NO, BUT THE INTERNET ONLY HAS A FRACTION OF THE KNOWLEDGE I CRAVE.
RIIIGHT...
血液型! 相性BOOK
ABO
Travel
BY THE WAY, DO YOU KNOW WHEN **MIYAMURA** IS COMING BACK FROM THE PRELIMINARY INSPECTION OF OUR SCHOOL TRIP **DESTINATION**?
HOW SHOULD I KNOW?
Mr. Not-Appearing-in-this-Chapter
I HEARD THE BIG DORK SUGGESTED HAWAII. PFFT! LIKE THE PRINCIPAL WOULD GO FOR THAT.
HAWAII
I didn't know that!
Idiot's Guide to Luck
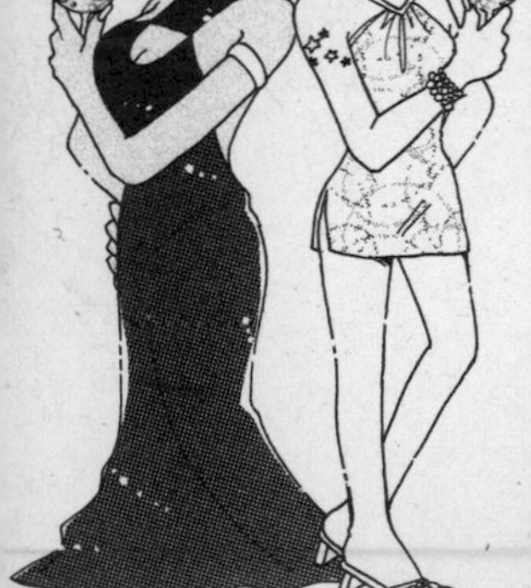

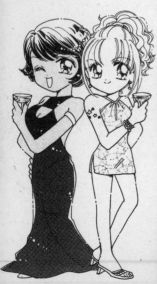

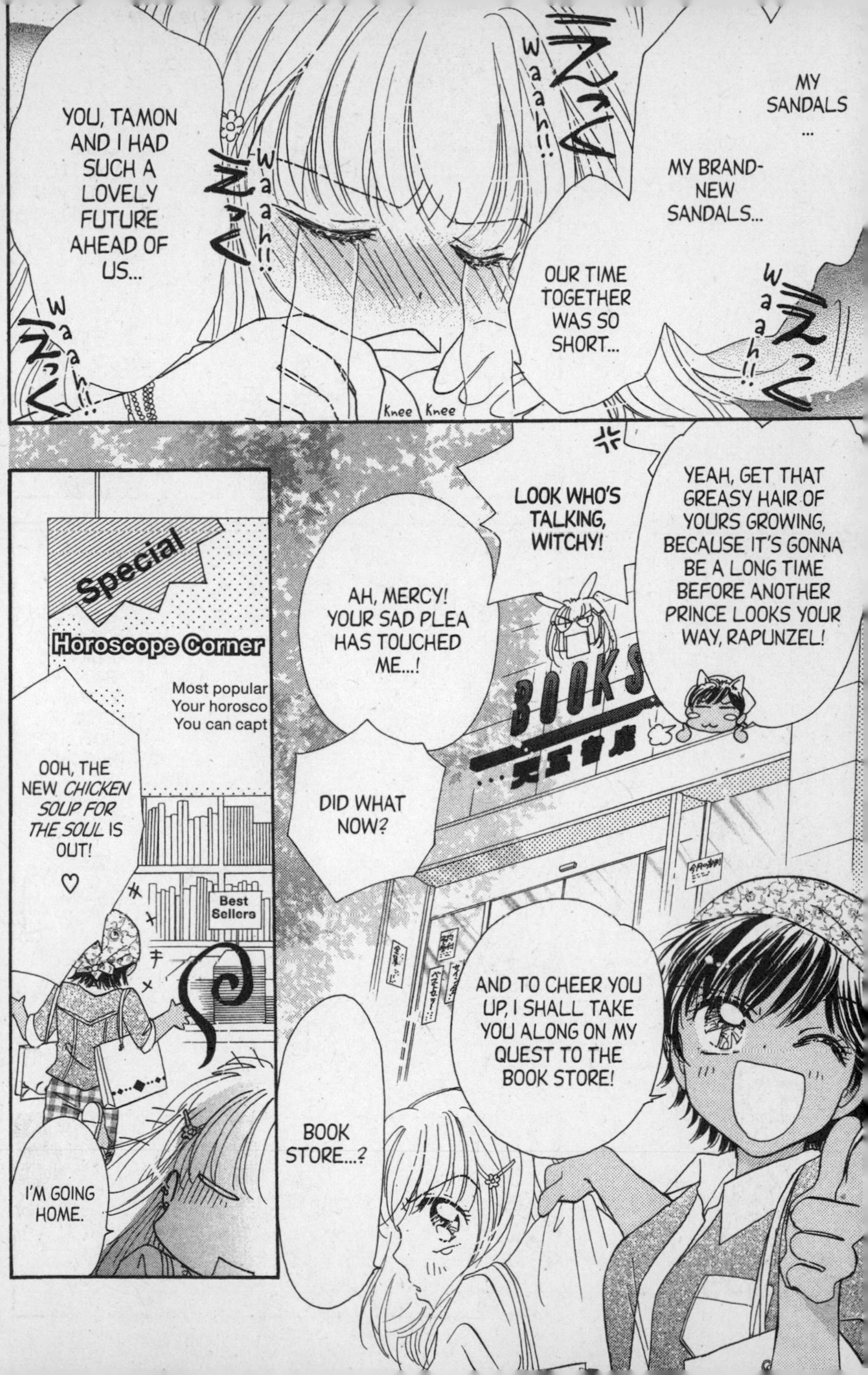
Waah!!
Waah!!
MY SANDALS ...
MY BRAND-NEW SANDALS...
OUR TIME TOGETHER WAS SO SHORT...
Waah!!
YOU, TAMON AND I HAD SUCH A LOVELY FUTURE AHEAD OF US...
Waah!!
Knee Knee
YEAH, GET THAT GREASY HAIR OF YOURS GROWING, BECAUSE IT'S GONNA BE A LONG TIME BEFORE ANOTHER PRINCE LOOKS YOUR WAY, RAPUNZEL!
LOOK WHO'S TALKING, WITCHY!
BOOKS
AH, MERCY! YOUR SAD PLEA HAS TOUCHED ME...!
DID WHAT NOW?
AND TO CHEER YOU UP, I SHALL TAKE YOU ALONG ON MY QUEST TO THE BOOK STORE!
BOOK STORE...?
Special
Horoscope Corner
Most popular
Your horosco
You can capt
OOH, THE NEW *CHICKEN SOUP FOR THE SOUL* IS OUT! ♡
Best Sellers
I'M GOING HOME.

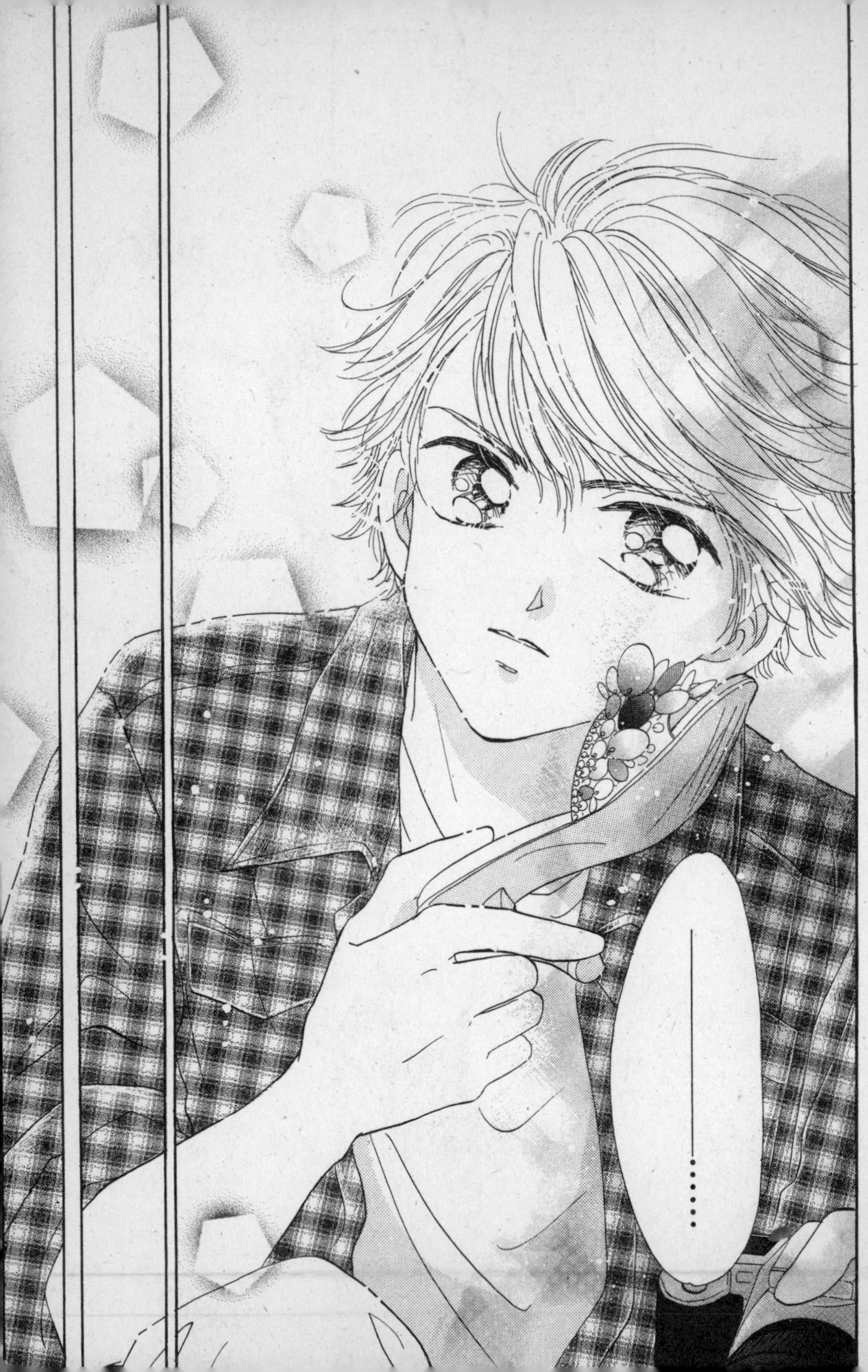
—......

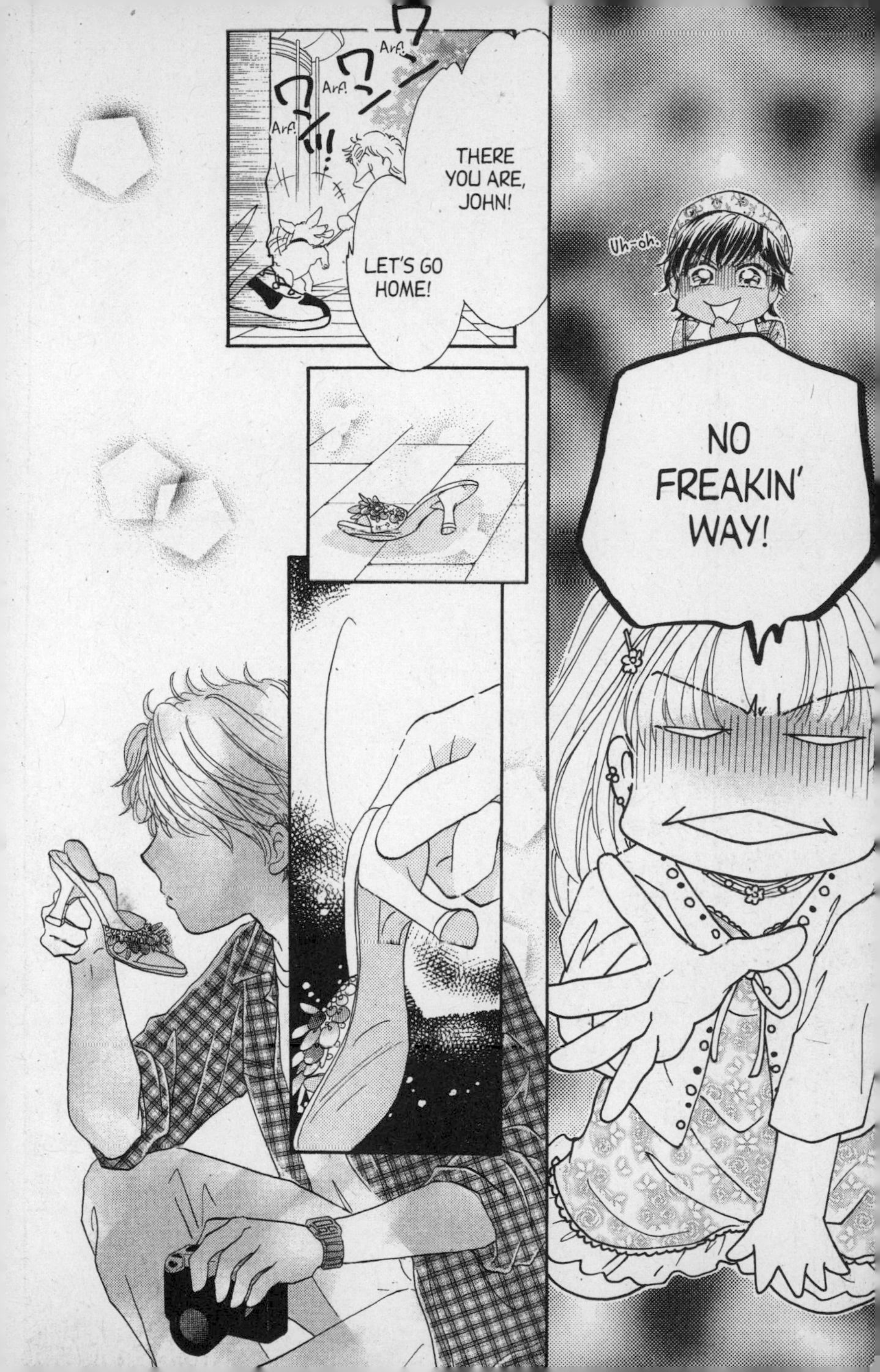
Uh-oh.
NO FREAKIN' WAY!
ワン
ワン
ワン!!
Arf!
Arf!
Arf!
THERE YOU ARE, JOHN!
LET'S GO HOME!

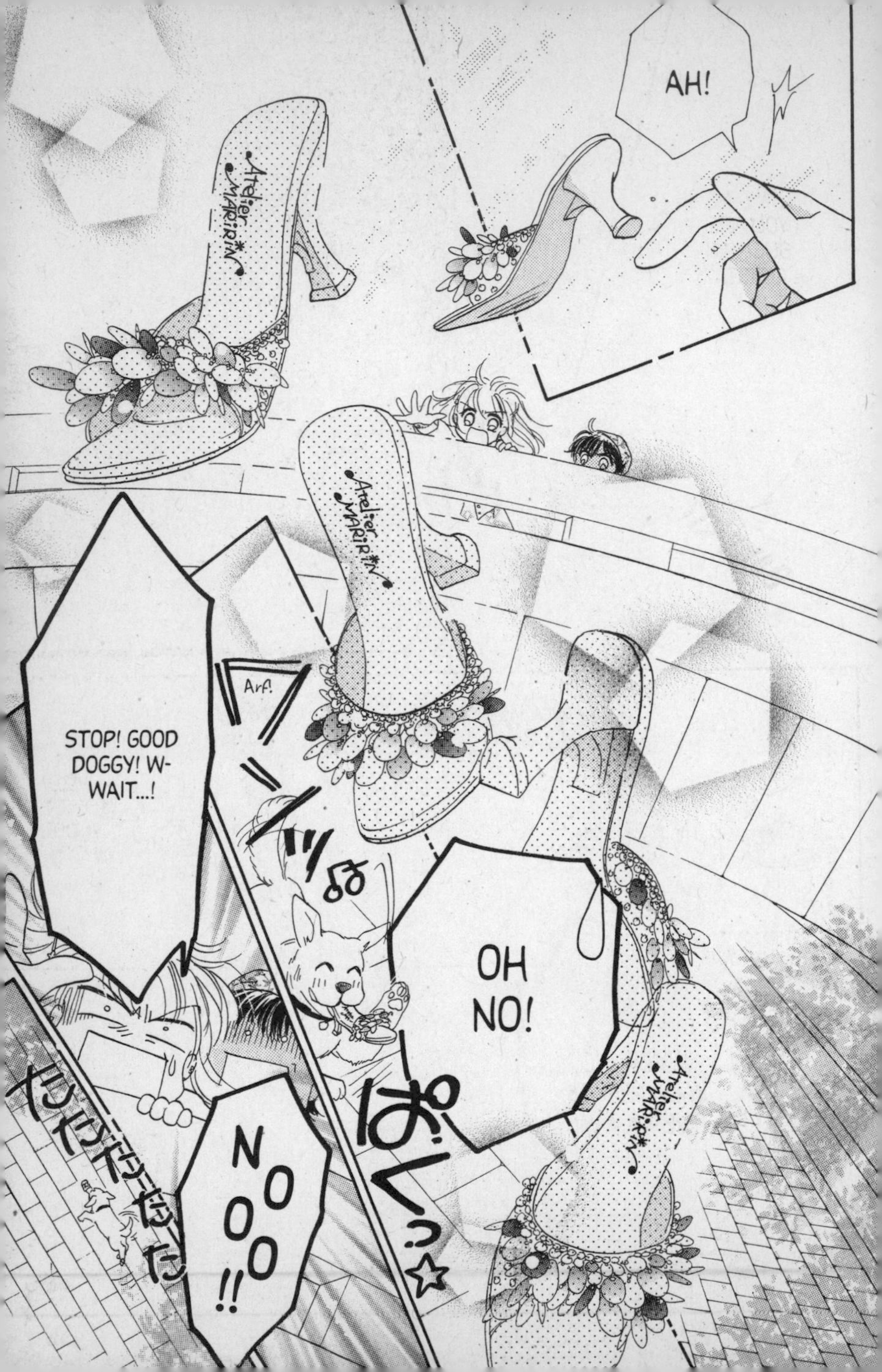
AH!
Atelier MARIRIN
OH NO!
STOP! GOOD DOGGY! W-WAIT...!
Arf!
ぱくっ☆
NOOOO!!

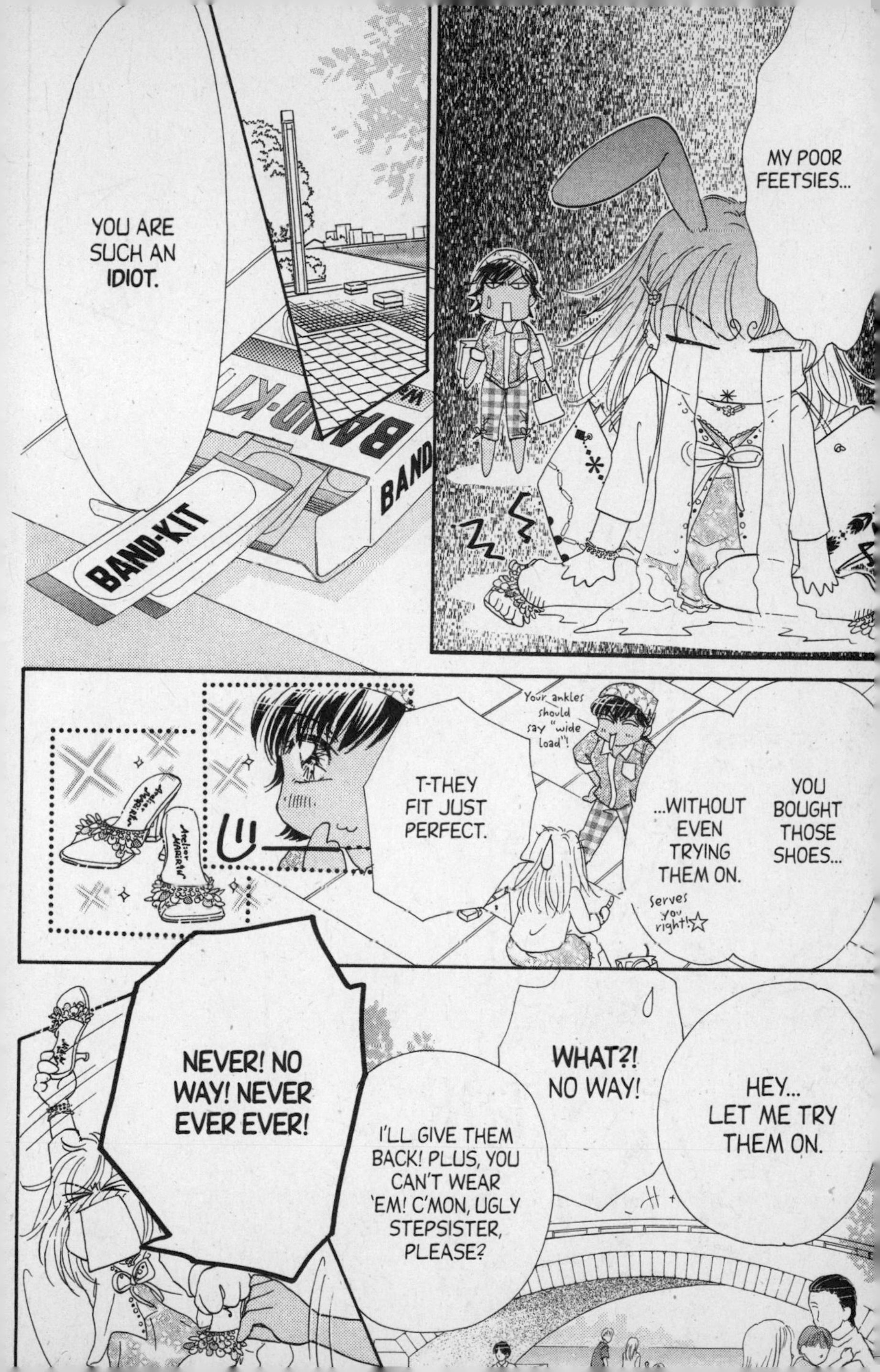
MY POOR FEETSIES...
YOU ARE SUCH AN IDIOT.
BAND-KIT
BAND-KIT
BAND
YOU BOUGHT THOSE SHOES...
...WITHOUT EVEN TRYING THEM ON.
Serves you right!☆
Your ankles should say "wide load"!
T-THEY FIT JUST PERFECT.
HEY... LET ME TRY THEM ON.
WHAT?! NO WAY!
I'LL GIVE THEM BACK! PLUS, YOU CAN'T WEAR 'EM! C'MON, UGLY STEPSISTER, PLEASE?
NEVER! NO WAY! NEVER EVER EVER!

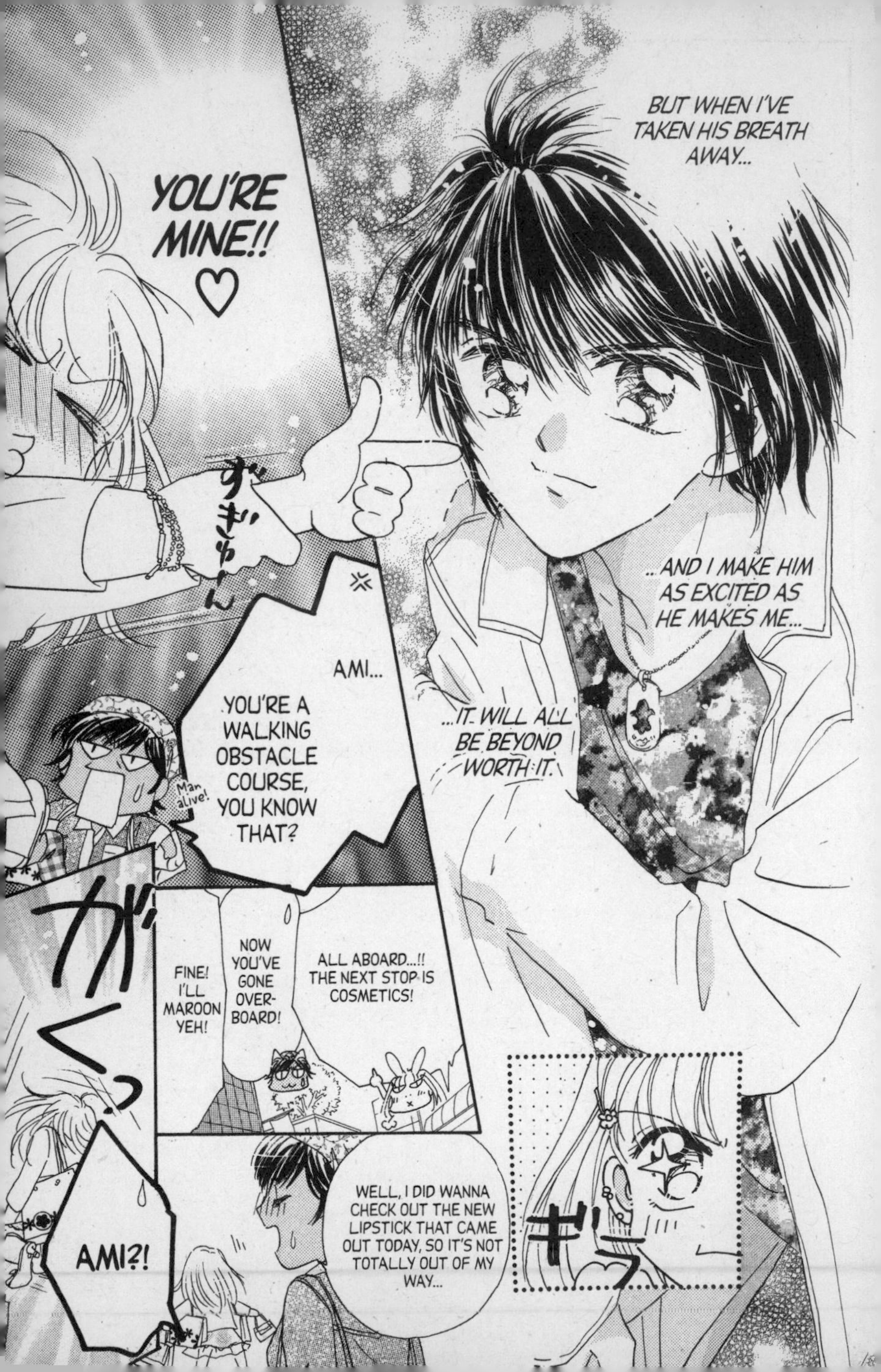
BUT WHEN I'VE TAKEN HIS BREATH AWAY...
...AND I MAKE HIM AS EXCITED AS HE MAKES ME...
...IT WILL ALL BE BEYOND WORTH IT.
YOU'RE MINE!! ♡
ずぎゅーん
AMI...
YOU'RE A WALKING OBSTACLE COURSE, YOU KNOW THAT?
Man alive!
ALL ABOARD...!! THE NEXT STOP IS COSMETICS!
NOW YOU'VE GONE OVER-BOARD!
FINE! I'LL MAROON YEH!
がくっ
ギラ
WELL, I DID WANNA CHECK OUT THE NEW LIPSTICK THAT CAME OUT TODAY, SO IT'S NOT TOTALLY OUT OF MY WAY...
AMI?!

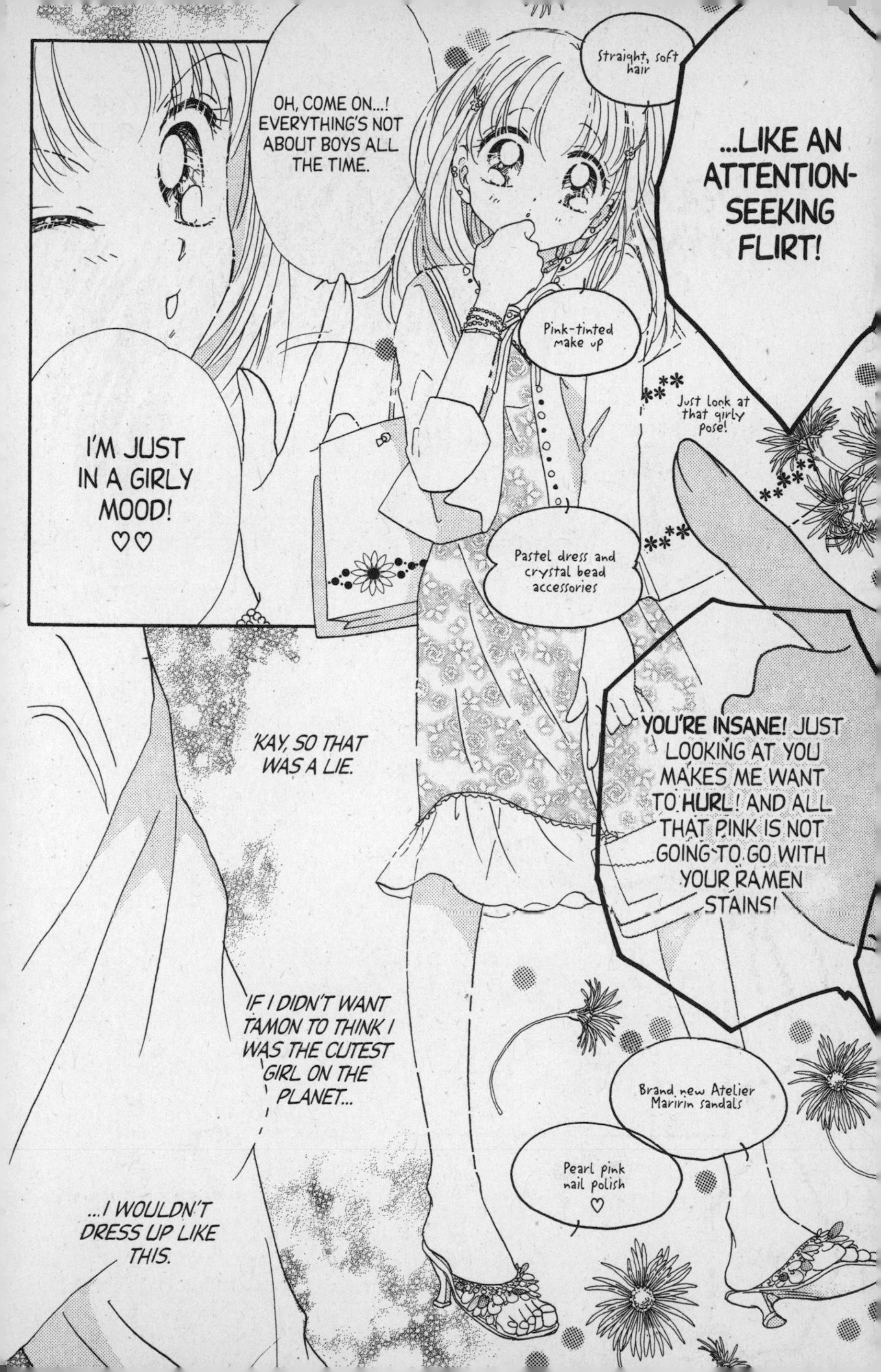
...LIKE AN ATTENTION-SEEKING FLIRT!
Straight, soft hair
Pink-tinted make up
Just look at that girly pose!
Pastel dress and crystal bead accessories
OH, COME ON...! EVERYTHING'S NOT ABOUT BOYS ALL THE TIME.
I'M JUST IN A GIRLY MOOD! ♡♡
YOU'RE INSANE! JUST LOOKING AT YOU MAKES ME WANT TO HURL! AND ALL THAT PINK IS NOT GOING TO GO WITH YOUR RAMEN STAINS!
Brand new Atelier Maririn sandals
Pearl pink nail polish ♡
'KAY, SO THAT WAS A LIE.
IF I DIDN'T WANT TAMON TO THINK I WAS THE CUTEST GIRL ON THE PLANET...
...I WOULDN'T DRESS UP LIKE THIS.

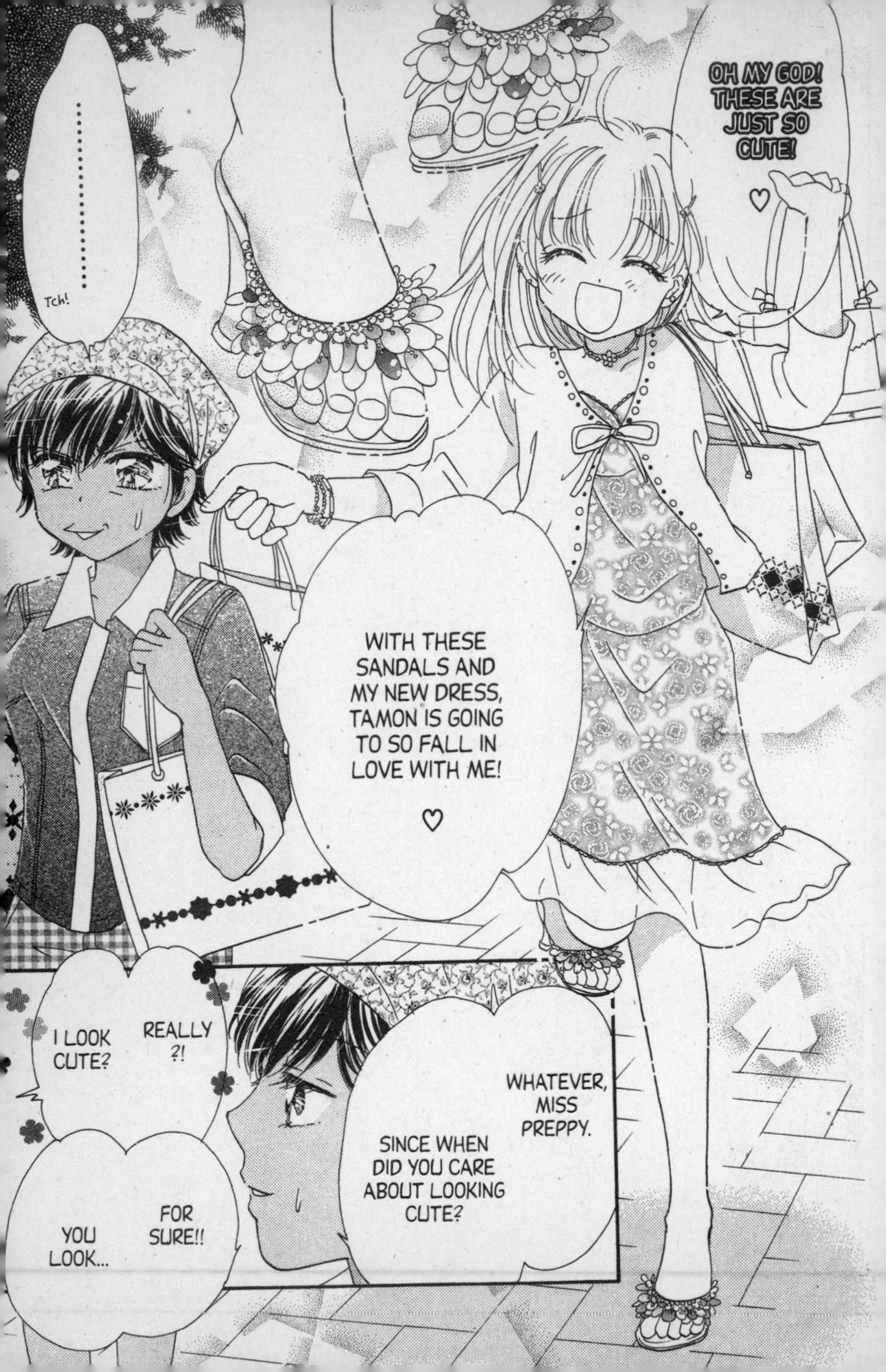
OH MY GOD! THESE ARE JUST SO CUTE! ♡
WITH THESE SANDALS AND MY NEW DRESS, TAMON IS GOING TO SO FALL IN LOVE WITH ME! ♡
......
Tch!
WHATEVER, MISS PREPPY.
SINCE WHEN DID YOU CARE ABOUT LOOKING CUTE?
REALLY?!
I LOOK CUTE?
FOR SURE!!
YOU LOOK...

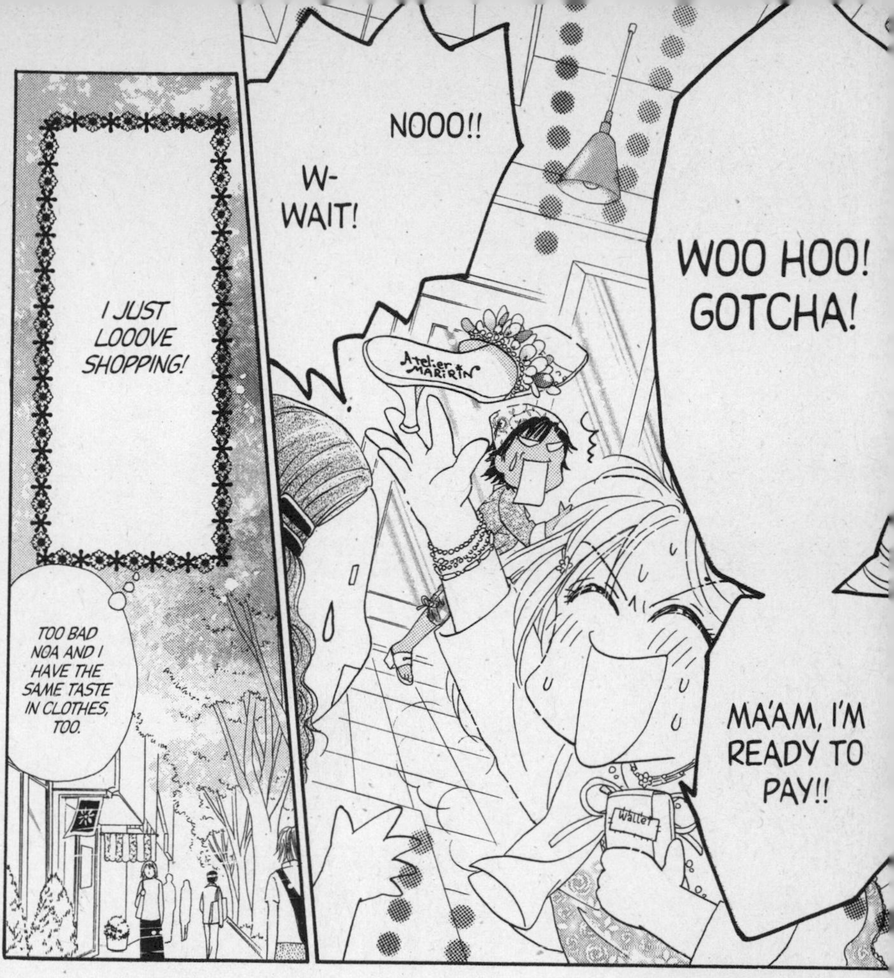
WOO HOO! GOTCHA!
NOOO!!
W-WAIT!
Atelier MARIRIN
MA'AM, I'M READY TO PAY!!
Wallet
I JUST LOOOVE SHOPPING!
TOO BAD NOA AND I HAVE THE SAME TASTE IN CLOTHES, TOO.

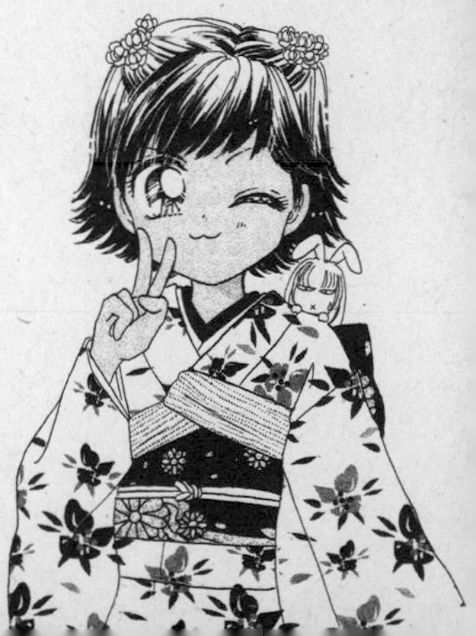

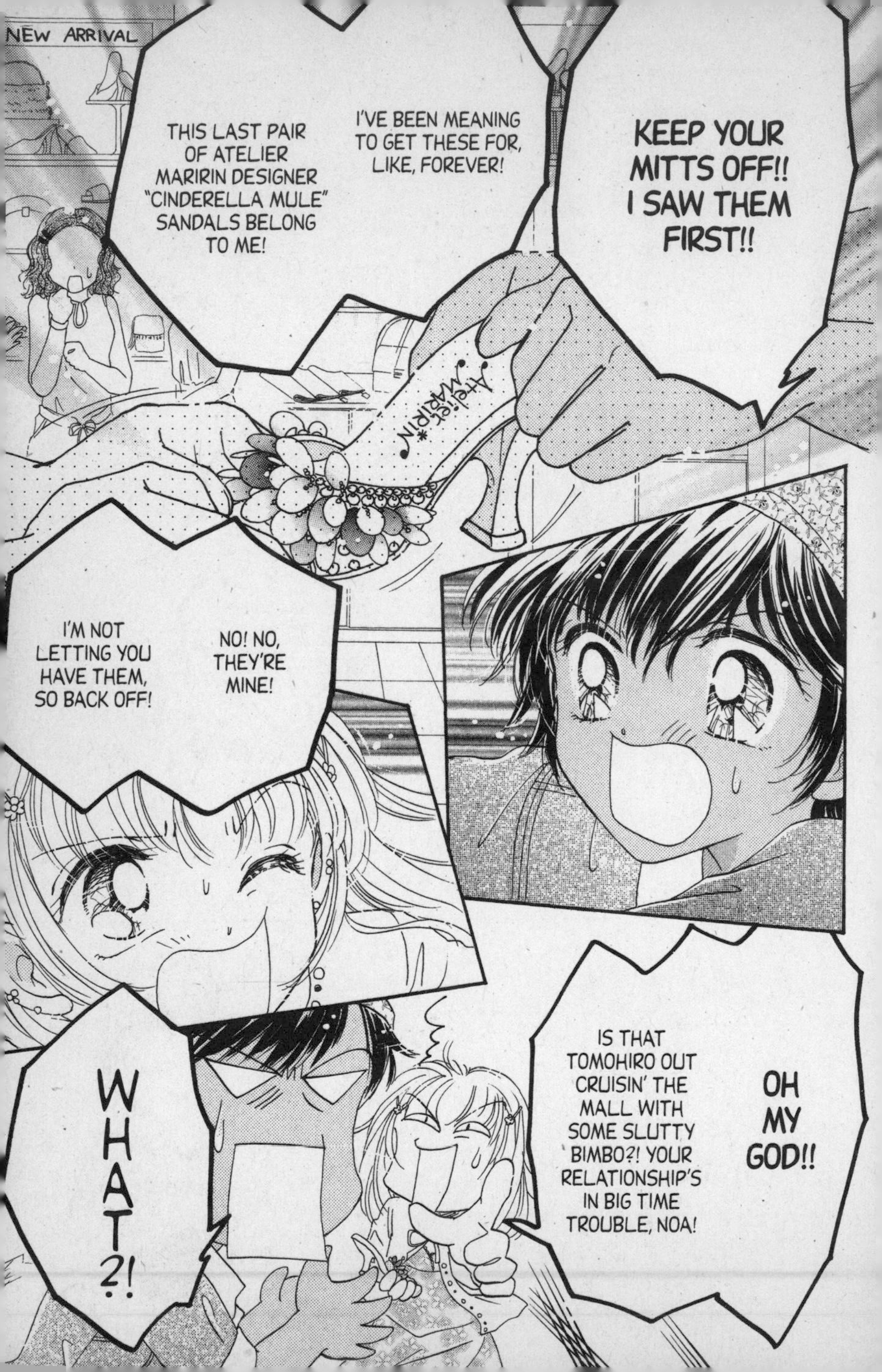
KEEP YOUR MITTS OFF!! I SAW THEM FIRST!!
I'VE BEEN MEANING TO GET THESE FOR, LIKE, FOREVER!
THIS LAST PAIR OF ATELIER MARIRIN DESIGNER "CINDERELLA MULE" SANDALS BELONG TO ME!
NEW ARRIVAL
Atelier MARIRIN
NO! NO, THEY'RE MINE!
I'M NOT LETTING YOU HAVE THEM, SO BACK OFF!
OH MY GOD!!
IS THAT TOMOHIRO OUT CRUISIN' THE MALL WITH SOME SLUTTY BIMBO?! YOUR RELATIONSHIP'S IN BIG TIME TROUBLE, NOA!
WHAT?!

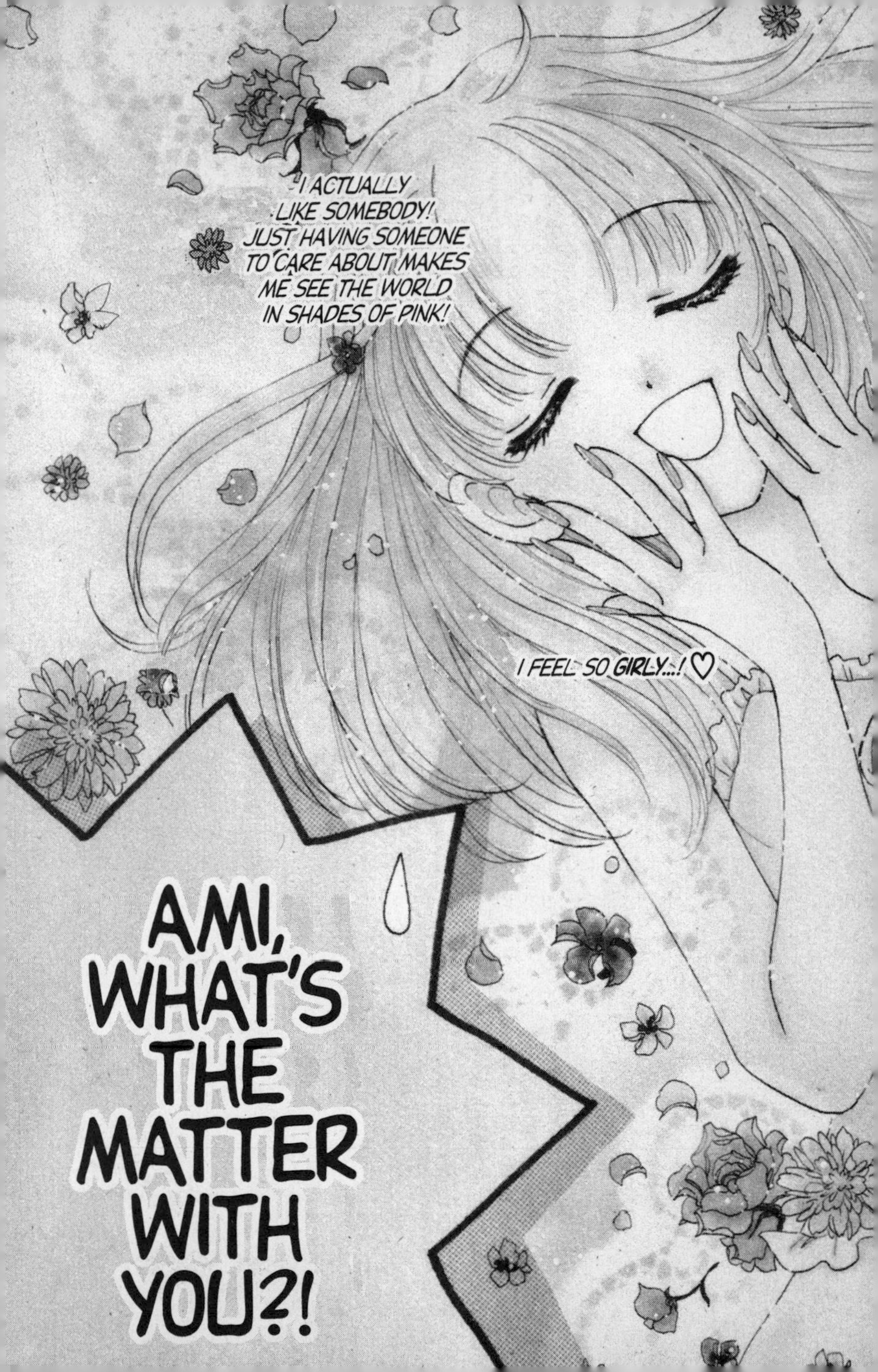
I ACTUALLY LIKE SOMEBODY! JUST HAVING SOMEONE TO CARE ABOUT MAKES ME SEE THE WORLD IN SHADES OF PINK!
I FEEL SO GIRLY...! ♡
AMI, WHAT'S THE MATTER WITH YOU?!

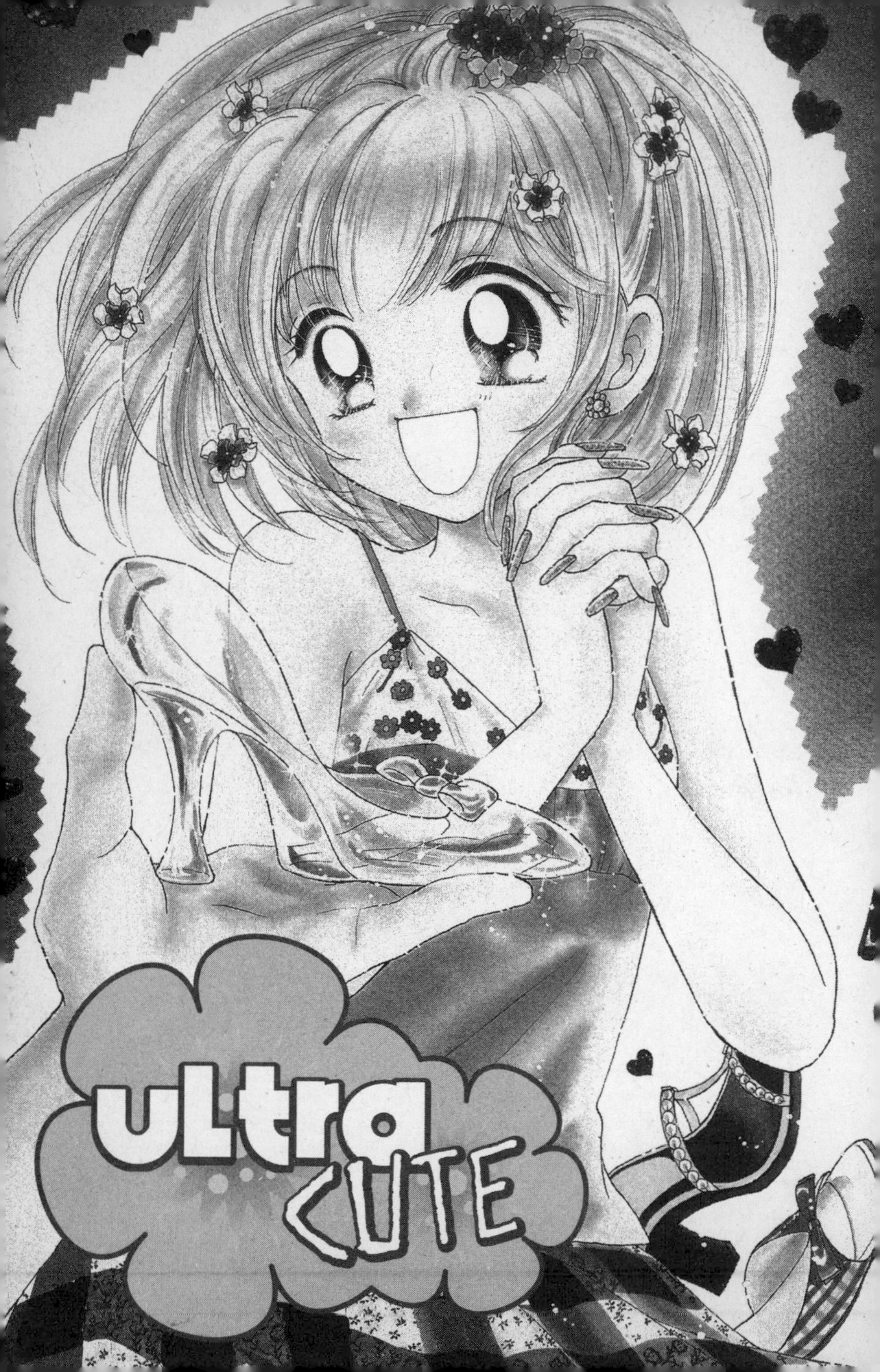
ultra
CUTE

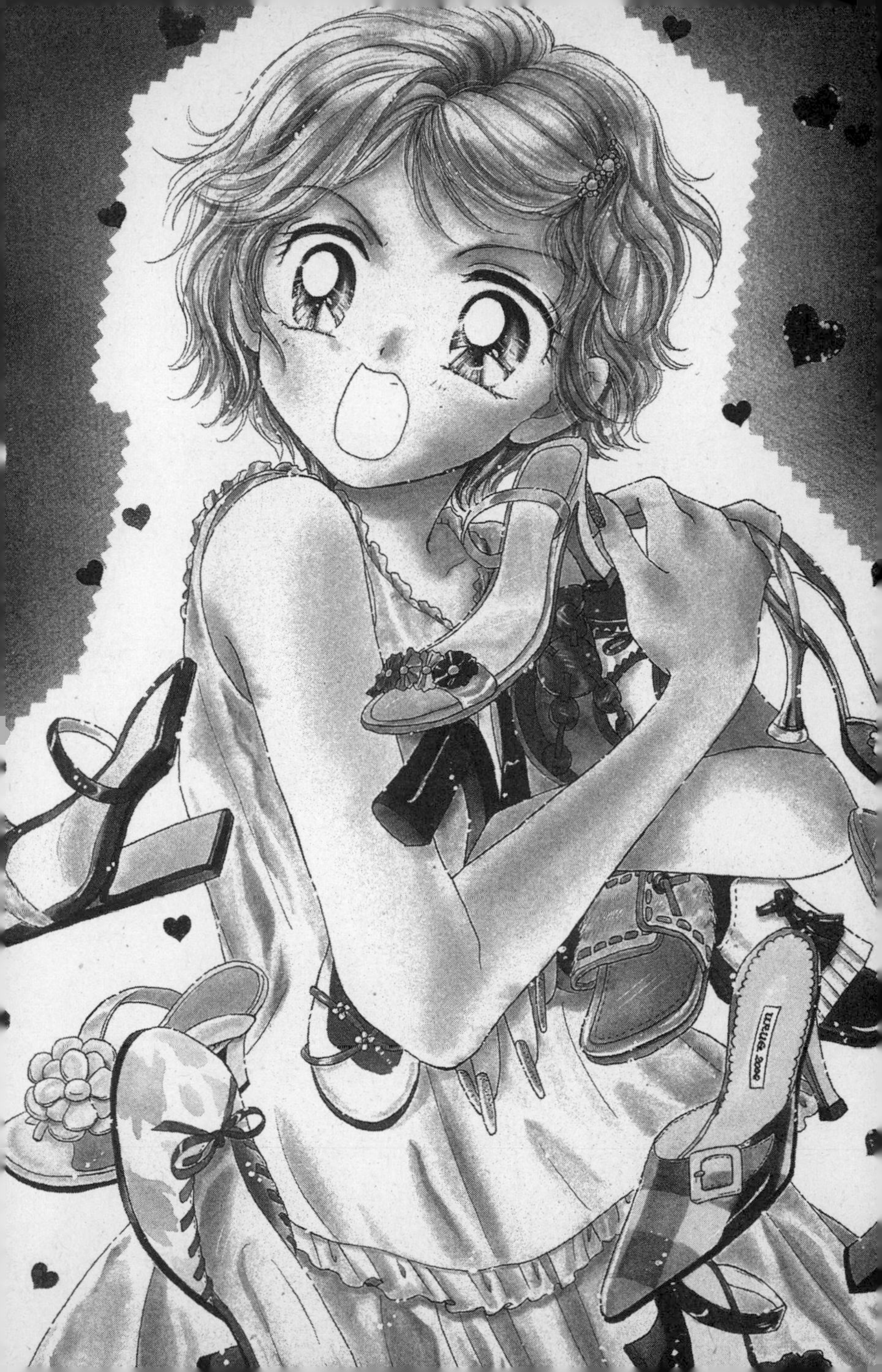

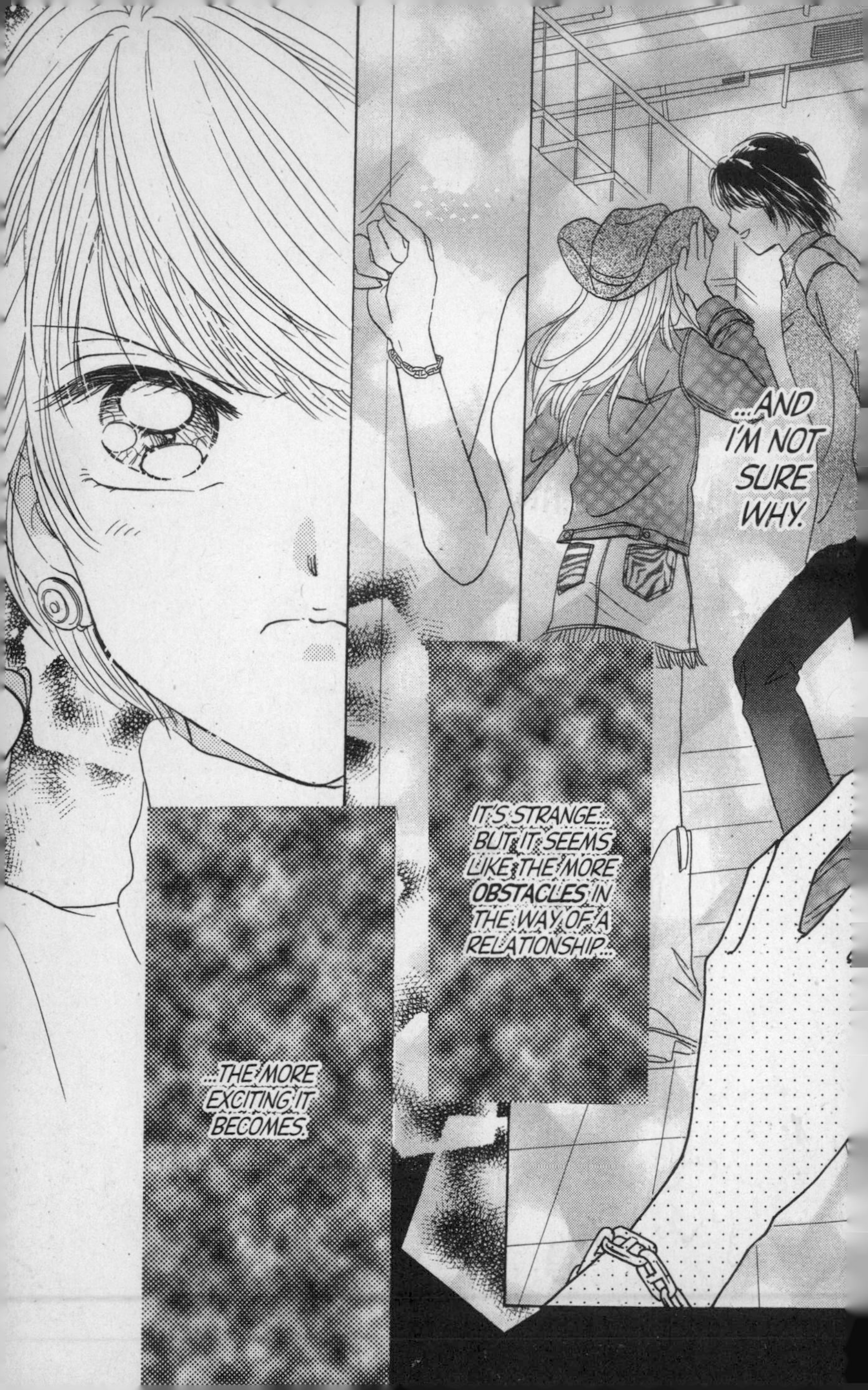
...AND I'M NOT SURE WHY.
IT'S STRANGE... BUT IT SEEMS LIKE THE MORE OBSTACLES IN THE WAY OF A RELATIONSHIP...
...THE MORE EXCITING IT BECOMES.

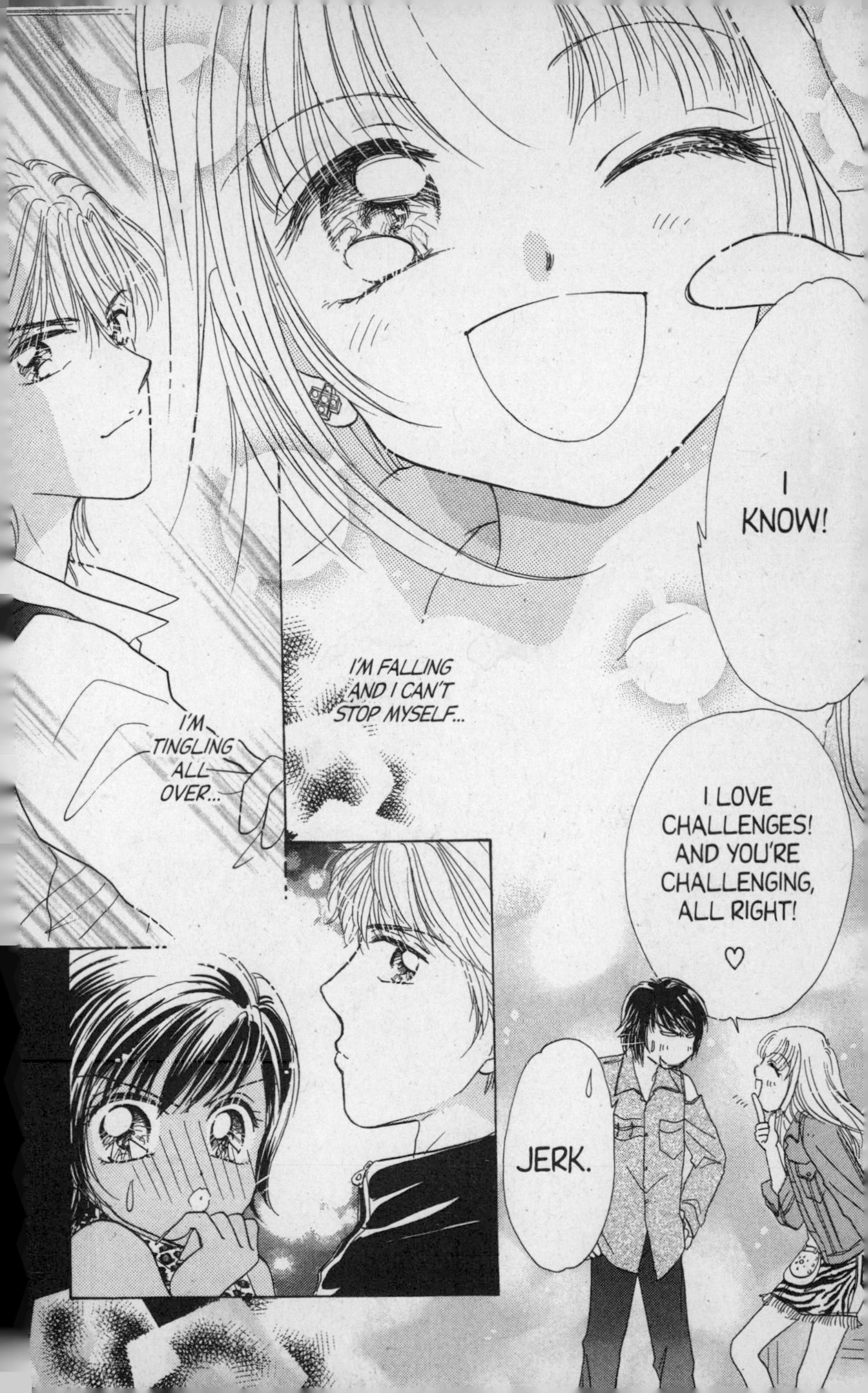
I KNOW!
I LOVE CHALLENGES! AND YOU'RE CHALLENGING, ALL RIGHT! ♡
JERK.
I'M FALLING AND I CAN'T STOP MYSELF...
I'M TINGLING ALL OVER...

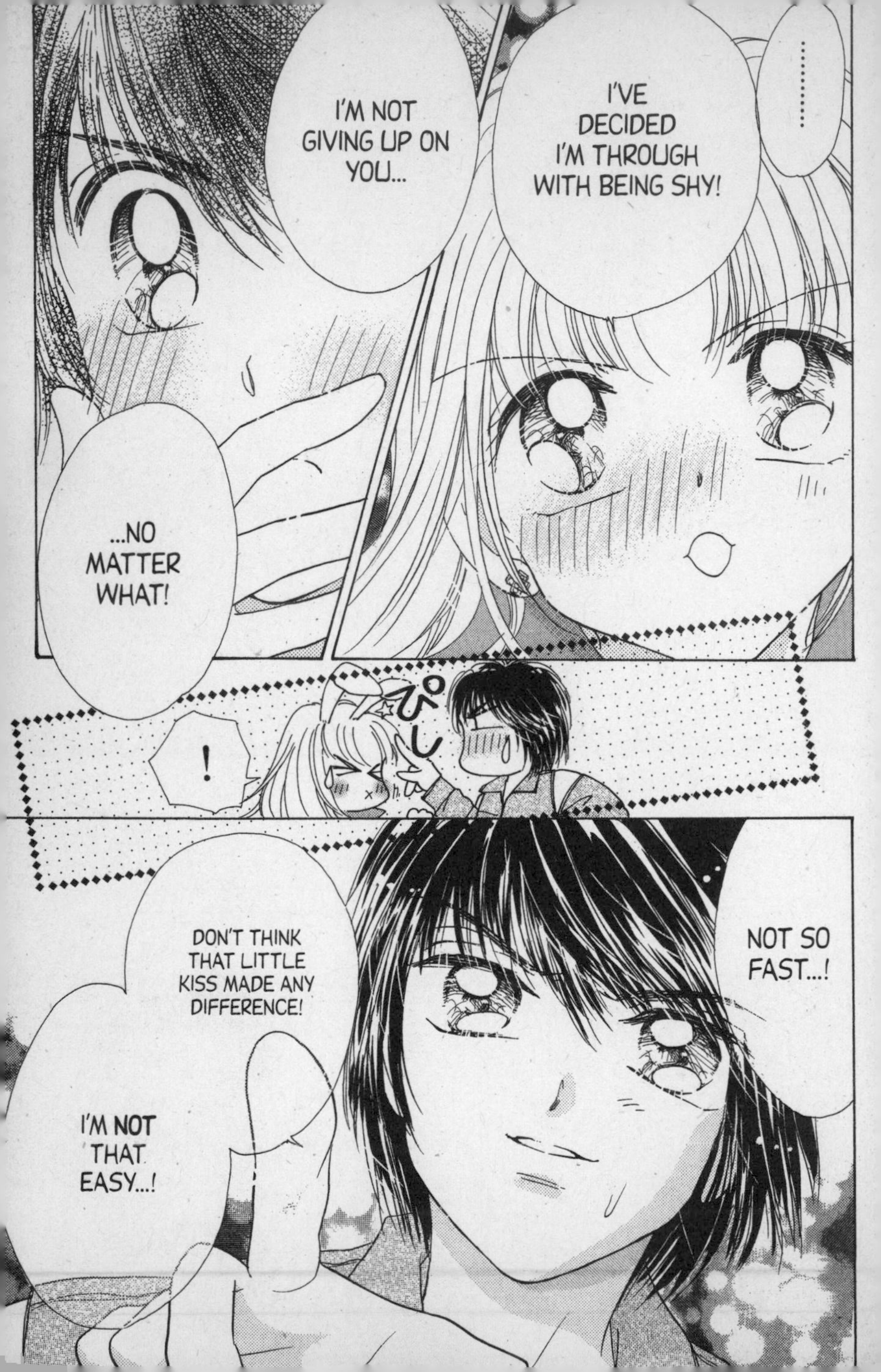

......
I'VE DECIDED I'M THROUGH WITH BEING SHY!
I'M NOT GIVING UP ON YOU...
...NO MATTER WHAT!
ぴし
!
NOT SO FAST...!
DON'T THINK THAT LITTLE KISS MADE ANY DIFFERENCE!
I'M NOT THAT EASY...!

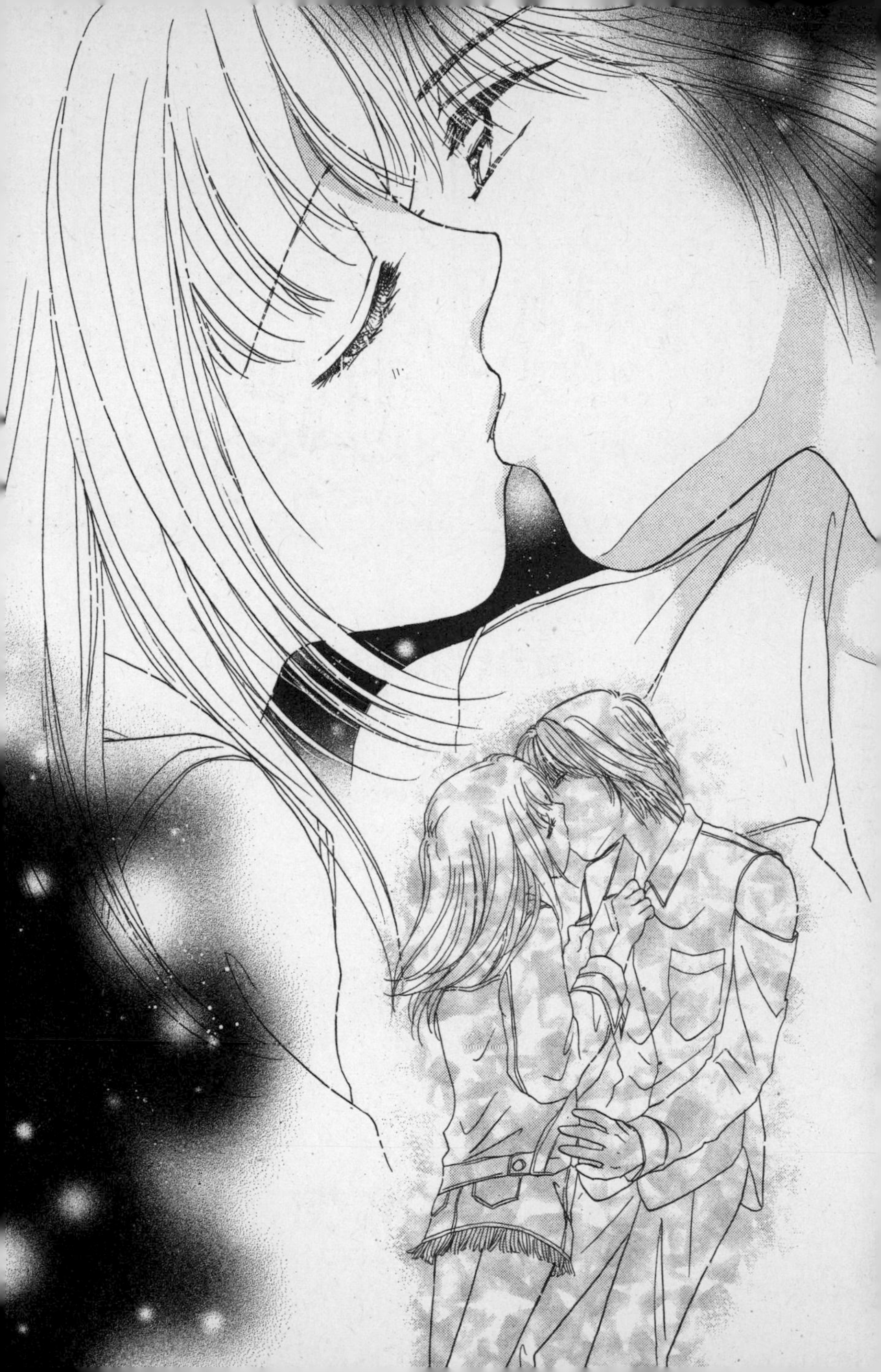

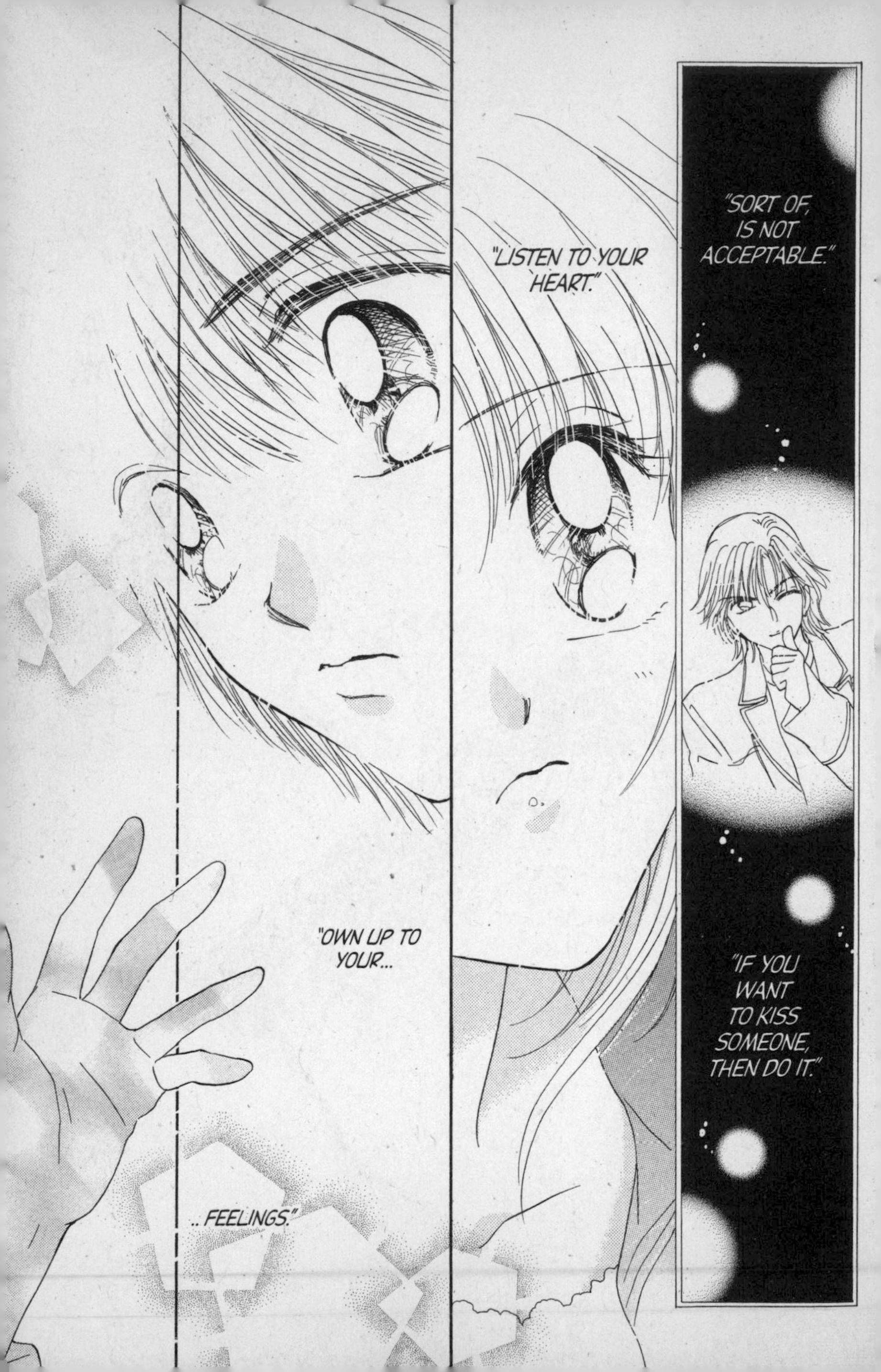
"SORT OF, IS NOT ACCEPTABLE."
"IF YOU WANT TO KISS SOMEONE, THEN DO IT."
"LISTEN TO YOUR HEART."
"OWN UP TO YOUR...
...FEELINGS."

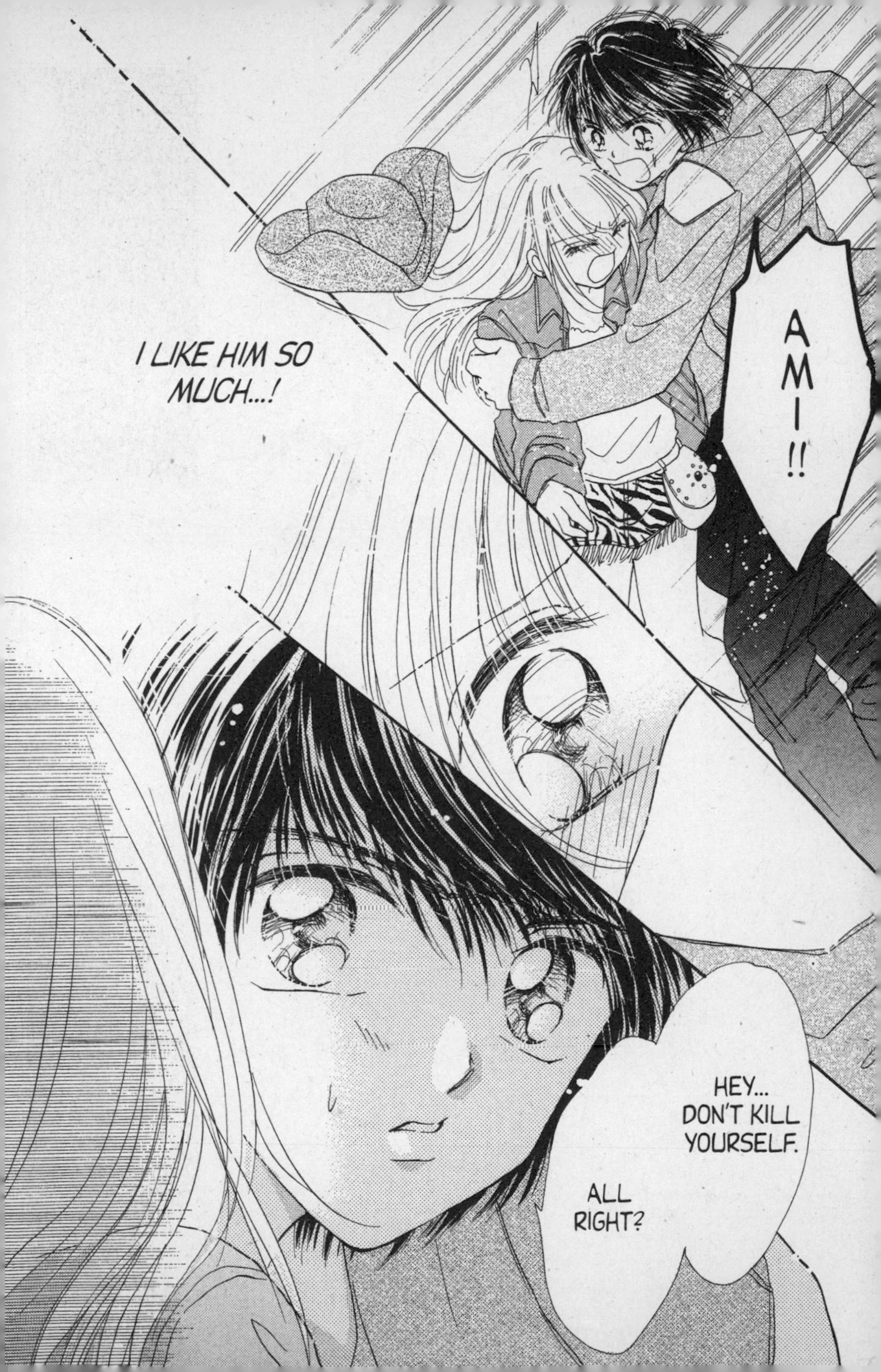
AMI!!
I LIKE HIM SO MUCH...!
HEY... DON'T KILL YOURSELF.
ALL RIGHT?

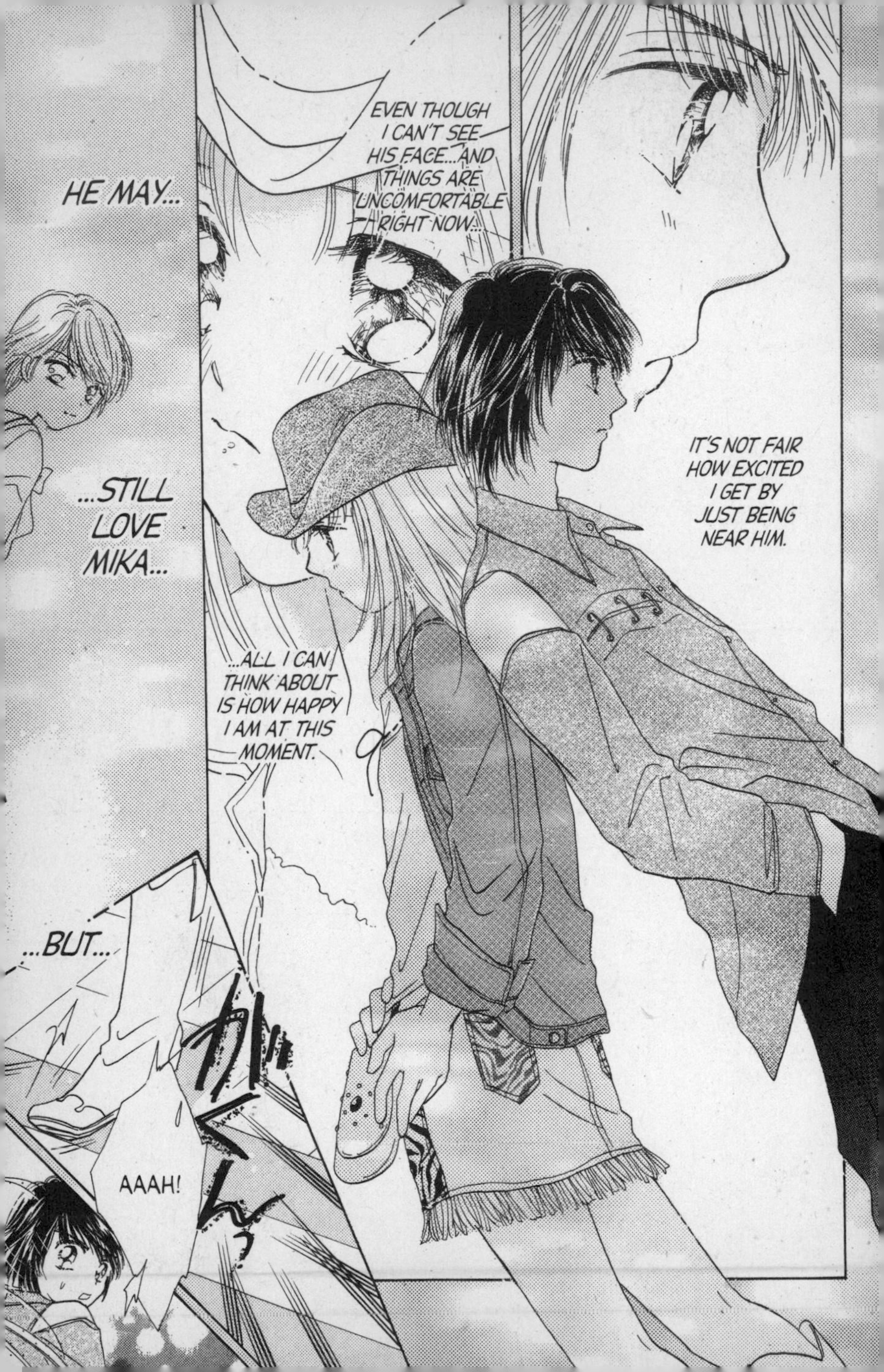
IT'S NOT FAIR HOW EXCITED I GET BY JUST BEING NEAR HIM.
EVEN THOUGH I CAN'T SEE HIS FACE...AND THINGS ARE UNCOMFORTABLE RIGHT NOW...
...ALL I CAN THINK ABOUT IS HOW HAPPY I AM AT THIS MOMENT.
HE MAY...
...STILL LOVE MIKA...
...BUT...
AAAH!

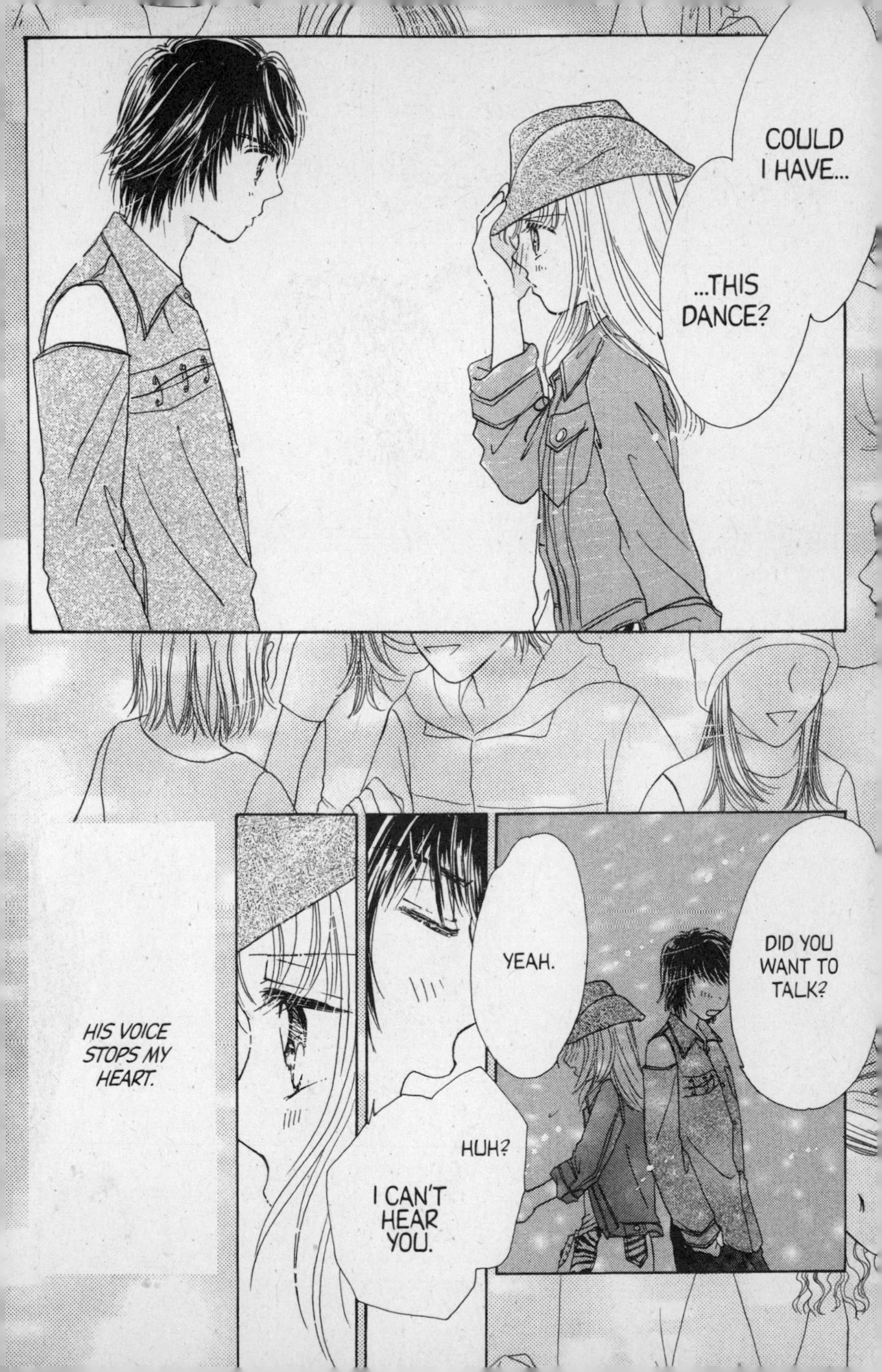
COULD I HAVE...
...THIS DANCE?
DID YOU WANT TO TALK?
YEAH.
HUH?
I CAN'T HEAR YOU.
HIS VOICE STOPS MY HEART.

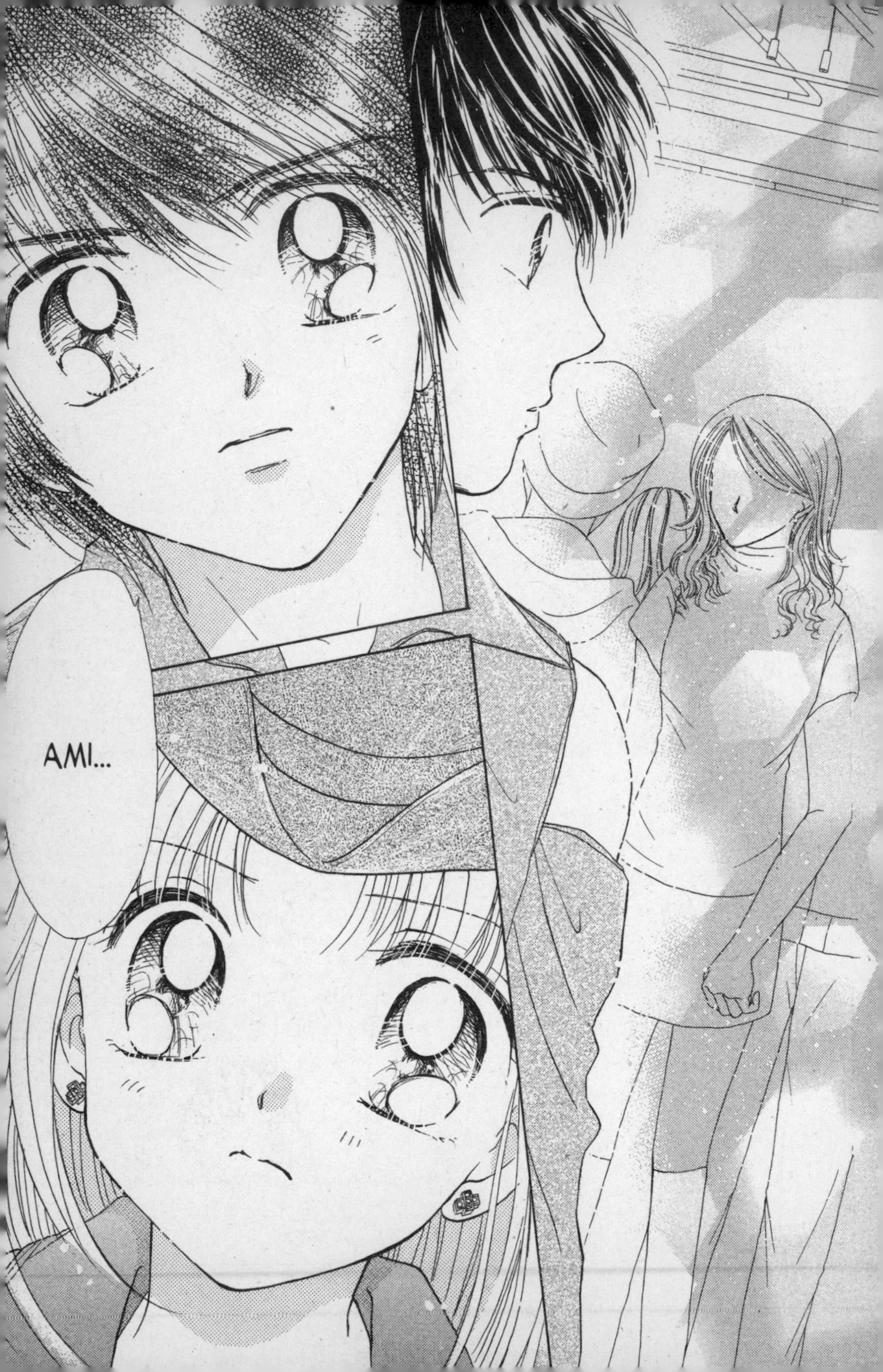
AMI...

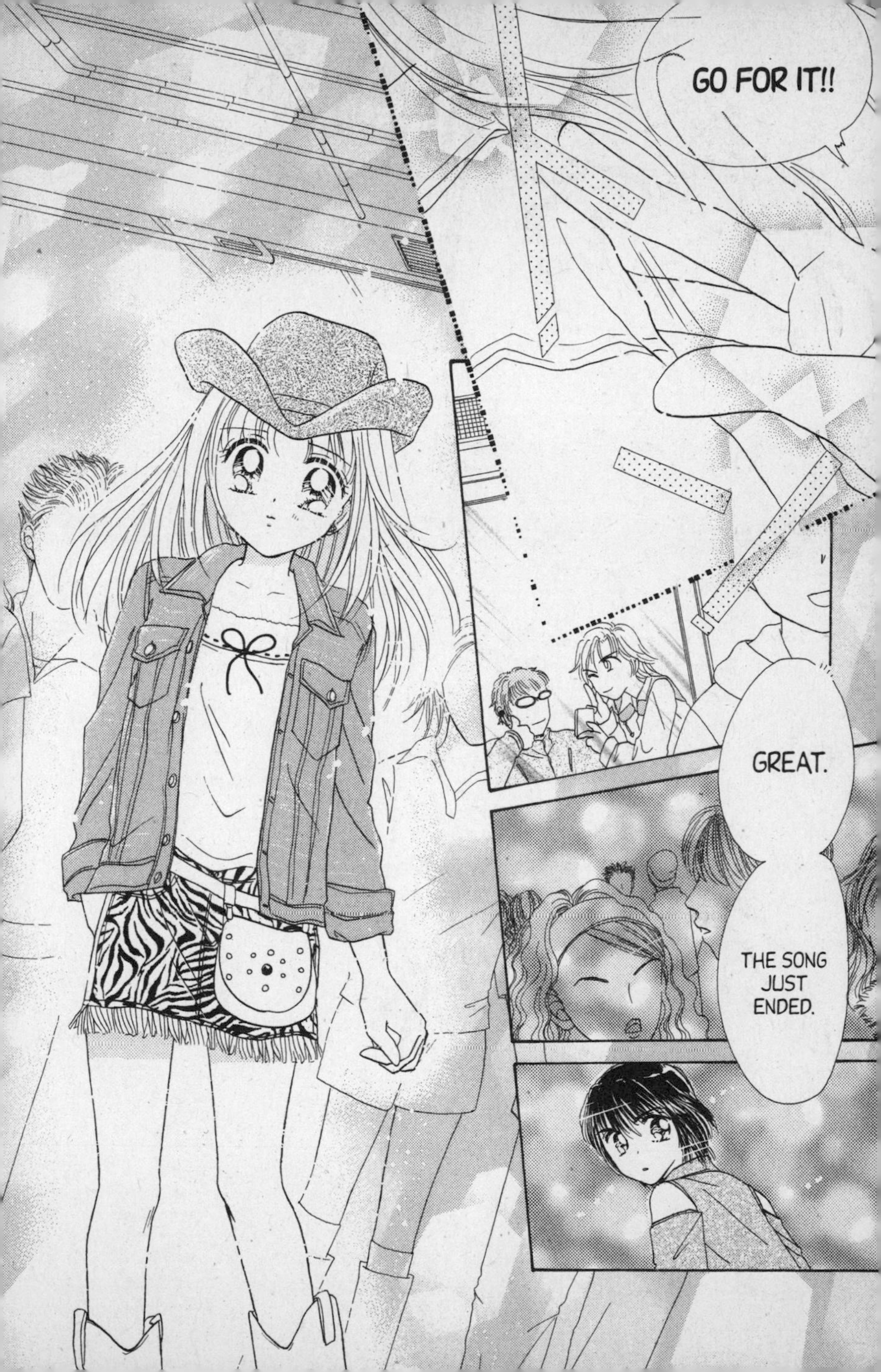
GO FOR IT!!
GREAT.
THE SONG JUST ENDED.

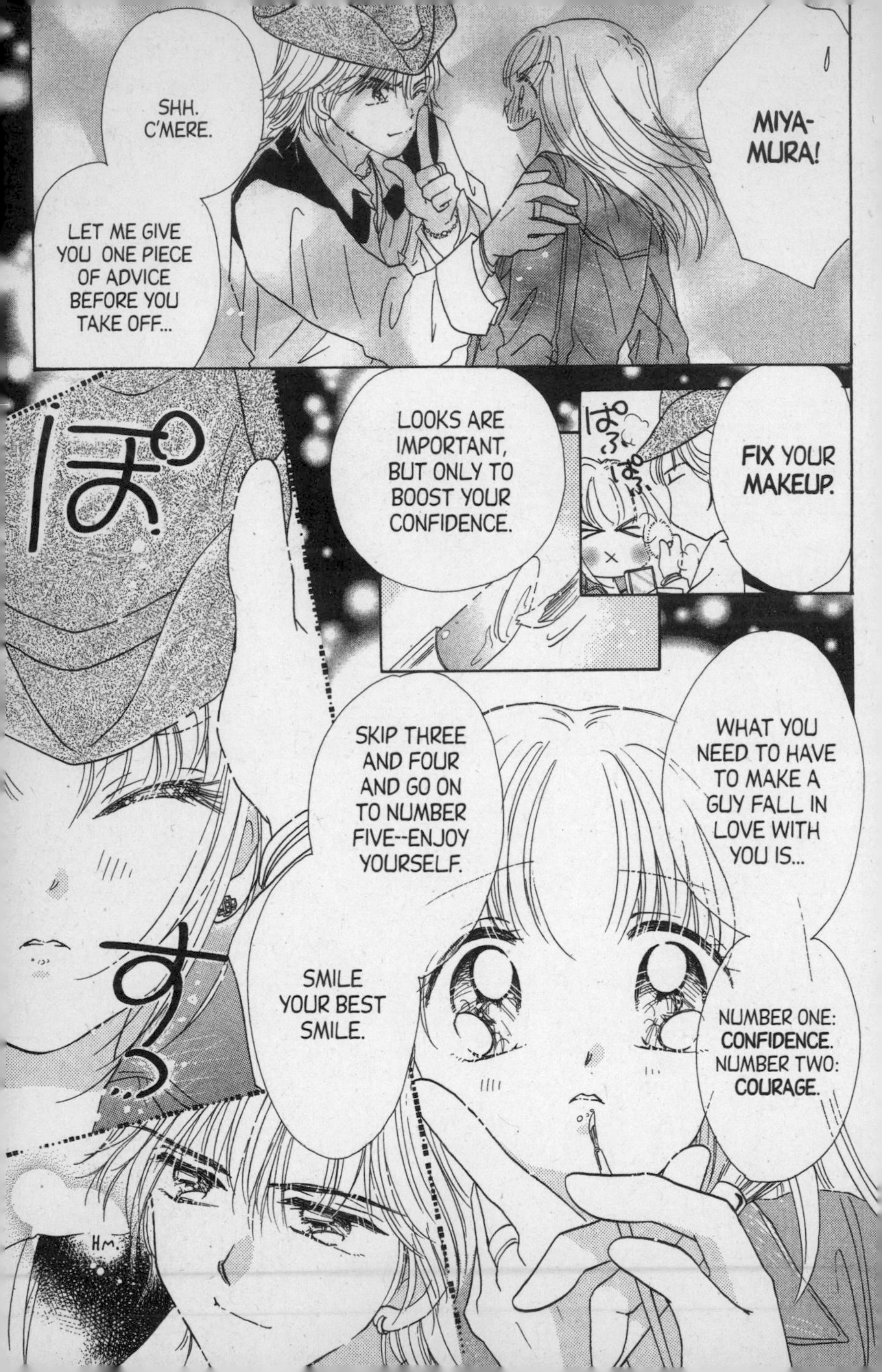
MIYA-MURA!
SHH. C'MERE.
LET ME GIVE YOU ONE PIECE OF ADVICE BEFORE YOU TAKE OFF...
FIX YOUR MAKEUP.
ぱふ ぱふ
LOOKS ARE IMPORTANT, BUT ONLY TO BOOST YOUR CONFIDENCE.
ぽ
WHAT YOU NEED TO HAVE TO MAKE A GUY FALL IN LOVE WITH YOU IS...
NUMBER ONE: CONFIDENCE. NUMBER TWO: COURAGE.
SKIP THREE AND FOUR AND GO ON TO NUMBER FIVE--ENJOY YOURSELF.
SMILE YOUR BEST SMILE.
すっ
HM.

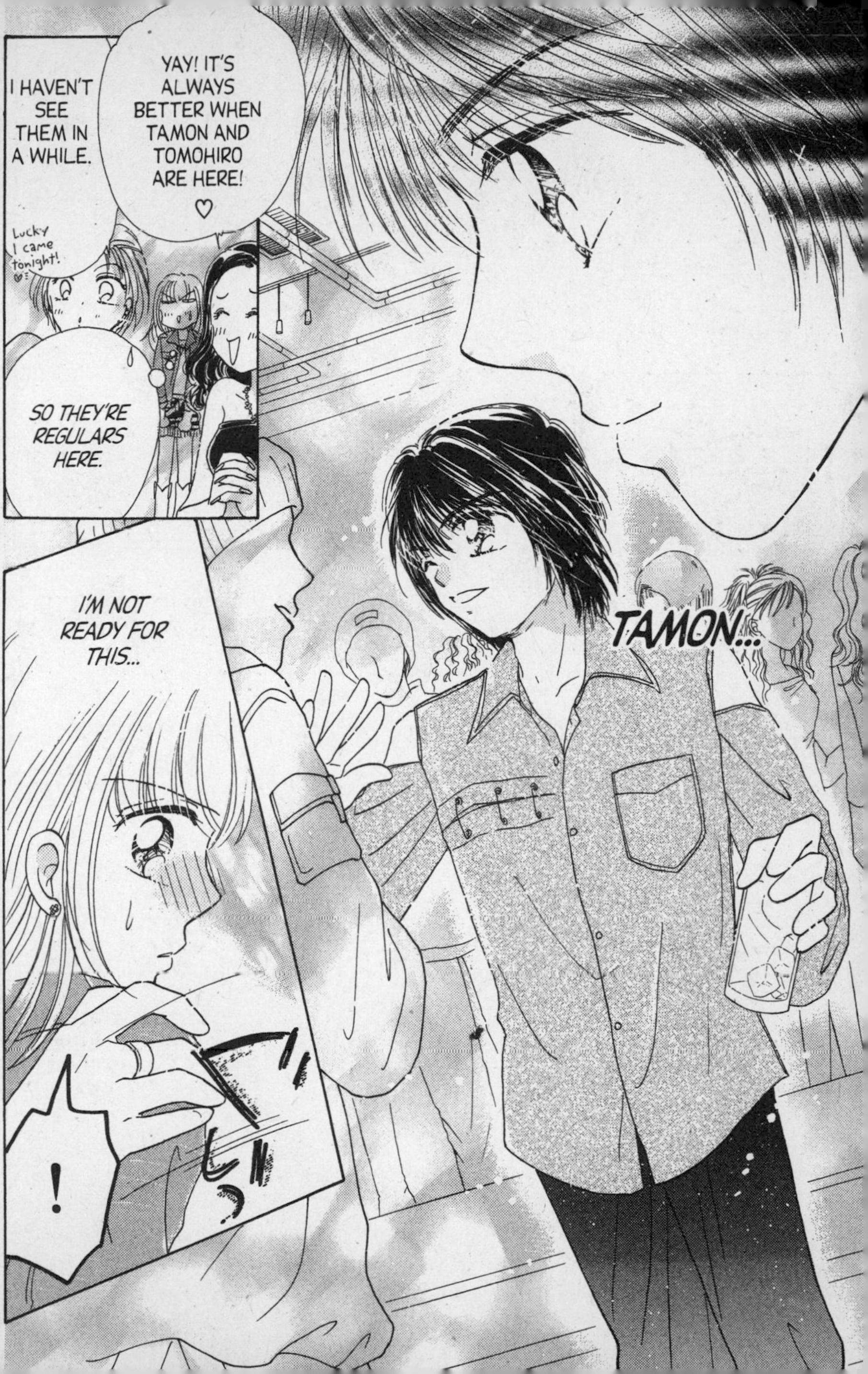
TAMON...
YAY! IT'S ALWAYS BETTER WHEN TAMON AND TOMOHIRO ARE HERE! ♡
I HAVEN'T SEE THEM IN A WHILE.
Lucky I came tonight!
SO THEY'RE REGULARS HERE.
I'M NOT READY FOR THIS...
!

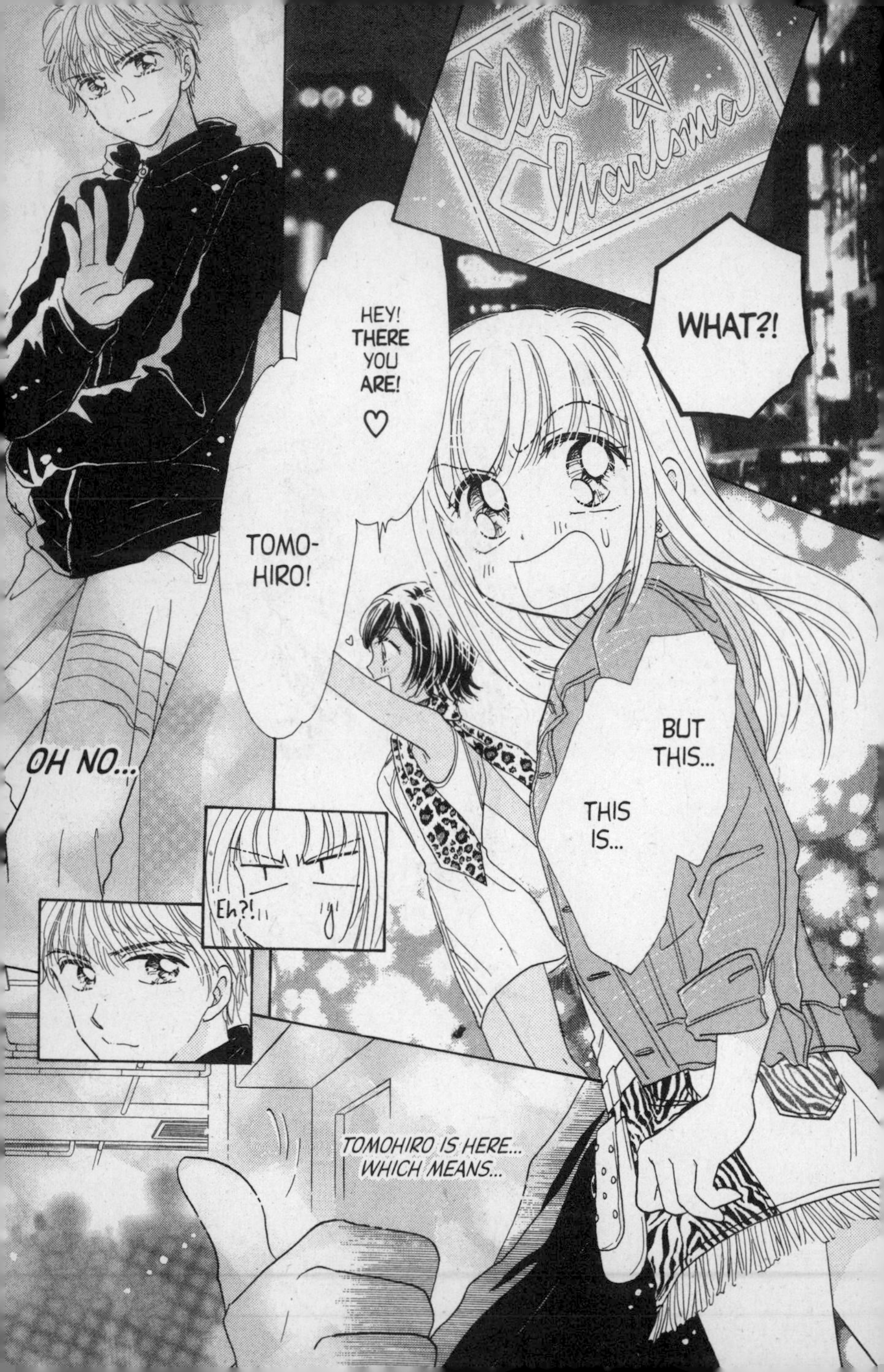
Club Charisma
WHAT?!
HEY! THERE YOU ARE! ♡
TOMO-HIRO!
BUT THIS...
THIS IS...
OH NO...
Eh?!
TOMOHIRO IS HERE... WHICH MEANS...

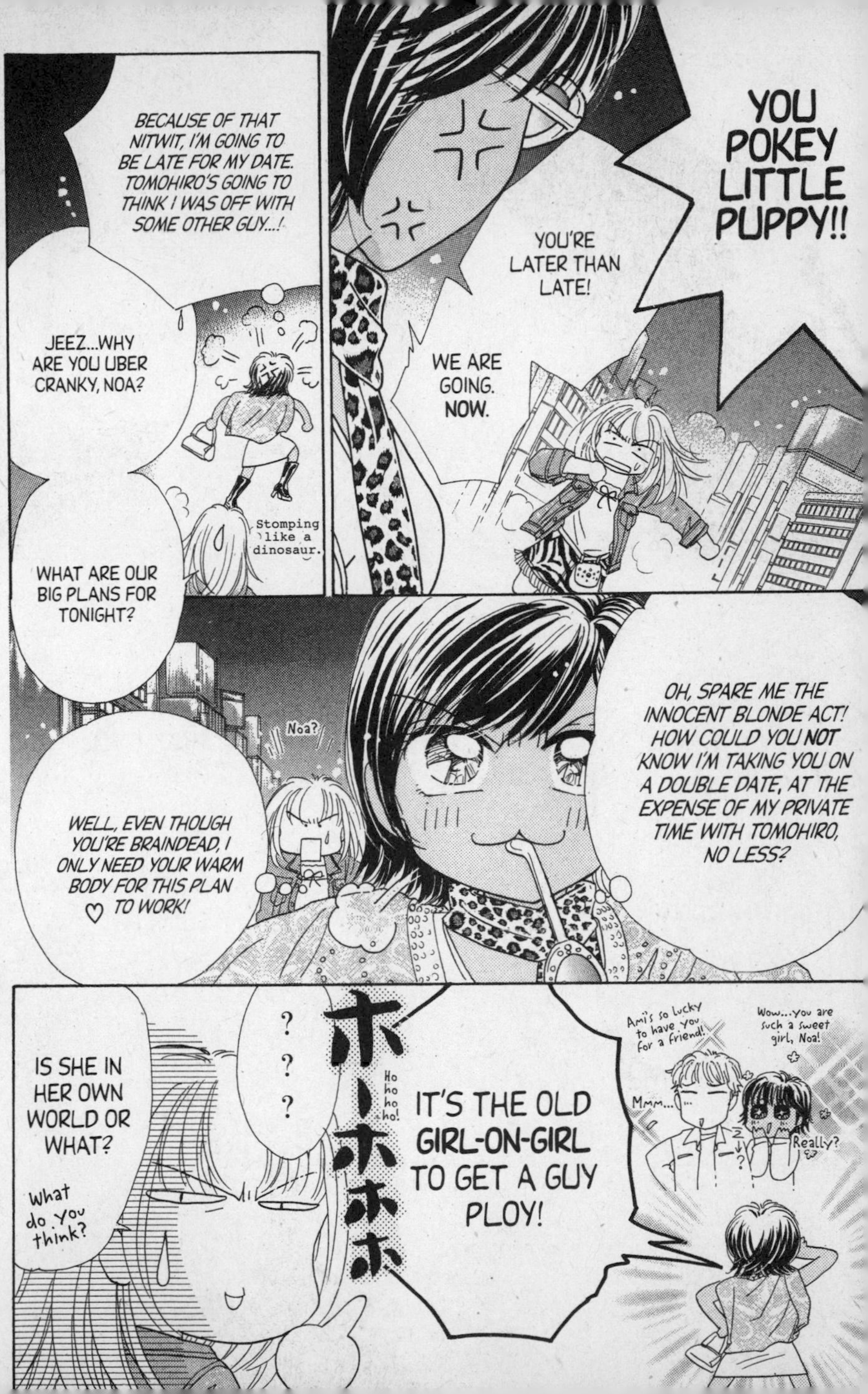
YOU POKEY LITTLE PUPPY!!
YOU'RE LATER THAN LATE!
WE ARE GOING. NOW.
BECAUSE OF THAT NITWIT, I'M GOING TO BE LATE FOR MY DATE. TOMOHIRO'S GOING TO THINK I WAS OFF WITH SOME OTHER GUY...!
JEEZ...WHY ARE YOU UBER CRANKY, NOA?
Stomping like a dinosaur.
WHAT ARE OUR BIG PLANS FOR TONIGHT?
OH, SPARE ME THE INNOCENT BLONDE ACT! HOW COULD YOU NOT KNOW I'M TAKING YOU ON A DOUBLE DATE, AT THE EXPENSE OF MY PRIVATE TIME WITH TOMOHIRO, NO LESS?
Noa?
WELL, EVEN THOUGH YOU'RE BRAINDEAD, I ONLY NEED YOUR WARM BODY FOR THIS PLAN TO WORK! ♡
Wow...You are such a sweet girl, Noa!
Ami's so lucky to have you for a friend!
Mmm...
Really?
IT'S THE OLD GIRL-ON-GIRL TO GET A GUY PLOY!
Ho ho ho ho!
ホーホホホ
???
IS SHE IN HER OWN WORLD OR WHAT?
What do you think?

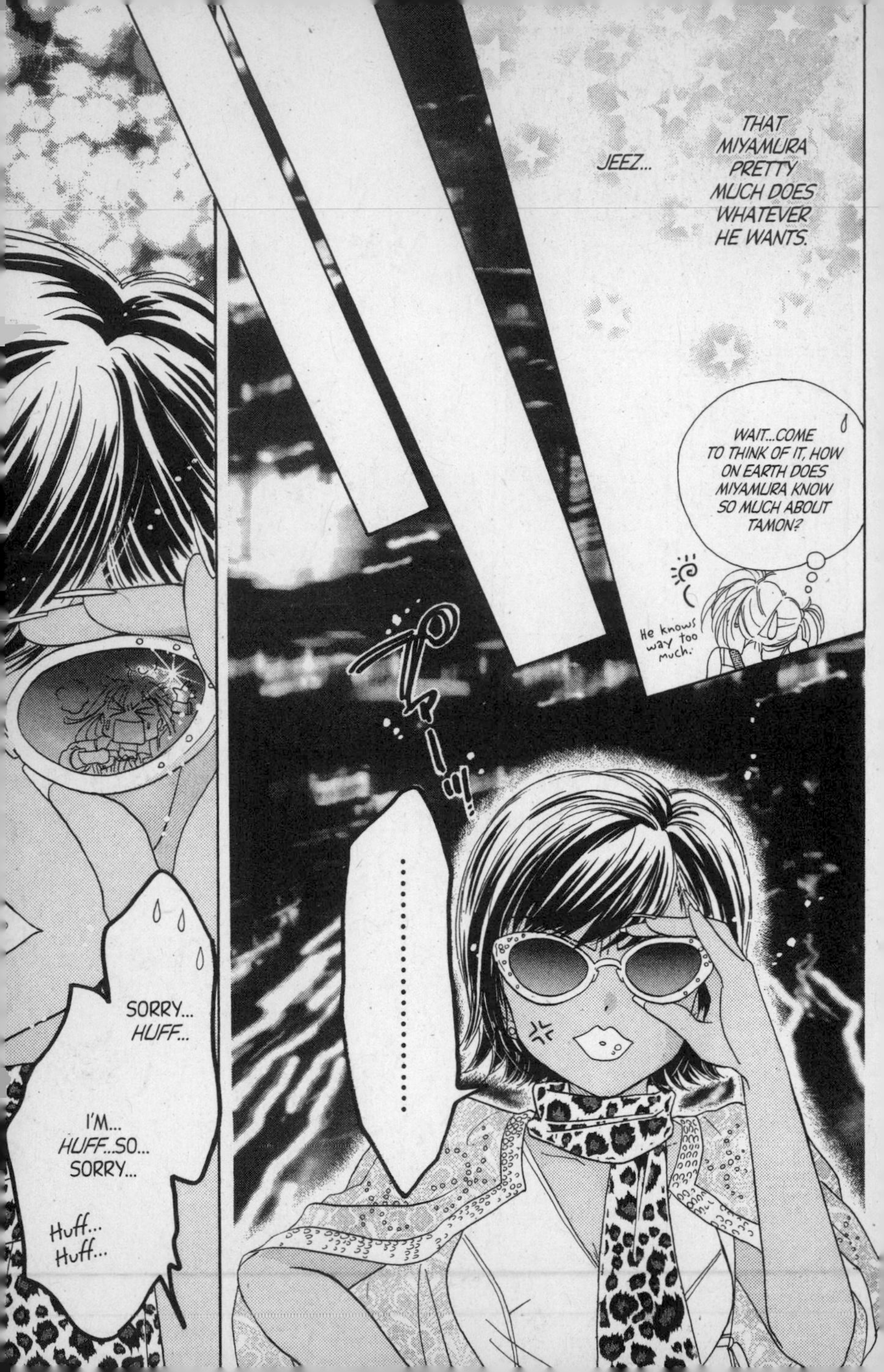
THAT MIYAMURA PRETTY MUCH DOES WHATEVER HE WANTS.
JEEZ...
WAIT...COME TO THINK OF IT, HOW ON EARTH DOES MIYAMURA KNOW SO MUCH ABOUT TAMON?
He knows way too much.
......
SORRY... HUFF...
I'M... HUFF...SO... SORRY...
Huff... Huff...

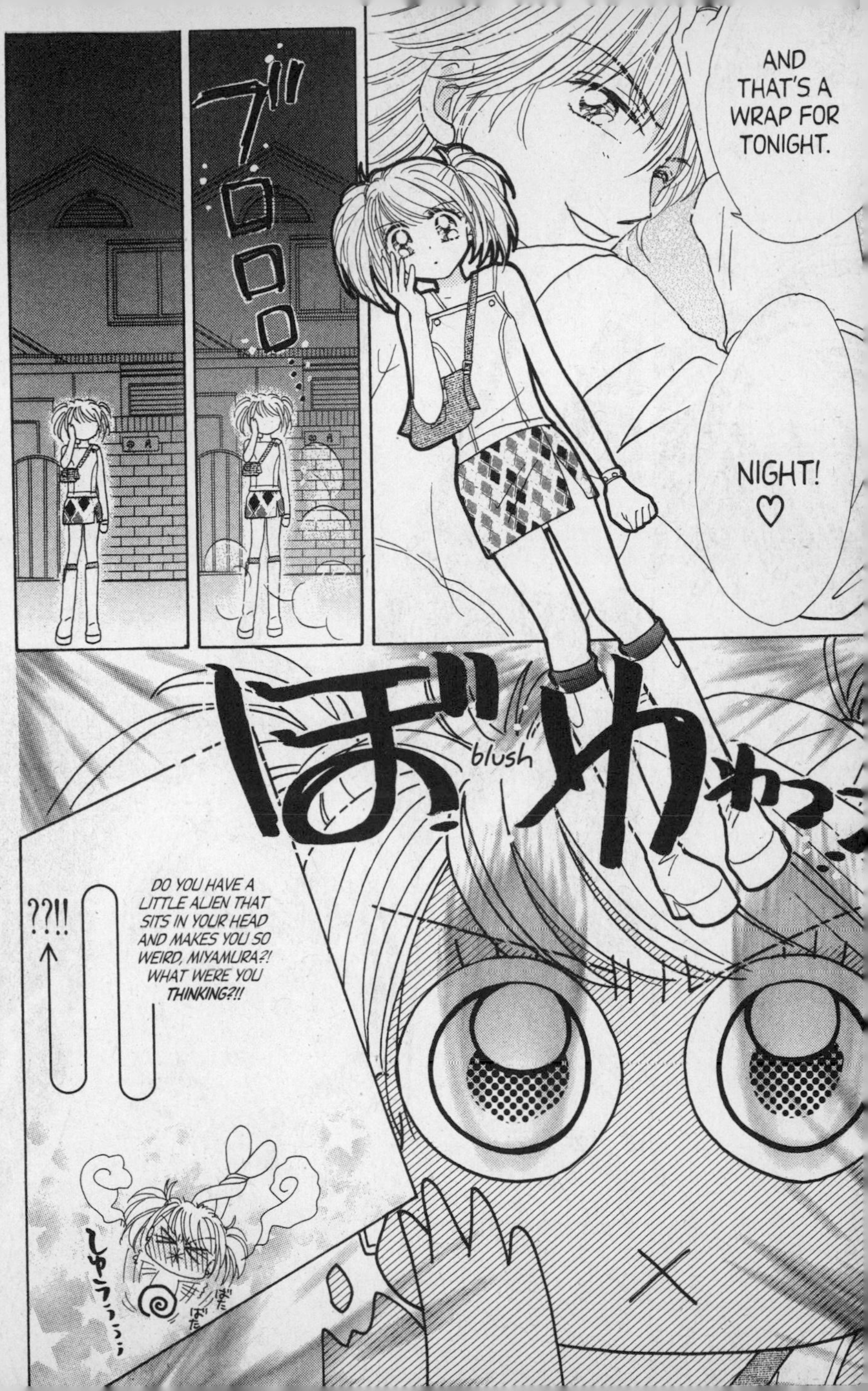
AND THAT'S A WRAP FOR TONIGHT.
NIGHT! ♡
ブロロロロ
ぽわっ
blush
DO YOU HAVE A LITTLE ALIEN THAT SITS IN YOUR HEAD AND MAKES YOU SO WEIRD, MIYAMURA?! WHAT WERE YOU THINKING?!!
??!!
ばた ばた
しゅ〜〜〜

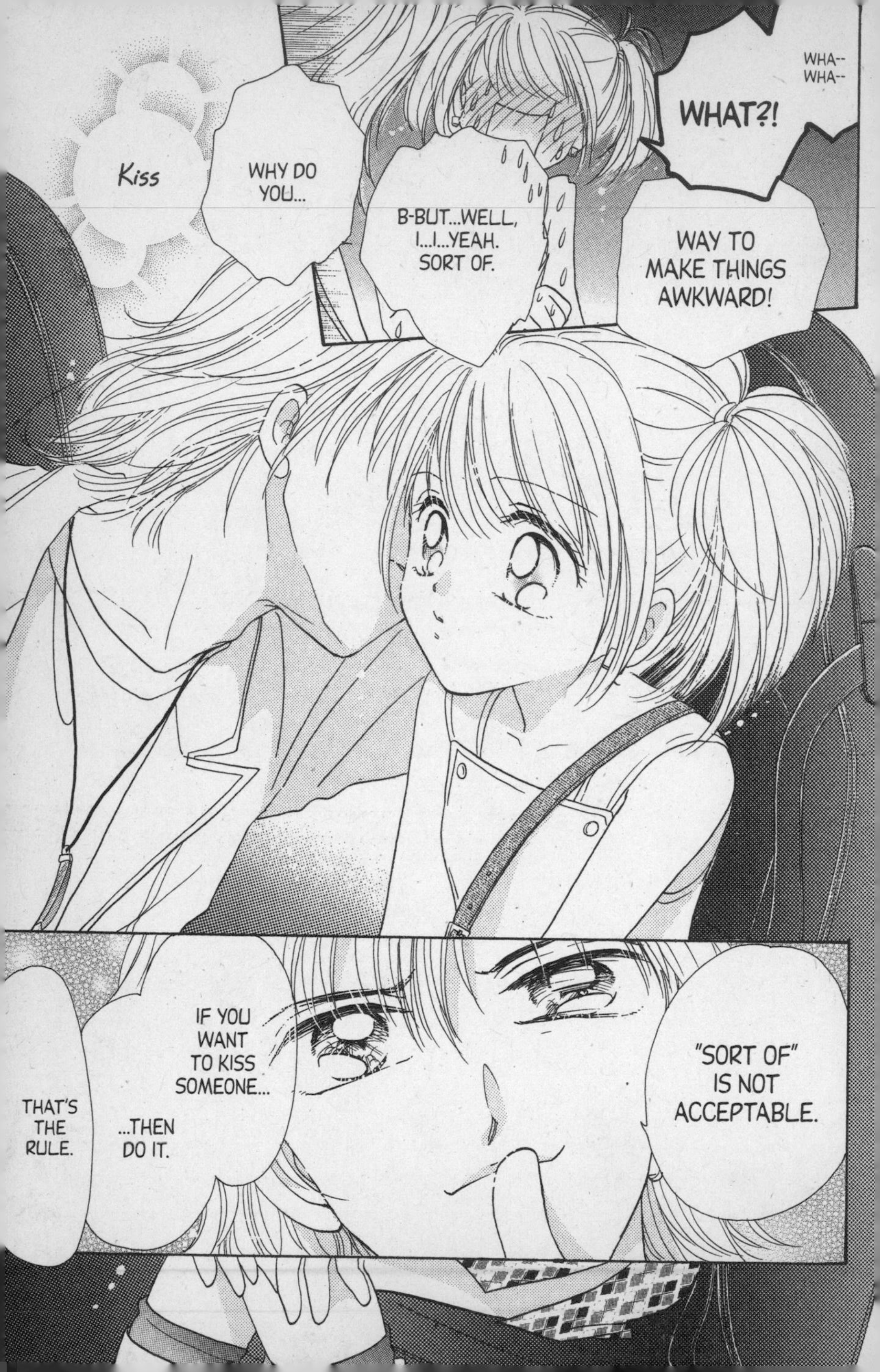
WHA-- WHA--
WHAT?!
WAY TO MAKE THINGS AWKWARD!
B-BUT...WELL, I...I...YEAH. SORT OF.
WHY DO YOU...
Kiss
"SORT OF" IS NOT ACCEPTABLE.
IF YOU WANT TO KISS SOMEONE...
...THEN DO IT.
THAT'S THE RULE.

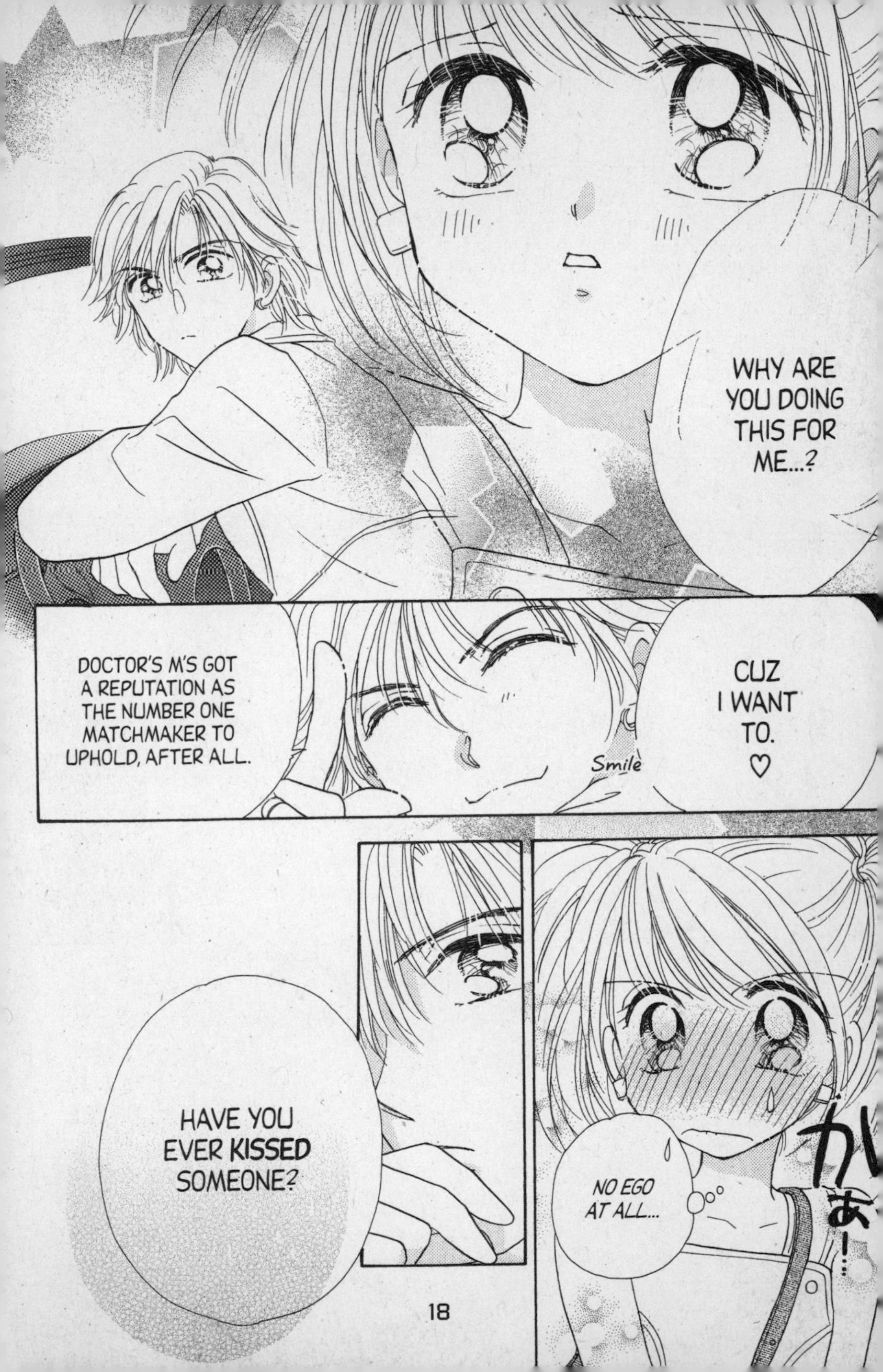
WHY ARE YOU DOING THIS FOR ME...?
CUZ I WANT TO. ♡
Smile
DOCTOR'S M'S GOT A REPUTATION AS THE NUMBER ONE MATCHMAKER TO UPHOLD, AFTER ALL.
かぁー…
NO EGO AT ALL...
HAVE YOU EVER **KISSED** SOMEONE?

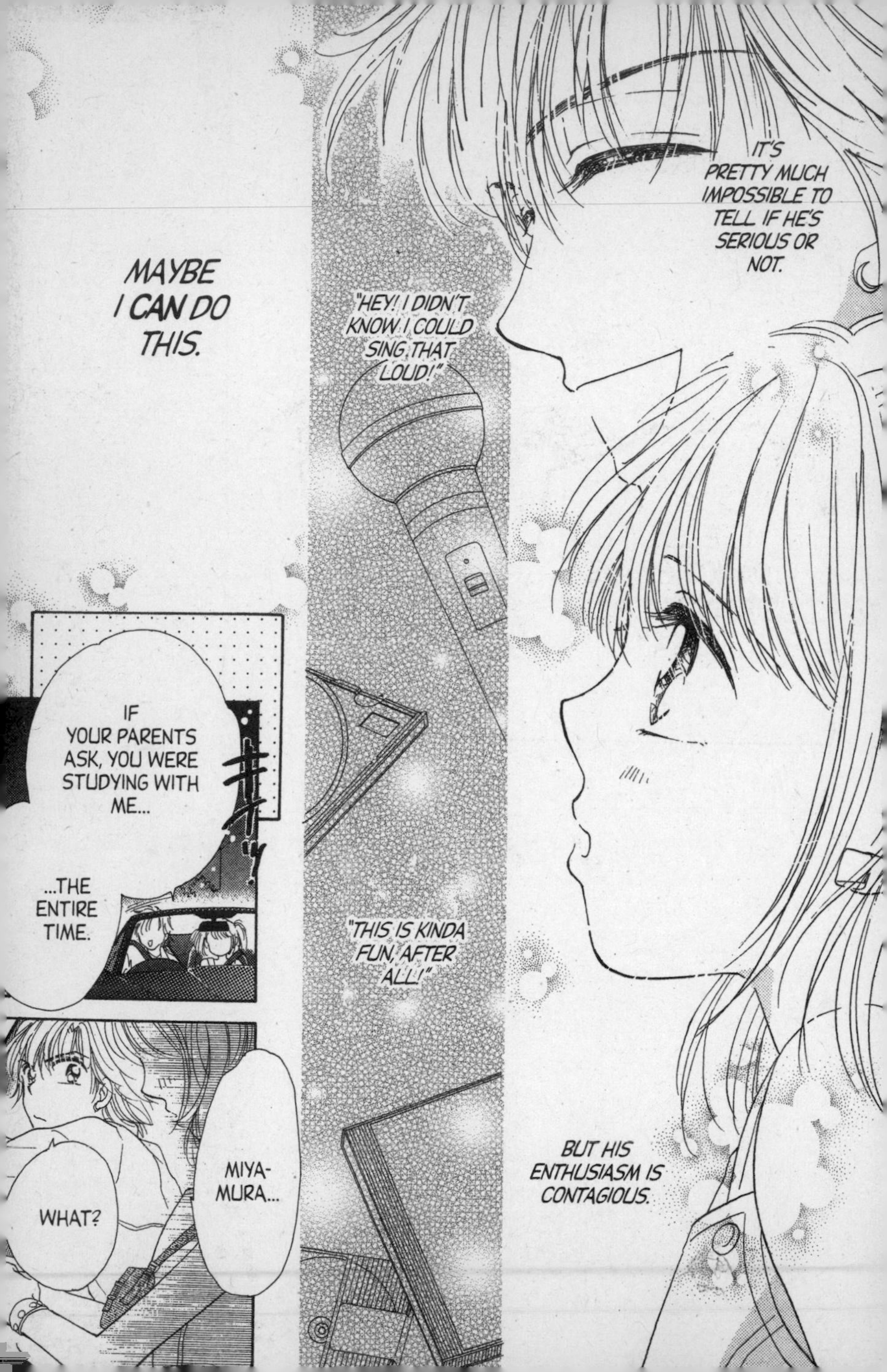
IT'S PRETTY MUCH IMPOSSIBLE TO TELL IF HE'S SERIOUS OR NOT.
BUT HIS ENTHUSIASM IS CONTAGIOUS.
"HEY! I DIDN'T KNOW I COULD SING THAT LOUD!"
"THIS IS KINDA FUN, AFTER ALL!"
MAYBE I CAN DO THIS.
IF YOUR PARENTS ASK, YOU WERE STUDYING WITH ME...
...THE ENTIRE TIME.
MIYA-MURA...
WHAT?

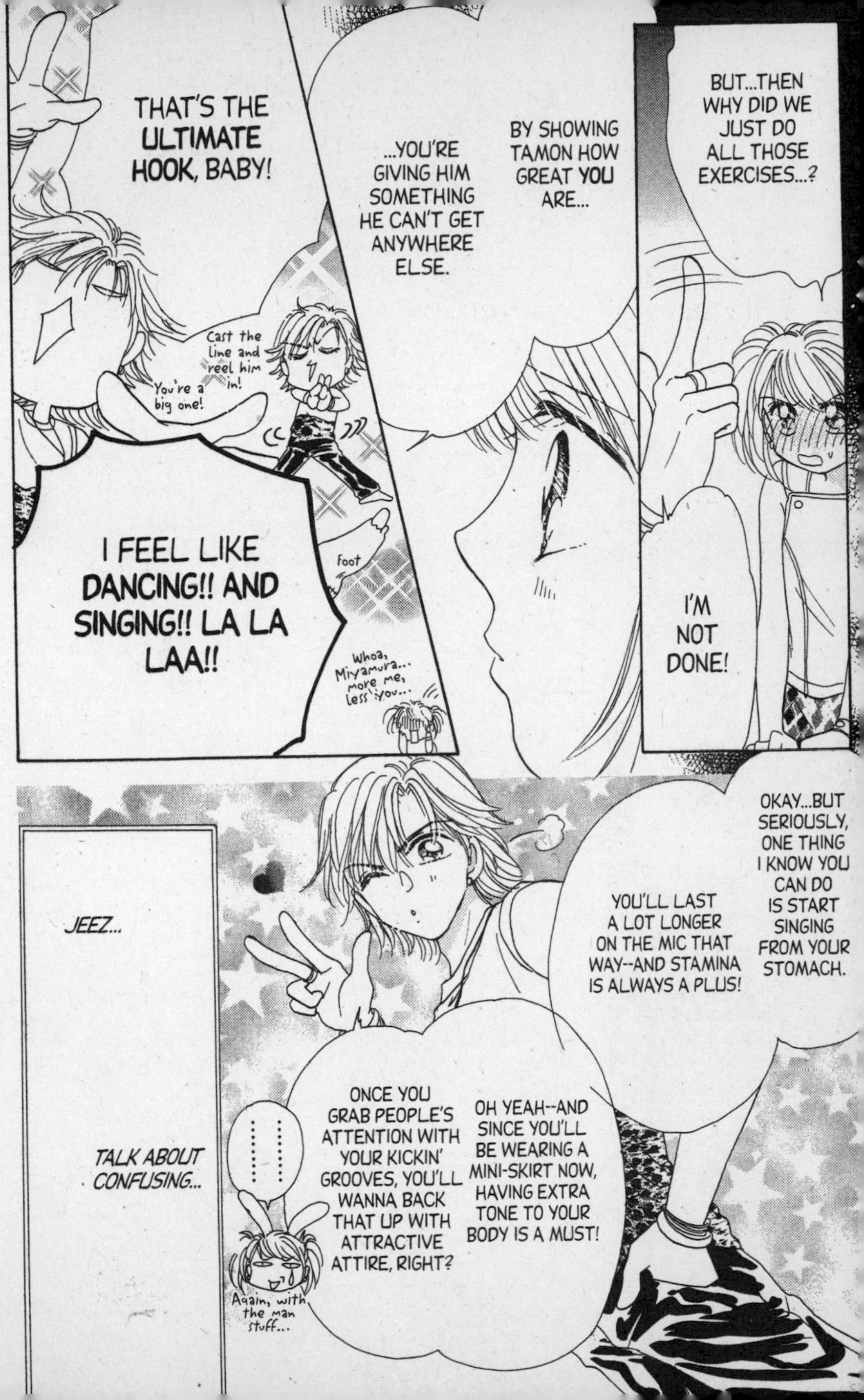
BUT...THEN WHY DID WE JUST DO ALL THOSE EXERCISES...?
I'M NOT DONE!
BY SHOWING TAMON HOW GREAT YOU ARE...
...YOU'RE GIVING HIM SOMETHING HE CAN'T GET ANYWHERE ELSE.
THAT'S THE ULTIMATE HOOK, BABY!
Cast the line and reel him in!
You're a big one!
I FEEL LIKE DANCING!! AND SINGING!! LA LA LAA!!
Foot
Whoa, Miyamura... more me, less you...
OKAY...BUT SERIOUSLY, ONE THING I KNOW YOU CAN DO IS START SINGING FROM YOUR STOMACH.
YOU'LL LAST A LOT LONGER ON THE MIC THAT WAY--AND STAMINA IS ALWAYS A PLUS!
OH YEAH--AND SINCE YOU'LL BE WEARING A MINI-SKIRT NOW, HAVING EXTRA TONE TO YOUR BODY IS A MUST!
ONCE YOU GRAB PEOPLE'S ATTENTION WITH YOUR KICKIN' GROOVES, YOU'LL WANNA BACK THAT UP WITH ATTRACTIVE ATTIRE, RIGHT?
......
Again, with the man stuff...
JEEZ...
TALK ABOUT CONFUSING...

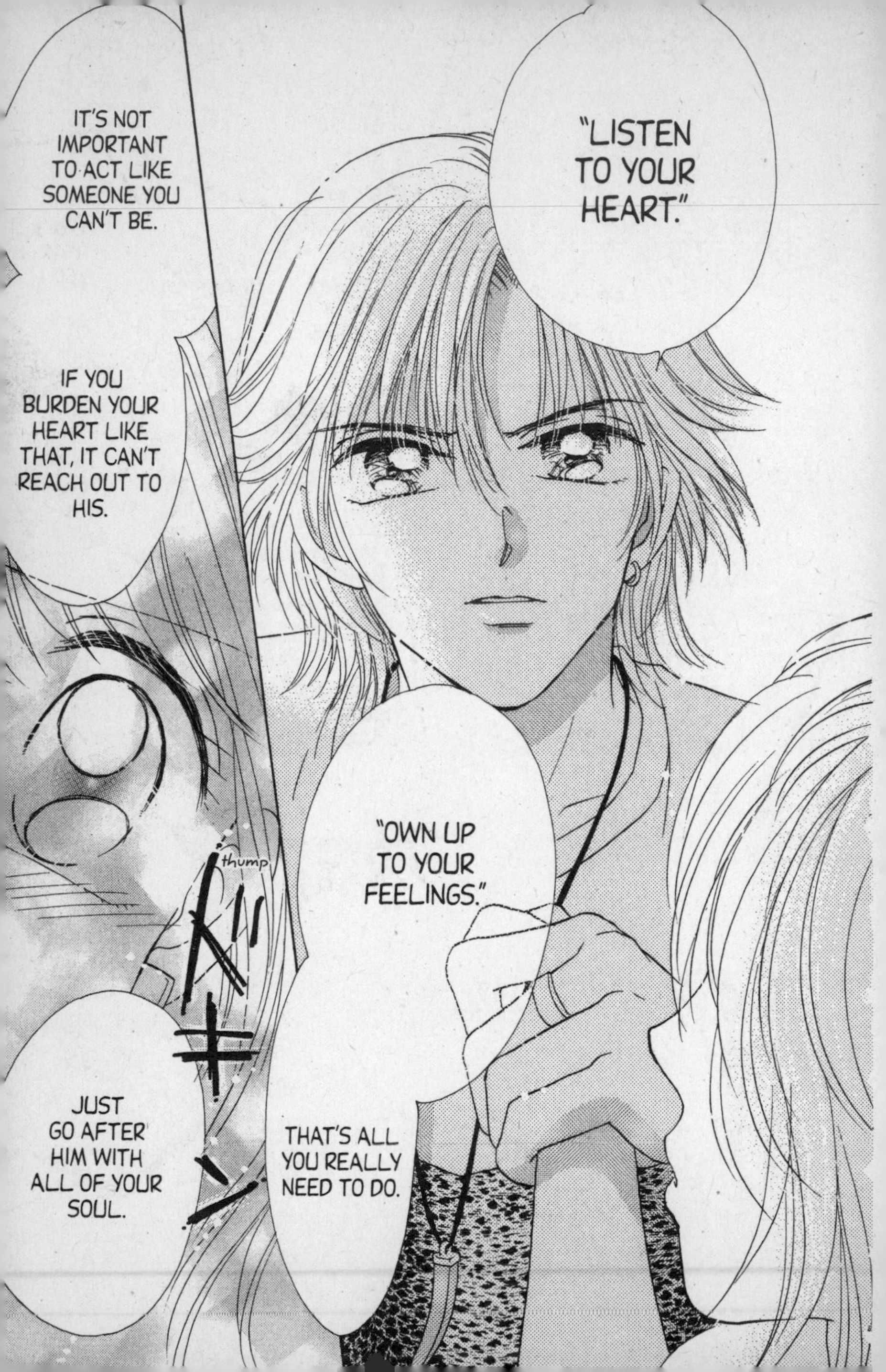
"LISTEN TO YOUR HEART."
"OWN UP TO YOUR FEELINGS."
THAT'S ALL YOU REALLY NEED TO DO.
IT'S NOT IMPORTANT TO ACT LIKE SOMEONE YOU CAN'T BE.
IF YOU BURDEN YOUR HEART LIKE THAT, IT CAN'T REACH OUT TO HIS.
thump
JUST GO AFTER HIM WITH ALL OF YOUR SOUL.

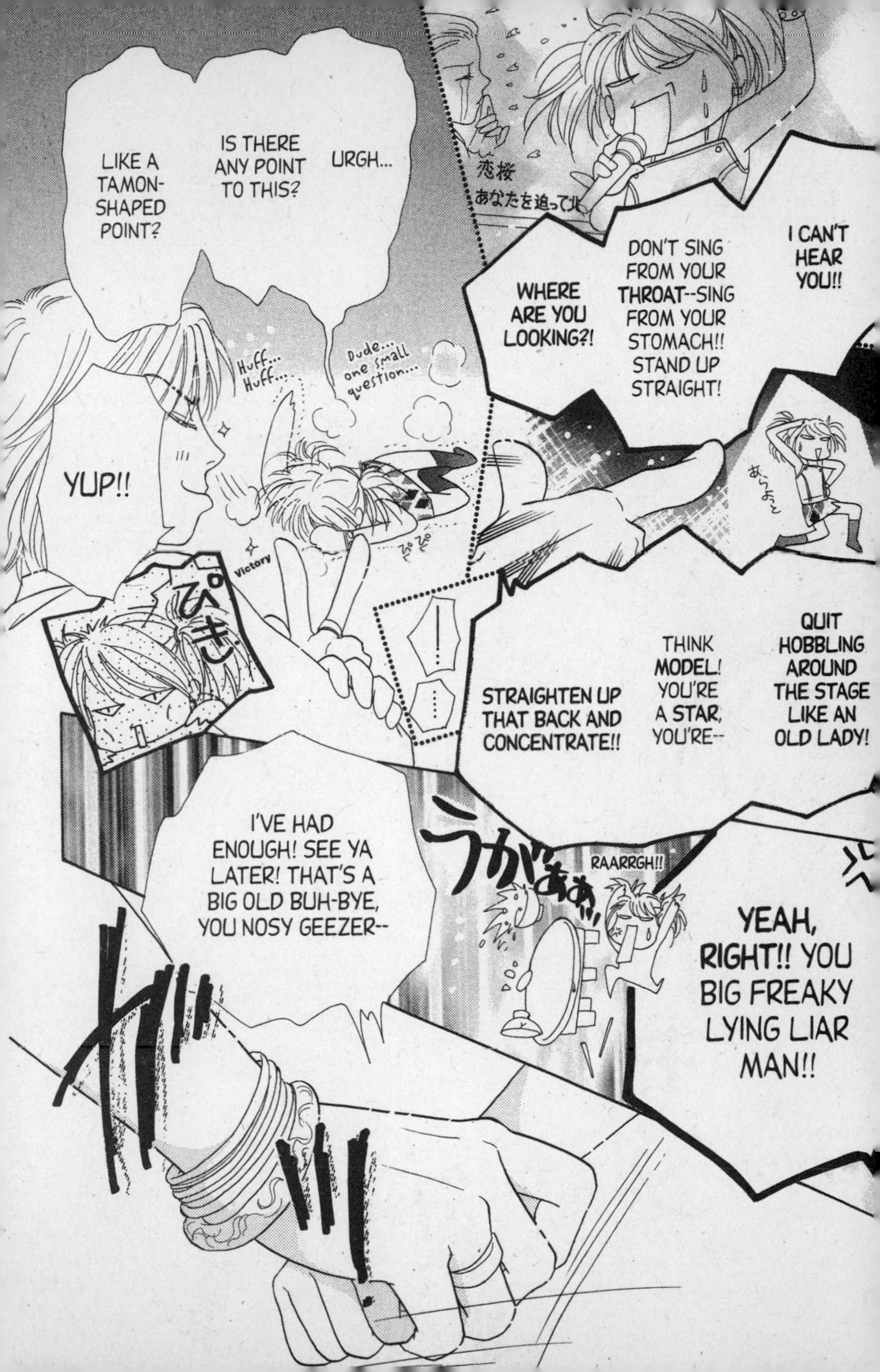
恋桜
あなたを追って
I CAN'T HEAR YOU!!
DON'T SING FROM YOUR THROAT--SING FROM YOUR STOMACH!! STAND UP STRAIGHT!
WHERE ARE YOU LOOKING?!
あらよっと
Huff... Huff...
Dude... one small question...
URGH...
IS THERE ANY POINT TO THIS?
LIKE A TAMON-SHAPED POINT?
YUP!!
Victory
ぴきっ
QUIT HOBBLING AROUND THE STAGE LIKE AN OLD LADY!
THINK MODEL! YOU'RE A STAR, YOU'RE--
STRAIGHTEN UP THAT BACK AND CONCENTRATE!!
!
……
YEAH, RIGHT!! YOU BIG FREAKY LYING LIAR MAN!!
うがぁあ
RAARRGH!!
I'VE HAD ENOUGH! SEE YA LATER! THAT'S A BIG OLD BUH-BYE, YOU NOSY GEEZER--

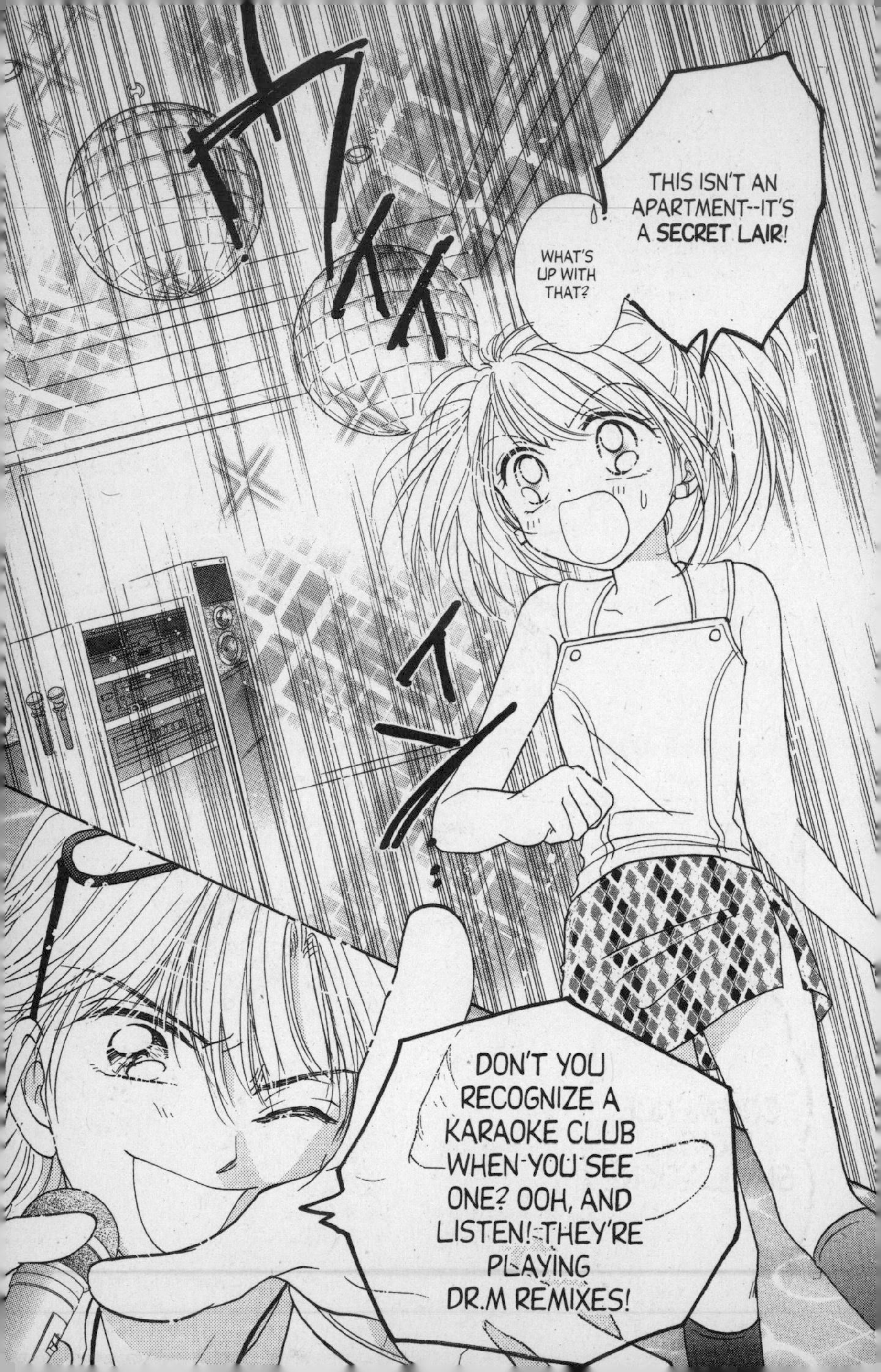
THIS ISN'T AN APARTMENT--IT'S A SECRET LAIR!
WHAT'S UP WITH THAT?
DON'T YOU RECOGNIZE A KARAOKE CLUB WHEN YOU SEE ONE? OOH, AND LISTEN! THEY'RE PLAYING DR.M REMIXES!

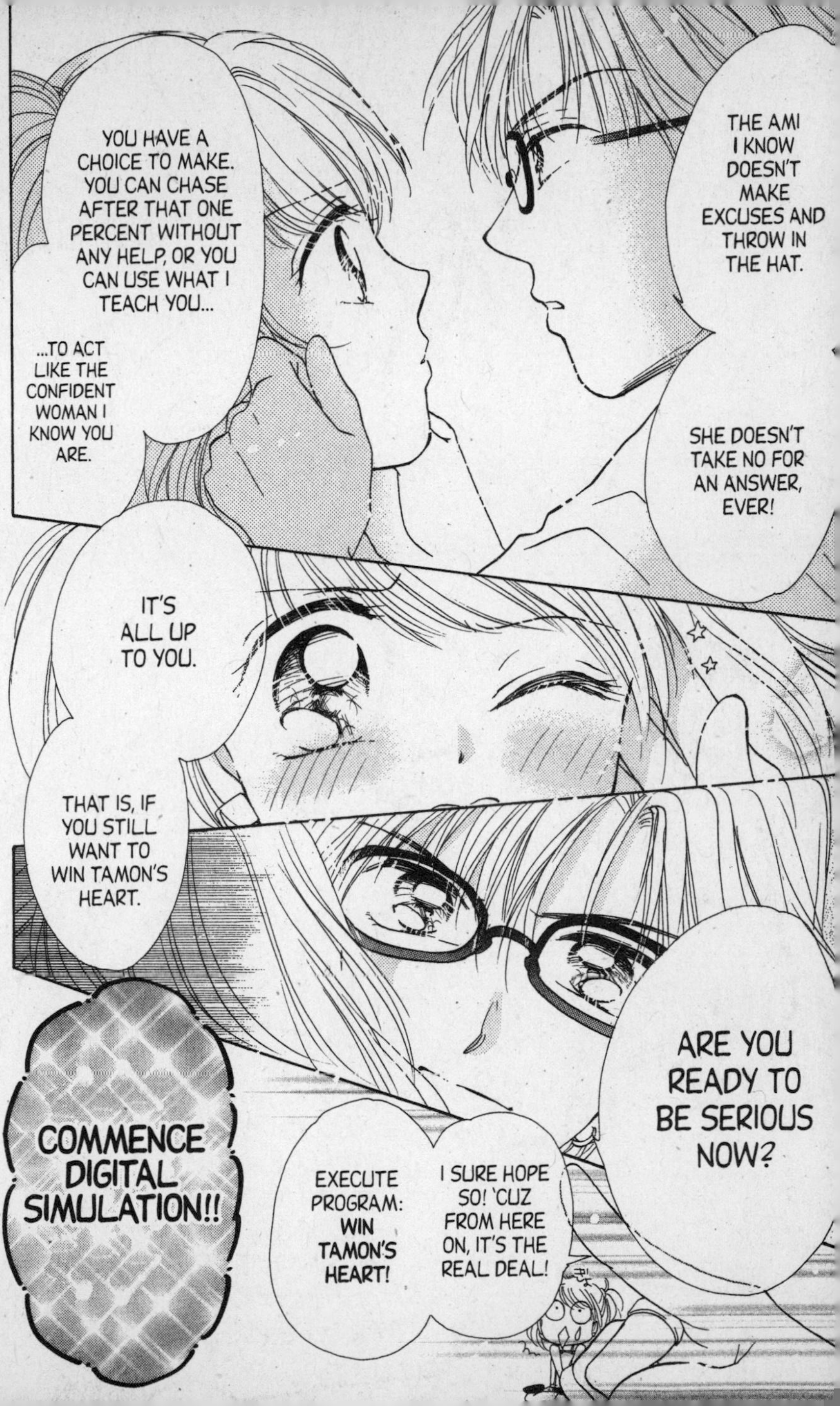
THE AMI I KNOW DOESN'T MAKE EXCUSES AND THROW IN THE HAT.
SHE DOESN'T TAKE NO FOR AN ANSWER, EVER!
YOU HAVE A CHOICE TO MAKE. YOU CAN CHASE AFTER THAT ONE PERCENT WITHOUT ANY HELP, OR YOU CAN USE WHAT I TEACH YOU...
...TO ACT LIKE THE CONFIDENT WOMAN I KNOW YOU ARE.
IT'S ALL UP TO YOU.
THAT IS, IF YOU STILL WANT TO WIN TAMON'S HEART.
ARE YOU READY TO BE SERIOUS NOW?
I SURE HOPE SO! 'CUZ FROM HERE ON, IT'S THE REAL DEAL!
EXECUTE PROGRAM: WIN TAMON'S HEART!
COMMENCE DIGITAL SIMULATION!!

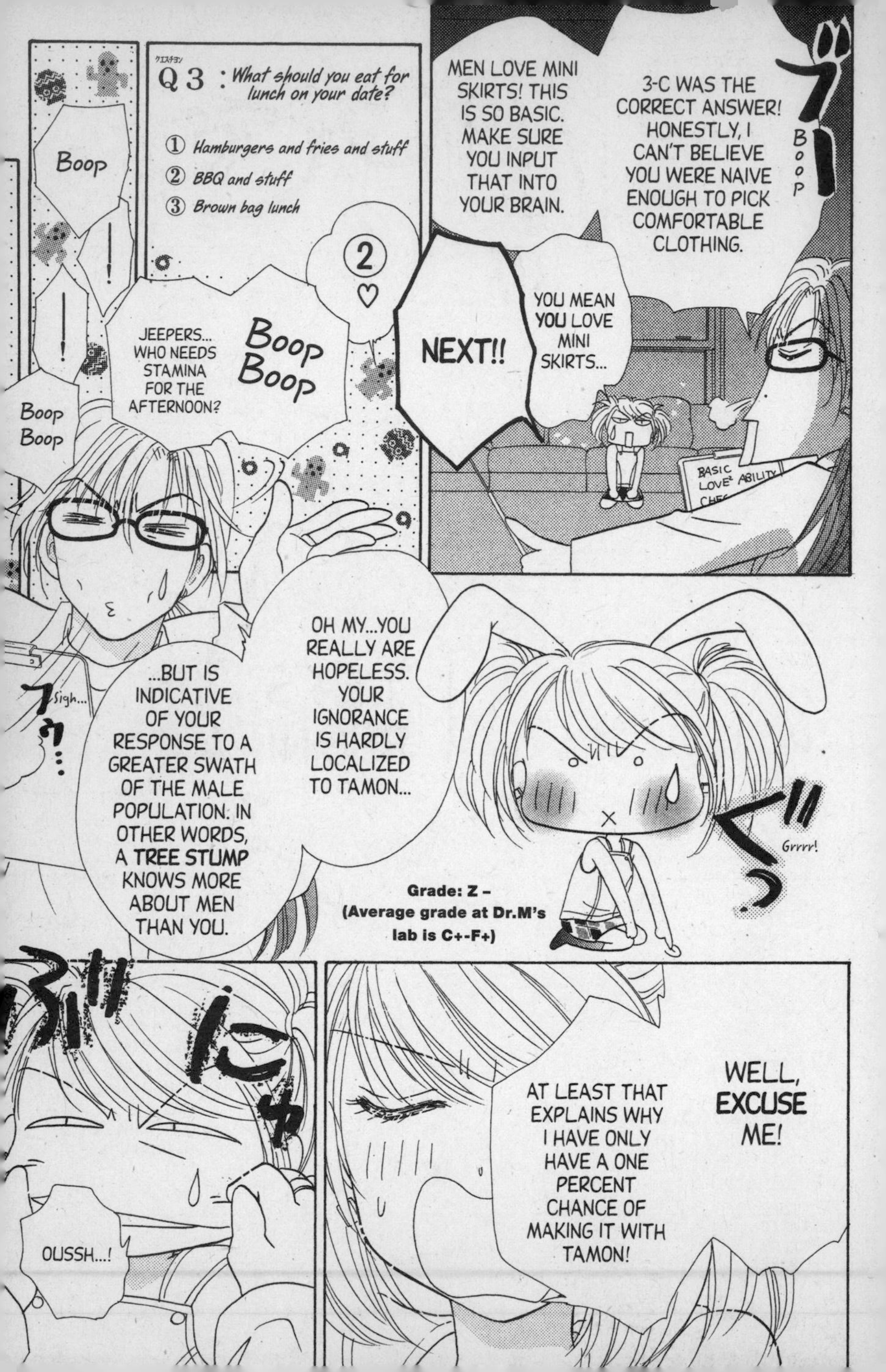

Boop
3-C WAS THE CORRECT ANSWER! HONESTLY, I CAN'T BELIEVE YOU WERE NAIVE ENOUGH TO PICK COMFORTABLE CLOTHING.
MEN LOVE MINI SKIRTS! THIS IS SO BASIC. MAKE SURE YOU INPUT THAT INTO YOUR BRAIN.
YOU MEAN **YOU** LOVE MINI SKIRTS...
NEXT!!
BASIC LOVE² ABILITY
Q3: What should you eat for lunch on your date?
① Hamburgers and fries and stuff
② BBQ and stuff
③ Brown bag lunch
② ♡
Boop Boop
JEEPERS... WHO NEEDS STAMINA FOR THE AFTERNOON?
Boop
Boop Boop
Grrrr!
OH MY...YOU REALLY ARE HOPELESS. YOUR IGNORANCE IS HARDLY LOCALIZED TO TAMON...
...BUT IS INDICATIVE OF YOUR RESPONSE TO A GREATER SWATH OF THE MALE POPULATION. IN OTHER WORDS, A **TREE STUMP** KNOWS MORE ABOUT MEN THAN YOU.
Sigh...
Grade: Z – (Average grade at Dr.M's lab is C+-F+)
WELL, **EXCUSE** ME!
AT LEAST THAT EXPLAINS WHY I HAVE ONLY HAVE A ONE PERCENT CHANCE OF MAKING IT WITH TAMON!
OUSSH...!

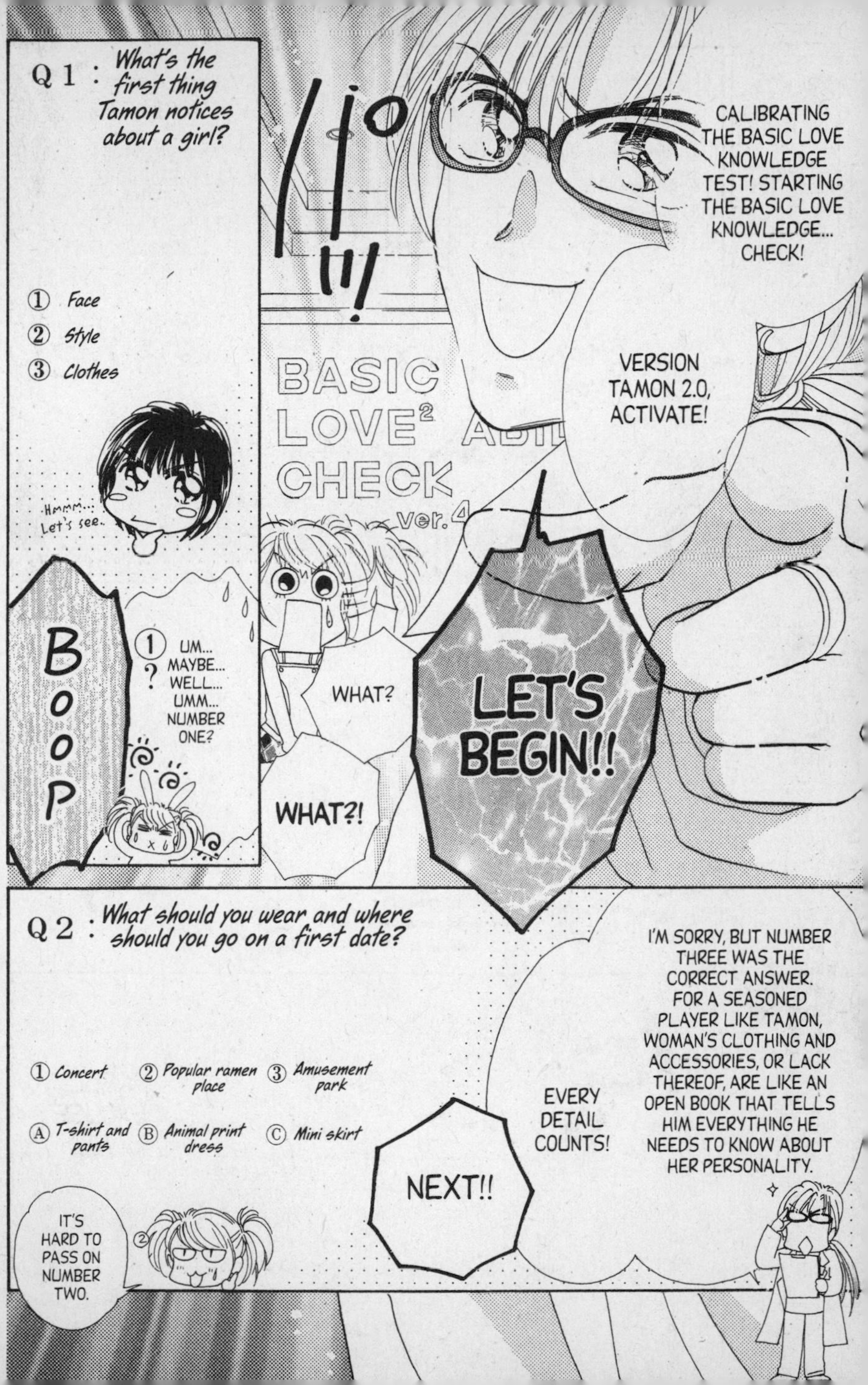
CALIBRATING THE BASIC LOVE KNOWLEDGE TEST! STARTING THE BASIC LOVE KNOWLEDGE... CHECK!
VERSION TAMON 2.0, ACTIVATE!
LET'S BEGIN!!
BASIC LOVE^2
CHECK ver.4
WHAT?
WHAT?!
Q1 : What's the first thing Tamon notices about a girl?
① Face
② Style
③ Clothes
Hmmm... Let's see.
BOOP
①?
UM... MAYBE... WELL... UMM... NUMBER ONE?
I'M SORRY, BUT NUMBER THREE WAS THE CORRECT ANSWER. FOR A SEASONED PLAYER LIKE TAMON, WOMAN'S CLOTHING AND ACCESSORIES, OR LACK THEREOF, ARE LIKE AN OPEN BOOK THAT TELLS HIM EVERYTHING HE NEEDS TO KNOW ABOUT HER PERSONALITY.
EVERY DETAIL COUNTS!
NEXT!!
Q2 : What should you wear and where should you go on a first date?
① Concert ② Popular ramen place ③ Amusement park
Ⓐ T-shirt and pants Ⓑ Animal print dress Ⓒ Mini skirt
②
IT'S HARD TO PASS ON NUMBER TWO.

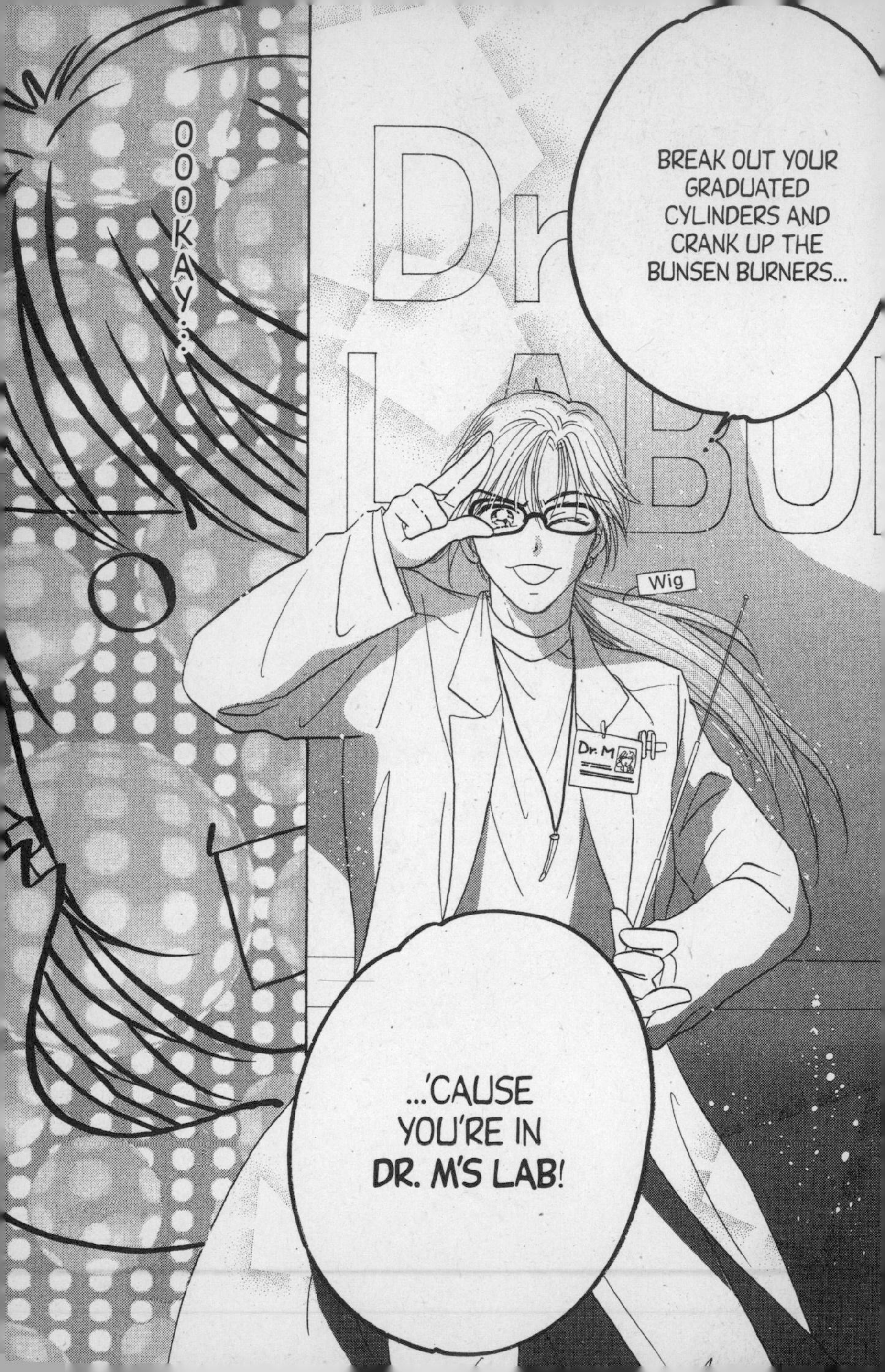
BREAK OUT YOUR GRADUATED CYLINDERS AND CRANK UP THE BUNSEN BURNERS...
Wig
Dr. M
...'CAUSE YOU'RE IN **DR. M'S LAB!**
OOOKAY...

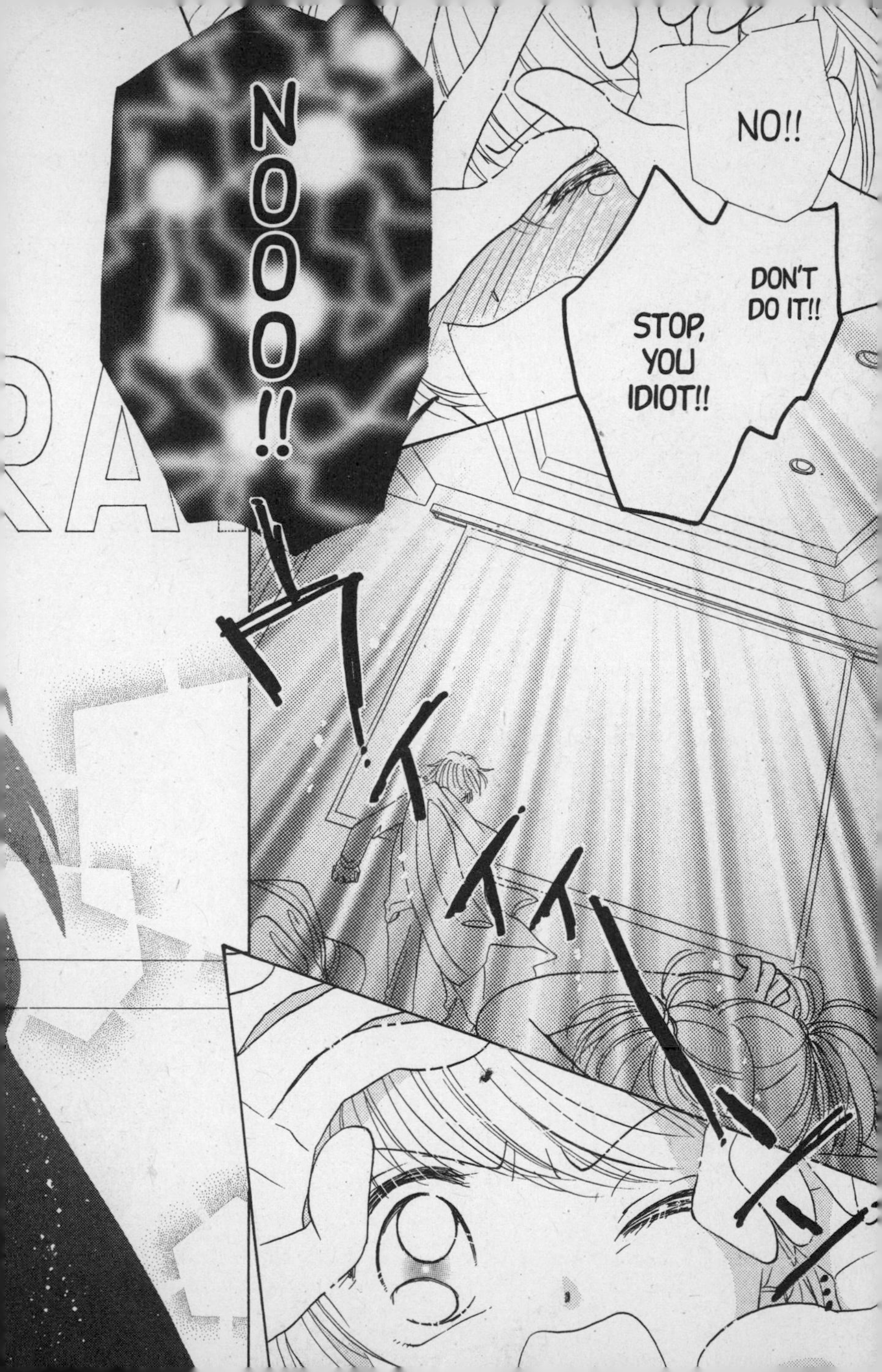
NO!!
DON'T DO IT!!
STOP, YOU IDIOT!!
NOOOO!!

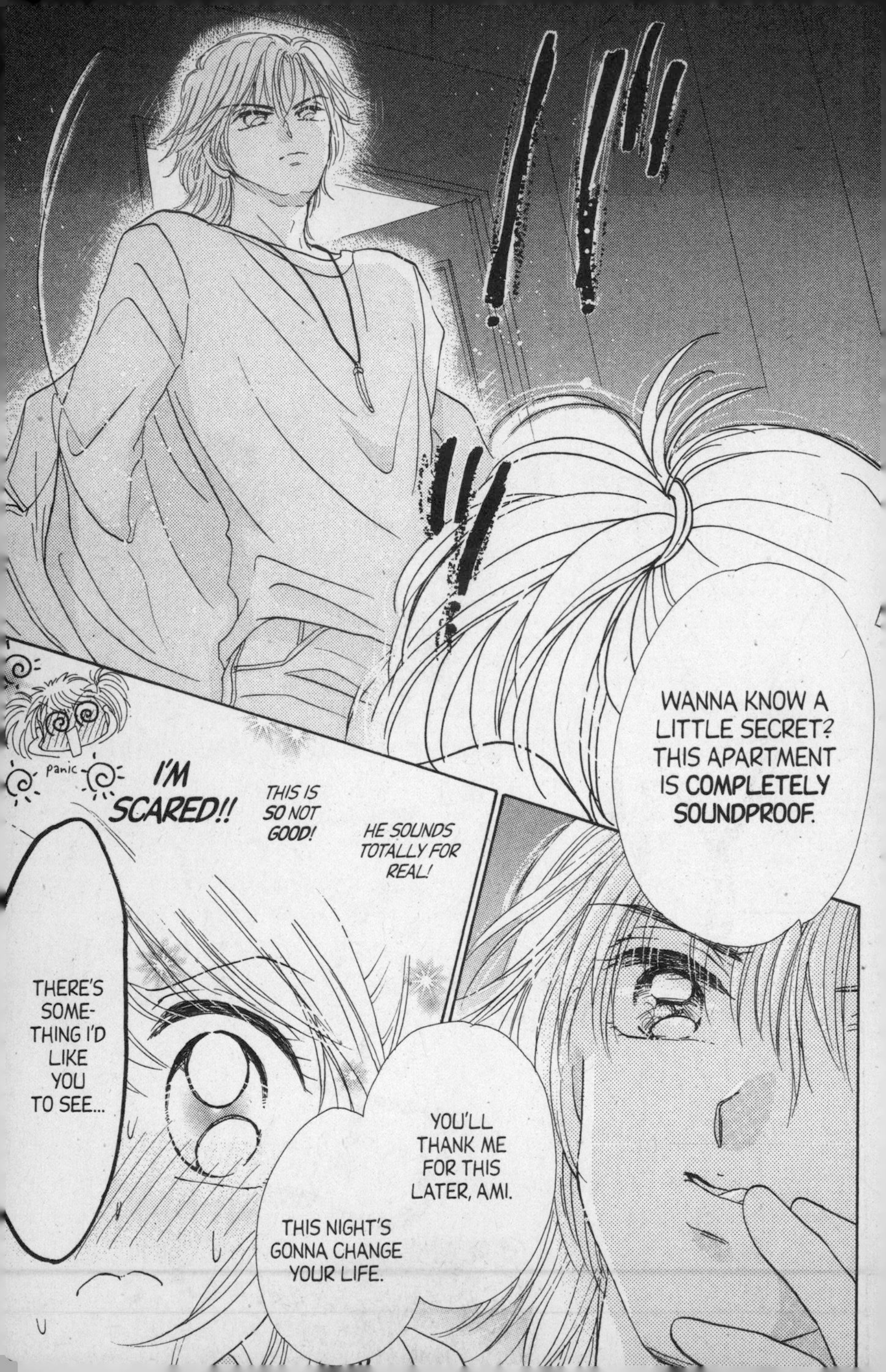
WANNA KNOW A LITTLE SECRET? THIS APARTMENT IS COMPLETELY SOUNDPROOF.
HE SOUNDS TOTALLY FOR REAL!
THIS IS SO NOT GOOD!
I'M SCARED!!
panic
THERE'S SOME-THING I'D LIKE YOU TO SEE...
YOU'LL THANK ME FOR THIS LATER, AMI.
THIS NIGHT'S GONNA CHANGE YOUR LIFE.

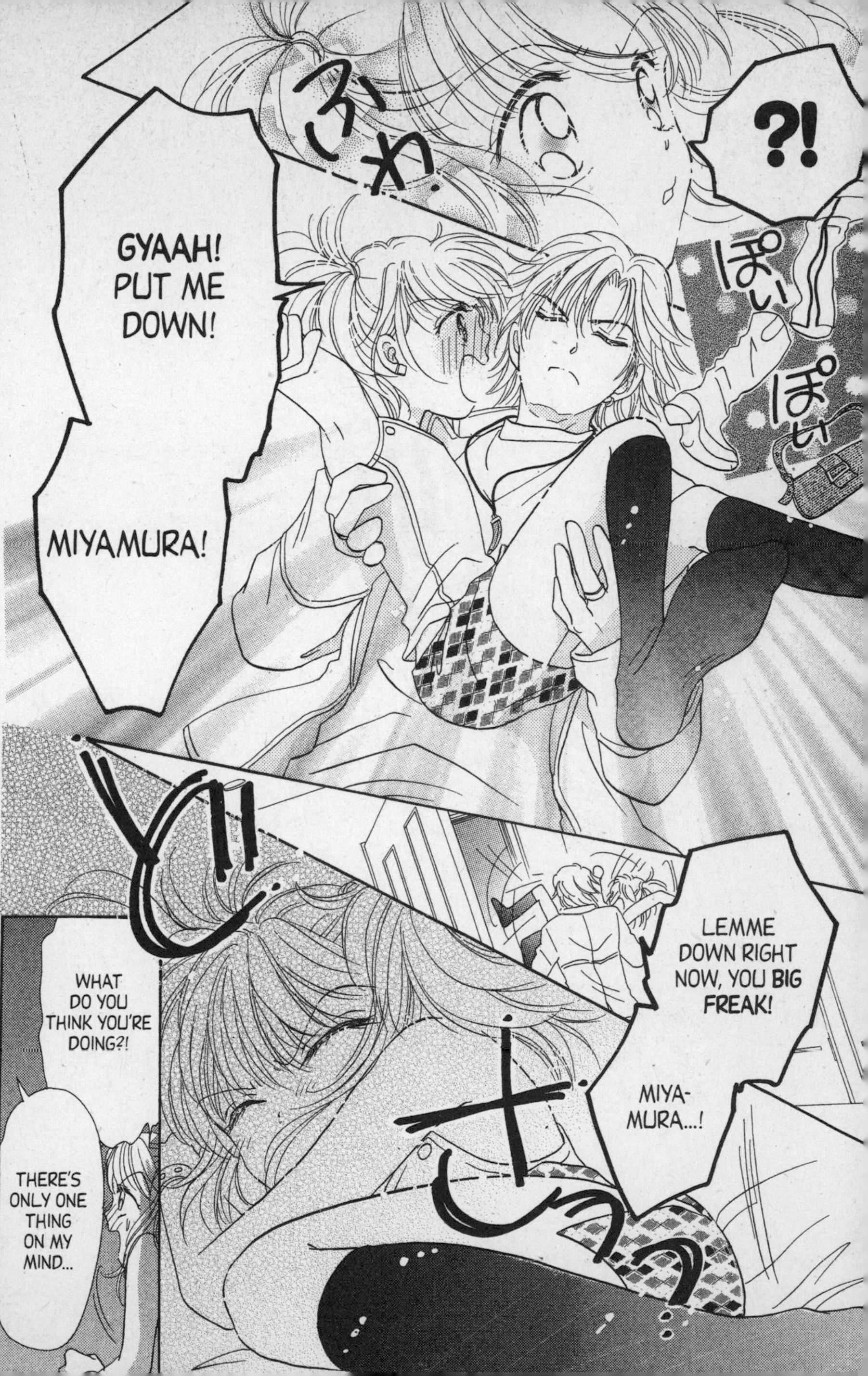
?!
ふわ
ぽい
ぽい
GYAAH! PUT ME DOWN!
MIYAMURA!
LEMME DOWN RIGHT NOW, YOU BIG FREAK!
MIYA-MURA...!
WHAT DO YOU THINK YOU'RE DOING?!
THERE'S ONLY ONE THING ON MY MIND...

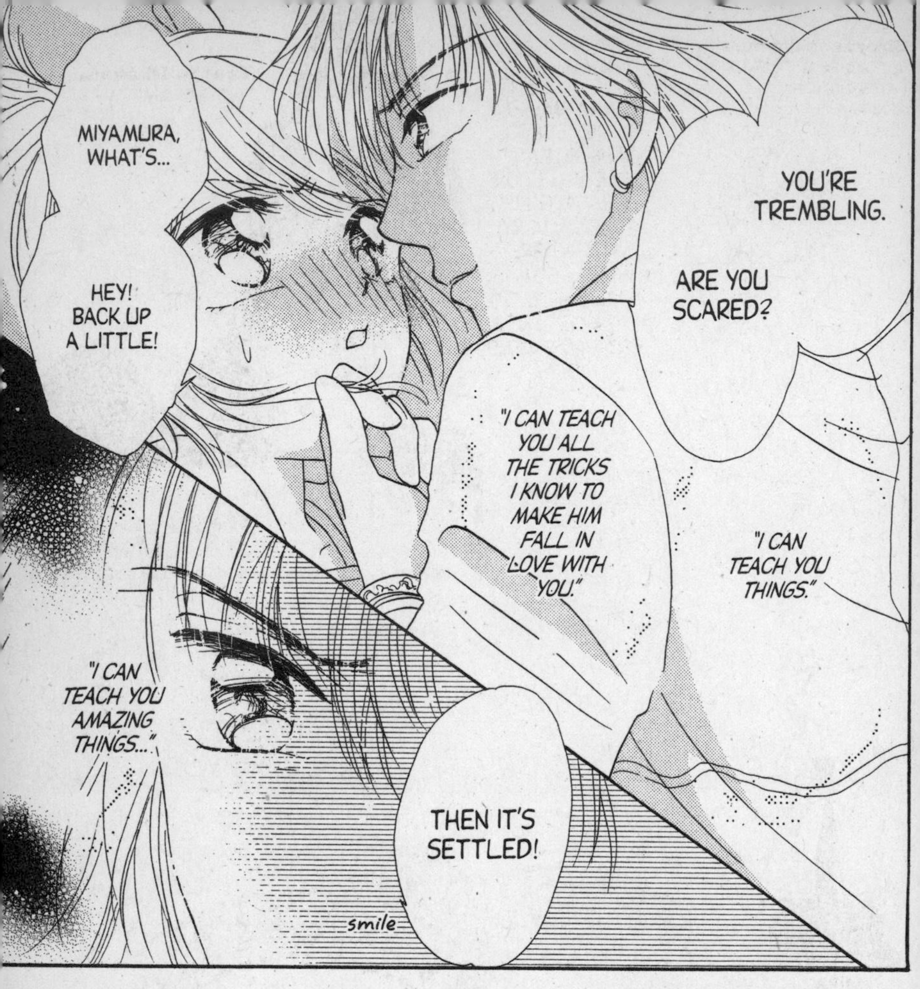
YOU'RE TREMBLING.
ARE YOU SCARED?
"I CAN TEACH YOU THINGS."
"I CAN TEACH YOU ALL THE TRICKS I KNOW TO MAKE HIM FALL IN LOVE WITH YOU."
MIYAMURA, WHAT'S...
HEY! BACK UP A LITTLE!
THEN IT'S SETTLED!
smile
"I CAN TEACH YOU AMAZING THINGS..."

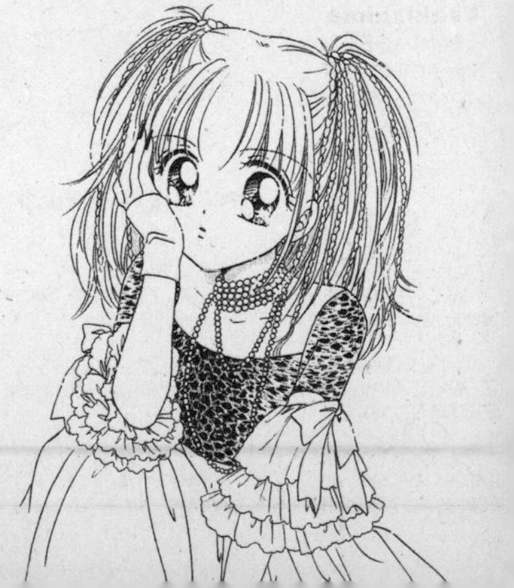

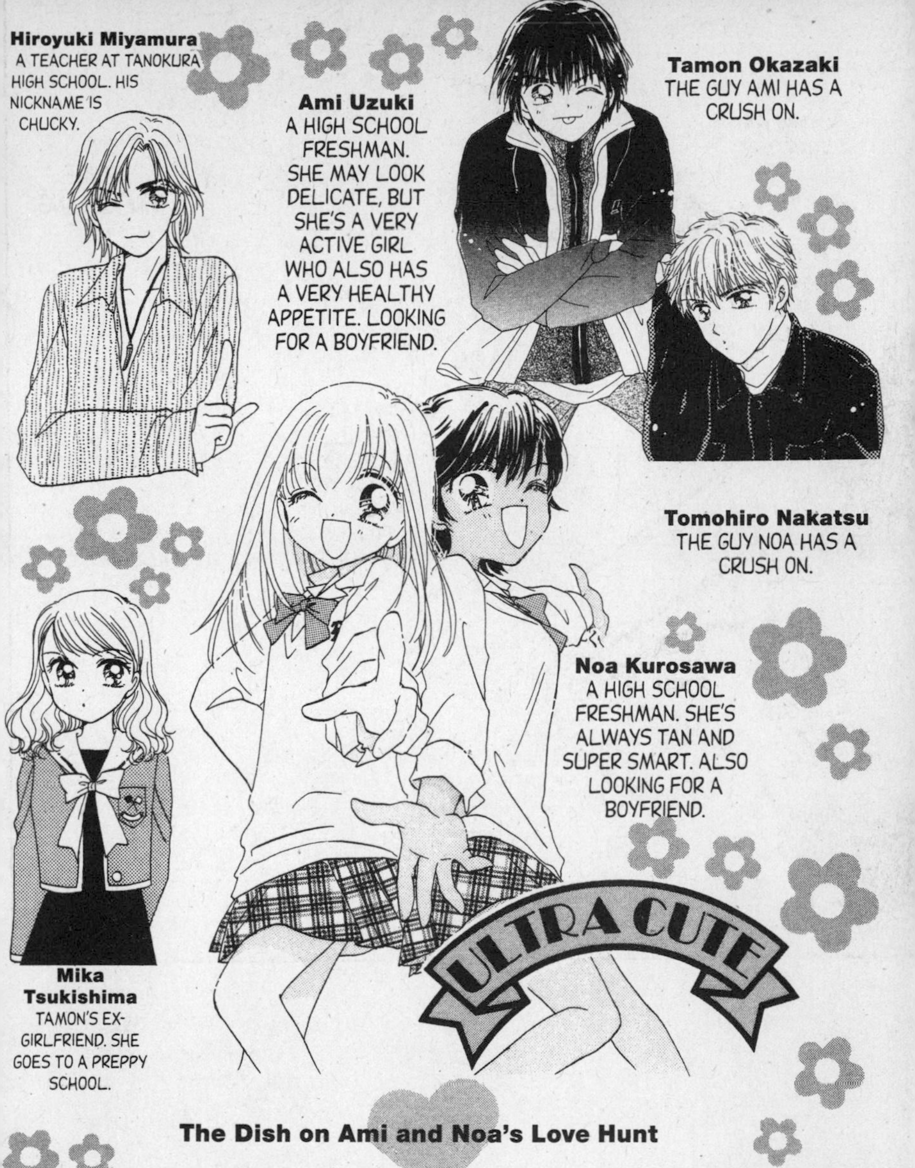
Hiroyuki Miyamura
A TEACHER AT TANOKURA HIGH SCHOOL. HIS NICKNAME IS CHUCKY.
Ami Uzuki
A HIGH SCHOOL FRESHMAN. SHE MAY LOOK DELICATE, BUT SHE'S A VERY ACTIVE GIRL WHO ALSO HAS A VERY HEALTHY APPETITE. LOOKING FOR A BOYFRIEND.
Tamon Okazaki
THE GUY AMI HAS A CRUSH ON.
Tomohiro Nakatsu
THE GUY NOA HAS A CRUSH ON.
Noa Kurosawa
A HIGH SCHOOL FRESHMAN. SHE'S ALWAYS TAN AND SUPER SMART. ALSO LOOKING FOR A BOYFRIEND.
Mika Tsukishima
TAMON'S EX-GIRLFRIEND. SHE GOES TO A PREPPY SCHOOL.
ULTRA CUTE

The Dish on Ami and Noa's Love Hunt

AMI AND NOA HAVE ALWAYS BEEN RIVALS WHEN IT COMES TO LOVE. HOWEVER, ONE DAY THEY WERE LUCKY ENOUGH TO MEET TWO SUPER HOT GUYS, TAMON AND TOMOHIRO, AT A KARAOKE CLUB AND NOT (FOR ONCE) BE ATTRACTED TO THE SAME ONE.

UNFORTUNATELY, TAMON AND TOMOHIRO ARE PLAYERS WHO TREAT RELATIONSHIPS LIKE A GAME. AMI'S DETERMINED TO MAKE TAMON FALL IN LOVE WITH HER FOR REAL, BUT IT SEEMS THAT HE'S STILL STUCK ON HIS MANIPULATIVE AND BITTER EX, MIKA.

DESPERATE FOR CONFIDENCE, AMI BEGINS VISITING A LOVE PREDICTION WEBSITE, RUN BY A "DR. M." AT HIS SUGGESTION, AMI MEETS DR. M IN PERSON AND IT TURNS OUT HE'S ACTUALLY THE TEACHER SHE AND NOA HAVE BEEN MAKING FUN OF FOR YEARS, CHUCKY. AND NOW SHE'S AT HIS PLACE IN A MOST AWKWARD SITUATION...

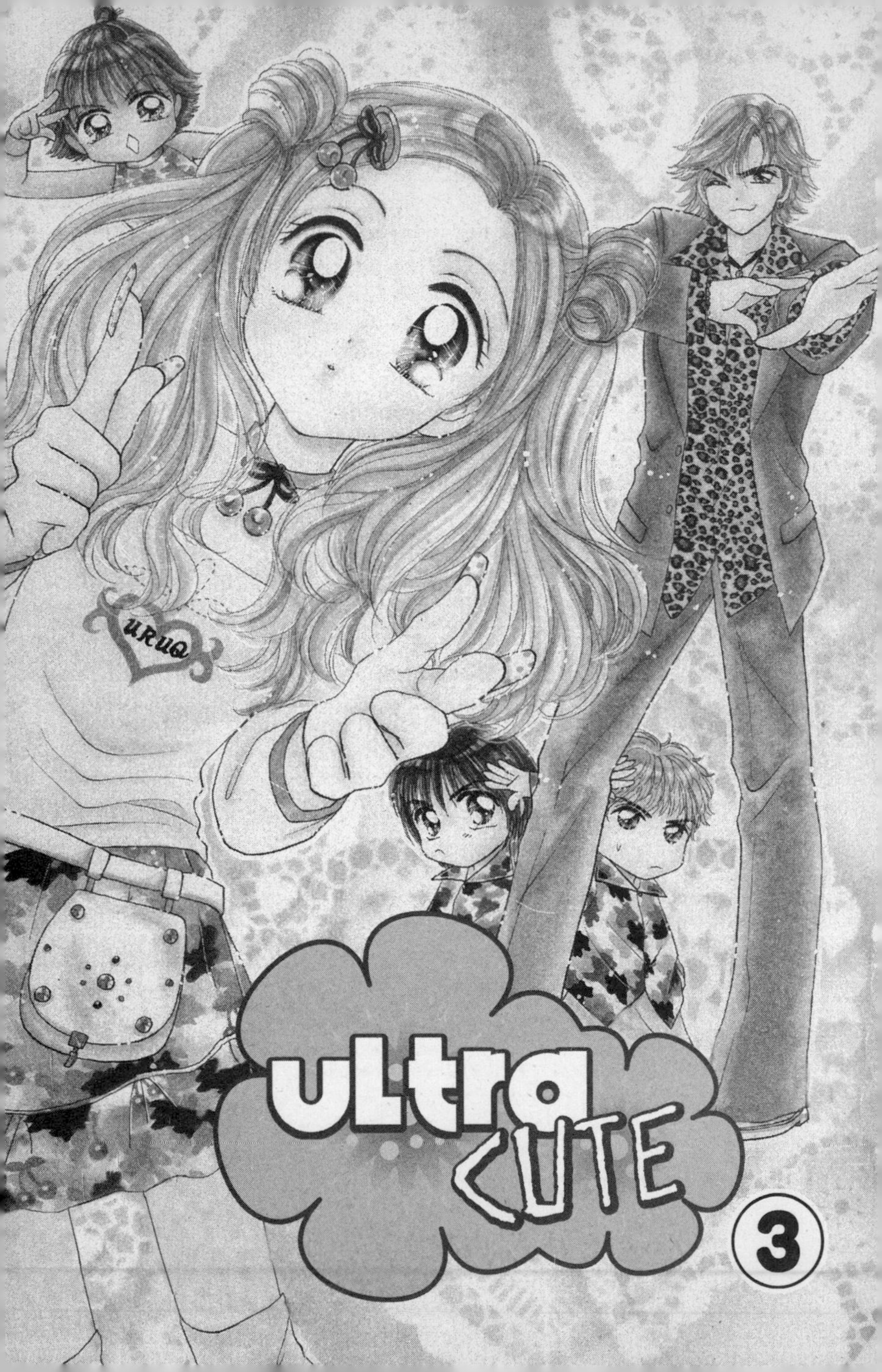
URUQ
ultra
CUTE
3

STOP!

This is the back of the book.
You wouldn't want to spoil a great ending!

This book is printed "manga-style," in the authentic Japanese right-to-left format. Since none of the artwork has been flipped or altered, readers get to experience the story just as the creator intended. You've been asking for it, so TOKYOPOP® delivered: authentic, hot-off-the-press, and far more fun!

DIRECTIONS

If this is your first time reading manga-style, here's a quick guide to help you understand how it works.

It's easy... just start in the top right panel and follow the numbers. Have fun, and look for more 100% authentic manga from TOKYOPOP®!